OXFORD PRIVATE INTERNATIONAL LAW SERIES

GENERAL EDITOR: JAMES J. FAWCETT

Professor of Law
University of Nottingham

THE ARREST OF SHIPS IN PRIVATE INTERNATIONAL LAW

OXFORD PRIVATE INTERNATIONAL LAW SERIES

General Editor: Professor James J. Fawcett FBA

The aim of the series is to publish work of quality and originality in a number of important areas of private international law. The series is intended for both scholarly and practitioner readers.

ALSO IN THIS SERIES

The Rome II Regulation
ANDREW DICKINSON

Cross-Border Divorce Law
MÁIRE NÍ SHÚILLEABHÁIN

The Anti-Suit Injunction
THOMAS RAPHAEL

Agreements on Jurisdiction and Choice of Law
ADRIAN BRIGGS

Conflict of Laws Within the UK
KIRSTY J HOOD

Civil Jurisdiction Rules of the EU and their Impact on Third States
THALIA KRUGER

Insolvency in Private International Law
Main Work and Supplement
IAN F FLETCHER

The Transfer of Property in the Conflict of Laws
JANEEN M CARRUTHERS

International Sale of Goods in the Conflict of Laws
JAMES J. FAWCETT, JONATHAN M HARRIS, and MICHAEL BRIDGE

Choice of Law for Equitable Doctrines
T M YEO

Procedural Law in International Arbitration
GEORGIOS PETROCHILOS

Foreign Law in Civil Litigation
SOFIE GEEROMS

Shares and Other Securities in the Conflict of Laws
MAISIE OOI

Forum Shopping and Venue in Transnational Litigation
ANDREW S BELL

Cross-Border Enforcement of Patent Rights
MARTA PERTEGÁS SENDER

Res Judicata, Estoppel, and Foreign Judgments
PETER BARNETT

Corporations in Private International Law
STEPHAN RAMMELOO

The Enforcement of Judgments in Europe
WENDY KENNETT

Claims for Contribution and Reimbursement in an International Context
KOJI TAKAHASHI

The Hague Convention on International Child Abduction
PAUL BEAUMONT AND PETER MCELEAVY

Autonomy in International Contracts
PETER NYGH

Foreign Law in English Courts
RICHARD FENTIMAN

Declining Jurisdiction in Private International Law
JAMES J. FAWCETT

THE ARREST OF SHIPS IN PRIVATE INTERNATIONAL LAW

VERÓNICA RUIZ ABOU-NIGM
Lecturer in Law, University of Sheffield

OXFORD
UNIVERSITY PRESS

OXFORD
UNIVERSITY PRESS

Great Clarendon Street, Oxford OX2 6DP

Oxford University Press is a department of the University of Oxford.
It furthers the University's objective of excellence in research, scholarship,
and education by publishing worldwide in

Oxford New York

Auckland Cape Town Dar es Salaam Hong Kong Karachi
Kuala Lumpur Madrid Melbourne Mexico City Nairobi
New Delhi Shanghai Taipei Toronto

With offices in

Argentina Austria Brazil Chile Czech Republic France Greece
Guatemala Hungary Italy Japan Poland Portugal Singapore
South Korea Switzerland Thailand Turkey Ukraine Vietnam

Oxford is a registered trade mark of Oxford University Press
in the UK and in certain other countries

Published in the United States
by Oxford University Press Inc., New York

First published 2011

British Library Cataloguing-in-Publication Data
Data available

Typeset by Cenveo, Bangalore, India
Printed in Great Britain
on acid-free paper by
CPI Group (UK) Ltd, Croydon, CRO 4YY

ISBN 978–0–19–958135–1

1 3 5 7 9 10 8 6 4 2

General Editor's Preface

Maritime law has an obvious and close relationship with private international law. It is surprising then to find that there has been a relative shortage of academic literature devoted to the private international law aspects of this area of substantive law. In particular, with the exception of Professor Jackson's *The Enforcement of Maritime Claims*, there is no specialist book on this topic. As far as the *Oxford Private International Law Series* is concerned, the only work which touches upon maritime law is Fawcett, Harris and Bridge's, *International Sale of Goods in the Conflict of Laws*, which has some coverage of jurisdictional and choice of law problems that arise in relation to bills of lading. Dr Verónica Ruiz Abou-Nigm's *The Arrest of Ships in Private International Law* goes to the very heart of maritime law and, as such, is not only a very valuable addition to the sparse literature in this area but also an especially welcome addition to the *Oxford Private International Law Series*.

It is not possible to understand the various private international aspects of the arrest of ships without first understanding the concept of arrest of a ship as a provisional and protective measure. This is examined in considerable detail, including the historical development of arrest, in the first part of the book. The second part considers the choice of law, jurisdictional and enforcement of foreign judgments aspects of arrest. These private international law matters are examined against the background of the ever–increasing Europeanization of private international law. The Brussels I Regulation is in the process of revision and the book contains timely suggestions for how a recast Regulation should deal with the arrest of ships. Further harmonization of the law on arrest is advocated. Although much attention is paid to arrest under English and Scots law, the European background means that this monograph should be of considerable interest to lawyers from elsewhere in the EU.

The stated aim of the *Oxford Private International Law Series* is to publish works of high quality and originality in a number of important areas of private international law. *The Arrest of Ships in Private International Law* conspicuously fulfils these criteria and is a sterling addition to the *Series*.

James Fawcett
Nottingham
April 2011

Acknowledgements

I would like to express my gratitude to my PhD supervisors at the University of Edinburgh, Professor Bill McBryde, whose motivation initiated me in the doctoral journey, and Professor Gerry Maher, whose expertise, understanding, and valuable suggestions added considerably to the development of this book. I would also like to thank my Uruguayan Professors, Dr Cecilia Fresnedo de Aguirre and Dr Didier Opertti Badán; having the honour of being their disciple has been as pivotal to my academic career as has been their friendship.

I would also like to acknowledge the support of the College of Humanities and Social Science of the University of Edinburgh, Overseas Research Scholarships Programme, and the School of Law of the University of Edinburgh, Edinburgh Legal Education Trust, Wilson Trust, The Max Planck Institute for Foreign Private and Private International Law, and Unidroit. These institutions provided me the financial support necessary to accomplish this research project. At the School of Law of the University of Edinburgh, at the Max Planck Institute in Hamburg, and at Unidroit Headquarters in Rome, I spent infinite hours surrounded by the greatest inspirational environment, therefore, to all my friends and mentors of those years I would like to show my appreciation.

My gratitude goes also to my colleagues and mentors at the School of Law of the University of Sheffield who encouraged me to publish this book, in particular, to Professor Tammy Hervey for her continued interest in this project and to Professor Duncan French for his helpful comments on the material at different stages throughout the preparation of the manuscript.

I am most grateful to the team at Oxford University Press for their support and assistance, and to Professor James Fawcett for his comments on the original manuscript.

Finally, my deepest debt of gratitude is to my family for the encouragement they have given me through my entire life. In particular, I must acknowledge my parents, my sister, my children, and most especially my husband and best friend, Juan Andrés, whose love and patience has made possible the realization of this project. I owe them my eternal thanks.

Verónica Ruiz Abou-Nigm
Sheffield
April 2011

Contents

Part II: The Arrest of Ships in Private International Law

Table of Cases

Tables of Legislation

Treaties and Conventions

Statutes

EU Instruments

Regulations

1

Introduction

I. THE THEME

1. The Arrest of Ships

1.01 The subject-matter of this book belongs to the overarching theme of enforcement of maritime claims.[1] In the modern global economy maritime commerce plays a key role in facilitating international trade. Since ancient times ship-related transactions are negotiated on the credit of the ship rather than that of the ship-owner. Ships are high value assets over which extensive debts can arise. In this context, the arrest of ships has become the

[1] For a treatise on the topic in English law see the authoritative work of DC Jackson, Enforcement of Maritime Claims (London, LLP, 1985; 2nd edn 1996; 3rd edn 2000; 4th edn 2005). Jackson refers to the tripartite nature of maritime claims, ie the interim or provisional remedy aspect, the jurisdictional aspect, and the security aspect. Arrest of ships is inextricably intermingled in these three facets of maritime litigation.

main mechanism of protection and security in the enforcement of maritime claims.

1.02 The traditional view is that the arrest of ships benefits both creditors and ship-owners;[2] this corresponds with the established view on rights in securities which are deemed to benefit creditor and debtor. In present times creditors often give paramount importance to the search for security for their claims and in times of economic crisis the number of ship arrests tends to increase worldwide.[3] Hence, the availability of the arrest of ships and related proceedings are of central importance in transactions involving ships.[4]

1.03 Furthermore, in shipping litigation conflict of laws and conflict of jurisdictions are likely to arise. Since its earliest developments, the law has been trying to provide a facilitative framework in this sphere for all those involved in shipping to do prosperous business. In this context, the arrest of ships, inherently connected with jurisdiction, has also played a key role since ancient times. It is the speed with which the defendant's main asset could leave the jurisdiction that arrest of ships has been always trying to counteract.

1.04 Thus, the arrest of ships is a very powerful interim measure of protection in maritime litigation. It is effective not only due to the eventuality of the judicial sale of the ship if the arrest is not released, but because in the commercial shipping industry the mere threat of a ship being paralysed due to its arrest is considerable: the arrest of a ship could generate significant losses for all those involved in the business. Strategically, that means that a claimant who has the possibility to arrest because of the nature of his claim has strong bargaining power.

1.05 Therefore, one of the *sine qua non* considerations in maritime litigation in present times is where to arrest a ship of the defendant; once arrested the ship will be detained until the defendant gives security to the claimant for his claim. On that basis, it has been argued that the arrest of the ship is not necessarily itself the security but it is the best mechanism of obtaining

[2] A Browne, *A Compendious View of the Civil Law and of the Law of the Admiralty: Being the Substance of a Course of Lectures Read in the University of Dublin*, vol 2 (New York, Halsted and Voorhies, 1840; reprint, New Jersey, The Lawbook Exchange Ltd, 2000) 76.

[3] M Davies, 'Choice of Law and U.S. Maritime Liens' (2009) 83 *Tulane Law Review* 1435, 1461.

[4] R Goode, H Kronke, E McKendrick, and J Wool, *Transnational Commercial Law* (Oxford, OUP, 2004) 437.

alternative security;[5] it has also been said that the most salient feature of arrest is its provisional character.[6]

The modern institution[7] of arrest of ships as recognized today by the international community is the result of the migration of legal ideas, institutions, concepts, and structures; the upshot of a chain of amalgamations over the centuries. In traditional English law, it is an institution generated from the efforts of the common lawyers to build upon the practices of a civil law court, the High Court of Admiralty. In traditional Scots law, it is the result of the mixture between original Scots law and Scotland's inheritance from the European systems, particularly that of the Netherlands, and to a lesser extent, France. Internationally, features of the arrest of ships are a compromise between common law and civil law conceptions and, in turn, it is this mixture that makes it unique as a legal institution. **1.06**

This study aims to facilitate the understanding of this distinctive provisional and protective measure and to shed some light on the advantages that private international law devices can bring to further harmonization of the current law on the arrest of ships in the international commercial sphere. **1.07**

2. The Scope of the Book

The book analyses the arrest of ships in English and Scots law in the light of the international Conventions in the field. It examines the three main functions of arrest of ships, ie its protective function, its security function, and its jurisdictional function, within the three classical domains of Private International Law or Conflict of Laws, ie applicable law, jurisdiction, and the recognition and enforcement of foreign judgments. **1.08**

The delimitation of the scope of this book is very much defined by the international Arrest Conventions' material scope of application. This leads to boundaries in the examination *inter alia* of the following matters: (i) arrest of ships in execution of a judgment is outside the scope of it; (ii) only privately owned ships will be included, leaving State-owned and **1.09**

[5] See eg *Oceanconnect UK Ltd v Angara Maritime Ltd* [2010] EWCA Civ 1050.

[6] R Herbert and C Fresnedo de Aguirre, 'El Arresto de Buques y el Principio de Jurisdicción más Próxima' [1993] *Revista de Transporte y Seguros* 158.

[7] The notion of 'legal institution' used throughout this book comes from N MacCormick and O Weinberger, *An Institutional Theory of Law* (Dordrecht, D Reidel Publishing Co, 1986) 49–76. Conceptualizing the arrest of ships as a 'legal institution' implies dynamism; hence, the different uses, applications, and developments across legal systems as well as the transmigration of ideas that distinguish the law on the arrest of ships make 'institution' an appropriate and useful conceptualization.

war ships out of the discussion; (iii) the various issues in relation to arrest of ships in the sphere of maritime arbitration is also left aside; and (iv) arrest of cargo will not be dealt with.[8]

1.10 In terms of the legal systems examined the study of the international Arrest Conventions is to be expected due to the very nature of the topic.[9] In contrast, the selection of English and Scots law is based on several considerations. First of all, the book intends to highlight the differences within Great Britain; such differences having sometimes been neglected due to the fact that treaty-making powers rest with the Crown. The United Kingdom is a signatory to the 1952 International Arrest Convention[10] which was originally enacted in the United Kingdom by the Administration of Justice Act 1956. Due to that statutory enactment, it has wrongly been assumed by some commentators that the United Kingdom has a singular system of arrest of ships in its territory. In fact the situation is quite the opposite; aware of the very different approach to arrest of ships in Scotland as compared with England the amendments made to Scots law were introduced in a separate self-contained section of the Act.[11] Moreover, it has been argued that the wording used in the provisions applicable to Scotland is much closer to that of the 1952 International Arrest Convention than those

[8] Arrest of cargo is part of the law of admiralty arrest/arrestment in English and Scots law and has received special treatment as far as its jurisdictional function in the European jurisdictional scheme. The Brussels and Lugano Conventions and currently Council Regulation (EC) 44/2001 (the Brussels I Reg) provide for arrest of cargo in Art 5(7) in relation to salvage. The reference in the European regime is indeed a consequence of the lack of treatment of arrest of cargo by the 1952 International Arrest Convention. Due to that gap, Art 57 of the Conventions (Art 71 of the Brussels I Reg) could not provide for a special jurisdictional basis in those circumstances, hence, Art 5(7) was introduced to fill that gap (JJ Alvarez Rubio, *Derecho Maritimo y Derecho Internacional Privado, Problemas básicos* (Vitoria-Gasteiz, Servicio Central de Publicaciones del Gobierno Vasco, 2000) 123). The aim of such inclusion was to adapt the benefits of *forum arresti* to the case of arrest of cargo as it is in respect of the arrest of the ship.

[9] There are other international instruments that deal with arrest of ships in the international sphere. The most important one in the United Kingdom apart from the 1952 International Arrest Convention is the Convention on Certain Rules concerning Civil Jurisdiction in Matters of Collision, Brussels, 10 May 1952. This Convention has been enacted into English and Scots law through the Administration of Justice Act 1956; replaced in English law by the Supreme Court Act 1981, now renamed as Senior Courts Act. The Collision Convention is concerned with jurisdiction based on arrest; it does not rule on arrest as a provisional measure, hence, is relevant only for the study provided in Ch 7 of this book.

[10] International Convention relating to the Arrest of Sea-Going Ships (Brussels, 10 May 1952).

[11] Administration of Justice Act 1956 Ch 46 Pt V (Admiralty Jurisdiction and Arrestment of Ships in Scotland) Arts 47–51/57.

which applied to England.[12] In England this statue has been superseded by the Supreme Court Act 1981, now renamed as Senior Courts Act 1981.

Hence, this book does not focus on domestic law. It is a study of the private international law effects of the arrest of ships. It examines issues of characterization, applicable law, jurisdiction, and recognition and enforcement of foreign judgments in relation to the arrest of ships. The book is organized in two parts. The analysis in the first part contributes to the characterization of arrest of ships as a provisional and protective measure, addressing the issue in different spheres, ie in transnational, international, and national law. The second part is divided into three chapters, and each chapter presents a specific function of the arrest of ships in relation to a specific question germane to private international law. **1.11**

In turn, the comparative law approach undertaken in this study represents very important assistance to the whole width of the book. Comparative analysis is the necessary first step in understanding different legal cultures and indispensable if the aim is to achieve further harmonization, and even more, unification of the law in a particular field. Comparative analysis is indeed of pivotal support to the private international law analysis of the arrest of ships. Modern times require a smooth blend between the common law and the civil law traditions in this field as in many others. **1.12**

II. THE AIM

1. Advancing Further Harmonization

The development of maritime law has always had the ideal of harmonization at its very centre. The inherent internationalism of the maritime adventure has fostered the trend towards uniform law at the international sphere and this tendency has been increasing since the early twentieth century. The arrest of ships as a typical admiralty institution is not alien to that process. This study provides an analytical framework that intends to advance further harmonization of the current law on the arrest of ships in the international commercial sphere. **1.13**

The arrest of ships as an institution used in civil and commercial matters does not have an exact equivalent in every legal system; nonetheless most **1.14**

[12] IG Inglis, 'Arrest of Ships in Scotland' in C Hill (ed), *The Arrest of Ships Series*, vol 4 (London, LLP, 1987) 83; *Owners of Cargo Lately Laden on Board the MV Erkowit v Owners of the Eschersheim (The Eschersheim, the Jade and the Erkowit)* [1976] 2 Lloyd's Rep 1 (HL) (Lord Diplock).

countries provide for the arrest of ships. In England it is known as ship arrest and in Scotland as ship arrestment. Neither of those institutions is identical to the French *saisie conservatoire* or the Spanish *embargo preventivo* or the Italian *sequestro conservativo* and certainly differs as well from the ancient English *maritime attachment* and the current North American *preliminary attachment* with regard to ships. All in all, what these measures have in common is their provisional nature and protective character, which have been the most salient features of arrest of ships since its very beginnings.

1.15 The international Arrest Conventions have attempted to harmonize the law in this field. These harmonization efforts were originally aimed at protecting the ship-owner from abuse as well as improving his position as to the ability to gain credit upon the ship.[13] Nevertheless, the success of the 1952 International Arrest Convention in achieving harmonization, despite its more than 80 ratifications, is still partial. Its successor, the 1999 International Arrest Convention, is just about to enter into force. By looking at this issue through the lens of private international law, this book identifies one of the problems that have led to this relative lack of 'harmonizing efficiency' of the international Arrest Conventions and suggests a way forward to furthering harmonization in this sphere based on the private international law theory of characterization.[14] The book therefore provides valuable insight to the theory of characterization as applied to uniform law provisions such as the ones of the international Arrest Conventions.

1.16 The characterization problems identified in this study derive from, and result in, different interpretations of the international Arrest Conventions in the State parties.[15] This study seeks to show that these problems are mainly created by the disruptive impact of the law of the *forum arresti* via the so-called law of the forum characterization. In practice the influence of the law of the forum in matters of characterization is unhelpful and poses problems for attaining uniformity in the application of the international Convention currently in force. This impact is apparent in English law where the framework in which arrest of ships currently develops is the *in rem* claim; the impossibility of separating the two concepts (ie on the one hand the arrest of ships as a provisional and protective measure and on the

[13] JJ Alvarez Rubio, *Derecho Marítimo y Derecho Internacional Privado, Problemas básicos* (Servicio Central de Publicaciones del Gobierno Vasco, Vitoria-Gasteiz, 2000) 91.

[14] Characterization is one of the fundamental pillars of private international law and yet the most difficult and unsettled issue. See Ch 3, paras 3.23–3.28 below.

[15] For several examples of such characterization problems and the lack of uniformity in the application of the 1952 International Arrest Convention in the State parties, see F Berlingieri, *Berlingieri on Arrest of Ships* (London, LLP, 2006).

other hand the *in rem* claim) has complicated matters in various ways. This intertwining between arrest and the *in rem* claim in English law has undermined the correct application of the 1952 International Arrest Convention in English law. The intrinsic connection between arrest of ships and the *in rem* claim in English law is discussed throughout the book.

Even though uniform Conventions such as the 1952 International Arrest Convention[16] affected positively the difficulties arising from the diversity of legal systems, it has not resolved all the problems that private international law aims to answer in this field. It is uncontested that uniform laws do not necessarily mean uniform application of such laws; and the 1952 International Arrest Convention is indeed an example of such disparity in application.[17] This study seeks to overcome these drawbacks by recognizing that the international Arrest Conventions provide an autonomous meaning of 'arrest of ships' as a private international law category, independent of the legal category 'arrest of ships' as provided for in national legal systems. The recognition of that autonomous meaning is paramount for advancing further harmonization in this field. **1.17**

In relation to the international Arrest Conventions the analysis pursued in this book concentrates on, first, the scope of application of the Conventions; secondly, the scope (*alcance extensivo*) of arrest of ships as a legal category (the characterization problem); thirdly, problems of interpretation of key Conventions' provisions; and fourthly, the necessary coordination of legal rules resulting from the coexistence of different (overlapping) legal systems. **1.18**

The book concludes that the only way to advance further harmonization in this particular field is to apply the Conventions' provisions bearing in mind the characterization of arrest of ships as a provisional and protective measure. However, such a characterization presents a problem in the case of arrest of ships to enforce maritime liens. In such cases arrest forms part of the enforcement procedure of a tacit right in security; it is not accessory or supportive to the case on the merits; it is indeed an essential element of the case on the merits. The intricacies of the relationship between arrest of ships and the action *in rem* (renamed as the *in rem* claim in English law), in the particular case of the enforcement of maritime liens, in English and in Scots law, is analysed throughout the book. **1.19**

[16] International Convention Relating to the Arrest of Sea-Going Ships signed in Brussels on 10 May 1952.

[17] For several examples of different applications of the 1952 International Arrest Convention in different countries, see F Berlingieri (2006) and JJ Alvarez Rubio (2000).

2. The Objectives

1.20 Thus, the present study has the following major objectives; first, the characterization of arrest of ships as a provisional and protective measure. Secondly, the review from a critical viewpoint of the indistinctive conceptualization of ship arrest in English law in modern times as an inherent part of the *in rem* claim. Thirdly, the systematization of the state of affairs regarding the legal framework applicable to the security function of arrest of ships, its distinction from maritime liens, and the examination of the conflict of laws issues in this respect in English, Scots, and international law. Fourthly, this book considers the position of *forum arresti* as a specific jurisdictional ground for maritime claims in the context of the Europeanization of private international law. Fifthly, the role of the law of the forum is examined throughout this book: its impact on characterization issues; its subtleties when applied as the governing (substantive) law of the forum (*qua lex causae*); and its so often too far-reaching scope when used as the law of the forum as such (*qua lex fori*) (in English law through a wide interpretation of the term 'procedure'). Finally, jurisdiction for the sole purpose of interim relief is distinguished from jurisdiction on the merits of the case in the context of arrest of ships. The underlying rationale of the proximity principle as a pivotal device of judicial cooperation is examined in this context.

III. THE KEY

1. Different Functions of Arrest of Ships

1.21 The arrest of a ship as a provisional and protective measure is available in most legal systems but is approached and effected differently in each country. The common features are its provisional character; its security function; its relationship with jurisdiction; and its inherently protective nature. These features and functions have become so intermingled, that it is difficult to draw lines and establish clear-cut categories between these different functions.

1.22 This study aims to show that the arrest of ships is a provisional measure that has throughout the centuries developed three main functions:[18] (i) as an interim measure of protection, ie a measure intended to ensure that the final

[18] Jackson refers to the three possible functions of the arrest of maritime property. See Jackson, *Enforcement of Maritime Claims* (4th edn, London, LLP, 2005) 393–4.

award or judgment can be enforced by safeguarding the defendant's assets or property; (ii) as a jurisdictional basis on the merits; and (iii) as security. It is at the crossroads of these three functions derived from different lineages where the core of the distinctive issues arising in relation to the arrest of ships lie.

2. The Protective Function

The protective function of arrest of ships is its most noticeable one,[19] so it is possible to refer to it as a provisional and protective measure, or as an interim measure of protection, even though the protective function is only one of its functions. The arrest of a ship places the *res* under judicial detention pending adjudication of the claim. This character is shared by most of the different institutions serving the same functions in the different legal systems. **1.23**

3. The Jurisdictional Function

Central to this study is the jurisdictional function of arrest of ships. Arrest and jurisdiction are indissolubly linked but not necessarily in the same way in different legal systems. The strongest link between arrest and jurisdiction is *forum arresti* and the possibility to found jurisdiction on the merits of the claim upon arrest. *Forum arresti* was originally a jurisdictional basis known only to a very small number of States, England and Scotland amongst them. Currently, it has been sustained that *forum arresti* constitutes a general trend in international procedural maritime law and that it is justified in terms of convenience, derived from the essentially moveable nature of the ship.[20] However, there are national legal systems that criticize severely this jurisdictional basis, particularly some civil law systems that do not provide for *forum arresti* as a consequence of a conservatory attachment (*saisie conservatoire*) effected on a ship before judgment is rendered. **1.24**

In this sphere, the book also distinguishes the different rationales underlying jurisdiction for the sole purpose of interim relief as compared to jurisdiction on the merits of the case. As far as the former, the book suggests that the proximity principle as the underpinning of the jurisdiction to arrest in support of foreign proceedings or arbitration should be enshrined as a pivotal device of private international law. In this era where so much attention has been devoted to banning exorbitant *fora*, this book proposes **1.25**

[19] DC Jackson, *Enforcement of Maritime Claims* (4th edn, London, LLP, 2005) 393.

[20] Herbert and Fresnedo de Aguirre, 'El Arresto de Buques y el Principio de Jurisdicción mas Próxima' [1993] 167.

a positive approach to jurisdictional issues through the lens of international judicial cooperation.

1.26 Despite the lack of recognition of the jurisdictional function of arrest of ships in some national legal systems, *forum arresti* has been recognized in the international Arrest Conventions and it has survived in the context of the European Union. This paradigmatic forum selection criterion in English and Scots law has acquired the status of a specific jurisdictional basis for maritime claims in the process of Europeanization of private international law. The triumph of *forum arresti* in the international maritime context has traditionally been justified by historical and practical reasons rather than theoretical ones. One of the main purposes of this book is to provide a framework within which *forum arresti* in the case of the arrest of ships gains legitimacy. Thus, the study purports to provide the theoretical underpinning that justifies the survival of *forum arresti* as a specific jurisdictional ground for maritime claims in the context of the Europeanization of private international law.

1.27 This enhancement of the position of *forum arresti* in the European jurisdictional scheme has been possible through the *lex specialis* provision of the then Brussels Convention, currently Article 71 of Council Regulation (EC) No 44/2001 (the Brussels I Regulation). Article 7 of the 1952 International Arrest Convention is considered as *lex specialis* in this context and prevails over the jurisdictional rules of the Regulation. The interface between the 1952 International Arrest Convention and the Brussels jurisdictional scheme is analysed in this study.

4. The Security Function

1.28 The nature and extent of the security function is understood differently in the diverse world of legal systems. It has been argued that this particular function of arrest is indeed its most relevant one. On this token the argument is that the ultimate rationale of arrest of ships is to give the creditor the chance to create a right in security over the ship, and in turn that possibility puts pressure on the debtor in order to comply with the eventual judgment; that is actually what makes it so effective.[21]

1.29 Internationally, the security function of arrest as such (independently from maritime liens) does not have a uniform framework. The issue is also not clearly framed in English or Scots law and this leads to uncertainty about the effect of arrest of ships on third party proprietary interests. The book provides an overview of the various elements of the legal framework

[21] Alvarez Rubio, *Derecho Maritimo y Derecho Internacional Privado* (2000) 102.

which does, or could, affect the security function of the arrest of ships and distinguishes this function from maritime liens. It explores the conflict of laws issues in this respect in English and Scots law taking into consideration the international Conventions in the field. However, the international Arrest Conventions leave the consequential rules relating to the security function of arrest to the law of the *forum arresti*.

IV. THE PERSPECTIVE

1. A Private International Law Study

1.30 Different legal systems have different understanding of the aims and objectives of private international law. The most extended conception, that of English and Scots law as well as most civil law systems, is that the subject includes the study of applicable law issues, conflict of jurisdictions, and the recognition and enforcement of foreign judgments. Therefore, as a study of the private international law effects of the arrest of ships, the major challenge of the book is to examine issues of characterization, applicable law, jurisdiction, and recognition and enforcement of foreign judgments in relation to the arrest of ships. In turn, English and Scottish private international law systems are formed respectively by three main pillars: national provisions; European rules (mostly Regulations); and international Conventions that are in force in the United Kingdom. In general terms, even though Scots domestic law differs substantially from English internal law, there is no such difference as to their respective principles of private international law.[22]

1.31 In the field of arrest of ships, international Conventions coexist with national law and regional law, together with the ever growing significance of the *lex mercatoria*, or the law of merchants. The application of such different sources of law is cumbersome and private international law comes into play to offer different alternatives to the applicable law issues and to the conflict of jurisdictions aimed ultimately at the juridical continuity of legal relations across national borders.[23]

1.32 This book takes advantage of the methodological pluralism characteristic of private international law as a scholarly discipline and considers both main private international law methods, namely 'substantivism' (or unification of

[22] E Crawford and J Carruthers, *International Private Law in Scotland* (Edinburgh, Green, 2006) 2.

[23] See R Herbert in D Opertti Badán et al, *Objeto y Método en el Derecho Internacional Privado* (2nd edn, Montevideo, Fundación de Cultura Universitaria (FCU), 1990) 93–118.

substantive law methodology), and 'conflictualism'[24] (or choice-of-law methodology) as central to the analysis of the conflict of laws related to the arrest of ships. Both approaches do not exclude but complement each other and the research undertaken, by considering the combination of both theoretical approaches, has enabled this book to offer different options to the conflict of laws in the field. This combination is paramount to achieve both depth and breadth of analysis, which a singular approach could not achieve. Moreover, the book shows that in this particular field of maritime claims, the traditional choice-of-law approach applied on its own is more often than not inefficient and unnecessarily sophisticated. 'Substantivism' has been the main approach of the international Arrest Conventions which constitute an essential part of this analysis.

2. Juridical Continuity of Legal Relations across National Borders

1.33 The dilemma that gives rise to private international law as a legal discipline is created by the confrontation between a world divided into different legal systems (each one with a defined territorial application), and private legal relations that go beyond frontiers. The specific aim of private international law is to solve the problem that arises when legal relations are confronted with the discontinuity that the diversity of legal systems throughout the world represents. Continuity should be therefore understood in this context as a relative (non-absolute) term as opposed to the discontinuity of legal orders.

1.34 The juridical continuity of legal relations is the dynamic rationale at the centre of concern of private international law.[25] This overarching aim founds its materialization in several objectives such as the mutual recognition of decisions in civil and commercial matters as a core principle in the Europeanization of private international law; and the decisional harmony sought by means of unification of private international law rules 'so as to ensure that a case containing a foreign element results in the same decision irrespective of the country of its trial.'[26] This ideal pertains to the classical theory of private international law as conceived by

[24] 'Conflictualism' refers to the method that purports to resolve conflicts of laws by selecting and applying the domestic law of one of the States connected to the case. In turn, 'substantivism' seeks to develop substantive rules for those conflicts of laws. See Symeon C Symeonides, 'American Choice of Law at the Dawn of the 21st Century' (2001) 37 *Willamette Law Review* 1.

[25] See n 23 above, 100.

[26] JJ Fawcett and J M Carruthers, *Chesire, North & Fawcett Private International Law* (14th edn, Oxford, OUP, 2008) 11.

Friedrich Carl von Savigny.[27] As a distinguished commentator has recognized, Savigny's rhetoric 'continues to be revered, his classical theory of private international law continues to hold sway'[28] in Europe.

Aims and objectives are always formulated in terms of ideals and it is in that sense that this dynamic purpose of private international law needs to be understood. The risk is not being idealistic in determining the goals; the risk is to use unrealistic methods when deciding on how to attain such goals. On that line of thought, this study aims to advance further harmonization of the law on the arrest of ships by taking recourse to private international law mechanisms in applying the provisions of the *existing* international Arrest Conventions.[29] **1.35**

V. THE CONTEXT

1. The Europeanization of Private International Law

One of the most important phenomena influencing the current development of private international law is market integration, particularly at the regional level. In Europe, such influence has generated a process known as Europeanization of private international law. This process poses various issues[30] and involves in many cases giving up national conflict rules in favour of harmonization and unification. Undoubtedly, integration processes between States such as the one undertaken by the European Union are leading to a degree of harmonization of law at a pace never experienced in modern legal history.[31] **1.36**

[27] Friedrich Carl von Savigny, *Private International Law and the Retrospective Operation of Statutes. A Treatise on the Conflict of Laws and the Limits of their Operation in Respect of Place and Time* (tr W Guthrie, 2nd edn, Edinburgh, Clark, 1880).

[28] See Symeon C Symeonides, 'The American Revolution and the European Evolution in Choice of Law: Reciprocal Lessons' (2008) 82 *Tulane Law Review* 1741, 1789. Symeonides explains that many authors and courts in the United States consider that even though 'uniformity is a laudable goal, it is largely unattainable, and consequently the theory and practice of [private international law] should recognize and support other goals', ibid, 1786.

[29] In the field of international maritime law, unfortunately, there are several examples of exhausted resources that did not come to fruition. The result is the proliferation of sterile international instruments that do not contribute to international harmonization but more worryingly do tend to hinder the success of their predecessors by generating disparity and uncertainty in the international legal scenario.

[30] See C van der Plas, 'The Limits of the Judicial Function and the Conflict of Laws' (2006) 53 *Netherlands International Law Review* 439.

[31] JA Jolowicz, 'On the Comparison of Procedures' in JAR Nafziger and SC Symeonides (eds), *Law and Justice in a Multistate World, Essays in Honor of Arthur T. von Mehren* (New York, Transnational Publishers, 2002) 721.

1.37 Before the Treaty of Amsterdam,[32] measures designed to secure the harmonization of conflict rules at European level had taken the form of international Conventions signed and ratified by the Member States. Important changes took place in this sphere during the life time of the Treaty of Amsterdam via the harmonization of conflict rules by means of Regulations adopted under Title IV (Articles 61–69) of the former EC Treaty. Currently, Article 81 of the Lisbon Treaty [33] extends the influence of the European Union over matters of private international law even further. Under the Lisbon Treaty the European Parliament and the Council are empowered to adopt measures in this field 'particularly when necessary for the proper functioning of the internal market' which suggests that legislation in this field need not be unequivocally necessary for the proper functioning of the internal market.[34] In this context, the European Parliament[35] has recently encouraged the European Commission to adopt a consistent framework in the field of private international law with a view to a 'comprehensive codification of private international law'.[36]

1.38 Furthermore, in the sphere of jurisdiction, in the revision process undertaken to evaluate the functioning of the Brussels I Regulation in the Member States, Schlosser in the 2005 *Heidelberg Report*[37] considered that '[t]he question remains whether the *forum arresti* is really justified in intra-European relationships, even if limited to the arrest of ships'.[38] The present study addresses this issue fully and concludes that *forum arresti* should be maintained in Europe as a private international law device that serves cooperation between Member States.

1.39 Therefore, what may the future hold for the arrest of ships in the European context? This book suggests that the accession of the European Union[39] to the 1999 International Arrest Convention would be advantageous in

[32] The Treaty of Amsterdam amending the Treaty of the European Union was signed on 2 October 1997, and entered into force on 1 May 1999.

[33] Treaty on the Functioning of the European Union signed at Lisbon, 13 December 2007 [2008] OJ C 115/01.

[34] J Harris, 'Understanding the English Response to the Europeanisation of Private International Law' (2008) *Journal of Private International Law* (Dec) 347, 359.

[35] Resolution of 7 September 2010 on the Implementation and the Review of the Brussels I Regulation (see European Parliament doc T7-0304/2010).

[36] Ibid.

[37] Schlosser in B Hess, T Pfeiffer, and P Schlosser, *Report on the Application of Regulation Brussels I in the Member States* (Study JLS/C4/2005/03) (hereafter *Heidelberg Report*).

[38] *Heidelberg Report*, para 310.

[39] With the new powers in the field of private international law recognized in the EU by the Treaty of Lisbon there is little doubt to consider accession to the 1999 International Arrest Convention as 'particularly necessary for the proper functioning of the internal market' (Art 81 of the Treaty on the Functioning of the European Union (OJ C 115, 9.5.2008). In the

many ways. Particularly in relation to the jurisdictional scheme of the European area of justice, it would represent the availability of a cooperative private international law device, *forum arresti*, to all Member States of the European Union regardless of their different domestic laws. If that happens, advancement would be brought to the enforcement of maritime claims within Europe. Moreover, in legal systems where the courts have discretion to exercise jurisdiction, such as English and Scots law, it would also represent the availability in this sphere of the doctrine of *forum non conveniens*,[40] as 'distilled in Scotland'[41] and matured in England; one of Great Britain's 'best known exports'.[42] Up to a certain extent, it would mean fitting the European admiralty scheme into English and Scottish traditions;[43] hence, the result would have a very recognizable British taste.

Heidelberg Report, Schlosser expressed that 'it would be worth contemplating that the EU as such accedes to the [1999 International Arrest] Convention' (*Heidelberg Report*, 136–7).

[40] Note, however, that according to Art 7(2) of the 1999 International Arrest Convention the exercise of discretion to decline jurisdiction based on the arrest of the ship is permitted only where a court of another State accepts jurisdiction.

[41] Lord Hope of Craighead (HL), '*Forum non conveniens*: where next?' Conference Paper, Journal of Private International Law Conference 2007, Birmingham 26 June 2007, 1. He referred to *forum non conveniens*, 'as distilled and matured in Scotland ... one of the country's best known exports'.

[42] Ibid.

[43] See DC Jackson, 'Fitting Maritime Jurisdiction into Europe or vice versa?' [2001] *Lloyd's Maritime and Commercial Law Quarterly* 219.

Part I

The Arrest of Ships as a Provisional and Protective Measure

2

The Arrest of Ships in International Commercial Litigation

I. INTRODUCTION

This study starts from the assumption that the arrest of ships in international commercial litigation can be said to be a truly private international law institution. Its rationale is to provide a useful device for international commerce and to compensate for the difficulty of enforcing judgments abroad. In the context of maritime claims, against the foreign defendant, the ship is in most cases the sole asset that the claimant is able to secure for the purposes of enforcing his claim. Thus, in practice, the possibility to arrest a ship in an appropriate jurisdiction is of paramount importance to the international shipping and trading community, and to their legal advisers. Ships trade worldwide; they spend their economic life moving between different jurisdictions often far from their country of registry; and their commercial management poses peculiar problems for those faced with an unpaid debt incurred in the course of shipping. Against this background, the arrest of ships, inherently connected with jurisdiction and security, has played a key role since ancient times. **2.01**

2.02 The traditional view is that the arrest of ships as a legal institution benefits both creditors and ship-owners. At the beginning of the sixteenth century Browne explained that if an Englishman was owed money by a foreign merchant, any ship of the latter coming into the jurisdiction was liable to arrest, the creditor not being obliged to look for his debtor in a foreign country due to the security that the ship itself represented. Moreover, such a security was considered as favouring as well the foreign merchant whom, on such security, was better enabled to gain credit in England upon occasion.[1] Thus, the harmonization efforts in the field of arrest of ships have been aimed at protecting the ship-owner from abuse as well as improving his position as to the ability to gain credit upon the ship.[2]

2.03 However, the actual arrest of a ship is not as frequent as the foregoing comments may suggest.[3] Nevertheless, the importance of the arrest of ships in international commercial litigation is not measurable by the number of ships effectively arrested but by the availability of such a measure. In modern times the arrest of ships has been regarded as 'the most effective provisional remedy' in maritime litigation.[4]

2.04 The international community has for a long time recognized the paramount importance of arrest of ships as a provisional and protective measure in the international commercial litigation sphere. Harmonization efforts have been developed and international Conventions have been agreed and are in force in most of the leading shipping countries. Nonetheless, the level of harmonization achieved by the international

[1] A Browne, *A Compendious View of the Civil Law and of the Law of the Admiralty: Being the Substance of a Course of Lectures Read in the University of Dublin*, vol 2 (New York, Halsted and Voorhies, 1840; reprint, New Jersey, The Lawbook Exchange Ltd, 2000) 76.

[2] JJ Alvarez Rubio, *Derecho Marítimo y Derecho Internacional Privado, Problemas básicos* (Servico Central de Publicaciones del Gobierno Vasco Vitoria-Gasteiz 2000) 91. Interestingly enough, this author has argued that the arrest of ships is the main mechanism of protection and security of ship financing transactions since obtaining possession upon default is naturally an essential first requisite in the realization of asset value through enforcement (ibid, 23).

[3] In England, undertakings in individual suits brought upon causes of action *in rem* are the usual practice since the 1960s (KC McGuffie, PA Fugeman, and PV Gray, *Admiralty Practice* (London, Stevens, 1964) 104), and this is reflected in the issue of warrants for arrest that then numbered less than 20% of the quantity of writs *in rem* issued (FL Wiswall, *The Development of Admiralty Jurisdiction and Practice since 1800: An English Study with American Comparisons* (Cambridge, CUP, 1970) 187). There are standard letters of undertaking usually provided by the protection and indemnity insurers (P&I Clubs) of the ship-owner or demise charterer, or by their banks.

[4] DC Jackson, *Enforcement of Maritime Claims* (4th edn, London, LLP, 2005) 3.

Convention currently in force, the 1952 International Arrest Convention,[5] despite more than 80 ratifications, is still partial and insufficient.

To fully understand the current law on the arrest of ships in international commercial litigation as a coherent set of interrelated rules it is vital to analyse the evolution of the arrest of ships as a legal institution over the centuries. After a very brief outline of the variety of approaches used in different legal systems, this chapter also looks briefly into the legal origins of arrest in general—not limited to the arrest of ships—in civil and commercial litigation. After that, the chapter follows a chronological order. First, it examines the arrest of ships in the ancient *lex maritima*. Then, along with the rise of jurisdictional sovereignty, it looks at the arrest of ships as practised in England and Scotland in the nineteenth century. The particular analysis of the arrest of ships in English and Scots law from the twentieth century up until present times is left to Chapters 4 and 5. **2.05**

1. The Variety of Approaches used in Different Legal Systems

As a legal institution used in civil and commercial matters, the arrest of ships pertains to most national legal systems. As a provisional and protective measure it has always been connected with litigation involving foreigners. Undoubtedly the differences between legal systems in relation to the arrest of ships are linked to the variety of approaches used in different legal systems in relation to provisional and protective measures. A brief description of the legal institutions across different national legal systems may contribute to present the general spectrum. **2.06**

Preliminary Attachment

The United States preliminary attachment[6] permits a claimant having an *in personam* claim in admiralty to attach property of the defendant (whether movable or immovable) within the district, when the defendant cannot be found in the district; the attachment thus serving as well as a jurisdictional basis founding jurisdiction where there is otherwise no *in personam* jurisdiction over the defendant.[7] Due to its civilian origins, this institution, which comes from the ancient maritime attachment originated in England, **2.07**

[5] International Convention for the Unification of Certain Rules Relating to the Arrest of Sea-Going Ships, Brussels 10 May 1952.

[6] The legal systems of the United States and Canada have similarities with English and Scots law; arguably as developments of both. The outstanding work of William W Tetley in those legal systems is noteworthy. See WW Tetley, 'Arrest, Attachment and Related Maritime Law Procedures' (1999) 73 *Tulane Law Review* 1895.

[7] Tetley, 'Arrest, Attachment and Related Maritime Law Procedures' (1999) 1934.

resembles in relation to its protective function, the *saisie conservatoire* of civil law systems such as the French.

Saisie Conservatoire

2.08 The *saisie conservatoire*—literally translatable as conservatory attachment—gives the claimant 'physical' security before judgment. In the case of ships the measure prohibits the ship from leaving port but does not otherwise affect the rights of the owner.[8] In that sense it differs from the Spanish *embargo preventivo*.

Embargo preventivo

2.09 In some other civil law systems including Spain and several South American legal systems, the type of arrest granted against a ship as a provisional and protective measure is known as *embargo preventivo*:[9] literally meaning a 'protective *embargo*', that restrains the defendant from selling the ship and sets up a privilege in the eventual posterior judicial sale of the ship ranking after mortgages but before subsequent *embargoes* and unsecured creditors.

2.10 All in all, what these measures have in common is their provisional nature and protective character, which have been the most salient features of arrest of ships since its very beginnings.[10] 'Arrest of ships' is the English language expression preferred by the international community. In the 1952 International Arrest Convention, the arrest of ships has been defined as 'any detention or restriction on removal of a ship by order of a Court to secure a maritime claim' and 'does not include the seizure of a ship in execution or satisfaction of a judgment or other enforceable instrument'.[11]

[8] Decree No 67-967 of 27 October 1967; R Rodière and E Du Pontavice, *Droit Maritime* (12th edn, Paris, Dalloz, 1997) 178.

[9] Cecilia Fresnedo de Aguirre, *'Embargo de Buques como Medida Cautelar en el Derecho Internacional Privado Uruguayo'* (1997) 14 *Anuario de Derecho Marítimo* 385; Ronald Herbert and C Fresnedo de Aguirre, *'El Arresto de Buques y el Principio de Jurisdicción mas Próxima'* [1993] *Revista de Transporte y Seguros* 158.

[10] P Miranda, *História e Prática do Arresto ou Embargo* (Sao Paulo, Saraiva, 1929; reprint, Campinas, Bookseller, 1999).

[11] Article 1(2) International Convention relating to the Arrest of Sea-Going Ships (Brussels, 10 May 1952). See also Art 1(2) International Convention on Arrest of Ships 1999 (Geneva, 12 March 1999).

2. Arrest in Civil and Commercial Litigation

There are different opinions as to the origins of arrest as a legal institution. According to Gierke,[12] arrest has a Germanic foundation. Nevertheless, Muther considered that arrest already existed in Roman law[13] and Wach distinguished the Germanic evolution from the Italian evolution, the first one from the Carolingian times, and the latter from Longobardish law.[14] In early times arrest was linked to enforcement processes and its compelling effects were against the person and not against the *res*.[15] In those early times arrest was voluntarily agreed between the litigating parties as a way to secure the accomplishment with the eventual judgment.[16] Later on it became compulsory in favour of the creditor, first against the person of the debtor, and afterward against his property. Arrest preserved only what was enough to cover the debt.[17] 2.11

II. THE ARREST OF SHIPS IN THE ANCIENT *LEX MARITIMA*

1. The Earliest Times of Maritime Navigation

The precise historical lineage of the arrest of ships is not entirely clear. Despite several scholarly attempts[18] to trace back this ancient process no definite source has appeared to be the original one. The need to provide security in the case of foreign defendants was already a requisite in the 2.12

[12] O Gierke, *Deutsches Privatrecht* (Leipzig, Duncker u. Humblot, 1895) (1) 330, '*Dieses dem römischen Recht unbekannte Rechtsinstitut hat sich aus deutschrechtlicher Wurzel im gemeinen Zivilprozess entwickelt*'. For a historic overview of arrest see Miranda, *História e Prática do Arresto ou Embargo* (1929).

[13] T Muther, *Sequestration und Arrest im Römischen Recht* (Leipzig, Hirzel, 1856) 304, 344. It is here submitted that as far as arrest of ships is concerned it is clear that it did exist already in the times of the Roman Empire.

[14] H von Rudorff, *Zur Rechtsstellung der Gäste im mittelalterlichen städtischen Prozess: vorzugsweise nach norddeutschen Quellen* (Breslau, Marcus, 1907) (88) 41.

[15] JW von Planck, *Das deutsche Gerichtsverfahren im Mittelalter: nach dem Sachsenspiegel und den verwandten Rechtsquellen* (Braunschweig, 1879; reprint, Olms Hildesheim, 1973) (2) 367. Planitz considered the arrest against the fugitive debtor as the main type of arrest in the past (H Planitz, *Studien zur Geschichte des deutschen Arrestprozesses, Der Arrest gegen den fugitivus* in *Zeitschrift der Savigny-Stiftung für Rechtsgeschichte* (germanische Abteilung, 1913 (34) 49.

[16] Miranda, *História e Prática do Arresto ou Embargo* (1929) 25.

[17] Ibid, 62.

[18] See eg Wiswall, *The Development of Admiralty Jurisdiction and Practice since 1800* (1970) 183.

practice of the ancient Athenian maritime procedure as early as in the fourth century. However, the arrest of ships is not mentioned there as a device used for such purposes.[19]

2.13 The ancient *lex maritima* originated from the customs of the early Egyptians, Phoenicians and Greeks, who carried an extensive commerce in the Mediterranean Sea. These rules enjoyed authority far beyond the ports where they were promulgated. Until the rise of modern nations, maritime law did not derive its force from territorial sovereigns but represented what was already conceived to be the customary law of the sea.[20] Nonetheless, no trace of the arrest of ships, or any institution thought to provide for similar functions, can be found in the substantive rules of the earliest times of maritime navigation. The very first rules related to the maritime adventure and its perils such as the *Hammurabi's Code of Laws* (c.1780 BC), the *Sumerian Laws Handbook* (c.1700 BC), and the *Laws of Manu (Manusmriti)* (1500 BC to AD 200) none of which provided for any such rule or procedure. Neither is the arrest of ships accounted for as a common practice in the Hellenic culture. However, it should be noted that the Athenian commercial maritime procedure of the fourth century, the *dikai emporiki*, was rigorous when it came to pre-trial bail for defendants.[21] This rigorousness was a consequence of the heavy participation of foreigners in those commercial cases.[22] Special provisions were available for assuring a defendant's appearance at the ensuing trial and measures such as imprisonment could be taken to enforce the judgment of maritime tribunals.[23] This shows that two of the three functions that eventually the arrest of ships came to fulfil at a later time, the jurisdictional and the security functions, were already part of commercial and maritime proceedings involving foreigners since at least the fourth century.

2.14 Notwithstanding the aforementioned, it is in Rhodian law[24] as compiled in the *Corpus Iuris Civilis* (Book XIV Title I–II of the *Justinian's Digest*) of the

[19] EE Cohen, *Ancient Athenian Maritime Courts* (New Jersey, Princeton University Press, 1973) 80.

[20] SS Jados (tr), *The Consulate of the Sea and Related Documents* (Alabama, University of Alabama Press, 1975).

[21] EE Cohen, *Ancient Athenian Maritime Courts* (New Jersey, Princeton University Press, 1973) 80.

[22] Ibid.

[23] Ibid, 8.

[24] Some commentators consider Rhodian Laws as the most ancient maritime laws in Europe, see GJ Bell, *Commentaries on the Law of Scotland and on the Principles of Mercantile Jurisprudence*, vol 2 (7th edn, Edinburgh, T&T Clark, 1870; reprint, Edinburgh, Butterworths, 1990) 547. Bell provides a good concise enumeration and description of authorities received by Scottish judges, ie The Rhodian Laws, *Il Consolato del Mare*, Rules of Oleron, Rules of

sixth century where the first evidences of the arrest of ships ever appeared. Romans did not have their own maritime law. They incorporated in the *Corpus Iuris Civilis* the famed *Rhodian Sea Law*. According to that law in the early times of the Roman Empire the ship or *res* could be arrested until bail was given and this arrest was not justified under the *tacita pignora* (tacit hypothec) of the Romans.[25] However, the origins of such practice are quite unsettled. No primary written specimen of the Rhodian law has survived, so it is impossible to tell whether this practice was already common in the law of Rhodes. Nonetheless, the majority seem to derive arrest as a process from the *processus contra contumacem* of Roman law. The first evidence of the arrest of ships as a procedure would emerge then from the transposition of the law of Rhodes—ie the practices of a small-shipping-experienced island—as incorporated in the magnificent compilation of Roman law and associated with the Roman *processus contra contumacem*. This could be seen as the very first merger in the long chain of amalgamations throughout the centuries that have led to what is known today as the arrest of ships.

2. The Arrest of Ships in the Medieval Era

Undoubtedly it was in medieval times where the blossoming of commerce within Europe led to the emergence of the *lex mercatoria*, a cosmopolitan mercantile law based upon customs and applied to cross-border disputes by the market tribunals[26] of the various European trade centres. This law resulted from the efforts of the medieval trade community to overcome the fragmentary and obsolete rules of feudal and Roman law which could not respond to the needs of the inter-local and international commerce.[27] Merchants created a legal system suitable to their needs, which constituted a solid legal basis for the great expansion of commerce. For almost 800 years uniform rules of law, those of the law merchant, were applied throughout Western Europe among traders. The *lex maritima* comprising the rules applied to shipping were an important part of such *lex mercatoria*. **2.15**

Wisby, *The Ordonnances of the Hanseatic Towns*, *Le Guidon de la Mer*, *Ordonnance de la Marine of Louis XIV*, *Code de Commerce*, the determinations of maritime and mercantile courts such as the ones of Genoa, Friesland, and Holland, and the decisions (of greatest authority) of the High Court of Admiralty of England; see Bell, *Commentaries on the Law of Scotland* (1990) 547–50.

[25] Browne, *A Compendious View of the Civil Law and of the Law of Admiralty*, vol 2 (2000) 35.

[26] In England these were the so-called *pie poudre* and staple courts (see G Baron, 'Do the UNIDROIT Principles of International Commercial Contracts Form a New *Lex Mecatoria*?' (1998) 15 *Arbitration International* (2) 117).

[27] AM Lopez Rodriguez, *Lex Mercatoria and Harmonization of Contract Law in the EU* (Copenhagen, DJOF Publishing, 2003).

However, the arrest of ships is not mentioned in many medieval sea laws. The first codes of the Medieval Era such as the *Maritime Ordinances of Trani* (AD 1063), the *Navigation Code of the Port of Arles* (1150), the Barcelona Navigation Act of 1227 or the Maritime Code of 1258 do not provide for the the arrest of ships as an interim measure of protection.

2.16 Nevertheless, the relation between the ship and its creditors as known in present times originated during those times. In *La Tabula de Amalfa* dated from AD 1095 the ship was already considered as the guarantee. There were provisions therein such as 'let the ship and the capital advanced on commission form one mass and one fund, and let the ship be responsible for the capital, and the capital for the ship, notwithstanding, any other ancient or modern obligation howsoever incurred';[28] or the faculty of the master to 'bind the ship to whomsoever he may please, expressly in accordance with the usage of the Strand of the aforesaid city, notwithstanding, any public or private agreement in the nature of a contract or a quasi-contract entered into between the parties'.[29] The relationship between the ship's equipment and the ship's creditors is found also in the first article of *The Rules of Oleron*[30] (c.1266), where interestingly enough, Scotland is expressly mentioned,[31] and it is established that the master may pledge part of the ship's equipment for necessaries.

2.17 It is in the Ordinances issued by King James of Spain (1213–1276) for the Island of Majorca where the first provisions regarding the arrest of ships appeared, but it was not until the end of the fifteenth century, when they were compiled in the *Consolato del Mare* (1494),[32] that they acquired broader

[28] *La Tabula de Amalfa* (1095), Art 6 see T Twiss (ed), *The Black Book of the Admiralty*, vol 4 (London, Longman, 1871–76); 2nd reprint (New Jersey, The Lawbook Exchange Ltd, 1998) 9.

[29] Ibid, Art 7.

[30] While travelling the eastern Mediterranean on the Crusades with her first husband, King Louis VII of France, Eleanor of Aquitaine discovered a complicated and advanced system of admiralty law. She brought back this admiralty law and administered it upon her people on the island of Oleron. Later, while acting as regent for her son King Richard the Lionheart in England, she founded the English system of admiralty law on such bases.

[31] *Rules of Oleron* (c.1266), Art I 'When several joint owners make a man master of a ship or vessel, and the ship or vessel departing from her own port, arrives at Bordeaux, Rouen, or any other such place, and is there freighted to sail for Scotland, or some other foreign country; the master in such case may not sell or dispose of that ship or vessel, without a special procuration from the owners: but in case he wants money for the victualling, or other necessary provisions of the said vessel, he may for that end, with the advice of his mariners, pawn or pledge part of the tackle or furniture of a ship.'

[32] *Il Consolato del Mare* (The Consulate of the Sea) is a compilation of ordinances. The first such codification was published in 1010 under the title of Customs of the City of Amalfitina; a second one was published in 1063 in the city of Trani. In 1509 an edited copy of the second one was incorporated into the statutes of the city of Fermo. It is also said that in the Hansa

recognition and acceptance. Arrest is therein expressly authorized by provision number 42[33] under the title 'Demand of a Guarantee When Seizure of a Vessel is Ordered'.

Therefore, it can be submitted without hesitation that even though arrest procedures were already practised in Roman law, the arrest of ships had its earliest developments in medieval times, in the context of shipping-credit and related to litigation involving foreigners. That is to say, two main functions were already then performed by arresting a ship. The first one related to the assertion of jurisdiction over a defendant who without such detention would not be submitted to it; and the second one, the security function, related to the ship as an asset guaranteeing the payment of debts. The third function identifiable in present times, the protective function, is indeed a pre-condition for these two to be operative; hence, arguably, the three functions have been part of the law of arrest of ships since its early origins. **2.18**

3. Ship Arrest in Early English Maritime Practice

In England admiralty courts were already functioning in the eleventh century. The greatest source to trace back the arrest of ships as practised in England is the *Black Book of the Admiralty*[34] which although only published in its modern form in 1871, was compiled as the definitive English collection of Admiralty sources dating from the middle ages. The *Black Book* shows that in the second year of the reign of King John (AD 1200) in **2.19**

Towns (Baltic, North Sea, Hanseatic League) some of these laws were adopted earlier and published under the auspicies of the Hanseatic League, under the title *Waterrecht* in 1407 (most commonly known as the Laws of Wisby). All these compilations contributed significantly to the later formation of *Il Consolato del Mare* of the fifteenth century (see Jados (tr), *The Consulate of the Sea and Related Documents* (1975)).

[33] *Il Consolato del Mare*, Ord 42, 'In all instances when the Consuls order seizure of a vessel and its cargo as a guarantee …'. Against the background of these ordinances, it looks as if this 'guarantee seizure' is the modern arrest of ships because 'guarantee' was only mentioned in these ordinances in such context. Ordinance No 30, under the title 'Posting a Bond to Assure the Execution of a Verdict' establishes 'If the summons demands that the defendant furnishes a guarantee in the action brought against him; … , and if he is a foreigner, he must furnish a guarantee bond at once …' (Jados (tr), *The Consulate of the Sea and Related Documents* (1975)).

[34] Twiss, *The Black Book of the Admiralty*, vol 2 (1998). Through the compilation of *The Black Book* Twiss succeeded to show that in the practice of shipping law the world rests firmly on the same roots; see J Hare, 'Of Black Books, White Horses and Sacred Cows: The Quest for International Uniformity in Maritime Law' address to the British Maritime Law Association, London, 11 November 1999.

Ipswich[35] there was a 'court sitting regularly from tide to tide to administer the Law Marine in England'.[36] This was a practice also in other regions of the country where 'courts sat in those boroughs from day to day, or from sea to sea, as the case might be, to administer justice between men of various nations, whom the spirit of commerce or the necessities of navigation happened to bring within their local jurisdiction'.[37] Later on, the courts of the Lord High Admiral dealt primarily with cases of piracy and naval discipline but gradually these tribunals extended their jurisdiction to commercial matters.

2.20 The arrest of ships is also an ancient institution in England even though it is not possible to determine with certainty when this practice started.[38] In the very first reports found in the oldest English admiralty manuscripts there are several references to arrest for the king's service[39] but it is difficult to assert when arrest procedures linked with commercial litigation started and what were the legal grounds for such a practice. In any case, at the beginning of the sixteenth century such a practice was common and was intrinsically linked with commercial cases with foreign elements (ie international commercial litigation). As no real right was necessary to found the Admiralty action *in rem* against ships in the medieval or early modern period, rather than it being derived from the *actio realis*[40] of Roman law, legal historians point to a procedural origin of the arrest of ships in English Admiralty jurisdiction.[41] In their opinion it derives from the

[35] See NSB Gras, 'A List of Local Customs Due in the Port of Ipswich' in *The Early English Customs System: A Documentary Study of the Institutional and Economic History of the Customs from the Thirteenth to the Sixteenth Century*, vol 18 (Cambridge, CUP, 1918) 159. Ipswich was an important maritime borough in the time of Edward the Confessor. The Domesday of Ipswich is the earliest extant record of any borough Court to sit daily to administer the law merchant.

[36] 'Domesday of Ipswich' in Twiss, *The Black Book of the Admiralty*, vol 2 (1998) viii '… When and how this practice originated does not appear. It was a legacy of the imperial Rome that maritime causes should be heard without any delay before the competent judges in each province, and there is good reason for believing that medieval Europe accepted this legacy, and never allowed it to lapse.'

[37] Twiss, *The Black Book of the Admiralty*, vol 2 (1998) vii–viii.

[38] In the old rules for the Lord Admiral (*Liber Niger Admiralitatis*) found in *The Black Book of the Admiralty* there are provisions regarding the arrest 'for the king's service or for any other reasonable cause' (Twiss, *The Black Book of the Admiralty*, vol 1 (1998) 65–7).

[39] See the Documents Connected with the Admiralty of John Holland, Duke of Exeter, 1443–46 in Twiss, *The Black Book of the Admiralty*, vol 1 (1998) 65, 250, 262. In these documents there are several precepts to arrest ships. One of them appears as 'precept to arrest certain aliens and their goods'.

[40] The *actio realis* of Roman law involved an action asserting a right of the claimant over a thing (*res*) in the possession of the defendant.

[41] Tetley, 'Arrest, Attachment and Related Maritime Law Procedures' (1999) 1900–1.

processus contra contumacem, 'a process of arrest of property to compel appearance of the defendant',[42] that was developed all over medieval Europe and practised in the City of London by the fifteenth century.[43]

The civilian judges of the High Court of Admiralty practised ship detention during the fourteenth and fifteenth centuries in the framework of the *processus contra contumacem*. Its primary purpose was to neutralize the effects of the defendant's contemptuous resistance to appear before the court.[44] This procedure could be exercised in two ways: against the person or against his property (any property, all the assets of the defendant were at stake, not only the ones related to the claim). As Tetley explains, the process was a summary one: first, the person and/or the property of the defendant were arrested at the same time that the defendant was cited to appear.[45] Secondly, the defendant received up to four citations to appear and if all were defaulted the claimant would formulate his claim in the form of a draft sentence or article upon first decree.[46] Finally, the admiralty court in its first decree (*primum decretum*) could award possession[47] of the property arrested to the claimant based on the defendant's contumacy.[48] In the original Continental procedure, a second decree was needed in an *actio personalis*, a personal right of action, different from the *actio realis*, where real rights were at stake, in order to transfer ownership of the arrested property to the claimant after a period of time. In England, the second decree rarely appeared in case law, paradoxically, due to the irrelevance of the distinction between *actio realis* and *actio personalis*[49] in English law. The arrest did not depend for its validity on the existence of any real right on the ship or the goods derived from a lien or a hypothec; the only requirements were that the ship or goods belonged to the defendant and were within the Court's jurisdiction.[50] **2.21**

The development in English law later abandoned these origins completely to reach the opposite pole: where the availability of arrest will depend on **2.22**

[42] Ibid.

[43] Ibid.

[44] Ibid.

[45] Ibid.

[46] Ibid.

[47] In the Continental original *processus contra contumacem* possession was granted only in *actio realis* and in *actio personalis* only custody of the property up to the amount of the indebtedness was granted (Tetley, 'Arrest, Attachment and Related Maritime Law Procedures' (1999) 1901).

[48] Browne, *A Compendious View of the Civil Law and of the Law of Admiralty*, vol 2 (1840) 352.

[49] Tetley, 'Arrest, Attachment and Related Maritime Law Procedures' (1999) 1901.

[50] Ibid, 1903.

the existence of a maritime lien (a real right on the ship) and where the relevance of the distinction between action *in rem* and action *in personam* will become not only paramount but—in the opinion of some—the *raison d'être* of the arrest of ships as a legal institution. In modern times, however, the situation of English law lies somewhere in the middle of this polarization, not without incongruities and inconsistencies difficult to overcome.

2.23 Hence, the English mark of the arrest of ships as a measure *in rem* lies elsewhere, not in the distinction between *actio realis* and *actio personalis* of Roman law. It can be said that the distinction *in personam/in rem* even though it originated undoubtedly from the Roman one, evolved as something completely different. It has been suggested that it owes its genesis to the long-lasting clash between the High Court of Admiralty jurisdiction and that of the common law courts started in the thirteenth and fourteenth centuries.[51]

2.24 The Court of Admiralty was a civil law court and during those times it was continuously confronted with the common law courts to determine the extent and limits of its jurisdiction. It took many centuries and more *prohibitions*[52] to settle this issue, unfortunately with not so good results for the Admiralty court.[53] One of the ways used by the common law courts to limit the scope of action of the High Court of Admiralty was to dwell upon

[51] A Mandaraka-Sheppard, *Modern Maritime Law and Risk Management* (2nd edn, London, Informa, 2009) 5.

[52] 'A prohibition is a writ issued by a [superior] court, directed to the judge and parties of a suit in an [inferior court], commanding them to cease from the prosecution of the same, upon a suggestion that the cause originally, or some collateral matter arising therein, does not belong to that jurisdiction, but to the cognizance of some other court' (WWC, 'The Function of Writs of Prohibition' (1919) 28 *The Yale Law Journal* 482). In the case of the clash between the court of admiralty and the common law courts the prohibitions were most of the time based on prejudice rather than on reason (Browne, *A Compendious View of the Civil Law and of the Law of Admiralty*, vol 2 (1840) 85).

[53] Already in 1632 the rules were as follows 'If suit should be commenced in the court of admiralty upon contracts made, or other things personal, done beyond the seas, or upon the sea, no prohibition to be awarded. If suit be before the admiral for freight, or mariners wages, or for breach of charter-parties, for voyages to be made beyond the seas; though the charter-party happen to be made within the realm, so as the penalty be not demanded, a prohibition is not to be granted: but it the suit be for the penalty; or if the question be, whether the plaintiff did release or otherwise discharge the same within the realm; this is to be tried in the King's courts at Westminster, and not in his court of admiralty. If suit be in the court of admiralty for building, amending, saving or necessary victualling of a ship, against the ship itself, and not against any party by name, but such as for his interest makes himself a party, no prohibition is to be granted, though this be done within the realm' (Browne, *A Compendious View of the Civil Law and of the Law of Admiralty*, vol 2 (1840) 78–9). For further analysis on the diminishing influence of the civil law tradition in the seventeenth century in England, see BP Levack, *The Civil Lawyers in England, 1603–1641: A Political Study* (Oxford, Clarendon, 1973).

the idea that admiralty jurisdiction was limited to causes of action involving the liability of the vessel, as opposed to the personal liability of the owner. At those times the device used in admiralty to compel the defendant to appear in court was to arrest the person of the defendant[54] or seize his assets within the jurisdiction (the ancient English maritime attachment).

The maritime attachment, originally adjunct to the writ *in personam*, fell into disuse in Admiralty by the beginning of the nineteenth century concurrently with the loss of jurisdiction *in personam* experienced by that court. The Admiralty Court's powers were only expanded by the Acts of 1840 and 1861 but by then the maritime attachment was already considered extinct as a legal procedure.[55] The High Court of Admiralty continued to arrest ships as part of its newly circumvented jurisdiction. From then on, the arrest of ships has been conceived in England as part of the action *in rem* nowadays renamed as *in rem* claim.[56] **2.25**

When the High Court of Admiralty lost its jurisdiction *in personam* (therefore to arrest the person of the defendant was no longer competent) arrest of the ship came to be seen as the exclusive mode in which admiralty process was exercisable in respect of such claims.[57] The advantage of having the ship as security was so manifest that common law courts were forced to yield and admiralty jurisdiction regained part of its lost jurisdiction in later times. Nevertheless, after those long centuries of struggle it was never again what it once was. From then on, an action *in rem* is one against the ship or *res* where an action *in personam* is against the owner or charterer of the ship, even though the border lines have never been and certainly are still not entirely clear.[58] This traditional *in rem/in personam* distinction—upon which all the admiralty law of England and its ex-colonies has been developing during the last 200 years—is full of inconsistencies. **2.26**

[54] The last known maritime attachment exercised as arrest of a person was in 1780 *The Clara* (1855) Swab 1.

[55] Tetley, 'Arrest, Attachment and Related Maritime Law Procedures' (1999) 1905. Tetley is of the opinion that the maritime attachment continued to exist after 1800 on the grounds of Fry LJ's speech in *Northcote v Owners of the Henrich Bjorn (The Henrich Bjorn)* (1885) LR 10 PD 44 (CA).

[56] Pt 61, Civil Procedure Rules (CPR) 1998.

[57] Tetley, 'Arrest, Attachment and Related Maritime Law Procedures' (1999) 1903.

[58] See *The Republic of India v India Steamship Co Ltd (No 2) (The Indian Grace (No 2))* [1998] 1 AC 878 (HL). See further analysis in paras 4.09–4.15 in Ch 4 below.

4. Arrestment of Ships in Early Scottish Maritime Practice

2.27 The first compilation to include a section on sea laws in Scotland appears to be Balfour's *Practicks*,[59] however this collection was not published until the eighteenth century. As early as in 1590 William Welwood published the first textbook of maritime law to be published in Great Britain under the title *Sea Laws of Scotland*.[60] In that book he commented that the first courts to exercise what it was later known as admiralty jurisdiction in Scotland were the courts of the water bailies of the maritime burghs.[61] These were superseded by the Court of Admiralty probably in the early fifteenth century even though the precise date of its establishment is unknown.[62]

2.28 The first Admiral of Scotland appears to have been the second Earl of Orkney in the early fifteenth century and the jurisdiction of the Court of Admiralty started to develop during the same time.[63] Its earliest records are the *Acta Curiae Admirallatus Scotioe*, dated 1557–62. In 1567 the Court was already established in Edinburgh.[64]

2.29 With a clear parallelism with what was happening in England, from 1532, when the Court of Session was instituted, the jurisdictions of the Court of Admiralty and the Court of Session clashed throughout the centuries.[65] There were various attempts to define the relation between the two courts: the 1609 Act expanded the jurisdiction of the Court of Admiralty; and the 1681 Act, which was enacted 'for the advancement and encouragement of trade and navigation', succeeded in affirming the independency of the jurisdiction of the Court of Admiralty in the first instance and the priority of maritime causes on appeal to the Court of Session. This Act continued to regulate the relations of the two courts until the abolition of the Court of Admiralty by the Court of Session Act 1830.[66]

[59] *The Practicks of Sir James Balfour of Pittendreich* (1583, published 1754, reprint Stair Society vol 21 (1962) and vol 22 (1963)); see also MC Meston, 'Admiralty' in *The Laws of Scotland, Stair Memorial Encyclopaedia*, vol 1, 197, para 402.

[60] W Welwood, *Sea Laws of Scotland* (Edinburgh, Robert Waldegrave, 1590). An expanded version written in English, not Scottish, appeared in 1613 (ADM Forte, 'Insurance' in KGC Reid and R Zimmermann, *A History of Private Law in Scotland*, vol 2, (Oxford, OUP, 2000) 333.

[61] ARG McMillan, *Scottish Maritime Practice* (Edinburgh, Hodge, 1926) xxxiii.

[62] Ibid, xxxiv.

[63] Ibid.

[64] The Acts of the Parliaments of Scotland (APS) III 41 (1567) Art 50, as cited by MC Meston, 'Admiralty' in *The Laws of Scotland, Stair Memorial Encyclopaedia*, vol 1, para 403.

[65] Ibid, para 404.

[66] McMillan, *Scottish Maritime Practice* (1926) xxxviii.

The Court of Admiralty was essentially a civil law court where the common law of Scotland was not administered but the general *lex mercatoria*. This had led some authors to affirm that the maritime law of Scotland is not Scottish but British.[67] This may be accurate in certain aspects of maritime law, such as the law of maritime liens which is indeed very much related to the law of arrest of ships, but it certainly does not apply to the law of arrest of ships itself where the two legal systems of Great Britain have developed differently. **2.30**

The arrestment of the ship played a key role in relation to the jurisdiction of the Court of Admiralty. Its jurisdiction was regarded as particularly applicable to foreigners due to the fact that it was only in admiralty cases that the court was capable of founding jurisdiction against a defender resident abroad through the arrestment of the ship (arrestment *ad fundandam jurisdictionem*[68]) (jurisdictional function).[69] In turn, arrestment of a ship was a summary procedure 'found to be necessary owing to the opportunities which ship-owners possessed for escaping diligence by merely sending their vessels to sea on receipt of notice that proceedings were contemplated'.[70] Due to this procedure, it was understood that 'the admiralty jurisdiction arises ratione rei sitae by reason of the res being situated within the maritime territory [of Scotland], and it is founded by the arrestment of the res'.[71] As McMillan explained, the arrestment was performed without calling the owners, whose names might have been unknown, and the precept was usually directed against the master alone. If the owners failed to enter, appearance decree might have proceeded in their absence and the vessel be judicially sold in extinction *pro tanto* of the debt in respect of which she had been arrested (security function).[72] In that case, which was frequent when the amount of the debt exceeded the value of the defender's interest in the ship, McMillan affirms that the proceedings 'were in no sense deemed to be directed against the defender, since the Court was, in fact, ignorant of his identity, and he was not before it but against the ship herself'.[73] Not surprisingly, McMillan does not give any further grounds for such an affirmation that disregards the personal **2.31**

[67] Ibid, 4.

[68] The arrestment *ad fundandam jurisdictionem* was first reported as used by the Court of Admiralty than by the Court of Session; see *Young v Arnold* 1683 M 4833.

[69] McMillan, *Scottish Maritime Practice* (1926) xxxiv.

[70] W Smith, *Maritime Practice, Adapted to the Sheriff Courts of Scotland* (Edinburgh, T&T Clark, 1832) 13 as cited by McMillan, *Scottish Maritime Practice* (1926) 57.

[71] McMillan, *Scottish Maritime Practice* (1926) 7.

[72] Ibid.

[73] Ibid, 19. Cf *The Indian Grace (No 2)* [1998] 1 AC 878 (HL). See further analysis in Ch 4 paras 4.09–4.15 below.

liability of the owner beyond the value of the vessel. The reason for that is probably that in the early twentieth century the personification theory, meaning that the action *in rem* was not a pure device for obtaining personal jurisdiction over ship-owners, but a unique proceeding directly against the ship, as firmly established in England by *The Bold Buccleugh* in 1852, was so unchallenged that it was taken for granted.[74]

2.32 The Court of Admiralty in Scotland considered the arrestment of ships as 'the appropriate machinery for proceeding *in rem* against the ship herself which is the subject of a claim'.[75] If the owners entered appearance they had to found caution the *judicio sisti* (to attend and appear during the pendency of the suit) and *judicatum solvi* (to pay the sum adjudged against them).[76] The ship was thereupon released and the action became a personal action against the owner, who was deemed to have voluntarily submitted to the jurisdiction.[77]

2.33 Moreover, the pursuer was required to find caution for damages for such liability as he might incur under the decree.[78] This cross-undertaking in damages is another typical feature of interim measures of protection as conceptually encoded universally in present times. Unfortunately it has been abandoned in the current practice of arrestment of ships in Scotland, probably in order to be in an equal position as a jurisdiction for the a rrestment of ships as compared to England.[79]

2.34 The creation of the United Kingdom of Great Britain in 1707 did not affect the way that admiralty jurisdiction was at those times exercised in Scotland.[80]

[74] Cf. *Morrison v Massa* 1866 5 M 130.

[75] McMillan, *Scottish Maritime Practice* (1926) 17. It is apparent that this jurisdiction based on arrestment is of a similar nature of the jurisdiction of an English Admiralty action *in rem* (now renamed as an *in rem* claim) as highlighted by McMillan, *Scottish Maritime Practice* (1926) 8, 'the form of action used in the Scottish Court of Admiralty [ie prior to 1830] was in substance an action *in rem* as now used in England'; see *The Dupleix* [1912] P 8 (PDAD).

[76] See C Farquhar Shand, *The Practice of the Court of Session: On the basis of the late Mr. Darling's Work of 1833* (Edinburgh, T&T Clark, 1848) 415.

[77] McMillan, *Scottish Maritime Practice* (1926) 8, 20.

[78] Ibid; see also R Boyd, *Judicial Proceedings before the High Court of Admiralty and Supreme Consistorial or Commissary Court of Scotland* (Edinburgh, C Elliot, 1779).

[79] See further discussion of this issue in Ch 5 paras 5.41–5.48 below.

[80] Act of Union 1707, Art 19 indicated that all admiralty jurisdictions shall be under the Lord Admiral or Commissioners of Admiralty in Great Britain. But the Court of Admiralty in Scotland shall be continued in maritime causes 'till the parliament of Great Britain make regulations as expedient for the whole United Kingdom so as in Scotland be always a court of admiralty for determining all maritime causes relating to private right in Scotland' (Browne, *A Compendious View of the Civil Law and of the Law of Admiralty*, vol 2 (1840) 31).

III. THE ARREST OF SHIPS IN THE NINETEENTH CENTURY IN GREAT BRITAIN

1. England

The Action *in rem*

Maxwell,[81] in giving the advantages of an Admiralty action *in rem* in his treatise of 1800, said 'the ship itself is responsible in the admiralty, and not the owners';[82] Browne, in 1802, said that 'no person can be subject to that [Admiralty] jurisdiction [*in rem*] but by his consent'.[83] In Tetley's opinion it was the need of the claimant, under the admiralty procedure of the Tudor/Stuart (1485–1714) period, to identify the arrested *res* in his draft sentence on first decree, and the fact that enforcement was limited to its value, that contributed to the concept that the ship itself, as opposed to its owner, was liable for certain claims, such as seamen's wages and salvage.[84] However, the liability of the ship is a more ancient concept than that, derived from the earliest *lex maritima* of medieval Europe.[85] **2.35**

The Intermingle of Theories in the Nineteenth Century in England

At the beginning of the nineteenth century, when the Admiralty Court had lost its *in personam* jurisdiction and acted only *in rem*, the struggle generated by the futile search of sources to understand, justify, and describe the one and only characteristic feature of the action *in rem*, made it unacceptable to conceive the different functions of the arrest of ships as equally important. The impression one has when analysing the unsettled dicta of the nineteenth century in Great Britain is that the different theories about the juridical nature of the action *in rem* have all contributed to a better understanding of the arrest of ships as a legal institution: whether it is a way to compel the defendant to appear in court/security-orientated device for accomplishing with the judgment (procedural theory); a way to enforce the liability of the ship as the wrongdoer (personification theory); or the way to establish the jurisdiction of the court (hereinafter called 'jurisdictional theory'). The problem, however, is that even when the **2.36**

[81] JI Maxwell, *The Spirit of Marine Law* (London, Bunney and Gold for T Chapman, 1800).

[82] Ibid, 8.

[83] Browne, *A Compendious View of the Civil Law and of the Law of Admiralty*, vol 2 (1840) 100.

[84] Tetley, 'Arrest, Attachment and Related Maritime Law Procedures' (1999) 1905.

[85] See para 2.17 above.

question addressed by these divergent theories is important, the answers should not be exclusive of one another.

The Jurisdictional Theory

2.37 The jurisdictional theory is constituted by all the decisions and comments that find the earliest antecedent of the arrest of ships in the *processus contra contumacem* as included into the *Black Book of the Admiralty*[86] as the *Ordo Judiciorum*.[87] The main aim of the procedure was to provide for a solution against the defendant's refusal to appear before the court to contest the suit brought against him. In England, the person and/or the property of the defendant in the jurisdiction of the Admiral could be arrested for such purposes. In the *Ordo Judiciorum* there could be no question of contumacy until the defendant had received the citation. However, by the time of Henry VIII, the arrest of the defendant's property was done concurrently with the citation of the defendant. It has been stressed that the practical reason which justified such alteration of the 'due process' was the speed with which the defendant's main asset, the ship, could leave the jurisdiction.[88] Already in 1823 Lord Stowell in *The Dundee* expressed that the arrest of ships was the ancient method of acquiring jurisdiction *in rem*.[89]

2.38 The jurisdictional theory contributed to the development of the arrest of ships as a legal institution by recognizing the medieval *processus contra contumaceum* as the origins of arrest and, particularly, the possibility of obtaining jurisdiction over the defendant through arrest, a function that has been carried on throughout the centuries.

The Personification Theory

2.39 In *The Bold Buccleugh*[90] Sir John Jervis rejected the idea that the action *in rem* was a purely procedural device intended to secure the appearance of the owners and thus to gain personal jurisdiction over them, similar to the manner of a foreign attachment.[91] He asserted that with attachment the process was directed initially at the person, and was thus in the nature of an action *in personam*, whereas the Admiralty action *in rem* was directed in

[86] T Twiss (ed), *The Black Book of the Admiralty*, vol 4 (London, Longman, 1871–76).

[87] Tetley, 'Arrest, Attachment and Related Maritime Law Procedures' (1999) 1900–1.

[88] Ibid.

[89] *The Dundee* (1823) I Hag Adm 109, 124.

[90] Daniel Harmer v William Errington Bell and Others (*The Bold Buccleugh*) (1851) 7 Moo. PCC 267, 282 (Sir John Jervis).

[91] Wiswall, *The Development of Admiralty Jurisdiction and Practice since 1800* (1970) 156; *The Bold Buccleugh* (1852) 7 Moo. PCC 267, 282 (Sir John Jervis).

the first instance at the ship. Hence, the Privy Council firmly established in *The Bold Buccleugh* that the action *in rem* was not a pure device for obtaining personal jurisdiction over ship-owners, but a unique proceeding directly against the ship.[92] At that time in Scotland the arrestment of ships was performed without calling the owners, whose names might have been unknown, and the precept was usually directed against the Master alone.[93]

The personification theory contributed to the development of the legal institution arrest of ships by considering the ship itself as the offender and by establishing a certain detachment between the ship and the ship-owner so as to allow proceedings against the ship even if there is no jurisdiction over the defendant personally. **2.40**

The Procedural Theory

The procedural theory was first advanced by Sir Francis Jeune in *The Dictator*.[94] In his opinion, arrest *in rem* was essentially intended to obtain security for any judgment that might be given. In evolving the procedural theory Jeune based his reasoning upon 'the early practice of the Admiralty Court'[95] and commenced his investigation in the early times when a proceeding to seize the *res* was available only when the defendant in a proceeding *in personam* was unavailable for personal arrest; failing to appear in response to a citation, the defendant was held in contempt and his *res* defaulted.[96] For an action *in rem* against the ship to be available, the procedural theory requires that the person who was the owner at the time when the facts giving rise to the cause of action occurred could have been answerable at common law. There is a person, not an asset, who is liable. Jeune's procedural theory was quickly accepted.[97] Jeune was not alone. Mardsen reached also the conclusion that the very early Admiralty action *in rem* was a security-orientated device because: 'Arrest of goods was quite as frequent as arrest of the ship ..., [and] the fact that goods and ships that had no connection with the cause of action, except as belonging to the **2.41**

[92] The personification theory has reached its utmost development in the United States. See *Tucker v Alexandroff* [1901] 183 US 424, 438.

[93] McMillan, *Scottish Maritime Practice* (1926)19.

[94] *The Dictator* [1892] P 304 (PDAD) 310; see also Wiswall, *The Development of Admiralty Jurisdiction and Practice since 1800* (1970) 159.

[95] *The Dictator* [1892] P 304 (PDAD) 310.

[96] F Clerke, *Praxis curiae admiralitatis Angli* (Dublin, 1666) Tit. 67–8 (Hall (1809) 115–18). For a translation of Clerke's Praxis, see JE Hall, *The Practice and Jurisdiction of the Court of Admiralty* (Geo. Dobbin and Murphy, Baltimore, 1809; reprint by New Jersey, The Lawbook Exchange, 2005) Part II, 3-118.

[97] *The Gemma* [1899] P 285 (CA) 292; *The Dupleix* [1912] P 8 (PDAD) 12.

defendant, were subject to arrest, points to the conclusion that arrest was mere procedure, and that its only object was to obtain security that judgment should be satisfied'.[98]

2.42 In turn, the procedural theory helped to neutralize the fictitious effects of the 'personification theory' by stressing that there is a person, not an asset, who is liable; and it has supported the possibility of sister-ship arrest. The procedural theory had one essential corollary, ie that in the original action *in rem* it was possible to arrest property of the defendant other than his ship. It was stated in 1885 by LJ Fry, that 'any property of the defendant within the realm' might be arrested to enforce a statutory right *in rem*.[99] This dictum was criticized as gratuitous and unsupported[100] due to confusion between the very early actions *in rem* with maritime attachment *in personam*. However, this aspect of the procedural theory eventually prompted the arrest in an action *in rem* of collateral property of a ship-owner, particularly sister-ships' arrests.

2.43 All in all, these three theories developed during the nineteenth century[101] in England are to a certain extent correct and all of them contributed to the development of the arrest of ships by a process of intermingling leading to what is today the unique institution at the centre of this analysis. However, after the revision of these different theories it is possible to argue that the confusion and complexities that still exist in the enforcement of maritime claims derive from the continued inaccurate reliance on historical admiralty practice. These different and sometimes opposing conceptual approaches reflect the difficulties that the conceptualization of the *in rem* claim poses in present times.[102] Particularly, in the case of arrest of ships, the lack of acknowledgement that the institution has been permanently changing, arguably adapting itself to the change of times, has jeopardized the understanding of its different functions.

[98] RG Marsden (ed), *Select Pleas of the Court of Admiralty. The court of the Admiralty of the West (A.D. 1390–1404) and The High Court of Admiralty (A.D. 1527–1545)*, vol 1 (London, B Quaritch, 1894–97) lxxi.

[99] *The Henrich Bjorn* (1885) LR 10 PD 44 (CA).

[100] Wiswall, *The Development of Admiralty Jurisdiction and Practice since 1800* (1970) 170.

[101] For a modern reassessment of these theories see *The Indian Grace (No 2)* [1998] 1 AC 878 (HL). See N Teare, 'The Admiralty Action *in rem* and the House of Lords' [1997] *Lloyds Maritime and Commercial Law Quarterly* 33.

[102] See eg Peter Gillies and Andrew Dahdal, 'Characterising the Action *In Rem* in Australia—Recent Perspectives' (2007) *Macquarie Law* (WP 2007–19) 1. The decision of the House of Lords in *The Indian Grace (No 2)* [1998] 1 AC 878 where an action *in rem* was considered to be—for jurisdictional purposes—an action against the owners and not merely an action against the ship, has represented a break through the conceptual dogma that considered the action *in rem* as inherently against the ship unless and until an owner liable *in personam* chooses to appear.

2. Scotland

Arrestment of Ships in Scotland after the Court of Session Act 1830

By the Court of Session Act 1830 the Court of Admiralty in Scotland was abolished and its civil jurisdiction transferred to the Court of Session and the Sheriff Court. From then on, arrestment can be made by the Court of Session or the Sheriff Court by virtue of their dual civil and common law jurisdiction. Same judges, same courts, but two distinct jurisdictions in their nature and in their law is the situation of administration of civil justice in Scotland since the Court of Session Act 1830. As the two jurisdictions had been cumulative and concurrently exercised since then, the maritime procedure in the early nineteenth century was more closely assimilated to that of a common law action in Scotland than was the case in England.[103] **2.44**

The most common form of action in Scotland was a petitory action for the payment of a debt directed against the ship-owner, and all his assets were liable to arrest in security.[104] Only if he failed to meet his personal obligations or allowed the action to go by default could proceedings *in rem* against the ship become necessary, by which the ship could be sold by order of the court in a process of sale. As McMillan explains, however, those proceedings *in rem* were ancillary to the main purpose of the action, which was one to enforce payment of a debt, and they were merely a form of diligence and not to be confused with the English action *in rem*. In the former the action was essentially a personal one and distinct from the latter where—in the opinion of most—the liability was primarily that of the ship and was only indirectly that of the owner.[105] On this distinction *The Bold Buccleugh*[106] was decided, and the two pending actions for damages out of the same collision, the one in Scotland and the other one *in rem* in England, were deemed to be essentially different; hence, the plea of *lis alibi pendens* was not upheld in England.[107] This has remarkably changed in present times.[108] **2.45**

At those times the distinctive features of the Scottish maritime procedure as compared with the English action *in rem* were as follows. First of all, in the case of a foreign ship-owner jurisdiction could be founded against **2.46**

[103] McMillan, *Scottish Maritime Practice* (1926) 19.
[104] Ibid, 21.
[105] *The Burns* [1907] P 137 (CA) 144.
[106] *The Bold Buccleugh* (1851) 7 Moo. PCC 267, 288.
[107] Ibid.
[108] See *The Indian Grace (No 2)* [1998] 1 AC 878 (HL).

him by arrestment *ad fundandam jurisdictionem* of any property or debts belonging to him situated within the jurisdiction. The jurisdictional ground was as simple as that and it disregarded how accidental the presence of this property within the jurisdiction could be.[109] In the case of existence of a maritime lien in favour of the pursuer, in addition to the warrant of arrestment obtained on the dependence against the defender (which was effectual only to attach his personal interest in the ship), a special warrant of arrestment *in rem* against the ship was also required in order to attach the ship itself. In an action in this form it was necessary to call all parties interested in the ship, and they were to be cited. However, this was not assimilated to the English action *in rem* because it was still based primarily on the liability of the ship-owner.[110]

Arrestment ad fundandam jurisdictionem

2.47 In contrast to the action *in rem*, which was (as the *in rem* claim still is) exclusively an Admiralty action, arrestment *ad fundandam jurisdictionem* was (and still is) not limited to admiralty arrestment but extends to all movable property of a defender not otherwise subject to the Scottish jurisdiction. If such property was in Scotland and it was arrested for the express purpose of founding jurisdiction such arrestment was (and still is) known as arrestment *ad fundandam jurisdictionem* or *jurisdictionis fundandae causa*.[111] In his *Treatise on the Law of Diligence* in 1898 Stewart offered a profound analysis of this particular 'diligence'.[112] Arrestment *ad fundandam jurisdictionem* does not provide for security in the terms that an arrestment of a ship on the dependence does; it has a very defined and narrow purpose: to found the jurisdiction of the Scottish courts.

2.48 The essential purpose of arrestment was understood to be 'as the term "arrest" itself implies, to fix the vessel in the place in which she is found',[113] operating as 'an interdict against the debtor himself and paralysing him in the use of the property in his own possession'.[114] It has always been the law of Scotland that jurisdiction exists over a defender not only in respect of his domicile but also in respect of his possession of property there; a

[109] McMillan, *Scottish Maritime Practice* (1926) 21.

[110] Ibid, 22–3.

[111] G Stewart, *A Treatise on the Law of Diligence* (Edinburgh, Green, 1898) 246.

[112] However, it has been alleged that this distinctive kind of arrestment is not proper diligence (GL Gretton, 'Diligence' in *The Laws of Scotland, Stair Memorial Encyclopaedia*, vol 8, 75 para 249); for a detailed analysis of this peculiar institution of Scots law see Ch 7 (Arrest of Ships and Jurisdiction) below.

[113] *Carlberg v Borjesson* 1877 5 R 188, 195.

[114] *Wolthekker v Northern Agricultural Society* 1862 1 M 211, 213.

jurisdictional ground nowadays considered exorbitant by the international community.[115] Stewart explained that this method of constituting jurisdiction was borrowed from Dutch law. There was always awareness that this jurisdictional ground was against the settled principle of Roman law that admits the maxim of *actor sequitur forum rei* but it was justified under the pressing needs of international commerce.[116]

It is from the amalgamation of the Scottish jurisdictional base and the Dutch method of 'fixing movable assets' that arrestment *ad fundandam jurisdictionem* emerged. By arresting movable property of the defender the property was rendered fixed in Scotland therefore it was possible through that mechanism to found jurisdiction over the owner of such property in Scotland.[117] As early as in 1683[118] the practice was an established one in the Admiralty Court and beyond it and it was accepted that where a foreigner had movable property in Scotland the creditor could prevent the possessor from handing it over until the owner gave security to submit to the jurisdiction.[119] Ultimately the effect was that arrestment *ad fundandam jurisdictionem* itself created jurisdiction.[120] **2.49**

In the earliest times of arrestment *ad fundandam jurisdictionem* it was considered that the security which could be demanded for releasing the goods was not only *judicio sisti* but *judicatum solvi*, hence, originally arrestment *ad fundandam jurisdictionem* served both functions, grounding jurisdiction and providing security for satisfaction of the eventual decree. **2.50**

[115] See Diego P Fernández Arroyo, *Compétence Exclusive et Compétence Exorbitante dans les relations privées internationales*, Recueil des cours, vol 323, 2006, (Leiden, Martinus Nijhoff, 2008) ch 3.

[116] Stewart, *A Treatise on the Law of Diligence* (1898) 246.

[117] Ibid, 247.

[118] *Young v Arnold* (1683) M 4833 is generally referred to as the leading case. Nevertheless, McMillan argues that the case showed that the practice was already common in the Admiralty Court. The importance of *Young v Arnold* in his opinion lies in the fact that it was the first application of the theory not in *re mercatoria* in the Admiralty Court but in the Court of Session in an ordinary case involving patrimonial rights. In that dictum the Court admits that the acceptance of the theory is foreign in principle to Scots law (McMillan, *Scottish Maritime Practice* (1926) 89).

[119] Stewart, *A Treatise on the Law of Diligence* (1898) 247. Interestingly enough the effects at those times seemed to be similar to the current effects of the English-crafted freezing injunction; but the purpose of the 'freezing effect' in the early arrestment *ad fundandam jurisdictionem* was to found jurisdiction and to make the goods available as security for the claim (jurisdictional and security function) the latter being actually the only purpose of the freezing effect of the English referred injunctions. Nowadays in Scots law both functions are displayed together in the frequent case of arrestment *ad fundandam jurisdictionem* and arrestment on the dependence being used concurrently.

[120] Further analysis of its current jurisdictional function is provided for in Ch 7 (Arrest of Ships and Jurisdiction).

However, already in the seventeenth century[121] this original view was departed from and only the jurisdictional function continued to be the effect of arrestment *ad fundandam jurisdictionem* up to the present time. Nowadays if it is necessary to obtain security in the terms of an interim measure of protection (*judicatum solvi*) an arrestment on the dependence must be served in addition.

2.51 This lack of *nexus* with the property meant also in practice—as it was established in 1896[122]—that the ship was entitled to sail away without committing any breach of arrestment. Surprisingly, even though this consequence expressed at the end of the nineteenth century ran counter to the former opinion on the issue, it was rapidly accepted, regarded as sound, and considered not to weaken the efficacy of the 'diligence'.[123] Undoubtedly, allowing the ship to sail was an unforeseeable feature of arrestment of ships to found jurisdiction when it was originally crafted in Scots law.

2.52 The general rule for arrestment *ad fundandam jurisdictionem* was that for jurisdiction to be found the defender needed to be the owner of the property arrested. The exception to that rule applied in the case of arrestment of ships. In contrast to English law, the justification for such departure from that general principle of law was not based on the personification theory but on the role of the Master as capable of representing and binding the owners and the ship. The dissenting opinion of Lord Curriehill in *Morrison v Masa* in 1866[124] shows that at those times the personification theory as developed earlier in England was not so well known in Scotland in the middle of the nineteenth century and that the possibility of raising an action against the ship as the 'wrongdoer' was far from clear.[125]

[121] *Lindsay v L & N-W Ry Co* 1860 22 D 571, 585 (Lord Press).

[122] *Craig v Brunsgaard, Kjosterud & Co* (1896) 3 SLT 265 (IH (1 Div)).

[123] Stewart, *A Treatise on the Law of Diligence* (1898) 272.

[124] *Morrison v Massa* 1866 5 M 130. Cf *The Bold Buccleugh* (1851) 7 Moo PCC 267.

[125] '... the argument ... comes very much to this: that the debt was ... the debt of the ship ... Now I do not know what is meant by a debt being called debt of the ship. It is not a real burden on the ship and the ship itself cannot personally be a debtor. And even if the ship were in the position of being the debtor I do not see how an arrestment of the ship could render her master personally subject to the jurisdiction of this Court on the ground that property belonging to him has been arrested ...' *Morrison v Massa* 1866 5 M 130 (Lord Curriehill). Cf with the situation in Scotland at the beginning of the twentieth century, see para 2.32 above.

IV. CONCLUSIONS

The arrest of ships never adjusted perfectly to the framework of arrest in general civil and commercial litigation. Its functions have always gone beyond the traditional functions of interim measures of protection.[126] Most of the inconsistencies of the law of arrest of ships as found today in England and in Scotland are owing to the lack of attempt to recognize that the institution has been forever changing since its earliest beginnings.[127] These changes have been in the way of 'transposition'[128] and cross-fertilization. Consequently, lack of historical accuracy was a common drawback found in many dicta in the nineteenth century in England and in Scotland, which created perplexity and inconsistency. From then on up to the present time Admiralty jurisprudence has been trying to reshape, to describe, and to understand the arrest of ships. The following chapter looks at the international Conventions on the arrest of ships to determine the key features of this mixed legal institution[129] in contemporary international commercial litigation. **2.53**

[126] The jurisdictional function of the arrest of ships clearly goes beyond the traditional purposes of provisional and protective measures.

[127] For instance, Wiswall highlighted that '... Marsden made no attempt to show or to intimate that the early jurisprudence of Admiralty endured without change until the 1890s and his remarks are entirely concerned with the Court's very early practice though they were subsequently cited in support of the historical accuracy of Jeune's scrutiny ...' (Wiswall, *The Development of Admiralty Jurisdiction and Practice since 1800* (1970) 162). A constant backwards-looking approach seems to be the rule when entertaining maritime litigation in England and such an attitude has been criticized (see Jackson, *Enforcement of Maritime Claims* (2005) 7–8). See eg *The River Rima* (1988) 2 Lloyd's Rep 193 (HL) where the House of Lords construed the 1952 International Arrest Convention in the light of English law prior to the Convention (the 1925 Supreme Court of Judicature (Consolidation) Act) (Lord Brandon of Oakbrook).

[128] E Örücü, 'Law as Transposition' (2002) 51 *International and Comparative Law Quarterly* 205.

[129] See V Ruiz Abou-Nigm, 'The Arrest of Ships as a Mixed Legal Institution', Conference paper, 2010 Society of Legal Scholars Conference (Southampton, September 2010).

3

The Arrest of Ships in the International Arrest Conventions

I. INTRODUCTION

3.01 The modern law on the arrest of ships is shaped, to a greater or lesser extent, by international uniform law. As international trade and commerce is more likely to thrive when it develops under a system of law which is predictable, one of the 'dominant legal leitmotifs'[1] of the late nineteenth, twentieth, and early part of the twenty-first centuries has been the desire to achieve international uniformity. This ideal has always been particularly important to maritime law; an area that is ruled by its international character. The ancient *lex maritima* provided a sound starting point for modern harmonization; it also fostered the expectation that uniformity in modern maritime law is realizable.

[1] Paul Myburgh, 'Uniformity or Unilateralism in the Law of Carriage of Goods by Sea?' (2000) 31 *Victoria University of Wellington Law Review* 355.

3.02 The arrest of ships has led the way in the use of uniform law in private international maritime law. Yet, conflict rules[2] are still necessary whenever uniform solutions have not been achieved, either because agreement was not obtained or because preference has been afforded to the law of the forum to rule on such issues. Uniformity has taken different paths in the field of arrest of ships: the 'transnational' level of the *lex mercatoria* since ancient times; the 'international' level of the traditional mechanism of international Conventions in the twentieth century; and more recently, allegedly, the 'supranational' level with regard to its jurisdictional effects within Europe, through the special position enjoyed by the jurisdiction-related provisions of the 1952 International Arrest Convention in the Brussels I Regulation.[3]

3.03 This chapter focuses upon the international level. It is a matter of fact that uniformity in this sphere is still partial, even after more than 50 years of application of the 1952 International Arrest Convention. In this chapter this study identifies certain drawbacks to uniformity and proposes to overcome these drawbacks by using the devices provided by private international law as a legal discipline. In particular, it proposes to take recourse in the doctrine of characterization[4] to clarify the scope of arrest of ships as a private international law category[5] in the 1952 and 1999 International Arrest Conventions. Following that line of thought it becomes possible to argue that the referred Conventions provide an autonomous meaning of

[2] For the relationship between these two main methods of private international law, ie the 'uniformist' and the 'conflictualist' methods, in international maritime law see C Fresnedo de Aguirre and V Ruiz Abou-Nigm, 'El Derecho Marítimo y El Derecho Internacional Privado' [2005] *Anuario de Derecho Marítimo* 189.

[3] Council Regulation (EC) 44/2001 on Jurisdiction and the Recognition and Enforcement of Judgments in Civil and Commercial Matters (Brussels I) [2001] OJ L 12.1.2001, Art 71. Note that this provision has been the object of numerous comments during the review of Brussels I (see eg Profs B Hess, T Pfeiffer, and P Schlosser, Report on the Application of Regulation Brussels I in the Member States (Study JLS/C4/2005/03) (the *Heidelberg Report*)) and in spite of that the European Commission Proposal for a Regulation of the European Parliament and of the Council on jurisdiction and the recognition and enforcement of judgments in civil and commercial matters (Recast) 14.12.2010 (COM (2010) 748/3) does not make any amendments of the current version of this article. See also Editorial comments, 'The Union, the Member States and International Agreements' (2011) 48 *Common Market Law Review* 1.

[4] The discoverer of the problem, Bartin (in 'De l'impossibilité d'arriver à la suppression definitive des conflits de lois' (1897) 24 *Clunet* 225), named it as of 'qualification' nonetheless the term 'characterization' proposed by Falconbridge (in 'Characterization in the Conflict of Laws' *Law Quarterly Review* (1937) 235) has been widely adopted as its English equivalent; 'classification' is also used in this sense, see, inter alia, Beckett, 'Classification in Private International Law' *British Yearbook of International Law*, vol 15 (1934) 59.

[5] JJ Alvarez Rubio identifies certain characterization problems in this sphere; see JJ Alvarez Rubio, 'El embargo preventivo de buques: Regulación Convencional y Problemas de Calificación' in *Derecho Marítimo y Derecho Internacional Privado: Algunos Problemas Básicos* (Servicio Central de Publicaciones del Gobierno Vasco Vitoria-Gasteiz 2000) 91.

arrest of ships, independent of the legal category 'arrest of ships' in national legal systems. It is submitted that the recognition of that autonomous meaning is paramount for further harmonization in this field.

3.04 In international maritime law the tendency has been to try to attain further harmonization through the adoption of new international instruments, aiming to achieve the sought after balance of interests between the different stakeholders involved in this field. In turn, this would facilitate obtaining the needed international acceptance that could foster uniformity. Experience shows that these goals are very difficult to realize.[6] This chapter proposes a different way of trying to reach further harmonization in the field of arrest of ships in the international sphere: by construing the terms of the existing international Conventions in a way that could enhance international uniformity.

3.05 In relation to the current degree of harmonization achieved by international uniform law on the arrest of ships, private international law can shed some light into the characterization (in the private international law sense[7]) of arrest of ships as a provisional measure. Thus, the purpose of this chapter is to put forward an autonomous meaning that arrest of ships has in the international Conventions with a view to advancing international uniformity in practice when applying the international Conventions' provisions. For this reason, the Conventions' provisions are only analysed insofar as helping to clarify the scope of arrest of ships as a private international law category. Furthermore, this chapter also looks into other private international law concerns in this field related to the scope of application of the international Conventions and to problems of interpretation currently raised by the 1952 International Arrest Convention.

II. THE INTERNATIONAL LEVEL

3.06 Certainly, the rationale underlying the first attempts to harmonize the law in this sphere was not to achieve uniformity for the sake of commercial prosperity generally but to protect ship-owners from the indiscriminate use of the arrest of ships as an interim measure of protection, purportedly as an indirect way to protect international trade. The ship-owners' protection

[6] In the field of international maritime law, unfortunately, there are several examples of exhausted resources that did not come to fruition. The result is proliferations of sterile international instruments that do not contribute to international harmonization but more worryingly do tend to hinder the success of their predecessors by generating disparity and uncertainty in the international legal scenario.

[7] See para 3.24 below.

as a purpose has been used to support the view that there is in fact no autonomous concept of arrest of ships in the international Conventions since the aim of the Conventions was just to limit the scope of arrest as practised by national courts before the 1952 International Arrest Convention entered into force. On that line of thought it could be argued that Article 1(2)[8] of that Convention is a mere delimitation of the scope of application of the Convention rather than a definition of the arrest of ships. This line of argument is not followed in this book; it is here submitted that for the sake of achieving further harmonization in this field Article 1(2) should be interpreted as providing for a substantive autonomous meaning.

The interest in international harmonization in the field arose in the 1930s in the *Comité Maritime International*[9] mores. As outlined in Chapter 2,[10] the arrest of ships as an institution used in civil and commercial matters did not have an exact equivalent in legal systems at the national level. One main difference between civil and common law systems needed to be aligned: in civil law countries a ship could be arrested as a security for any claim, even for claims that were of a non-maritime nature, and in common law countries, especially in England, ships could only be arrested in the limited cases where the claimant was entitled to a right *in rem*. Certainly, the chase for uniformity at the international level constituted a further link in the long chain of amalgamations that have formed the arrest of ships as the modern mixed legal institution[11] that it is today. 3.07

The first product of the harmonization efforts[12] was the Convention Relating to Arrest of Sea Going Ships adopted in Brussels on 10 May 1952, which entered into force on 24 February 1956, where a degree of harmonization 3.08

[8] Article 1(2) International Convention relating to the Arrest of Sea-Going Ships (Brussels, May 10, 1952) '"Arrest" means the detention of a ship by judicial process to secure a maritime claim, but does not include the seizure of a ship in execution or satisfaction of a judgment.'

[9] Historically the *Comité Maritime International* was the first private international organization concerned with the unification of private international maritime law. In the middle of the twentieth century, however, the United Nations created the International Maritime Organization (IMO) and then the United Nations Conference on Trade and Development (UNCTAD) and the United Nations Commission on International Trade Law (UNCITRAL). Nowadays the IMO has become the primary forum for harmonization in the field of private international maritime law. The *Comité Maritime International* continues to work on its own initiatives and acts as a consultant to IMO, UNCTAD and UNCITRAL.

[10] See Ch 2, para 2.05 above.

[11] On arrest as a mixed legal institution see V Ruiz Abou-Nigm, 'The Arrest of Ships as a Mixed Legal Institution', Conference paper, 2010 Society of Legal Scholars Conference (Southampton, September 2010).

[12] The International Convention Relating to the Arrest of Sea-Going Ships was signed in Brussels on 10 May 1952 and was preceded by several conferences: Paris (1937), Antwerp (1947), Amsterdam (1948), and Naples (1951).

was achieved via the definition of 'maritime claim'; the *ex facie* conceptualization of the arrest of ships as an interim measure of protection; and the recognition of *forum arresti* as an acceptable jurisdictional ground subject to certain conditions. The 1952 International Arrest Convention has at present more than 80 ratifications and accessions.[13]

3.09 Discussions as to the possible review of the 1952 International Arrest Convention were initiated at the *Comité Maritime International* Annual Conference in Lisbon in 1985.[14] The International Maritime Organization (IMO) and the United Nations Conference on Trade and Development (UNCTAD) established a 'Joint Intergovernmental Group of Experts on Maritime Liens and Mortgages and Related Subjects' (JIGE) in December 1986 to work on a new convention on Maritime Liens and Mortgages and to review the 1952 International Arrest Convention. After prolonged considerations, on 12 March 1999 in Geneva the UN/IMO Diplomatic Conference updated the 1952 International Arrest Convention by the adoption of the 1999 International Convention on the Arrest of Ships.

3.10 The 1999 International Arrest Convention aims to achieve further unification in the field by providing a widely acceptable legal instrument promoting international trade and transport. It strives to strike a balance between the interests of cargo-owners and of ship-owners in securing the free movement of ships, and the right of the claimant to obtain security for his claim. Undoubtedly, the 1999 International Arrest Convention represents advancement in various ways analysed in this chapter and throughout this book.[15]

III. THE ARREST OF SHIPS AND DRAWBACKS TO UNIFORMITY FROM A PRIVATE INTERNATIONAL LAW PERSPECTIVE

3.11 Experience reveals that in order to achieve international uniformity in the regulation of a certain field of law, reaching consensus on certain provisions to be included in a particular international Convention is just a first

[13] The status of ratification of the 1952 International Arrest Convention is published in the *Comité Maritime International Yearbook* (2009) 462–6, accessible through the CMI website <http://www.comitemaritime.org> (last accessed 9 August 2010).

[14] 33rd International Conference of the *Comité Maritime International*, 19–25 May 1985.

[15] At the time of writing the 1999 International Arrest Convention is just about to enter into force on 14 September 2011 according to its Art 14(1). The countries that have so far ratified or acceded to it are: Albonia, Algeria, Benin, Bulgaria, Ecuador, Spain, Estonia, Latvia, Liberia, and the Syrian Arab Republic.

step towards accomplishing such goal. More difficult to attain in practice is the necessary uniformity of application of such provisions in the different State parties to the Convention. For such purposes there must be certain criteria to be followed by courts, judges, and arbitrators for the interpretation of conventional provisions in accordance with the aims and objectives of the respective international Convention.

In that sense the results of the application of the 1952 International Arrest Convention have been, and still are, relatively unsuccessful.

The reasons for such lack of uniformity are manifold. From a private international law perspective the drawbacks to uniformity in the case of the law of arrest of ships relate to the following issues: the scope of application of the 1952 International Arrest Convention; the different interpretation of this Convention's provisions in the State parties; and last but not least the 'disruptive' recourse to the law of the forum taken by some of these provisions. The latter undermines the uniform application of the Convention by brushing aside the process of characterization. In practical terms that means that when, under the 1952 International Arrest Convention, an Italian judge is ordering a *sequestro conservativo* of a ship, or a Spanish court is ordering an *embargo preventivo* of a ship, or a Swedish court is ordering a *kvarstad*, or a French court is ordering a *saisie conservatoire* of a ship, or a Scottish court is ordering a ship arrestment, or an English court is ordering a ship arrest, they generally do not take into consideration that they are ordering 'the detention of a ship to secure a maritime claim' and that they should do so according to the provisions and the purposes of the 1952 International Arrest Convention. **3.12**

That is to say that the scope of the legal category 'arrest of ships' should be examined *in ordinem*, ie against the provisions of the 1952 International Arrest Convention itself; *extra ordinem* characterization, ie based on concepts not pertaining to that international Convention, is best avoided. However, it appears clear that in many cases the 1952 International Arrest Convention is seen just as a limitation imposed in terms of the kind of claims that entail the right to arrest the ship; that is the Convention is seen purposively as its Article 2.[16] Therefore, *dicta* in the different State parties to the Convention show that in accordance with the limitations and extensions established by the Convention, courts, judges, and arbitrators usually continue to apply their own 'arrest of ships' in terms of scope of the **3.13**

[16] Article 2 'A ship flying the flag of one of the Contracting States may be arrested in the jurisdiction of any of the Contracting States in respect of any maritime claim, but in respect of no other claim; ...' (International Convention relating to the Arrest of Sea-Going Ships (Brussels, 10 May 1952)).

legal category, ie based on the regulation of the arrest of ships as an interim measure of protection in the internal law of the forum, and disregarding the fact that the Convention is a uniform scheme by itself.[17] Several factors can be identified as contributing to that misapplication, as follows.

1. Scope of Application of the International Conventions

3.14 One of the weaknesses of the 1952 International Arrest Convention in relation to its scope of application is that the Convention applies in a different manner to ships flying the flag of one of the Contracting States and to ships flying the flag of non-Contracting States.

3.15 Article 2 of the Convention establishes that:

> A ship flying the flag of one of the Contracting States may be arrested in the jurisdiction of any of the Contracting States in respect of any maritime claim, but in respect of no other claim; but nothing in this Convention shall be deemed to extend or restrict any right or powers vested in any governments or their departments, public authorities, or dock or harbor authorities under their existing domestic laws or regulations to arrest, detain or otherwise prevent the sailing of vessels within their jurisdiction.

As 'maritime claim' in the Convention means necessarily one of the claims listed in Article 1(1) of the Convention, and this is a closed list, there is no scope for the application of the internal law of the Contracting States to determine what constitutes a maritime claim. From a civil law perspective this is a protective rule—protecting ship-owners—as it limits the right of arrest to certain types of claims. The strongest controversy arises in relation to this provision in relation to the unfortunate provision of Article 8(2) of the 1952 International Arrest Convention.

3.16 *Article 8(2).* This provision establishes the application of the Convention to ships flying the flag of a non-Contracting State except for the 'protective' rule of Article 2. The rationale of this provision seems to have been to extend the burdens of the Convention to every sea-going ship but to avail the benefits of it only to ships and claimants closely connected to any of the State parties. The provision is the result of a British proposal in order not to leave ships of non-Contracting States in a better position in English ports than the ships of State parties. As for English law before the adoption of the

[17] An illustration of that is to be found in the Scottish Law Commission, *Report on Diligence on the Dependence and Admiralty Arrestment* (Scot Law Com Report No 164 (1998)) where it was expressed that the harmonization introduced through the enactment of the Administration of Justice Act 1956 did not change the nature of arrestment of ships in Scots law; it merely limited its scope or field of competence to a list of particular claims (at 116).

Convention the right of arrest was limited to claims enforcing a maritime lien; if the Convention could not be applied to ships of non-Contracting States that would have implied that those ships in English ports would have been 'safer' than the rest. The application of the 1952 International Arrest Convention to ships flying the flag of non-Contracting States in this different manner is an extended one in the Contracting States.[18] This situation generates double standards in relation to the application of the Convention's provisions that do not but jeopardize uniformity.

In the 1999 International Arrest Convention these double standards have been erased in principle and paragraphs 1 and 2 of Article 8 have been replaced by a provision according to which the Convention shall apply to any ship, whether or not flying a flag of a State party; and this is without any qualifications insofar as to the availability of 'protective rules' whatsoever.[19] This modification is to be welcomed. The wider the scope of application of the Convention the more uniformity that is going to be achieved in the field, and the less chances of characterization based on internal law conceptual structures interfering with a proper characterization (based on the Convention's provisions) of the legal category. **3.17**

Article 8(3). Also controversial are the two exceptions to the general rule of Article 2 provided for in Article 8 paragraphs 3 and 4 of the 1952 International Arrest Convention. Article 8(3) provides that State parties may exclude from the benefits of the Convention any person who does not at the time of the arrest have his habitual residence or principal place of business in a State party. This provision is actually entitling Contracting States to make an exclusion that would have the nature of a reservation to the Convention. This has been also amended in the 1999 International Arrest Convention. **3.18**

Article 8(4). Furthermore, Article 8 (4) establishes that 'Nothing in this Convention shall modify or affect the rules of law in force in the respective Contracting States relating to the arrest of any ship within the jurisdiction of the State of her flag by a person who has his habitual residence or principal place of business in that State.' The exclusion is directed towards cases where there are no foreign elements, ie a purely domestic case. On balance, the technique used in Article 8(4) of the 1952 International Arrest Convention is regrettable since as well as the two previous provisions **3.19**

[18] Belgium, Denmark, Croatia, Finland, France, Germany, Haiti, Norway, Poland, Slovenia, Spain, Sweden, Nigeria, and the United Kingdom (F Berlingieri, *Berlingieri on Arrest of Ships* (4th edn, London, Informa, 2006) 310–11).

[19] States may, however, reserve the right to exclude the application of the Convention to ships not flying the flag of a State party to the Convention via a formal reservation.

referred to above it also encourages State parties to keep double standards.[20] Unfortunately this provision has been reproduced in Article 9(6) of the 1999 International Arrest Convention. In the opinion of Berlingieri this provision limits the global character of the new International Arrest Convention.[21] In his opinion the exclusion from the scope of application of purely national cases is sensible in private international law Conventions adopting the methodology of choice-of-law, ie in a 'conflictualist' approach. However, in his opinion, if the 'uniformist' method (referred as 'substantivism' in Chapter 1[22]) is adopted and therefore the final aim of the Convention is to achieve uniformity of application of the substantive rules of the Convention in the State parties, it advances such a goal better to apply the substantive rules of the Convention to domestic as well as international cases.[23]

3.20 It is here submitted that for the sake of international uniformity keeping a double standard, that is, keeping two different schemes of arrest of ships depending on whether the case is domestic or international, places further difficulties for judges and those in charge of applying the law; and, in a certain way, it enhances the possibility of the law of the forum to display a disruptive interference. Moreover, this is not a field where double standards would be justifiable in terms of the need to protect forum policies.

[20] Sweden, for example, has a dual system when it comes to arrest of ships. It has ratified the 1952 International Arrest Convention and it keeps its domestic legislation regarding the *kvarstad* institute. *Kvarstad* is a Swedish term and may be defined as an ordinary attachment. Under Art 8(4) of the Convention the rules relating to the *kvarstad* procedure found in ch 15 of the Swedish Code of Judicial Procedure may still be used to arrest ships (see O Egerström, 'Securing Maritime Claims: The Ship Arrest Regimes in Sweden and England' (2004/2005) Thesis, Faculty of Law, University of Lund). Other examples include Germany and France. In the German *Handelsgesetzbuch* (Commercial Code) the internal provisions on arrest still apply to the arrest of ships granted under the 1952 International Arrest Convention on the ground that the internal provisions are not in conflict with those of the Convention because they require conditions for an arrest that are stricter than those set out in the Convention. This interpretation is criticized by Berlingieri (Berlingieri, *Berlingieri on Arrest of Ships* (2006) 16). In France the national regime applicable to French ships in the cases set out in Art 8(4) and to ships flying the flag of a non-Contracting State party to the Convention where the arrester elects to apply it, is Decree No 67-967 of 27 October 1967.

[21] Berlingieri, *Berlingieri on Arrest of Ships* (2006) 319.

[22] See Ch 1, para 1.32 above.

[23] He explains that this provision may give rise to problems, for example where a ship is arrested by two claimants one to whom the Convention applies and one to whom it does not (or it does not completely) because the uniform rules and the national rules may be in conflict with one another (Berlingieri, *Berlingieri on Arrest of Ships* (2006) 316).

Contrarily, a field such as the arrest of ships should be a prosperous sphere to advance harmonization in the procedural mores.[24]

2. Problems of Interpretation of the 1952 International Arrest Convention

Another stumbling block to uniformity,[25] probably the most significant one, is that the 1952 International Arrest Convention has been implemented differently in the States parties to the Convention.[26] In some countries it has been given force of law directly as a consequence of its ratification.[27] However, in most of the countries some sort of implementing legislation was necessary.[28] These different methods of implementation have affected the uniform interpretation of the Convention. Inconsistencies are manifest,[29] even after more than 50 years since its entry into force. **3.21**

These differences became apparent from the various titles that the 1952 International Arrest Convention received in the different languages that it has been drafted in or translated into. The arrest of ships has been defined **3.22**

[24] JA Jolowicz, 'On the Comparison of Procedures' in JAR Nafziger and SC Symeonides (eds), *Law and Justice in a Multistate World, Essays in Honor of Arthur T von Mehren* (New York, Transnational Publishers, 2002) 721, 740.

[25] Clearly, this is not a downside particular to the 1952 International Arrest Convention but to international Conventions more generally; however, it is material to this study in the sense that it does affect directly the characterization problem.

[26] It is worth mentioning in this context that the International Maritime Law Institute (IMLI) in Malta provides an excellent source for governments in the understanding and implementing international Conventions in this field.

[27] That is the case of Belgium, Croatia, France, Germany, Greece, Haiti, Italy, The Netherlands, Poland, Portugal, Slovenia, Ireland, and Spain (Berlingieri, *Berlingieri on Arrest of Ships* (2006) 15–23).

[28] States where the provisions of the Convention have been incorporated into national law include Denmark, Finland, Nigeria, Norway, Sweden, Scotland, and England (Berlingieri, *Berlingieri on Arrest of Ships* (2006) 24). The Administration of Justice Act 1956 was enacted with the purpose of giving effect to the 1952 International Arrest Convention in English and Scots law. In England it has been superseded by the Supreme Court Act 1981 (now renamed as England and Wales' Senior Courts Act 1981 by the Constitutional Reform Act 2005, s 59 and Sch 11 in force since 1 October 2009). In Scotland, even though the 1956 Act remains in force, it has had several amendments and further modifications have been introduced by the Bankruptcy and Diligence, etc (Scotland) Act 2007.

[29] Berlingieri's work is the clearest evidence of the many inconsistencies that still exist in the law of arrest of ships when applied in the States parties to the Convention. See Berlingieri, *Berlingieri on Arrest of Ships* (2006).

by the Conventions as 'any detention of a ship to secure a maritime claim'.[30] However, the English term 'arrest' and the French term *saisie conservatoire*, both official languages of the Convention, have been translated, for example, in Spanish, as *embargo preventivo*[31] which has particular implications in terms of the requirements and functions of ship arrest that do not necessarily coincide with the autonomous meaning of the Convention.[32]

3.23 As recognized by Berlingieri, 'when the provisions of a Convention are enacted into national law the danger arises that they are interpreted on the basis of national rules rather than on the basis of the Convention from which they originate, no account being taken of the need for their uniform interpretation'.[33] The text of the Conventions consists of concepts formed out of negotiations between states delegates based on several systems of law; not only the *saisie conservatoire* of French law or the ship arrest of English law but many more. It is, therefore, paramount to avoid the use of traditional methods of national law in interpreting international uniform Conventions; the restrictive bases that they use make them unsuitable for interpreting international uniform law.

IV. CHARACTERIZATION AND AUTONOMOUS INTERPRETATION OF INTERNATIONAL UNIFORM LAW: THE DEVICES

3.24 Every private international law rule has two elements: the category (the situations covered by the norm) and the provision (the legal consequence). This structure is common to conflict rules and uniform rules.[34] However,

[30] Article 1(2) International Convention relating to the Arrest of Sea-Going Ships (Brussels, 10 May 1952) ' "Arrest" means the detention of a ship by judicial process to secure a maritime claim, but does not include the seizure of a ship in execution or satisfaction of a judgment'; Art 1(2) International Convention on Arrest of Ships 1999 (Geneva, 12 March 1999) ' "Arrest" means any detention or restriction on removal of a ship by order of a Court to secure a maritime claim, but does not include the seizure of a ship in execution or satisfaction of a judgment or other enforceable instrument.'

[31] In Spain jurists have to distinguish between the nature of *embargo preventivo* in the general frame of provisional and protective measures from the particular nature of *embargo preventivo* in the maritime law mores; see Alvarez Rubio, 'El embargo preventivo de buques: Regulación Convencional y Problemas de Calificación' (2000) 102.

[32] The *embargo preventivo* of a ship may restrain the defendant from selling the ship and set up a privilege in the eventual posterior sale of the ship ranking after mortgages but before posterior embargoes and unsecured creditors.

[33] Berlingieri, *Berlingieri on Arrest of Ships* (2006) 14.

[34] JR Talice in D Opertti Badán et al, *Objeto y Método en el Derecho Internacional Privado* (2nd edn, Montevideo, FCU, 1990) 29, 59.

the scope of research of private international law as a legal discipline in relation to uniform rules is limited to the first element of this normative structure: the category, where the internationalism of the rule remains. Hence, the central concern of this chapter is the characterization of the arrest of ships as a legal category in the international Arrest Conventions.

Characterization is one of the fundamental pillars of private international law[35] and yet the most difficult and unsettled issue.[36] It is often discussed in the sphere of choice-of-law rules (ie conflict rules); however, the process is common to all methods in private international law.[37] The process of characterization seeks to allocate a certain legal issue into a private international law category.[38] This process goes unnoticed if the legal relation is easily 'classifiable' and the private international law category has a scope of application clearly established. Whenever these two circumstances do not coincide the problem of characterization arises. **3.25**

When applying international uniform law the process of characterization goes sometimes unobserved within the process of autonomous interpretation;[39] though, in the construal process, this autonomous interpretation **3.26**

[35] Q Alfonsin, *Teoría del Derecho Privado Internacional* (Montevideo, Editorial Martin Bianchi Altuna, 1955) 386; E Rabel, 'La Problème de la Qualification' (1933) *Revue de Droit International Privé* 1; AH Robertson, *Characterization in the Conflict of Laws* (Cambridge, MA, Harvard University Press, 1940); J Unger, 'The Place of Classification in Private International Law' (1937) 19 *The Bell Yard* 3.

[36] T de B Maekelt, *Teoría General del Derecho Internacional Privado* (Caracas, Academia de Ciencias Políticas y Sociales, 2005) 285. There seems to be consensus on two main aspects of characterization: (a) what is to be characterized is a legal relation confronted with a certain system or systems of law; and (b) the aim of the process of characterization is to reveal the function and purpose of those norms as far as that legal relation is concerned (K Lipstein, 'Characterization' (1999) 3 *International Encyclopaedia of Comparative Law* (ch 5) 8).

[37] For a discussion on the importance of characterization in relation to uniform law, see Alfonsin, *Teoría del Derecho Privado Internacional* (1955) 385–407.

[38] As for the importance of characterization in English private international law and the need to undertake such process in a broad internationalist spirit in accordance with the principles of private international law, see *Raiffeisen Zentralbank Osterreich AG v Five Star General Trading LLC (The Mount I)* [2001] EWCA Civ 68, [2001] 1 Lloyd's Rep 597 (CA) (Mance LJ) paras 26–7.

[39] The standard principles of interpretation of international uniform Conventions are nowadays clearly established. A leading example is Art 7(1) of the 1980 United Nations Convention on Contracts for the International Sale of Goods. More recently the Cape Town Convention on International Interest in Mobile Equipment, Art 5 expressly recognizes those standards by stating that in the interpretation of the Convention regard is to be had to its purposes as set forth in the preamble, to its international character and to the need to promote predictability in its application. Furthermore, questions concerning matters governed by the Convention which are not expressly settled in it are to be settled in conformity with the general principles on which it is based or, in the absence of such principles, in conformity with the applicable law. See R Goode, *Official Commentary to the Cape Town Convention on International Interest in*

is preceded by characterization.[40] In turn, an autonomous interpretation of international uniform law provisions implies that the traditional grammatical, systematic, and historical method of interpretation must be supplemented by a comparative approach.[41]

3.27 In the case of the arrest of ships in the international Arrest Conventions the conflict arises due to the fact that different legal systems attach different meanings to the term 'arrest of ships'. This is the problem identified by Freund as the 'hidden homonym' or 'latent conflict'.[42] Taking the Conventions as the system of law against which characterization is to be performed, and bearing in mind that there is an autonomous meaning of arrest of ships in the Conventions, this conflict should be easily resolved. But it is not. It is misleading to assume that because there is an autonomous definition within an international uniform law Convention, the characterization problem is totally avoided. Probably, it is possible to expect a greater degree of harmonization arising out of the consensus that States parties to the Convention achieved at the law-making stage. However, it is still necessary to characterize at the stage of the application of such uniform rules.

3.28 That is to say, that an 'autonomous definition' does not guarantee uniformity of application of the Conventions. The difficulty lies in freeing the concepts advanced by the Conventions from its interpretation according to the different internal laws of the States parties. Therefore, uniformity of application would be advanced if courts bear in mind that in a private international law case characterization is always part of the decision-making process.[43]

Mobile Equipment and Protocol thereto on Matters Specific to Aircraft Equipment (Rome, Unidroit, 2002) 63.

[40] This opinion is not unanimous. Alfonsin understood that characterization and interpretation were the two phases of a one and only process. In his opinion the difference is one of perspective: from the point of view of the rule of law it is interpretation; from the point of view of the legal relation is characterization (Q Alfonsin, *Teoria del Derecho Internacional Privado* (2nd edn, Montevideo, Idea, 1982) 389.

[41] F Diedrich, 'Mantaining Uniformity in International Uniform Law Via Autonomous Interpretation' (1996) 8 *Pace International Law Review* 303, 311. An excellent source of information for the comparative approach that is necessary to achieve an 'autonomous interpretation' in this regard is Berlingieri, *Berlingieri on Arrest of Ships* (2006).

[42] Elizabeth B Crawford and Janeen M Carruthers, *International Private Law in Scotland* (Edinburgh, Green, 2006) 52.

[43] For arguments to the contrary, aiming to minimize the effect of characterization in modern English private international law, see A Briggs, 'Conflict of Laws and Commercial Remedies' in A Burrows and E Peel (eds), *Commercial Remedies: Current Issues and Problems* (Oxford, OUP, 2003) 274 '... And the elimination of the line which separates right from remedy would have the advantage of negating the exercise in characterization which the existence of

V. CHARACTERIZATION *IN ORDINEM* OF ARREST OF SHIPS: THE RESULTS

The arrest of ships under the Conventions is the detention of a ship under the authority of a court as a provisional and protective measure. Hence, the extent of the private international law category includes arrest as a protective measure to secure payment of a maritime claim; arrest as a preventive measure to enforce maritime liens; and arrest as a provisional measure 'to secure the *res*'. Bearing in mind that these three different types of measure have different functions, it is indeed its provisional character and not its functions that provides the scope of arrest of ships as a private international law category insofar as its characterization in the international Arrest Conventions. **3.29**

1. The Arrest of Ships as a Provisional Measure

Better harmonization results in relation to the practice of arrest of ships in international commercial litigation could be attained if the characterization of arrest of ships in the international Conventions is taken to its utmost comprehension. That is to say, recognizing that the arrest of ships is first and foremost a provisional measure in the international Arrest Conventions should imply that the internationally recognized criteria to grant such provisional measures apply to the arrest of ships as a consequence of the autonomous definition included in the Conventions. **3.30**

In international commercial litigation the distinctive features of provisional measures are to be supportive of the case on the merits and consequentially reasonable and proportional. Bearing in mind that measures are to be granted '... without however adversely affecting the other guarantees of a fair trial',[44] proportionality is vital. In English law proportionality is part of the overriding objective that interim remedies purport to obtain.[45] **3.31**

At present there are certain universal standards of what constitutes a provisional measure; there is also a good enough basis for international consensus as to what is necessary for the claimant to fulfil in terms of **3.32**

such a line requires to be undertaken ...' 277–8; see also DC Jackson, *Enforcement of Maritime Claims* (2005) '... classification is a first step away from reality ...' at 717.

[44] Resolution No 1 adopted by the 20th Conference of European Ministers of Justice Budapest 11–12 June 1996.

[45] H Brooke (ed), *Civil Procedure* (London, Sweet & Maxwell, 2004) 547.

requirements for a court to order any such measures. The most authoritative achievements in this regard internationally are the 'Resolution on Provisional and Protective Measures in International Litigation' prepared by the International Law Association at its Helsinski Conference in 1996 and the 'Principles of Transnational Civil Procedure ALI/Unidroit' as adopted in 2004.[46] Both international instruments agree on the core issues in relation to provisional measures. These measures are generally discretionary, and to assess the convenience of granting them it is usually necessary for the party requesting it to prove that the cause of action has a reasonable prospect of success (*fumus boni iuris*); that there is risk in waiting (*periculum in mora*), in most cases because the defendant is intending to dispose of his assets; and generally a cross-undertaking in damages needs to be provided by the party that requests the measure.

The Disruptive Recourse to the Law of the Forum

3.33 However, these requirements are not necessarily fulfilled in the current practice of arrest of ships in international commercial litigation. Article 6(2) of the 1952 International Arrest Convention provides that the law of the forum applies to all matters of procedure which the arrest may entail.[47] If this provision is interpreted as including not only the rules that are intrinsically procedural relating to the application for obtaining the arrest, such as the manner in which to present the pleadings and supporting documentation, but also within that concept of 'procedure' the criteria to assess such application is included, this makes it even more difficult to free the concepts advanced by the Convention from their meanings in the respective internal laws of the State parties to the Convention. In other

[46] (2004) 4 *Uniform Law Review* 758–809. For a comprehensive study of provisional and protective measures see L Collins, *Provisional and Protective Measures in International Litigation* (1992) 234 *Recueil des Cours* 19.

[47] Regardless of the convenience of this choice-of-law rule and the good example that this represents of the supportive role of private international law in harmonization processes what is here submitted is that in relation to the 'uniformist' methodology recourse to the law of the forum should be left as a last resort for issues where forum policies are germane or where the lack of consensus in terms of legal principles jeopardizes the possibility of achieving a substantive solution. Following that, what is to be avoided is recourse to the law of the forum in areas where consensus was achievable. At the time of the adoption of the 1952 International Arrest Convention, it was felt that it was 'indeed undesirable to unify the law of procedure' (see Miller's comments in relation to the definition of arrest in this Convention, *Comité Maritime International* Bulletin (104) 535). It is here submitted, however, that in modern times the harmonization of procedural laws is desirable, particularly in the field of procedural requirements for the granting of provisional and protective measures. This harmonization is indeed achievable as the 'Principles of Transnational Civil Procedure ALI/Unidroit' adopted in 2004 have shown.

words, if the courts have to take recourse to their internal law criteria to solve issues such as whether it is necessary for the party requesting the measure to prove the urgency of the measure (*periculum in mora*) and/or to prove a reasonable prospect of success on the merits of the case (*fumus boni iuris*), necessarily, the autonomous interpretation is jeopardized.

However, to a certain extent, Article 6(2) of the 1952 International Arrest Convention is consistent with an internationally recognized principle of private international law according to which procedural issues are always to be governed by the law of the forum. In that sense, the law of the forum has been regarded as universal and exclusive in its application; *ab initio* every question has to be decided by reference to the law of the forum and this dogma applies to every national court.[48] Hence, the law of the forum always interferes with the governing law, unavoidably. This happens whether the governing law is international uniform law or domestic law selected by a choice-of-law rule; it is something to be assumed rather than discussed.[49] **3.34**

What is unfortunate is not recourse to the law of the forum within an international uniform Convention; in that sense it could be argued that total uniformity is a utopia and that the 'uniformist' and the 'conflictualist' methods do complement each other in private international law. This is apparent in international maritime law where, even though there is a considerable degree of unification, conflict rules still have a very important role to play.[50] What is unfortunate is the way in which this provision of Article 6 has been interpreted and applied in many legal systems. In that sense, the supportive role of conflict rules within an international uniform convention implies that such rule should not be used in a way that undermines the harmonization purposes of the Convention. **3.35**

Conversely, if reference to the law of the forum in Article 6(2) was interpreted together with the autonomous definition of arrest of ships as provided for in Article 1(2) of the 1952 International Arrest Convention, ie essentially as a provisional measure, the need to apply the international recognized criteria to grant such provisional measures would derive from the definition of arrest **3.36**

[48] A court should as a matter of course look to the law of the forum as the source of the rules of decision; see B Currie, *Selected Essays on the Conflict of Laws* (Durham, NC, Duke University Press, 1963) 183; O Kahn-Freund, 'General Problems of Private International Law' 143 *Recueil des Cours* 139 (1974) 167; GC Petrochilos, *Procedural Law in International Arbitration* (Oxford, OUP, 2004) 6.

[49] The author does not want to fall in the trap that many private international law scholars do, devoting enormous energy to square the circle (see FK Juenger, *The Problem with Private International Law* (Roma, Centro di Studi e Ricerche di Diritto Comparato e Straniero, 1999).

[50] On the particular theme, see C Fresnedo de Aguirre and V Ruiz Abou-Nigm, 'El Derecho Marítimo y El Derecho Internacional Privado' (2005).

of ships itself. Therefore, Article 6(2) would have a more restrictive scope possibly resulting in further harmonization in the field.

Periculum in mora

3.37 There are important differences of perspective in common law systems as opposed to civil law ones in relation to the need to prove the *periculum in mora* in relation to the arrest of ships. *Periculum in mora* literally means 'risk in waiting' and, therefore, in most civilian legal systems urgency is an element to be proved by the claimant. Nonetheless, it has been argued that the risk in waiting is in fact inherent to the movable character of the ship.[51] In Lord Jeffrey's words 'in maritime causes the parties are always supposed to be in *meditatione fugae*; they have their sails spread, and are, as it were, on the wing, and ever ready to depart'.[52] For that reason, it has been argued that in the case of the arrest of ships it is not necessary to prove *periculum in mora* because it is always presumed.[53]

3.38 The issue of *periculum in mora* in relation to the arrest of ships has been thoroughly discussed in Italy[54] and Spain. In the latter the need to prove the *periculum in mora* has been provided for in relation to protective measures in general in the new Spanish Code of Civil Procedure[55] in force since January 2001. Despite that, the law that established (following the ratification by Spain of the 1952 International Arrest Convention) that the right of arrest exists in respect of maritime claims on the basis of a mere allegation of a claim[56] has remained in force as a *lex specialis*[57] based on the understanding that the definition of arrest as contained in Article 1(2) of the 1952 International Arrest Convention does not include *periculum in mora* as a requirement.

[51] F Aguirre Ramirez, 'Embargo y Arresto de Buques en Uruguay' [2005] *Revista de Transporte y Seguros* (2005) 280.

[52] *Gray v Sutherland* 1847 10 D 154,156.

[53] In German law there is a statutory provision that provides for such presumption when the defendant does not have any other assets, see S Nieschulz, *Der Arrest in Seeschiffe: Eine rechtsvergleichende Untersuchung des deutschen, niederländischen und englischen Rechts* (Hamburg, Lit, 1997) 18 (Arrestgrund des § 917 I ZPO bei one ship companies).

[54] See M Orione, 'Breve rassegna di orientamenti giurisprudenziali su alcuni aspetti del sequestro conservativo di nave' (1995) *Diritto marittimo* 1076.

[55] *Ley de Enjuiciamiento Civil* 1/2000, Art 728.

[56] *Ley* 2/1967.

[57] Berlingieri, *Berlingieri on Arrest of Ships* (2006) 22. In the eighth session of the Joint UNCTAD/IMO Intergovernmental Group of Experts (hereinafter JIGE) held on 9–10 October 1995 one delegate suggested that new language should be added to the definition of arrest to ensure that arrest can only be ordered in cases where there was a risk for the alleged claim not to be satisfied. See the *travaux préparatoires* of the 1999 International Arrest Convention in *Berlingieri on Arrest of Ships* (Berlingieri, *Berlingieri on Arrest of Ships* (2006) 526).

Fumus boni iuris

By the same token, the allegation of a maritime claim suffices to justify the arrest of ships in some legal systems, whereas in others, such as Italy, for example, the general rule is that in order to obtain an order of arrest it is sufficient to provide a *prima facie* evidence of the claim which is described as *fumus boni juris*. Italian courts have applied this rule also in respect of the arrest of ships governed by the 1952 International Arrest Convention.[58] This 'presumption of sufficient legal basis' relates both to the likelihood of success of the claim and to the amount of the claim.[59] The request is assessed in similar terms in Poland and Portugal for the purposes of ordering the arrest of a ship under the 1952 International Arrest Convention.[60] In France and Spain, however, the burden of proof resting on the claimant is less onerous in the cases of the arrest of ships under the 1952 International Arrest Convention than under internal procedural rules.[61] **3.39**

Cross-undertaking in damages

Article 6(1) of the 1952 International Arrest Convention establishes that '... all questions whether in any case the claimant is liable in damages for the arrest of a ship or for the cost of the bail or other security furnished to release or prevent the arrest of a ship, shall be determined by the law of the State party in whose jurisdiction the arrest was made or applied for ...'. In this regard the differences were not solved but circumvented by '... abandoning any attempt to provide uniform rules in that respect and merely inserting a private international law rule ...'.[62] Advancement in this matter has been achieved in the 1999 International Arrest Convention, where arrest may be subject to provision of security by the claimant for wrongful arrest or excessive security (Article 6). This shows that the remission to the law of the forum in the 1952 International Arrest Convention was not justified by 'forum connections' but was indeed a point where further consensus was necessary. With regard to this issue the newest Convention intends to bring the arrest of ships in line with the latest trends of interim measures of protection in international commercial litigation. **3.40**

[58] *Martingale Trading Group v Azovske Morske Paroplavsto (The Mekhanik Yuzvocich)* [2005] Dir Mar 200 (Court of Appeal of Rome).

[59] Berlingieri, *Berlingieri on Arrest of Ships* (2006) 99.

[60] Ibid, 100.

[61] Ibid, 101.

[62] Ibid, 9.

Proportionality

3.41 The consideration of 'proportionality'[63] in the 1952 International Arrest Convention prohibits more than one arrest or bail or other security in respect of the same maritime claim by the same claimant in any one or more of the Contracting States unless the claimant shows 'good cause'.[64] It does not appear, however, that an absolute prohibition of multiple arrests is established by the Convention, following the reference to 'good cause for maintaining the arrest' at the end of Article 3(1).[65] In the 1999 International Arrest Convention, Article 5(2) clarifies that another ship may be arrested for the same claim only if the security provided by the first arrest is inadequate or defective.

2. The Arrest of Ships as a Protective Measure

3.42 The protective function of arrest of ships is its most conspicuous one, so it is possible to refer to arrest as a provisional and protective measure, even though it is provisional in character and the protective function is only one of its functions. The particularities of the protective function of arrest of ships in the international Arrest Conventions are as follows.

The Ship-claim Connection

3.43 For the right of arrest to arise it does not suffice that the ship is the property of the defendant to the action; it must also be identifiable as the ship in connection with which the claim arose.[66] Only that ship or a sister ship[67] of that ship are liable to arrest under the Conventions in respect of

[63] It needs to be noted that in many cases the value of the ship will greatly exceed the value of the claim; hence, the consideration of proportionality in the international Arrest Conventions is set up to a minimum.

[64] 1952 International Arrest Convention, Art 3(1).

[65] Scottish Law Commission, *Report on Diligence on the Dependence and Admiralty Arrestment* (Scot Law Com Report No 164 (1998) 135).

[66] *Owners of Cargo Lately Laden on Board the MV Erkowit v Owners of the Eschersheim (The Eschersheim, the Jade and the Erkowit)* [1976] 2 Lloyd's Rep 1 (HL) (Lord Diplock).

[67] A sister ship is any other ship which is owned by the person who was, at the time when the maritime claim arose, the owner of the particular ship (Art 3(1) 1952 International Arrest Convention). Ships shall be deemed to be in the same ownership when all the shares therein are owned by the same person or persons (Art 3(2)). Furthermore, in this context, a sister ship may be also any other ship in the ownership of the charterer by demise (Art 3(4)). In the 1999 International Arrest Convention, Art 3(2) establishes that a sister ship is any other ship which, when the arrest is effected, is owned by the person who is liable for the maritime claim and who was, when the claim arose, either the owner of the ship in respect of which the maritime claim arose, or the demise charterer, time charterer, or voyage charterer of that ship.

that claim. Consequently, claims that are not against a particular ship cannot be protected by arrest.[68]

Arrest of a Ship in Respect of a Person Other than the Owner

The arrest of ships would not present any particularities in this regard if it **3.44** was available only when the owner of the ship is liable at the moment of arrest; this would be in line with general principles of law in respect of personal obligations. However, even though this is the general rule also in the case of arrest of ships,[69] there are some exceptions. Article 3(4) of the 1952 International Arrest Convention grants the claimant who has a maritime claim against the demise charterer[70] of the ship the right to arrest the ship in respect of which the claim arose. Such right is unrestricted and exists irrespective of the claim being secured by a maritime lien or not. The last sentence of paragraph 4 extends the right of arrest to any case in which a person other than the registered owner is liable in respect of a maritime claim relating to the ship (including, for instance, the time charterer or the voyage charterer).[71]

Article 3(4) appears to derive from the fact that, in certain legal systems,[72] **3.45** maritime claims needed in certain cases to be brought against the *armateur*

[68] '[C]laims against a ship-owner that relate to the maintenance and operation of his ships but which are not related to a particular ship cannot be secured by means of the arrest of one of the ships owned by him. If, for example, the owner purchases stores or spare parts for his fleet and uses them for his ships when the need arises' (Berlingieri, *Berlingieri on the Arrest of Ships* (2006) 127). The same would happen if he leases containers for use by an entire fleet since the claim of the supplier for the payment of such contracts has not arisen in respect of a particular ship and therefore does not give right of arrest in terms of the Convention.

[69] The limits have been clarified in the same article of the 1999 International Arrest Convention. The latter provides that arrest is permissible of any ship in respect of which a maritime claim is asserted if the person who owned the ship at the time when the maritime claim arose is liable for the claim and is owner of the ship when the arrest is effected.

[70] A 'demise' or 'bareboat' charter is a charterparty 'under which the charterer not only has the use of the vessel, but also engages its own crew' (Simon Baughen, *Shipping Law* (4th edn, London, Routledge, 2009) 200).

[71] This could be the case in relation to the maritime claims listed in Art 1(1)(b) (loss of life or personal injury); Art 1(1)(e) (agreements relating to the carriage of goods); Art 1(1)(f) (loss of or damage to goods); ie in most of the cases it will be related to a maritime claim against 'the carrier' when such carrier is neither the owner nor the demise charterer. It has been revealed by Berlingieri that this provision was added on request of Norway and The Netherlands but he argues that the provision goes beyond what was required to bring it in line with Dutch and Norwegian law (Berlingieri, *Berlingieri on Arrest of Ships* (2006) 139). Indeed, in those legal systems arrest of a ship is permissible if the owner is not personally liable only in the cases where a maritime lien exists.

[72] eg this was the case in The Netherlands at the time of the adoption of the 1952 International Arrest Convention. At present under Art 360 Book 8 of the Dutch Civil Code of

gerant (manager) or the demise charterer of the ship. The concept seems to unravel if Article 3(4) is read together with Article 9.[73] Probably the intention was to provide for arrest to follow the ship in the case of maritime liens; but Article 3(4) goes far beyond those cases.

3.46 This provision has given rise to interpretation problems.[74] Arrest of a ship in respect of a person other than the owner is permitted under the 1952 International Arrest Convention, regardless of the existence of a maritime lien, inter alia, in France (demise charterer); Germany (*Ausruster*);[75] Greece (any kind of charterer); Italy (demise charterer and time charterer); and the Netherlands (demise charterer).[76]

3.47 The situation has been clarified in the 1999 International Arrest Convention. Article 3(1)(b) establishes that 'arrest is permissible of any ship in respect of which a maritime claim is asserted if the demise charterer of the ship at the time when the maritime claim arose is liable for the claim and is demise charterer or owner of the ship when the arrest is effected'. Article 3(3) adds: 'Nonetheless, the provisions of paragraphs 1 and 2 of this article, the arrest of a ship which is not owned by the person liable for the claim shall be permissible only if, under the law of the State where the arrest is applied for, a judgment in respect of that claim can be enforced against that ship by judicial or forced sale of that ship.' Paragraph 3 refers generally to the arrest of a ship which is not owned by the person liable for the claim and is formulated as an exception to the provisions of paragraphs 1 and 2; the exception, therefore, applies not only in respect of claims against the demise charterer but also in respect of claims secured by a maritime lien, a mortgage, hypothec, or other charge, and claims relating to the ownership or possession of the ship.[77]

3.48 Article 3(3) of the 1999 International Arrest Convention was intended to reinforce the 'protective' character of the arrest of ships. And it has been

1991 the owner of a ship is personally liable in respect of claims against the demise charterer (Berlingieri, *Berlingieri on Arrest of Ships* (2006) 140).

[73] Even though Art 3 wrongly refers to Art 10; this is a recognized mistake (Berlingieri, *Berlingieri on Arrest of Ships* (2006) 131).

[74] Berlingieri, *Berlingieri on Arrest of Ships* (2006) 144.

[75] The *Ausruster* pursuant to para 510 of the HGB is the operator. This concept would include the demise charterer but not the time charterer (Berlingieri, *Berlingieri on Arrest of Ships* (2006) 145).

[76] At present Art 8(360) of the Dutch Civil Code of 1991 provides that if a ship is demise chartered the owner is jointly liable with the demise charterer in respect of all contractual obligations of the demise charterer relating to the operation of the ship (F Berlingieri, *Berlingieri on Arrest of Ships* (2006) 147).

[77] Berlingieri, *Berlingieri on Arrest of Ships* (2006) 150.

welcomed by expert commentators.[78] As such the arrest of ships can only be effective as a 'security' measure if it can ensure the availability of judicial sale. Doubtless this provision was included to suppress the potentially oppressive effect of the arrest of ships in the cases where the eventual judgment would not be enforceable against the ship. And it certainly links the protective function with the security function of arrest of ships as referred to in Chapter 1.[79] At the time of the adoption of such a rule it was suggested that the issue was a question of national law which was not expected to have a significant impact in common law countries.[80] However, Scots law, where the property of a third party is not generally affected to satisfy the debts of another, has already been modified in respect of arrestment of ships against demise charterers to allow judicial sale of the ship in the cases provided for in the 1999 International Arrest Convention.[81]

VI. CONCLUSIONS

Under the 1952 and 1999 International Arrest Conventions, the arrest of ships is the detention of a ship under the authority of a court as a provisional and protective measure. This characterization provides a broad framework for the development of the arrest of ships as a legal institution in international commercial litigation. **3.49**

The protective and security functions of the arrest of ships are invariably intermingled up to such a point that it is very difficult to distinguish one from the other. From the autonomous definition of arrest of ships in the international Arrest Conventions as the detention of a ship to secure a maritime claim it follows that the security function is inevitably the root of the protective measure. **3.50**

However, the apparent conceptualization of arrest of ships as a provisional and protective measure has not been as effective as it could have been since it was not provided for with consistency in the Conventions. Particularly, leaving the requirements related to the granting of the provisional and protective measure entirely to the law of the *forum arresti* in Article 6(2) of the 1952 International Arrest Convention has jeopardized the harmonization of the law in this field and has left the arrest of **3.51**

[78] See especially Jackson, *Enforcement of Maritime Claims* (2005) 396–7.

[79] See Ch 1, paras 1.21–1.29 above.

[80] N Gaskell and R Shaw, 'Arrest Convention 1999' [1999] *Lloyds Maritime and Commercial Law Quarterly* 1,10.

[81] See Administration of Justice Act 1956, Ch 46, s 47E, as introduced by Sch 4 to the Bankruptcy and Diligence (Scotland) Act 2007.

ships behind the internationally recognized standards[82] with regard to provisional and protective measures.

3.52 It is submitted that better harmonization results could be obtained if courts turned to the process of characterization as advanced in this chapter to distinguish between the private international law category in the Conventions and the measure as provided for in the domestic law of the forum. Clearly, the general rationale of international uniform law, ie the creation of international uniform statutory rules between State parties that support stability and predictability in international legal relations, is not fostered by 'homewards' methods of interpretation.[83] Therefore, an autonomous interpretation is paramount if real harmonization is to be achieved in this field.

[82] See eg the 'Resolution on Provisional and Protective Measures in International Litigation' (1996) *International Law Association* (Helsinski) and the 'Principles of Transnational Civil Procedure ALI/Unidroit' (2004) 4 *Uniform Law Review* 758–809.

[83] F Diedrich, 'Mantaining Uniformity in International Uniform Law Via Autonomous Interpretation' (1996) 8 *Pace International Law Rev* 303, 310.

4

Ship Arrest in England

I. INTRODUCTION

Ship arrest in modern English law is an inherent part of the *in rem* claim. **4.01** The *in rem* claim can be entertained only for claims within Admiralty jurisdiction hence an *in rem* claim[1] must be started in the Admiralty Court.[2] The relationship between claims *in rem* and the arrest of ships is clearly established by Jackson in the following terms 'the action *in rem* [now the *in rem* claim][3] is the method of enforcement [of maritime or statutory liens] and arrest a powerful measure of interim relief'.[4] Hence, as the *in rem* claim is how ship arrest has developed in England, understanding the nature of the *in rem* claim becomes pivotal to the analysis of ship arrest in

[1] An *in rem* claim form can be issued naming more than one ship, but according to s 21(8) of the Senior Courts Act 1981 only one ship can be arrested. In practice once one of the ships named comes within the jurisdiction the claimant amends the claim form and serves it on that particular ship (Aleka Mandaraka-Sheppard, *Modern Maritime Law and Risk Management* (2nd edn, London, Informa, 2009) 115). It is also admissible to issue separate *in rem* claim forms against different ships belonging to the same owner for the same claim (*The Berny* [1977] 2 Lloyd's Rep 533).

[2] Civil Procedure Rules 1998 (SI 1998/3132) Pt 61 (Admiralty Claims), r 61.2(1).

[3] Civil Procedure (Amendment No 5) Rules 2001 (SI 2001/4015).

[4] DC Jackson, *Enforcement of Maritime Claims* (4th edn, London, LLP, 2005) 257.

English law.[5] Moreover, since ship arrest is a 'powerful measure of interim relief', general consideration of interim measures of protection in English law would also seem relevant in this regard. Nonetheless, ship arrest and interim relief are treated separately in English law, hence, the examination of the general provisions related to interim relief in English law[6] is outside the scope of this study.

4.02 This chapter and the following one aim to signal the current differences between English and Scots law[7] in the law of arrest of ships and to assess their consistency, respectively, with the international Arrest Conventions. Ultimately, the theoretically-driven approach characteristic of the civilian tradition expresses itself in this particular field in treating the arrestment of ships in Scots law as pertaining to a broader category (interim relief/diligence/provisional and protective measures). On the other hand, the practice-driven approach of the English common law emphasizes the need to adjust ship arrest to the particular needs of maritime commerce; therefore, the institution is treated as a category of its own. Neither of these approaches is without hindrances.

4.03 The previous chapter has shown how the arrest of ships in the international Arrest Conventions is first and foremost a provisional and protective measure. This chapter and the following one will, in particular, examine English and Scots law, respectively, in relation to that characterization. Hence, the difficulties in this regard generated by the current law on the arrest of ships in each of the legal systems of Great Britain are the focus of the analysis.[8]

[5] For an account of the English dicta concerned with the nature of the action *in rem* in the twentieth century, see N Teare, 'The Admiralty Action *in rem* and the House of Lords' [1997] *Lloyds Maritime and Commercial Law Quarterly* 34.

[6] See Civil Procedure Rules 1998, Pt 25.

[7] Due to the fact that the power to ratify international Conventions rests with the Crown, most of the international literature on the subject-matter tends to erroneously assume that the United Kingdom has at present a single system of arrest of ships. For the discussion on arrestment of ships in Scotland, see Ch 5 below.

[8] Note that, as explained in Ch 1 (Introduction), this book does not focus on domestic law. It is a study of the private international law effects of the arrest of ships. Hence, the study of the arrest of ships in England and Scotland is necessarily limited to the relevant issues that contribute to the analysis of issues of characterization, applicable law, jurisdiction, and the recognition and enforcement of foreign judgments. Therefore, the study of the domestic law in this chapter and the following one is not intended to be comprehensive of the current law on the arrest of ships in each of these legal systems.

II. ADMIRALTY JURISDICTION IN ENGLAND

As essential background to this discussion, it is necessary to present an overview of the Admiralty jurisdiction in England to set the scene. The Admiralty Court in England is part of the Queen's Bench Division of the High Court. Admiralty proceedings in England may be brought *in personam* against a named defendant or *in rem* against a *res* (in most cases, a ship). It is possible to commence proceedings both *in rem* and *in personam* in relation to the same claim, even though two claim forms must be issued in this case.[9] Since the beginning of the nineteenth century, ship arrest is available in English law in the frame of *in rem* claims only. Admiralty proceedings in English law (in fact, Admiralty claims *in rem*) are subject to the Civil Procedure Rules Part 61 (Admiralty Claims) and the associated Practice Direction. In turn, *in personam* Admiralty claims are dealt with in accordance with the Civil Procedure Rules Part 58 (Commercial Claims). **4.04**

The subject-matters over which the Admiralty Court has jurisdiction are established in section 20 of the Supreme Court Act 1981 (now renamed as Senior Courts Act 1981) and all claims therein included are closely connected to the maritime activity.[10] The right to proceed against a ship *in rem* is governed by sections 20 to 24 of the same Act. According to section 20(7), Admiralty jurisdiction is exercisable in relation to all ships for all claims enumerated in section 20(2). **4.05**

The claims enumerated in section 20(2) are: **4.06**

(a) any claim to the possession or ownership of a ship or to the ownership of any share therein;
(b) any question arising between the co-owners of a ship as to possession, employment, or earnings of that ship;
(c) any claim in respect of a mortgage of or charge on a ship or any share therein;

[9] *The Berny* [1977] 2 Lloyd's Rep 533.

[10] (i) under s 20(1)(a) of the Senior Courts Act 1981 claims are largely coincident with the list of maritime claims as provided for in the 1952 International Arrest Convention; these claims are listed in s 20(2); (ii) under s 20(1)(b) of the same Act any application to the High Court under the Merchant Shipping Act 1995; any action to enforce a claim for damage, loss of life, or personal injury arising out of several circumstances enunciated therein; and any action by ship-owners or other persons under the Merchant Shipping Act 1995 for the limitation of the amount of their liability in connection with a ship or other property; (iii) under s 20(1)(c) of the Act any other Admiralty jurisdiction which it had immediately before the entry into force of the Act; (iv) under s 20(1)(d) of the Act any jurisdiction connected with ships or aircraft which is vested in the High Court apart from that section and is for the time being by rules of court made or coming into force after the commencement of the Act assigned to the Queen's Bench Division and directed by the rules to be exercised by the Admiralty Court.

(d) any claim for damage received by a ship;
(e) any claim for damage done by a ship;
(f) any claim for loss of life or personal injury sustained in consequence of any defect in a ship or in her apparel or equipment, or in consequence of the wrongful act, neglect, or default of
    (i) the owners, charterers, or persons in possession or control of a ship; or
    (ii) the master or crew of a ship, or any other person for whose wrongful acts, neglects, or defaults the owners, charterers, or persons in possession or control of a ship are responsible, being an act, neglect, or default in the navigation or management of the ship, in the loading, carriage, or discharge of goods on, in, or from the ship, or in the embarkation, carriage, or disembarkation of persons on, in, or from the ship;
(g) any claim for loss of or damage to goods carried in a ship;
(h) any claim arising out of any agreement relating to the carriage of goods in a ship or to the use or hire of a ship;
(i) any claim
    (i) under the Salvage Convention 1989;
    (ii) under any contract for or in relation to salvage services; or
    (iii) in the nature of salvage not falling within (i) or (ii) above; or any corresponding claim in connection with an aircraft;
(j) any claim in the nature of towage in respect of a ship or an aircraft;
(k) any claim in the nature of pilotage in respect of a ship or an aircraft;
(l) any claim in respect of goods or materials supplied to a ship for her operation or maintenance;
(m) any claim in respect of the construction, repair, or equipment of a ship or in respect of dock charges or dues;
(n) any claim by a master or member of the crew of a ship for wages (including any sum allotted out of wages or adjudged by a superintendent to be due by way of wages);
(o) any claim by a master, shipper, charterer, or agent in respect of disbursements made on account of a ship;
(p) any claim arising out of an act which is or is claimed to be a general average act;
(q) any claim arising out of bottomry;
(r) any claim for the forfeiture or condemnation of ship or of goods which are being or have been carried, or have been attempted to be carried, in a ship, or for the restoration of a ship or any such goods after seizure, or for droits of Admiralty.

III. THE FRAMEWORK IN WHICH SHIP ARREST HAS DEVELOPED

1. The *in rem* Claim

4.07 As analysed in Chapter 2,[11] the action *in rem* (now renamed as the *in rem* claim) has a long history in the administration of Admiralty law in England. In this context, the particular features of the *in rem* claim are material, as the legal framework in which ship arrest has developed in English law. Traditionally, several features were adjudicated to the old action *in rem* in English law. It was considered that the *in rem* proceedings were primarily a means of obtaining security for the claim and also a means of obtaining jurisdiction on the merits of the claim by arresting the ship within the jurisdiction. In relation to maritime liens, the action *in rem* was viewed as the only way of making good the lien, ie the means of enforcing a right in security already accrued on the ship. Furthermore, the value of the ship had always been the limit for satisfaction of maritime claims *in rem*.[12] Most of these advantages adjudicated in English law to the action *in rem* are due to functions displayed in fact by the arrest of the ship. Hence, the benefits of the arrest of ships as the most powerful provisional and protective measure used in international shipping litigation are invariably treated in English law as features not of ship arrest (as they are) but of the *in rem* claim. In other words, in English law ship arrest as such only displays the protective function; it is for the *in rem* claim as a distinctive Admiralty procedure to display the three, in this order: the security function (by the issuance of the *in rem* claim form), the protective function (with the ship arrest), and the jurisdictional function (by the service of the *in rem* claim).

4.08 In 1997 the House of Lords in *The Indian Grace (No 2)*[13] recognized that in reality an action *in rem* is an action against the owner, and not the ship.[14] This decision of the House of Lords has been criticized both in England[15]

[11] See Ch 2, paras 2.36–2.44 above.

[12] See *The Longford* (1889) 14 PD 34; *The Burns* [1907] P 137. Cf *The Conoco Britannia* [1972] 2 QB 543, 555 (Brandon J). See also Mandaraka-Sheppard, *Modern Maritime Law and Risk Management* (2009) 79.

[13] *The Republic of India v India Steamship Co Ltd (No 2)(The Indian Grace (No 2))* [1998] 1 AC 878 (HL).

[14] Cf with the personification theory in Ch 2 paras 2.39–2.40 above.

[15] See, inter alia, N Teare, 'The Admiralty Action *in rem* and the House of Lords' [1998] *Lloyd's Maritime and Commercial Law Quarterly* 33; SC Derrington and JM Turner, *The Law and*

and elsewhere.[16] However, in the opinion of Jackson this decision helped significantly to replace fiction with reality. It contributed to the understanding that an *in rem* claim 'is an action against a defendant with particular benefits for the claimant rather than an action against the ship as the "wrongdoer"'.[17]

4.09 On first examination, considering an *in rem* claim as a claim against the owner goes against the traditional[18] and world-wide extended understanding that, as the literal expression itself indicates, an *in rem* claim is a claim against the *res*.[19] In Admiralty, the distinctive feature of the old action *in rem* has always been the ability of the maritime claimant to proceed directly against the ship; if the person interested in defending the claim appears in the proceedings, or acknowledges service of the *in rem* claim form, an *in personam* claim may materialize in addition against the defendants.[20] This has an important effect in practice: if the claim exceeds the value of the ship and Admiralty jurisdiction is also being exercised *in personam* in relation to that claim by virtue of the appearance of the defendant, the defendant could be eventually personally liable beyond the value of the ship.[21] If, however, the claim is only *in rem* and no jurisdiction

Practice of Admiralty Matters (Oxford, OUP, 2007) Ch 2; S Derrington, 'The Continuing Utility of the Action *in rem*' (2007) *Law Quarterly Review* 358.

[16] See, inter alia, *Kuo Fen Ching v Dauphin Offshore Engineering & Trading Pte Ltd* [1999] 3 SLR 721; *The Irina Zharkikh and Ksenia Zharkikh* [2001] 2 NZLR 801, [2001] 2 Lloyd's Rep 319; *Comandate Marine Corp v Pan Australia Shipping Pty Ltd* [2006] FCAFC 192.

[17] DC Jackson, *Enforcement of Maritime Claims* (4th edn, London, LLP, 2005) 2–3.

[18] In the words of Sir George Jessel MR, 'You may in England and in most countries proceed against the ship. The writ [now claim form] may be issued against the owner of such a ship, and the owner may never appear, and you may get your judgment against the ship without a single person being named from beginning to end. That is an action *in rem*, and it is perfectly well understood that the judgment is against the ship' (*The City of Mecca* (1881) 5 PD 106, 112). Cf *The Indian Grace (No 2)* [1988] AC 878 (HL).

[19] The *in rem/in personam* distinction derives ultimately from Roman law; see B Nicholas, *An Introduction to Roman Law* (Oxford, Clarendon, 1975) 99–104. Nonetheless, the strict Roman dichotomy becomes difficult to maintain in modern legal systems where the law is construed in terms of rights and duties. An action *in personam* may operate to protect a right *in rem* (as it is in fact the case in Scots law in some admiralty actions) hence, the Roman dichotomy is blurred. It is also blurred in English law in the sister-ship 'allowance' which is only permitted for those claims under paragraphs (e)–(r) of s 20(2) of the Senior Courts Act 1981. Thus, as examined in Ch 2, in admiralty actions, the modern dichotomy of *in rem/in personam* claims finds its routes elsewhere but in the Roman distinction.

[20] *The Dictator* [1892] P 304; *The Gemma* [1899] P 285 (CA); *The Burns* [1907] P 137; *The Dupleix* [1912] P 8; *The Joannis Vatis (No 2)* [1922] P 213; *The Beldis* [1936] P 51; *The Banco* [1971] P 137; *The August 8* [1983] 1 Lloyd's Rep 351((PC) Singapore); *The Nordglimt* [1988] 1 QB 183; *The Maciej Rataj* [1992] 2 Lloyd's Rep 552; *The Anna H* [1995] 1 Lloyd's Rep 11.

[21] *The Dictator* [1892] PD 304 (Jeune J).

in personam is exercised against a named defendant, the maximum that the claimant is able to recover is the value of the ship.

The decision of the House of Lords in *The Indian Grace (No 2)* may have altered this important distinction between *in rem* and *in personam* claims. Mandaraka-Sheppard explains that '[i]n theory, the value of the ship will no longer be the limit of liability for the satisfaction of maritime claims, which arose in connection with the ship because, once the *in rem* claim form is served, the action becomes also an action *in personam* from that moment, whether or not the defendant chooses to acknowledge service'.[22] This personal jurisdiction arises only in relation to the person liable for the claim and it does not extend to a bona fide purchaser of the ship.[23] **4.10**

There is a further distinction to be considered in English Admiralty jurisdiction in this context and refers to the difference between claims that are 'truly *in rem*' and 'non-truly *in rem*'.[24] The latter ones are also known as statutory rights to proceed *in rem*. These rights were first created by the Admiralty Court Act 1840. The list of claims giving the claimant this procedural advantage (to proceed *in rem* and consequently to arrest the ship) was subsequently expanded by the Judicature (Consolidation) Act 1925, the Administration of Justice Act 1956 (giving effect to the 1952 International Arrest Convention in English and Scots law) and finally by the Supreme Court Act 1981 (now renamed as Senior Courts Act 1981). **4.11**

Claims that are substantively *in rem* can be brought against the relevant ship without considerations of who would be liable *in personam* for that claim at the time when the *in rem* claim form is issued or who is the beneficial owner of the ship to be arrested. On the other hand, such considerations are paramount when a non-truly *in rem* claim is brought against the relevant ship.[25] These different scenarios are examined later in this chapter.[26] **4.12**

The intermingling of theories surrounding the action *in rem* during the nineteenth century in Great Britain (as discussed in Chapter 2) perpetuated into the twentieth century. In 1907 in *The Burns*[27] the nature of the action *in rem* was explained by counsel for the appellants 'upon the contention that the process of arrest of a vessel ... is merely a method of **4.13**

[22] Aleka Mandaraka-Sheppard, *Modern Maritime Law and Risk Management* (2nd edn, London, Informa, 2009) 91.

[23] Ibid, 93.

[24] Ibid, 69.

[25] Mandaraka-Sheppard, *Modern Maritime Law and Risk Management* (2009) 69.

[26] See paras 4.20–4.21 below.

[27] *The Burns* [1907] P 137.

enforcing an appearance in an action. In other words, that an action *in rem* in no way differs in its nature from an action *in personam*; save that there is attached to it a means of compelling the appearance of the defendant by arrest of the vessel'.[28] It is certainly arguable that the various theories, particularly the personification theory and the procedural theory, still constitute today an integral part of the analysis when it comes to the conceptualization of the *in rem* claim in English law. And they have also played an important role in the conceptualization of the action *in rem* in common law legal systems.[29]

4.14 More recent jurisprudence has focused on whether actions *in rem* were to be understood as procedural in nature—aimed at compelling appearance by an individual subject to an action *in personam*—or alternatively, deriving from a substantive right against the ship. Ship arrest and its functions are at the centre of the contrasting arguments used to support one position or the other. This controversy has been settled in English law by the above-mentioned decision of the House of Lords in *The Indian Grace (No 2)*.[30] Lord Steyn considered that 'the procedural theory stripped away the form and revealed that in substance the owners were parties to the action *in rem*'.[31]

4.15 The procedural advantages of the *in rem* claim have ship arrest at the very core; by commencing the *in rem* claim and arresting the ship three distinct functions are merged: namely, (a) it has the consequence of preventing the ship from leaving the jurisdiction; (b) it is possible to establish jurisdiction on the merits, even if there is no substantive link between the claim and the jurisdiction other than the presence of the arrested ship in the jurisdiction; and (c) it secures the position of maritime claimants as preferred creditors over unsecured ones in the eventual sale of the ship. These features of the *in rem* claim apply equally in English and in Scots law.

4.16 As outlined earlier in this chapter,[32] in English law it is necessary to distinguish claims which are inherently *in rem* from claims that are procedurally *in rem* but substantially *in personam*, which are sometimes referred as *quasi*

[28] Ibid, 148 (per Lord Justice Fletcher Moulton). The dictum in this case dismissed this argument of the appellant but the quote mentioned above is illustrative to show the relationship between the most disputed features of the action *in rem* and the arrest of ships and its functions.

[29] See eg Peter Gillies and Andrew Dahdal, 'Characterising the Action *In Rem* in Australia—Recent Perspectives' (2007) *Macquarie Law* WP 2007-19.

[30] *The Indian Grace (No 2)* [1998] 1 AC 878.

[31] Ibid, at 909.

[32] See paras 4.09–4.10 above.

in rem claims.[33] Claims that are inherently *in rem* include claims that attract a traditional maritime lien[34] and claims related to ownership, possession, or mortgages, ie proprietary rights in a ship. All these *in rem* claims are registered in the Admiralty Registry.[35]

From the moment an *in rem* claim form has been issued, an *in rem* claim crystallizes on the ship as a statutory lien *in rem*, which constitutes a form of security in the event that the ship is sold to a bona fide purchaser[36] before service of the claim form; in that case, the claim will still be enforceable against the ship by service and arrest. **4.17**

The service of the *in rem* claim form on the ship does not constitute a ship arrest. A separate application must be made for the issue of a warrant of arrest. Only the Admiralty Marshal or his substitute may effect the arrest of the ship.[37] To prevent arrest it is possible to file a caution against arrest in the Admiralty and Commercial Registry accompanied by an undertaking to file an acknowledgement of service and to give sufficient security to satisfy the claim; however, the entry of a caution against arrest is not considered to be a submission to the jurisdiction of the English courts and, in any case, property may be arrested notwithstanding a caution against arrest.[38] These procedural features reinforce the different functions of ship arrest. **4.18**

IV. DIFFERENT TYPES OF SHIP ARREST

Three different 'types' of ship arrest may be distinguished in English law, ie (a) ship arrest to enforce a maritime lien; (b) ship arrest to protect proprietary rights on the ship; and (c) ship arrest to secure a maritime claim when there are no maritime liens or proprietary rights at stake but just a statutory right to proceed *in rem*. Even though it is possible to draw these **4.19**

[33] N Meeson, *Admiralty Jurisdiction and Practice* (3rd edn, LLP, London, 2003) 17. Contrarily, Mandara-Sheppard considers that the phrase *quasi in rem* is best avoided because it was used in relation to the ancient maritime attachment referred to in Ch 2 para 2.26 above. See Aleka Mandaraka-Sheppard, *Modern Maritime Law and Risk Management* (2nd edn, London, Informa, 2009) 69.

[34] For the consideration of maritime liens, its relation with the arrest of ships, and its particular position in relation to the conflict of laws, see Ch 6 below.

[35] The administrative office for the Admiralty Court and the Commercial Court is the Admiralty & Commercial Registry which is located in the Royal Courts of Justice, London.

[36] Aleka Mandaraka-Sheppard, *Modern Maritime Law and Risk Management* (2009) 11.

[37] Civil Procedure Rules 1998, Pt 61 (Admiralty Claims) r 61.5(8).

[38] Civil Procedure Rules 1998, Pt 61 (Admiralty Claims), r 61.7(5).

distinctions, ship arrest in English law is treated indistinctively as an inherent part of the *in rem* claim.[39]

4.20 Technically, statutory rights *in rem* include all claims that can be enforced in the Admiralty Court according to the provisions of the Senior Courts Act 1981. Some of the claims listed in the Act attract a traditional maritime lien, ie a substantive right in security against the ship that arises upon the incident that generates the cause of action. Other claims, however, refer to proprietary rights on the ship. Moreover, the residual category within this list of claims do not attract a maritime lien or refer to a proprietary right on the ship but are claims generally related to maritime commerce. Nonetheless, the differences are not associated to the effect of ship arrest as such, but with the nature of the right that the arrest is connected to, ie the difference is between rights *in rem* (or 'truly *in rem*') and rights to proceed *in rem* (namely, as a procedural device).

4.21 According to English law, traditional maritime liens are rights *in rem* on the ship that exist irrespective of an *in rem* claim and in relation to them the *in rem* claim is just the way of enforcing the maritime lien. By contrast, in the case of rights to proceed *in rem*, which are not maritime liens, the procedural right crystallizes on the ship upon commencement of proceedings *in rem*.[40] The latter are known as statutory liens.

1. Different Functions of Ship Arrest

4.22 Due to the indistinctive treatment of ship arrest in English law, regardless of the different functions that the arrest may display in the three different scenarios outlined above, it becomes necessary to distinguish these different 'types' of ship arrest in relation to their functions. This delineation may bring about clarity in the characterization of ship arrest in English law and contribute to the understanding of the conceptual distinction between the arrest of ships and the *in rem* claim as different legal institutions.

The Jurisdictional Function

4.23 The jurisdictional function operates the same way in all these types of ship arrest, since it is technically not the arrest that displays this function in English law but the *in rem* claim form when served on the defendant. The interaction of the other two functions, however, varies more significantly and will be analysed in turn.

[39] See Civil Procedure Rules 1998, Pt 61 (Admiralty Claims), r 61.5.
[40] *The Monica S* [1967] 2 Lloyd's Rep 113.

The Protective Function

In cases where the ship to be arrested is the one in connection with which the claim arose, and provided the claim does not attract a maritime lien, and is not one of a proprietary character, the person who would be liable for such claim *in personam* when the cause of action arose should be either the beneficial owner[41] of that ship in all shares, or the demise charterer at the time of the issue of the *in rem* claim form. **4.24**

The determination of the beneficial ownership of foreign ships has presented problems in practice.[42] The proliferation of one-ship companies and complex corporation structures usually represent a hindrance in this sphere. Furthermore, the common law distinction between legal and equitable ownership has no counterpart in many legal systems.[43] **4.25**

For the arrest of a sister ship, the person who would be liable for such claim *in personam* when the cause of action arose should be the beneficial owner of that other ship in all shares at the time of the issue of the *in rem* claim form. A sister ship is only permitted for those claims under paragraphs (d) to (r) of section 20(2), which include the claims which give rise to maritime liens, but not claims related to mortgages, ownership, or possession of a particular ship. However, when a sister ship is arrested for a claim attracting a maritime lien, the lien is lost and therefore its priority in satisfaction of the claim will rank in the same category as that of the other statutory rights *in rem*.[44] **4.26**

In relation to the possibility to arrest more than one ship with regard to the same *in rem* claim in England, the Senior Courts Act 1981, section 21(8) enacts a mandatory prohibition for claims mentioned in s 20(2)(e) to (r) of the same Act.[45] Where a ship has been served with a claim form or arrested **4.27**

[41] Beneficial ownership means equitable ownership; it does not include possession and control (as a charterer has under a bareboat or demise charterparty). In *The Andrea Ursula* [1973] Q B 265 Brandon J held that demise charterers were beneficial owners in this context but this position was struck down in *The I Congreso del Partido* [1978] 1 All ER 1169, followed by *The Father Thames* [1979] 2 Lloyd's Rep 364. See also *The Nazym Khikmet* [1996] 2 Lloyd's Rep 362.

[42] See *The Aventicum* [1978] 1 Lloyd's Rep 184; *The Maritime Trader* [1981] 2 Lloyd's Rep 153; *The Evpo Agnic* [1988] 1 WLR 1090; *The Nazym Khikmet* [1996] 2 Lloyd's Rep 362; *The Tjaskemolen* [1997] 2 Lloyd's Rep 465; *The Giuseppe di Vittorio* [1998] 1 Lloyd's Rep 136.

[43] Jonathan Hill and Adeline Chong, *International Commercial Disputes, Commercial Conflict of Laws in English Courts* (Oxford, Hart, 2010) 256.

[44] *The Leoborg (No 4)* [1964] 1 Lloyd's Rep 380 (PDAD).

[45] However, in *Centro Latino Americano de Commercio Exterior SA v Owners of the Kommunar (The Kommunar) (No 2)* [1997] 1 Lloyd's Rep 8 (QBD (Admlty)) it was held that s 21(8) of the (now) Senior Courts Act 1981 is not to be seen as implementing the more

to enforce that claim no other ship may be served with such a form or arrested in that or any other *in rem* proceedings brought to enforce that claim. Notwithstanding this prohibition, when the security provided is insufficient[46] or when the security given is ineffective, the court has discretion to allow re-arrest if the particular circumstances of the case so request to balance the interests of claimant and defendant.[47] However, English courts will strive to avoid oppression and unfairness in this sphere,[48] consequently, a second arrest is exceptional.

No ship arrest as a protective measure for in personam claims

4.28 In England it is not possible to arrest a ship as an interim measure of protection in relation to *in personam* claims under present law. As examined in Chapter 2,[49] this was not always the case. In the early days of the Admiralty jurisdiction in England it was possible to arrest a ship in the framework of an action *in personam*. The measure was known as a maritime attachment, and allegedly it fell into disuse in Admiralty by the beginning of the nineteenth century concurrently with the loss of jurisdiction *in personam* experienced by the Admiralty Court.[50] However, this does not mean there are no other forms of interim security available to maritime claimants in relation to *in personam* claims in present times.

Freezing orders

4.29 It has often been noted that '[a]n unsatisfied judgment against an assetless defendant is a pyrrhic victory'.[51] This applies generally in relation to any type of dispute in civil and commercial matters. In English law, in the sphere of enforcement of maritime claims, there are currently two principal methods of obtaining interim security available to the claimant to ensure that any possible judgment in his favour will be complied with. These two methods are ship arrest, available only in relation to *in rem* claims,

flexible but wide prohibition on re-arrest provided for in the 1952 International Arrest Convention Art 3(3).

[46] *The Hero* (1865) B&L 447.

[47] *Owners of the Carbonnade v Owners of the Ruta (The Ruta)* [2000] 1 Lloyds Rep 359 (QBD (Admlty)) (Steel J).

[48] See Mandaraka-Sheppard, *Modern Maritime Law and Risk Management* (2009) 126 and 130.

[49] See Ch 2, para 2.26 above.

[50] W Tetley, 'Arrest, Attachment and Related Maritime Law Procedures' (1999) 73 *Tulane Law Review* 1905. Tetley is of the opinion that the maritime attachment continued to exist after 1800 on the grounds of Fry's speech in *The Northcote v Owners of the Henrich Bjorn (The Henrich Bjorn)* (1885) LR 10 PD 44 (CA).

[51] DR Thomas, *Maritime Liens* (London, Stevens, 1980) 73.

and freezing orders, available in relation to *in personam* claims.[52] The former, as discussed in this chapter, is exclusive to maritime claims; the latter, conversely, is common to civil and commercial cases in general.

The English freezing order is a relatively recent common law creation formerly known as a *Mareva* injunction.[53] At present, the jurisdiction of the English courts to grant a freezing order derives from the Senior Courts Act 1981 and is set out in the Civil Procedure Rules 1998 along with interim measures of protection.[54] The purpose of a freezing order is to prevent a defendant from moving, hiding, or otherwise unjustifiably dissipating his assets so as to render himself judgment proof.[55] A freezing order does not give an applicant security for his claim, and in particular does not create any proprietary rights against the ship as an asset covered by the order.[56] Freezing orders take effect against the respondent personally, rather than attaching to the assets themselves. **4.30**

The analysis of freezing orders in the context of this book is necessarily very limited. It is theoretically possible to consider that a freezing order involving a ship is within the private international law category 'arrest of ships' as provided for in the international Arrest Conventions Article 1(2). However, this has not been the approach taken by the English courts in relation to the definition of arrest of ships in the 1952 International Arrest Convention.[57] **4.31**

[52] In 1972 in *The Conoco Britannia* [1972] 2 QB 543 Brandon J held that equitable remedies *in personam* could be awarded in an action *in rem*. However, in 1980 in *The Stolt Filia* [1980] LMLN 15 Sheen J held that the [then] *Mareva* injunction could not be granted in an action *in rem* since there was no defendant against whom it could be ordered.

[53] The freezing order is another example of the common law ingenuity. Created by Lord Denning in *Nippon Yusen Kaisha v Karageorgis* [1975] 2 Lloyd's Rep 137 and *Mareva Compañia Naviera SA v International Bulk Carriers SA* [1975] 2 Lloyd's Rep 509. In these two cases Lord Denning took recourse to a discretionary power vested in the High Court under s 45 of the Supreme Court of Judicature Act 1925.

[54] Section 37(1) and (3) of the Senior Courts Act 1981; Civil Procedure Rules 1998, r 25(1)(f).

[55] *Gangway Ltd v Caledonian Park Investments* [2001] 2 Lloyd's Rep 715, 717 (Colman J, para 14). See also *TTMI Ltd of England v ASM Shipping* [2006] 1 Lloyd's Rep 401, 406 (paras 24 *et seq*).

[56] See *The Angel Bell* [1980] 1 Lloyd's Rep 632; *A/S Admiral Shipping v Portlink Ferries Ltd* [1984] 2 Lloyd's Rep 166; *Gangway Ltd v Caledonian Park Investments* [2001] 2 Lloyd's Rep 715.

[57] Jackson, *Enforcement of Maritime Claims* (2005) 436. See further discussion in para 4.35 below.

The Security Function

4.32 In relation to its security function as referred to in Chapter 1,[58] it has been argued that ship arrest in English law 'is simply an early step ensuring physical retention of an asset in that process'[59] and that the permanent security effects of a maritime process arise in connection with the 'lien'[60] rather than in connection with ship arrest in English law. However, as explained in the previous paragraphs, the issuance of an *in rem* claim form also displays a security function in English law. Hence, the distinction between the different 'types' of ship arrest remain paramount in this sphere to fully understand the effects of these as far as the claimant status of a preferred creditor.

Arrest in rem *to enforce a maritime lien*

4.33 In English law maritime liens arise out of collision, salvage, crew's wages, master's disbursements, and bonds of *bottomry* and *respondentia*. A maritime lien is a security which gives the security-holder a right *in rem* on the ship, and takes priority over mortgages. This right arises by operation of law, without registration or other formalities. It is indeed a right in security. This kind of security must be enforced by an *in rem* claim, in which the arrest of the ship is an essential component. In this context, ship arrest as an early step ensuring physical retention of the *res*, is a pre-emptive measure linked with a real right in security on the object. It displays the protective function of arrest of ships as referred to in Chapter 1, ie it counteracts the speed with which the *res* could leave the jurisdiction, but it does not have a security function as such; the priority afforded lies in the nature of the cause of action.

Arrest in rem *to enforce statutory rights* in rem

4.34 As explained by Tetley,[61] the statutory right to proceed *in rem* differs from a maritime lien in at least three major ways, all of them related to the security function. First, the right arises only from the time of the issue of the *in rem* claim form, where the maritime lien arises when the cause of action arises, eg in a collision scenario when the damage is done by the ship concerned. Secondly, for a statutory right *in rem* to follow the ship into whomever's

[58] See Ch 1, paras 1.28–1.29 above.

[59] Jackson, *Enforcement of Maritime Claims* (2005) 404.

[60] For a detailed analysis of the security function of ship arrest and its connection with maritime liens, see Ch 6 below.

[61] Tetley, 'Arrest, Attachment and Related Maritime Law Procedures' (1999) 1895.

hands it passes, an *in rem* claim form needs to be issued before the ship is sold.[62] Once the *in rem* claim form is issued, the claimant acquires a status of a preferred creditor and the claim will follow the ship even in the hands of an innocent purchaser. The potential purchaser can protect himself against such encumbrance by looking at the court's register of *in rem* claims. This is a further difference from ships 'affected' by maritime liens, because traditional maritime liens are invisible (non-registrable). Thirdly, the holder of a statutory right *in rem* has a much lower priority than the maritime lien-holder in the distribution of the proceeds of the judicial sale, ranking after, rather than before, the ship's mortgagee.[63]

V. CONSISTENCY WITH THE INTERNATIONAL CONVENTIONS

As explained in Chapter 3, Article 1(2) of the 1952 and 1999 International Arrest Conventions contain an autonomous definition of arrest of ships as formed by various parts: (i) arrest (the detention of a ship; the detention or restriction on removal of a ship); (ii) how it is effected (judicial process; order of a court); (iii) its purpose (to secure a maritime claim); and (iv) what is not arrest (the seizure of a ship in execution or satisfaction of a judgment or other enforceable instrument). In the following paragraphs the consistency of ship arrest as practised in England with such an autonomous definition is scrutinized. **4.35**

(i) Arrest Means Physical Detention of a Ship

According to established practice, ship arrest in England generally prevents the ship from sailing;[64] that is, the ship in question can be legally prevented from moving or indeed trading pending the resolution of a court action (an *in rem* claim). In that sense ship arrest as practised in England fits within the Convention's category. **4.36**

The only question in relation to English law concerns the possible inclusion of the English freezing orders mentioned above within the international Arrest Conventions' category of 'arrest of ships'. The position of English courts has clearly rejected this interpretation of the definition of **4.37**

[62] Section 21(4)(b)(i) of the Senior Courts Act 1981.

[63] Tetley, 'Arrest, Attachment and Related Maritime Law Procedures' (1999) 1895.

[64] According to the Civil Procedure Rules 1998, Pt 61, r 61.5(9) 'Property under arrest, (a) may not be moved unless the court orders otherwise; and (b) may be immobilised or prevented from sailing in such manner as the Marshal may consider appropriate.'

arrest of ships in the 1952 International Arrest Convention.[65] The issue becomes more relevant in the 1999 International Arrest Convention than under the Convention currently in force. Notably, the wording of this provision in the Conventions is different, ie as the 'detention of a ship' in the 1952 International Arrest Convention and as the 'detention or restriction on removal of a ship'[66] in the 1999 International Arrest Convention.[67] The latter points to a broader scope of the arrest of ships as a private international law category in the latest Convention that might eventually be understood as including freezing orders involving ships.[68]

(ii) Arrest is a Judicial Remedy

4.38 Article 1(2) of both international Conventions refers to the detention of a ship by judicial process and Articles 4 and 2, respectively, provide that a ship 'may only be arrested [or released from arrest] under the authority of a court [or of the appropriate judicial authority] of the State party in which the arrest is made [effected]'. In English law, according to the Civil Procedure Rules,[69] on application by a claimant in an *in rem* claim, 'the court' will issue an arrest warrant. However, in fact, an *in rem* claim form and subsequently an arrest warrant will be issued by an official of the Admiralty and Commercial Registry. The arrest warrant may only then be effected by the Admiralty Marshal. The judicial intervention is very limited: the rules do not enable the courts to refuse an arrest warrant if an *in rem* claim form has been issued. Judicial control may be exercised only if the claim form has been challenged;[70] and setting aside an *in rem* claim form removes in principle the basis for the arrest.[71] In consequence, the possibility to arrest is initially under minimal if any judicial scrutiny in English law.

[65] See Jackson, *Enforcement of Maritime Claims* (2005) 436.

[66] The selection of the term 'removal' in the English version has been criticized. In the French version the more appropriate term 'depart' was used. In the Spanish text the term used is *restricción a la salida de un buque* (F Berlingieri, *Berlingieri on Arrest of Ships* (London, Informa, 2006) 93).

[67] It was inserted to clarify the situation of any encumbrance over a ship that does not imply physical detention. For instance, the so-called 'ship-register arrest' in Danish law, whereby the warrant of arrest is not executed on the ship but is only endorsed in the ship's register.

[68] See Jackson, *Enforcement of Maritime Claims* (2005) 436.

[69] Civil Procedure Rules 1998, Pt 61, r 61 and PD 5.2.

[70] Acording to Civil Procedure Rules 1998, r 11(6) the courts have power to set aside a claim form.

[71] Jackson, *Enforcement of Maritime Claims* (2005) 414.

(iii) Arrest is a Provisional Measure; it is Not Seizure in Execution

Arrest of ships can be used in English law before a court has reached a decision on the merits of a maritime claim; arrest in execution is also available, but it has been set apart from the characterization of arrest of ships in the international Conventions.[72] This point is made clearly in Article 1(2) of the Conventions. Seemingly, the characterization of arrest of ships is centred on two premises: on the one hand, arrest is a provisional measure requested before the claim is subject to a decision on its merits by a court. To be provisional in nature means that it can be recalled at the instance of the defendant and alternative security may replace that of the ship herself. On the other hand, seizure in execution is permanent, and a manner of enforcing a judgment and satisfying the claim out of the proceeds of sale. In this event a ship is not different from any other assets of the debtor, and due to its exclusion from the definition of arrest of ships under the 1952 International Arrest Convention, is liable to seizure irrespective of the nature of the claim, whether maritime or not.[73] **4.39**

(iv) Arrest is a Measure intended to 'Secure a Maritime Claim'

In the international Arrest Conventions the security function of arrest of ships is part of the autonomous definition included in Article 1(2). In English law, however, several *dicta* have disregarded such function.[74] In *The Prinsengracht*[75] it was held that the claimant is entitled to arrest a ship even after bail has been provided when the owner has declined to agree expressly to submit to the jurisdiction of the court. On the same line of thought in *The Anna H*[76] the Court of Appeal argued that the purpose of the arrest of ships as indicated in its definition in the 1952 International Arrest Convention does not mean that where there is alternative security, an arrest to establish jurisdiction is not within that Convention. It was argued that despite the definition of arrest as a measure 'to secure a maritime claim' the commercial motive of the arrester was irrelevant. **4.40**

[72] Arrest/arrestment in execution is outside the scope of this book since it has been expressly excluded from the international framework (Art 1(2) 1952 and 1999 International Arrest Conventions). In relation to seizure of a ship in execution in English law, see M Tsimplis and N Gaskell, 'Admiralty Claims and the New CPR Part 61' [2002] *Lloyds Maritime and Commercial Law Quarterly* 520, 527.

[73] Berlingieri, *Berlingieri on Arrest of Ships* (2006) 88.

[74] *The Prinsengracht* [1993] 1 Lloyd's Rep 41; *The Anna H* [1995] 1 Lloyd's Rep 11. In fact, in the latter it became clear as to English case law, the multiplicity of functions that the arrest of a ship entails as a single procedural act.

[75] *The Prinsengracht* [1993] 1 Lloyd's Rep 41 (QBD (Admlty)) (Sheen J).

[76] *The Anna H* [1995] 1 Lloyd's Rep 11 (CA).

This argument is in plain contradiction with the principles of characterization as advanced in Chapter 3.[77] The only explanation for that departure from the autonomous interpretation of arrest of ships as a private international law category in the 1952 International Arrest Convention is that the characterization of 'arrest of ships' based on the law of the forum (*extra ordinem* characterization, ie based on concepts not pertaining to that international Convention), and consequentially, the association of ship arrest with the action *in rem* (now renamed as *in rem* claim), distorted the application of the Convention in such a way.

1. Ship Arrest as a Provisional Measure

4.41 The 'provisional' character of the arrest of ships in the international Arrest Conventions is related to its temporary condition and to its supportive role to the case on the merits. Due to these features, provisional measures are generally discretionary, and can always be recalled under the provision of alternative security. The universally recognized criteria to assess the convenience of granting such interim remedies require the party requesting it to prove that the cause of action has a reasonable prospect of success (*fumus boni iuris*); that there is risk in waiting (*periculum in mora*), in most cases because the defendant is intending to dispose of his assets; and generally, also for that party, to provide a cross-undertaking in damages. However, as explained in Chapter 3, in the long chain of amalgamations that led to arrest of ships as the modern mixed legal institution that it is today, several legal systems have departed from the universally recognized criteria mentioned above. In English law, the reason why these generally recognized criteria are not applicable to the arrest of ships is because ship arrest is considered exclusively as a component part of the *in rem* claim and thus viewed very much as legal entitlement rather than a discretionary remedy.[78]

Arrest *in rem*

4.42 In English law, ship arrest to enforce a maritime lien is currently a legal right rather than a discretionary remedy.[79] On the one hand, it needs to be borne in mind that if the 'court' were to refuse to grant an arrest warrant

[77] See Ch 3, para 3.13 above.

[78] Note that according to s 25(1) of the Civil Jurisdiction and Judgments Act 1982 these criteria apply to the granting of freezing injunctions in relation to ships.

[79] In English law it used to be conditional upon the claimant making full and frank disclosure of material facts at the time it applied for the arrest (see *Owners of the Vasso v Owners of Cargo Lately Laden on Board the Vasso (The Andria, The Vasso)* [1984] 1 Lloyd's Rep 235 (CA)).

in relation to a claim that attracts a maritime lien it would be depriving the claimant of the benefit of his maritime lien.[80] On the other hand, the latter point does not take into consideration that even though the court is enforcing a real right it is doing so 'in advance', ie before considering the case on its merits; hence, there should be an 'essential justification for the impatience of a tribunal granting relief before it has reached a final decision'.[81] None of the benefits of a maritime lien as a real right in security justifies the 'anticipation' of the remedy; the only justification is that it is an essential part of the *in rem* claim, a special admiralty scheme the development of which does not have other than historical explanation as discussed in Chapter 2.[82]

Arrest (*quasi*) *in rem*

In English law, this feature of it being a legal right rather than a discretionary remedy applies not only to ship arrest to enforce a maritime lien but to ship arrest in general. Arrest is described as an inherent part of the *in rem* claim,[83] a characterization that seems to prevail over its provisional and protective nature. At present, the general understanding is that as there is an entitlement to arrest, subject to compliance with procedural requirements, there is no room for any discretion to impose any condition.[84] Nevertheless, it has been argued that due to the strength in nature and effect of ship arrest it might be fairer to both parties if it were viewed as discretionary rather than a legal entitlement.[85] **4.43**

This view of arrest as a legal entitlement was not always so. Before 1986, ship arrest was considered to be a discretionary remedy and the court had **4.44**

[80] Ibid.

[81] E Jimenez de Aréchaga in the *Aegean Sea Continental Shelf case (Greece v Turkey) International Court of Justice Reports* 3 (1976) 15–16.

[82] See Ch 2, paras 2.35–2.43 above.

[83] R Goode, H Kronke, E McKendrick, and J Wool, *Transnational Commercial Law* (Oxford, OUP, 2004) 440.

[84] Jackson, *Enforcement of Maritime Claims* (2005) 405. However, when Pt 61 of the Civil Procedure Rules 1998 and its associated PD entered into force in 2002, there was some scope for doubt as to whether there was any intention to return to the position prior to 1986 (Tsimplis and Gaskell, 'Admiralty Claims and the New CPR Part 61' (2002) 525). The widely held position is that there was no such intention and arrest remains a legal entitlement rather than a discretionary remedy under current English law. Surprisingly, the issue has not been examined in the light of the European Convention on Human Rights in English law, as it has been in Scots law. See Ch 5 paras 5.35–5.40 below.

[85] Tsimplis and Gaskell, 'Admiralty Claims and the New CPR Part 61' (2002) 525. Furthermore, these authors argue that this may be particularly true if the 1999 International Arrest Convention is enacted, as it increases the scope of arrest.

the power to refuse the application to arrest.[86] Furthermore, in the case of *ex parte* proceedings there was the requirement of full and frank disclosure by the claimant.[87] Ship arrest shifted from a discretionary remedy to a legal right due the changes introduced in the Rules of the Supreme Court in 1986.[88] This change of character enhanced the power of ship arrest as a 'weapon' in the hands of a claimant; doubtless due not only to the protective and the security function of arrest of ships but also to its jurisdictional one. From then on the entitlement to arrest has been further reaffirmed by subsequent legislation.[89]

4.45 The only sphere where discretion still exists is with regard to ancillary jurisdiction in support of foreign proceedings.[90] Where in England a court stays or dismisses Admiralty proceedings on the ground that the dispute in question should be submitted to the determination of the courts of another part of the United Kingdom or of an overseas country, the court may, if in those proceedings a ship has been arrested, order that the ship arrested be retained as security for the satisfaction of any award or judgment which is given in respect of the dispute in the legal proceedings in favour of which those proceedings are stayed or dismissed. Alternatively, the court may order that the stay or dismissal of those proceedings be conditional on the provision of equivalent security for the satisfaction of any such award or judgment.[91]

4.46 Moreover, the provisions in section 26 of the Civil Jurisdiction and Judgments Act 1982 authorize the starting of proceedings *in rem* for the sole purpose of obtaining security in support of substantive proceedings to be heard in a foreign court or in arbitration. A claimant who successfully uses the *in rem* procedure to secure its claim is not thereby obliged to have the substantive claim heard by the Admiralty Court. It may apply to stay the substantive proceedings, in the same manner as this possibility is open to the defendant. As referred to above, where a stay is ordered, the relevant procedural rules[92] provide for the continuance of any arrest or the

[86] Ibid, 523; *The Vasso* [1984] 1 Lloyd's Rep. 235; *The Vanessa Ann* [1985] 1 Lloyd's Rep 549 (QBD (Admlty)).

[87] Ibid.

[88] See also *The Varna* [1993] 2 Lloyd's Rep 253 (CA).

[89] See the former 1999 PD 49F [6.1] as enacted by Civil Procedure Rules 1998 and the current PD 61 as supplementary to Pt 61 (Admiralty Claims) of the Civil Procedure Rules 1998 as amended by the Civil Procedure (Amendment No 5) Rules 2001.

[90] For a detailed analysis of the exercise of jurisdiction in support of foreign proceedings in relation to ship arrest see Ch 8.

[91] Section 26 of the Civil Jurisdiction and Judgments Act 1982.

[92] Civil Procedure Rules 1998, Pt 61, r 61.12.

maintenance of any security, unless the court orders otherwise. This provision is further discussed in Chapter 8.[93]

Fumus boni iuris

4.47 *Fumus boni juris* refers to the requirement to show a good arguable case on the merits (ie that the claim has a reasonable prospect of success). As explained in Chapter 3, proof of *fumus boni iuris* is not an express requirement under the international Arrest Conventions since requirements more generally are left to the law of the *forum arresti* according to the Conventions' provisions.[94] Consequently, since ship arrest is considered as a legal entitlement in English law, judicial discretion to assess the prospects of success is beyond the powers of English courts when it comes to ship arrest, except when exercising ancillary jurisdiction in support of foreign proceedings or arbitration. However, and even though showing a reasonable prospect of success is not a condition at the moment of arrest, the lack of foundation to ask for such a measure may amount to gross negligence in the eventuality of the defendant claiming damages for wrongful arrest.[95]

Periculum in mora

4.48 The *periculum in mora* is literally the 'risk in waiting' and, therefore, the claimant needs to prove urgency or at least allege that the enforcement of the eventual judgment may be frustrated or prejudiced by the defendant's insolvency or by him removing or concealing his assets.[96] In English law, along with the characterization of ship arrest as an inherent part of the *in rem* claim, there is no need to show *periculum in mora*.

No Cross-undertaking in Damages

4.49 In the 1952 International Arrest Convention, the issue of cross-undertakings is left to the law of the *forum arresti*, whereas the 1999 International Arrest Convention expressly empowers courts with discretionary powers

[93] See Ch 8, paras 8.23–8.25 below.

[94] With the exception of the issue of cross-undertaking in damages that is provided for in Art 6 of the 1999 International Arrest Convention.

[95] Jackson, *Enforcement of Maritime Claims* (2005) 424; *The Evangelismos* (1858) Swab 378; *The Chesire Witch* (1864) B & L 362; *The Margaret Jane* (1869) LR 2 A&E 345; *The Strathnaver* (1875) 1 App Cas 58 (PC); *The Saqr Jubail* [1985] LMLN 140; *The Kommunar (No 3)* [1997] 1 Lloyd's Rep 22. See also Mandaraka-Sheppard, *Modern Maritime Law and Risk Management* (2009) 121.

[96] G Maher, 'Diligence on the Dependence: Reform Needed' (2004) 27 *Scots Law Times* (news) 168.

in this regard.[97] In English law there is in principle no requirement to provide an undertaking for damages by the applicant in the case of ship arrest. The only sphere where discretion is sometimes exercised in relation to this issue is in the context of ancillary jurisdiction in support of foreign proceedings or arbitration under section 26(2) of the Civil Jurisdiction and Judgments Act 1982.[98]

4.50 The absence of a cross-undertaking in damages in the case of ship arrest may leave without a remedy a defendant ship-owner who has suffered loss by an unjustifiable arrest but who is unable to establish malice or gross negligence (the only grounds for awarding damages for wrongful arrest under English law).[99] In present times it is very difficult for a defendant who has suffered injustice due to the wrongful arrest of the ship to prove malice or gross negligence.[100] The need for reform has been recognized by commentators, who see no justification for the different procedural treatment given to ship arrest and freezing orders in this context.[101]

2. Ship Arrest as a Protective Measure

4.51 The arrest of a ship places the *res* under judicial detention pending adjudication of the claim to ensure that the final award or judgment can be enforced. In traditional English law the only claimant who had the right to arrest the ship in the hands of a *bona fide* purchaser was the holder of a maritime lien. This position has been adopted in the 1952 International Arrest Convention.

4.52 Furthermore, under section 21(4) of the Senior Courts Act 1981, if a person who would be liable in an action *in personam* is, when the cause of action arises, the owner or charterer of, or is in possession or control of, the ship, an *in rem* claim may be brought against: (a) the offending ship, if at the time when the action is brought, that person is either the owner or demise

[97] 1999 International Arrest Convention, Art 6.

[98] Section 26(2) reads: 'Where a court makes an order under subsection (1), it may attach such conditions to the order as it thinks fit, in particular conditions with respect to the institution or prosecution of the relevant legal proceedings.' See *Greenmar Navigation v Owners of Ships Bazias 3 and Bazias 4 and Sally Line (The Bazias 3 and The Bazias 4)* [1993] QB 673 (CA). Cf *The Havhelt* (1993) 1 Lloyd's Rep 523.

[99] *The Evangelismos* (1858) Swab 378; *Walter D Wallett* [1893] P 202.

[100] See Mandaraka-Sheppard, *Modern Maritime Law and Risk Management* (2009) 123.

[101] Jackson, *Enforcement of Maritime Claims* (2005) 417, 'It would seem that tradition in this regard should not be allowed to continue a somewhat one sided practice—particularly in the light of the opposite and regular imposition of a cross-undertaking on a person obtaining a freezing injunction.'

charterer; (b) a sister ship, if that person is the owner at the time when the action is brought.

According to English law, the cause of action 'arises' when the incident occurs, and the action is 'brought' when the *in rem* claim form is issued. The effect of these provisions is that if, when the claim form is issued, the person liable for the claim was either the owner or demise charterer of the ship, the ship may be arrested whoever owns her at the date the arrest is actually effected; this was clearly established in *The Monica S*.[102] To fully understand the impact of such a rule it is important to bear in mind that arrest can happen in England several months, and exceptionally years, after the issue of an *in rem* claim form. **4.53**

To be consistent with the international framework, however, English law should change the relevant moment in time from the issue of the claim form to when arrest is effected,[103] returning the situation arguably back to the state of affairs in English law prior to the Judicature Acts 1873 to 1875. In that sense Jackson is of the opinion that this link is a substantive aspect of the regulation of arrest of ships, and therefore, it cannot be left to English domestic rules.[104] This is another example of interference of the law of the forum when the line between procedure and substance is stretched out to allow for issues that are inherently connected with the substantive aspects of the legal institution at stake to be considered as 'procedural'. If the purpose of the Convention is to allow for the ship in relation to which the claim arose—except for the case of claims attracting a maritime lien—to be arrested only when the person liable *in personam* is at the time of the arrest the owner or demise charterer of the ship, changing that 'relevant time' from the moment when the arrest is effected to the moment when the *in rem* claim is issued certainly goes against the purpose of the 1952 International Arrest Convention. **4.54**

VI. CONCLUSIONS

In present times, it is possible to draw a distinction between three different types of ship arrest in English law, ie arrest of ships to enforce a maritime lien; arrest of ships to protect the *status quo* in the case of claims related to proprietary rights on the ship; and arrest of ships as a true provisional and protective measure, ie a measure to secure a maritime claim. These differences **4.55**

[102] *Owners of Cargo Laden on Board the Monica Smith v Owners of the Monica Smith* [1967] 2 Lloyd's Rep 113 (QBD (Admin)).

[103] Jackson, *Enforcement of Maritime Claims* (2005) 404; *The Po* [1991] 2 Lloyd's Rep 206.

[104] Ibid.

are rarely made distinctive within English law (and also within the international Arrest Conventions); arguably in the latter due to the influence of the former. It is the *in rem* claim (and its intrinsic connection with the concept of lien) that gives the arrest of ships to enforce maritime liens singularly characteristic features which should not be extended to other cases where such a 'real' linkage between the *res* and the claim does not exist. Indeed, the main functions of arrest of ships as identified in this book are attributed to the *in rem* claim rather than to ship arrest in English law.[105]

4.56 The conceptual and jurisprudential association between ship arrest and the *in rem* claim has thus many disadvantages: it creates confusion between the different functions of ship arrest: the protective function, on the one side, and the jurisdictional function, on the other side, by making ship arrest dependent on merits jurisdiction.[106] This linkage has especially undermined the correct application of the 1952 International Arrest Convention in English law.[107] In the opinion of Jackson, the intricacies of English law in this respect show the 'schizophrenic approach of English law to maritime claims'.[108]

4.57 Moreover, this relationship has left ship arrest outside the framework of interim measures of protection. The consequences of that exclusion are usually explained as recognizing the particular needs of maritime commerce, where any delay in the exercise of the right to arrest should be avoided. On that line of thought, judicial discretion is considered as threatening to jeopardize the position of ship arrest as the most effective remedy in shipping litigation. This is a debatable proposition.

4.58 Interestingly enough, Irish law represents a good example of a different approach. The 1952 International Arrest Convention was directly enacted in Ireland by the Jurisdiction of Courts (Maritime Conventions) Act 1989, hence recognizing arrest as distinct from the *in rem* claim.[109] Moreover, it is not even necessary to cross the Irish Sea. Scots law has always recognized the difference between the arrestment of ships and the action *in rem*, and the enactment of the 1952 International Arrest Convention in a self-contained section of the Administration of Justice Act 1956 for Scotland has not blurred that distinction. Scots law has all the possibilities,

[105] See Mandaraka-Sheppard, *Modern Maritime Law and Risk Management* (2009) 11.

[106] See Jackson, *Enforcement of Maritime Claims* (2005) 402.

[107] In Jackson's words '[Arrest of ships] necessary connection with the action *in rem* seems to have led to a failure to put national law into a form which complies fully with the international obligations undertaken through ratification of the Arrest Convention', Jackson, *Enforcement of Maritime Claims* (2005) 402.

[108] Ibid, 240.

[109] Ibid, 402.

and makes a clearer distinction between the different categories. The following chapter analyses the position of Scots law in this field. As will be noted, just as Scots law itself might do well to reflect some elements of English law on this matter, it should not be thought that English law should be held up as the paradigmatic example in all respects. The international Conventions themselves are arguably testimony to that.

5

Arrestment of Ships in Scotland

I. INTRODUCTION

5.01 England and Scotland have always had different legal systems, even when they shared a common Parliament.[1] As it is well-known, Scots law[2] is a mixed legal system with strong civilian roots[3] and influence from the common law of England.[4] In the past, the earliest Admiralty Courts in England and in Scotland recognized and applied the law merchant,

[1] By the Act of Union 1707 when the United Kingdom of Great Britain was formed express provision was made for the preservation of Scots law and Scottish courts. Pursuant to the Scotland Act 1998, ch 46, Scotland has had its own Parliament since 1999 with legislative competence in relation to matters that are not reserved to the UK Parliament.

[2] See KGC Reid, 'While One Hundred Remain: TB Smith and the Progress of Scots Law' in E Reid and DL Carey Miller (eds), *A Mixed Legal System in Transition: T.B. Smith and the Progress of Scots Law* (Edinburgh, EUP, 2005); R Evan-Jones, 'Mixed Legal Systems, Scotland and the Unification of Private Law in Europe' in JM Smits (ed) *The Contribution of Mixed Legal Systems to European Private Law* (Antwerp, Intersentia, 2001).

[3] See PBH Birks, 'More Logic and Less Experience: The Difference between Scots and English Law' in DL Carey Miller and R Zimmermann (eds), *The Civilian Tradition and Scots Law* (Berlin, Dunker und Humblot, 1997) 167.

[4] See HL MacQueen, *Common Law and Feudal Society in Medieval Scotland* (Edinburgh, EUP, 1993).

particularly the *lex maritima*—a general maritime law common to all maritime nations[5]—the same in England and in Scotland.[6] Nonetheless, even then, uniformity of principle did not necessarily imply uniformity of practice;[7] it is undeniable though that there has been direct and indirect cross-fertilization between both legal systems since ancient times.

Arrest (under English law) and arrestment (under Scots law) correspond **5.02** to the same legal institution;[8] therefore, they share the same origins. However, the approach and language used in Scotland is different from that of English law. In Scotland arrestment is a special kind of diligence. Diligence[9] is the Scots law term used to indicate the legal measures to secure or enforce compliance with court decrees, primarily decrees for payment.[10] Arrestment of ships as a provisional and protective measure has developed in Scots law within the framework of diligence on the dependence.[11] Diligence can be used on the dependence of an action, ie when the court has not yet reached a decision on the merits, to provisionally secure the pursuer's claim. In the nineteenth century, these measures used on the dependence used to be called 'diligence for intermediate

[5] *Currie v McKnight* [1897] AC 97 (HL). See also Kirsty J Hood, *Conflict of Laws within the UK* (Oxford, OUP, 2007) 15–17.

[6] See AN Sack, 'Conflicts of laws in the history of the English law' in New York University School of Law, *Law: A Century of Progress 1835–1935* (New York, New York University Press, 1937) vol 3 342, 355. See also the section on 'Sea lawis, betwixt Scotland and Ingland' in J Balfour, *Practicks*, 642–4 (see Peter GB Mcneill, *The Practicks of Sir James Balfour of Pittendreich Reproduced from the Printed Edition of 1754* (Edinburgh, The Stair Society, 1962).

[7] *Sheaf Steamship Co Ltd v Compania Trasmediterranea* (1930) 36 Lloyd's Law Rep 197 (IH (2 Div)). Although the Scottish and English Admiralty Courts administered the same maritime law the procedure which each Court adopted as a condition of exercising its jurisdiction was not necessarily the same (ARG McMillan, *Scottish Maritime Practice* (Edinburgh, Hodge, 1926)). It has been argued that the *lex mercatoria* as applied in England was predominantly procedural, see JH Baker, 'The Law Merchant and the Common Law Before 1700' (1979) 38 *Cambridge Law Journal* 295, 300–2.

[8] 'The effect of an Admiralty arrestment, as the term 'arrest' itself implies, is to fix the vessel in the place in which she is found …' *Carlberg v Borjesson* 1877 5 R 188, 195.

[9] As Gretton mentions in 'Diligence' *The Laws of Scotland, Stair Memorial Encyclopaedia*, vol 8, 17, para 102, how a word meaning carefulness or assiduity came to mean execution for debt is unclear. He mentions W Ross, *Lectures on the History and Practice of the Law of Scotland relative to Conveyacing and Legal Diligence* (2nd edn, Edinburgh, Bell & Bradfute, 1822)), and his derivation from the French usage *diligentia*, and ascertains that modern French law does not use the word in this sense any more.

[10] The exception to that general rule is arrestment of ships *in rem* to secure non-pecuniary claims under s 47(3) of the Administration of Justice Act 1956.

[11] For a recent analysis of diligence on the dependence in Scots law, see G Maher and BJ Rodger, *Civil Jurisdiction in the Scottish Courts* (Edinburgh, Green, 2010) Ch 9.

security',[12] particularly, 'arrestment in security',[13] and operated in a way that seemed to be unknown in England at the time.[14]

5.03 The deeper differences between English and Scots law in the field of arrest/arrestment of ships were harmonized in the United Kingdom by the 1952 International Arrest Convention as enacted by the Administration of Justice Act 1956.[15] This enactment introduced the compromise achieved in the international sphere into both legal systems. Before this enactment a ship could be arrested in Scotland as a security for any claim, even for claims that were of a non-maritime nature, and in England, ships could only be arrested in the limited cases where the claimant was entitled to a right *in rem*. The degree of harmonization was affected by the very different approach to the arrestment of ships in Scotland as compared with England prior to the Convention. In view of such divergences the amendments made to Scots law were introduced in a separate self-contained section of the Act.[16] This enactment narrowed down the wide powers of arrestment of a ship on the dependence previously available in Scots law.

II. ADMIRALTY JURISDICTION IN SCOTLAND

5.04 In present times there are many similarities between Scots and English Admiralty law although they have always been distinguished from each other.[17] Most Admiralty actions in Scotland can be initiated either in the sheriff court or in the Court of Session in Edinburgh.[18] Admiralty actions can be either *in rem* or *in personam*. As well as in English law it is possible

[12] GJ Bell *Commentaries on the Law of Scotland and on the Principles of Mercantile Jurisprudence*, vol 1 (7th edn, Edinburgh, T&T Clark, 1870; reprint Edinburgh, Butterworths, 1990) 7.

[13] Ibid, vol 2 (1870) 64–8. However, Gretton criticizes that usage as confusing, since technically arrestment in security refers to a debt which is contingent or future (Gretton, 'Diligence', *The Laws of Scotland, Stair Memorial Encyclopaedia*, vol 8, para 257).

[14] Bell, *Commentaries on the Law of Scotland and on the Principles of Mercantile Jurisprudence*, vol 1 (1870) 7.

[15] See *Gatoil International Inc v Arkwright-Boston Manufacturers Mutual Insurance Co (The Sandrina)* [1985] 1 Lloyd's Rep 181 (HL).

[16] Administration of Justice Act 1956, Ch 46, Pt V (Admiralty Jurisdiction and Arrestment of Ships in Scotland) (47–51/57).

[17] See D MacLean, 'Ship Arrest in Scotland' (2010) *Lloyd's Maritime and Commercial Law Quarterly* 579. However, in the nineteenth century Bell expressed that 'the Scottish Court of Admiralty is so far different from that of England' in Bell, *Commentaries on the Law of Scotland and on the Principles of Mercantile Jurisprudence*, vol 2 (1870) 546.

[18] The Sheriff Court has exclusive jurisdiction in Admiralty causes below a certain amount of money in value, and otherwise, concurrent jurisdiction with the Court of Session except in relation to salvage, where there are very particular provisions, the discussion of which is outwith the scope of this analysis; see MC Meston, 'Admiralty' in *The Laws of Scotland,*

for an action to be both *in rem* and *in personam*; but differently from the latter, in Scots law arrestment of a ship is available in the two types of Admiralty actions. That is, actions *in rem*, where the claim is pursued against the *res* as such and actions *in personam* against the owner (or demise charterer[19]) of the ship, where a ship is arrested to secure the claim.

As well as in England, the arrestment of ships in Scotland (with the only exception of arrestment to found jurisdiction[20]) is only available in relation to maritime claims. In Scots law those claims are the ones listed in section 47 of the Administration of Justice Act 1956. For arrestment to be competent the ship must be within Scotland, in port or in a recognized anchorage; section 47(6) of the Act provides that arrestment of a ship on passage is forbidden. **5.05**

In Scots law an action *in rem* is 'truly *in rem*'[21] and is only competent to enforce a maritime lien;[22] all other forms of admiralty actions are *in personam*. An action *in rem* is directed against the ship (or cargo) itself. Proceedings *in rem* enable the claimant to obtain an arrestment *in rem* of the ship. An arrestment *in rem* founds jurisdiction in such actions, even if the owner or other parties with an interest in the ship are not otherwise amenable to the jurisdiction of the Scottish courts.[23] **5.06**

Stair Memorial Encyclopaedia, vol 1, para 407. See also Maher and Rodger, *Civil Jurisdiction in the Scottish Courts* (2010) para 16-09.

[19] See the Administration of Justice Act 1956, Ch 46, s 47E as introduced by Sch 4 to the Bankruptcy and Diligence etc (Scotland) Act 2007.

[20] Arrestment of ships to found jurisdiction is treated elsewhere, see Ch 7, paras 7.59 *et seq* below. Note, that warrant to arrest the ship to found jurisdiction is also available in actions against the demise charterer of the ship; see the Administration of Justice Act 1956, Ch 46, s 47H as introduced by Sch 4 to the Bankruptcy and Diligence etc (Scotland) Act 2007. See also Sheriff Courts (Scotland) Act 1907, Ch 51, s 6(c) (Competence of Arresting a Ship to Found Jurisdiction in Sheriff Court) as amended by Sch 4 to the Bankruptcy and Diligence etc (Scotland) Act 2007.

[21] See Ch 4, paras 4.12–4.13 above.

[22] Administration of Justice (Scotland) Act 1933, s 17(iii) consolidated in the Court of Session Act 1988, s 6(iii). This provision requires the Court of Session to provide by act of sederunt 'for enabling the enforcement of a maritime lien over a ship by an action *in rem* directed against the ship and all persons interested therein without naming them and concluding for the sale of the ship and the application of the proceeds in extinction *pro tanto* of the lien and for enabling arrestment of the ship on the dependence of such an action, and for the regulation of the procedure in any such action'.

[23] Maher and Rodger, *Civil Jurisdiction in the Scottish Courts* (2010) 334.

III. THE FRAMEWORK WHERE ARRESTMENT OF SHIPS DEVELOPS AS A PROVISIONAL AND PROTECTIVE MEASURE

1. Diligence on the Dependence

5.07 Most legal systems provide for measures to be granted before a court has reached a decision on the merits so as to secure compliance with the eventual judgment, primarily in relation to pecuniary claims. In Scots law, admiralty arrestment[24] as a provisional measure is part of the law of such measures more generally,[25] that of diligence on the dependence.

5.08 As it is easily observed from the concept of diligence, the line between 'to secure' and 'to enforce' seems to be drawn at the moment when the court proceeds to judgment; before that, the action is depending (ie progressing through the courts) and, therefore, measures are provisional, ie subject to recall on security being given for the debt. Once there is a decree on the merits, diligence may be available in execution to enforce it, and in the case of arrestment in execution, the object arrested can only be relieved by payment.[26] Arrestment of ships to enforce maritime liens lies somewhere in the middle of the two, its function is to enforce rather than to secure, but it is granted before a decision on the merits has been taken by the courts.

5.09 The law of diligence more generally, and Admiralty arrestment in particular, have been the object of recent law reform in Scotland. Part 14 of, and Schedule 4 (Admiralty Actions and the Arrestment of Ships) to, the Bankruptcy and Diligence etc (Scotland) Act 2007 came into force on 1 July 2010.[27]

5.10 The Bankruptcy and Diligence etc (Scotland) Act 2007 draws from much consideration over more than two decades. In 1989 the Scottish Law

[24] Due to the many specialities of arrestment of ships as compared with ordinary arrestment in Scots law, Gretton considers that it should be perhaps considered as a separate diligence though he recognizes that most texts deal with it as a special kind of arrestment (Gretton, 'Diligence' in *The Laws of Scotland, Stair Memorial Encyclopaedia*, vol 8, para 322).

[25] For a general discussion on diligence in Scots law, see JG Stewart, *Treatise on the Law of Diligence* (Edinburgh, Green, 1898); G Maher and DJ Cusine, *The Law and Practice of Diligence* (Edinburgh, Butterworths, 1990); Gretton, 'Diligence' in *The Laws of Scotland, Stair Memorial Encyclopaedia*, vol 8, paras 101–399.

[26] Gretton, 'Diligence' in *The Laws of Scotland, Stair Memorial Encyclopaedia*, vol 8, paras 101–399.

[27] Bankruptcy and Diligence etc (Scotland) Act 2007 (Commencement No 6 and Savings) Order 2010 (SI 2010/249) (Scottish SI).

Commission launched the debate with a Discussion Paper,[28] followed by a Consultation Paper.[29] Later on in 1998 the Scottish Law Commission produced a Report[30] on the subject-matter and it was followed by a Consultation Document[31] issued by the Scottish Executive on this topic as well as others. Finally Part 14 of and Schedule 4 to the Bankruptcy and Diligence etc (Scotland) Act 2007 received the Scottish Parliament consent on 30 November 2006. It received Royal Assent at the beginning of 2007 and Part 14 (Admiralty Actions and Arrestment of Ships) and Schedule 4 (Modifications of enactments relating to admiralty actions and the arrestment of ships) were brought into effect on 1 July 2010. The objective of the reform more generally is to modernize the law of diligence and to bring it into line with international commitments already undertaken. The current law of diligence in Scots law is in general consistent with the latest international developments in the sphere of diligence on the dependence.[32]

As far as diligence on the dependence is concerned, the underlying policy is to prevent an unscrupulous creditor from using provisional and protective measures to put undue pressure on the debtor when the creditor does not in fact need any security for the claim. The procedure for obtaining a warrant to arrest on the dependence of an action is now governed by the Debtors (Scotland) Act 1987, Part 1A.[33] Insofar as the arrestment of ships, Schedule 4 to the 2007 Act, introduced by section 213, modifies various enactments relating to Admiralty actions and the arrestment of ships. **5.11**

The functions of diligence more generally, and the functions of the arrestment of ships as a special kind of diligence, coincide to a certain extent. As Stewart[34] explained, diligence has three main functions: (i) forcing the **5.12**

[28] Scottish Law Commission, *Diligence on the Dependence and Admiralty Arrestments* (Scot Law Com DP No 84, December 1989).

[29] Scottish Law Commission, *Arrestment of Ships Securing Claims against Demise Charterers* (Scot Law Com CP, March 1990).

[30] Scottish Law Commission, *Report on Diligence on the Dependence and Admiralty Arrestments* (Scot Law Com No 164, March 1998).

[31] Scottish Executive, *Enforcement of Civil Obligations in Scotland: A Consultation Document* (April 2002).

[32] eg proportionality as the main criterion for granting permission to use interim measures of protection, as recognized in the *ALI/Unidroit Principles of Transnational Civil Procedure* (2004) (see (2004) 4 *Uniform Law Review* 758–809) is also a main criterion in Scots law, particularly since the coming into force of the Human Rights Act 1998.

[33] As inserted by the Bankruptcy and Diligence etc (Scotland) Act 2007 s 169.

[34] Stewart, *A Treatise on the Law of Diligence* (1898) 1. As Gretton explains (Gretton, 'Diligence' in *The Laws of Scotland, Stair Memorial Encyclopaedia*, vol 8, para 101), the first of these three functions refers to arrestment to found jurisdiction, and also to the now obsolete *fugae* warrant (*meditatio fugae warrant*, a device of ancient Scots law to stop the debtor from escaping from the country; under this warrant the debtor could be imprisoned unless he

debtor to appear in court to answer an action at the creditor's instance (the 'compelling' effect); (ii) finding security to satisfy the eventual judgment (the security function); and (iii) enforcing a judgment already pronounced (diligence in execution).

5.13 The benefit of being part of a more general framework is that there are certain legal effects that belong to the general category, for example the *nexus* (attachment) that arrestment lays over the property arrested, thus, the real right in security that arrestment implies;[35] which in turn gives a preference to the creditor over acts of the debtor and of the competing creditors.[36] On the contrary, it is arguable that the arrest of ships as developed in England,[37] where ship arrest is seen exclusively as part of its Admiralty scheme, is better suited to meet the particular needs of maritime commerce.

IV. DIFFERENT TYPES OF ARRESTMENT OF SHIPS

5.14 There are four types of provisional arrestment of ships to be considered in Scots law:

(1) arrestment *in rem* in an Admiralty action *in rem* to enforce a maritime lien;
(2) arrestment *in rem* in an Admiralty action *in personam* to enforce a statutory right *in rem*;[38]
(3) arrestment on the dependence in an Admiralty action *in personam*;
(4) arrestment to found jurisdiction.

1. Arrestment *in rem*

5.15 There may be an arrestment *in rem* of a ship in Scots law:

(a) in an Admiralty action *in rem* to enforce a maritime lien over that ship. In this type of action there are no differences between Scots law and English law. The claim needs to be arising out of a collision, salvage,

relieved himself by finding bail to remain in the country); see Bell, *Commentaries on the Law of Scotland and on the Principles of Mercantile Jurisprudence*, vol 1 (1870) 7.

[35] Gretton, 'Diligence' *The Laws of Scotland, Stair Memorial Encyclopaedia*, vol 8, para 286.

[36] Scottish Law Commission, *Report on Diligence on the Dependence and Admiralty Arrestments* (Scot Law Com No 164, 1998) 186.

[37] For ship arrest in English law see Ch 4 above.

[38] ie a non-pecuniary claim to that ship; being one of the specified claims in paras (p)–(s) of s 47(2) of the 1956 Act.

or for master and/or crew's wages or master's disbursements, bottomry, or respondentia;[39]

(b) in an Admiralty action *in personam* involving a non-pecuniary claim related to ownership and possession, or mortgage or hypothecation of a ship. The claim needs to be arising out of
   (i) any dispute as to the ownership or right to possession of any ship or as to the ownership of any share in a ship;
   (ii) any dispute between co-owners of any ship as to the ownership, possession, employment, or earnings of that ship; the mortgage or hypothecation of any ship or any share in a ship;
   (iii) or any forfeiture or condemnation of any ship, or of goods which are being, or have been, carried, or have been attempted to be carried, in any ship, or for the restoration of a ship or any such goods after seizure.[40]

Arrestment *in rem* to Enforce Maritime Liens

In Scots law a maritime lien[41] gives the creditor a security without possession from the moment when the circumstances occur out of which the lien arises. The effect of an arrestment *in rem* to enforce a maritime lien is, therefore, not to create a nexus or security over the *res* (which already exists) but to fix the *res* in the place where it is when the arrestment *in rem* is executed.[42] That is to say that the protective function of arrest of ships is the central one in this case. In addition, in an action *in rem* an arrestment *in rem* founds jurisdiction;[43] ie it displays also the jurisdictional function. **5.16**

With regard to the protective function, already in the late nineteenth century Lord Shand in *Carlberg v Borjesson*[44] used the expression 'real diligence' **5.17**

[39] These claims are in the list provided for in s 47(2) of the Administration of Justice Act 1956, as claims arising out of (a) damage done or received by any ship; (c) the Salvage Convention, 1989; (h) any bottomry bond; (n) liability for payment of wages of a master or member of the crew of a ship; or (o) master's disbursements, including disbursements made by shippers, charterers, or agents on behalf of a ship or her owner.

[40] These are the claims included in the list provided for in s 47(2)(p)–(s) of the Administration of Justice Act 1956.

[41] In Scots law a 'maritime lien' over a ship means a hypothec over a ship (see s 48 of the Administration of Justice Act 1956 (c 46) as amended by the Bankruptcy and Diligence etc (Scotland) Act 2007.

[42] Scottish Law Commission, *Report on Diligence on the Dependence and Admiralty Arrestments* (Scot Law Com Report No 164, 1998) 124.

[43] Civil Jurisdiction and Judgments Act 1982, Sch 5[7], Sch 9[6]. See also AE Anton, *Private International Law: A Treatise from the Standpoint of Scots Law* (Edinburgh, Sweet & Maxwell, 1967) 115.

[44] *Carlberg v Borjesson* 1877 5 R 188, 195.

in this sense; arrest of ships has the effect of fixing the object in a particular place, preventing the defender from disposing of it.[45] As well as in English law, an arrestment *in rem* to enforce a maritime lien is not only competent, but also an essential incident of an admiralty action *in rem*.[46] Warrant of arrestment *in rem* should be executed before service of the summons.[47]

Arrestment *in rem* to Secure Non-pecuniary Claims

5.18 By virtue of section 47(3)(b) of the Administration of Justice Act 1956, certain non-pecuniary claims[48] encumber the right to arrest *in rem* in an action *in personam*. As it was highlighted by the Scottish Law Commission in its *Report on Diligence on the Dependence and Admiralty Arrestments*,[49] this kind of arrestment is distinctive in terms of its nature and functions. It is a unique example in Scots law of an arrestment which secures non-pecuniary claims, and in that sense sits uneasily with settled principles of the Scots law of diligence.[50] It is the only example in Scots law of an arrestment which is neither an arrestment on the dependence of an action nor an arrestment *in rem* enforcing a maritime lien. Although it is an arrestment *in rem*, it is competent only in Admiralty actions *in personam* or combined actions, but not in actions which are purely *in rem*.

5.19 Furthermore, it does not display the functions of arrest of ships as described in Chapter 1.[51] It does not have a jurisdictional function, therefore,

[45] In Lord Shand's words: 'Its effects, as the term "arrest" itself implies, is to fix the vessel in the place in which she is found, and, if there is any danger of her being removed from that place, the power to dismantle may be exercised.' As Gretton explains, the term 'real diligence' indicates an open-ended concept since it has been used in different senses in English and Scots law, and even within the latter, with more than one meaning; hence it is not helpful to distinguish one type of arrestment from the others (Gretton, 'Diligence' in *The Laws of Scotland, Stair Memorial Encyclopaedia*, vol 8, paras 118 and 322).

[46] Consequentially, the expenses of an arrestment *in rem* are recoverable as part of the expenses of process because they are essential to the obtaining of decree *in rem*; see *Hatton v A/S Durban Hansen* 1919 SC 154 (IH (1 Div)).

[47] Implementing a proposal (Proposition 30(2), para 3.48) of the Scottish Law Commission, *Diligence on the Dependence and Admiralty Arrestments* (Scot Law Com DP No 84, 1989), the current Rules of Court make it possible to convert an Admiralty action *in personam* into an action *in rem* after signeting (Rules of the Court of Session 1994, r 13.8).

[48] These claims are the ones listed in para 5.15 above as included in s 47(2)(p)–(s) of the Administration of Justice Act 1956.

[49] Scottish Law Commission, *Report on Diligence on the Dependence and Admiralty Arrestments* (Scot Law Com No 164, 1998).

[50] In his *Commentaries*, Bell established that arrestment 'is an incompetent diligence for enforcing obligations which are not of a pecuniary nature', Bell, *Commentaries on the Law of Scotland and on the Principles of Mercantile Jurisprudence*, vol 2 (1870) 68.

[51] See Ch 1, paras 1.21–1.29 above.

arrestment of a ship to found jurisdiction is competent in addition to that ship being arrested *in rem* to secure a non-pecuniary claim.[52] Moreover, this kind of arrestment is not followed by a process of sale, that is, the security function does not operate to safeguard the defendant's assets to eventually create a fund against which to enforce the judgment, but to safeguard the *res* itself. Following that, and contrary to the situation of arrestment on the dependence and arrestment *in rem* to enforce a maritime lien, this kind of arrestment does not appear to have any effect on the ranking of creditors, or in competition with *bona fide* purchasers or mortgagees, or generally on the substantive rights of parties, other than the right to interim possession.

In terms of juridical nature, however, it is a provisional and protective **5.20** measure. A distinction must be made between measures such as preliminary attachment, arrest/arrestment or freezing orders, on the one side, where the protective function operates to ensure that the final award or judgment can be enforced by safeguarding the defendant's assets or property;[53] and, on the other side, provisional measures relating directly to the subject-matter of the case. This second kind of measures have as their main function the preservation of the *res*, ie the preservation of the status quo until the merits of the case are settled.

In that sense, arrestment *in rem* to enforce non-pecuniary claims is an order **5.21** regulating interim possession pending decree in a petitory action determining the right of parties. It is for this reason that it may be used whether or not the ship belongs to the defender (defendant), and even if it belongs already to the pursuer (the party bringing the claim).[54] Furthermore, it has been argued that being an ancillary interim remedy in an action the court granting it should have jurisdiction on the substance of the principal action.[55] For this reason, the possibility of arresting a ship in these circumstances while exercising ancillary jurisdiction for the sole purpose of granting interim relief to support foreign proceedings or arbitration seems to be excluded in Scots law.

[52] *PTKF Kontinent v VMPTO Progress* 1994 SLT 235 (OH).

[53] CA McLachlan, 'Second Interim Report on Provisional and Protective Measures in International Litigation', Report of the Sixty-Seventh Conference, Helsinski (London, ILA, 1996) 185, 202.

[54] Inglis explains, for instance, that 'under s 47(2)(p) an owner may wish to obtain possession of a ship which he has chartered to the defender because, for example, of a breach of the defender of a material obligation in the charter', IG Inglis, 'Arrest of Ships in Scotland' in C Hill (ed), *The Arrest of Ships Series*, vol 4 (London, LLP, 1987) 87. In this situation the ship-owner would be entitled to arrest his own ship to obtain possession.

[55] Scottish Law Commission, *Report on Diligence on the Dependence and Admiralty Arrestments* (Scot Law Com No 164, 1998) 31.

2. Arrestment on the Dependence

5.22 *Arrestment on the dependence in general law.* The arrestment on the dependence as it stands today in Scots law was already a very familiar and well-known form of diligence at the beginning of the twentieth century.[56] Its rationale is to keep fixed some asset of the debtor, the defender in the action, so it may be made good to satisfy the decree which the pursuer is seeking (protective function).[57] With the exception of arrestment of ships, arrestment could never be in the hands of the debtor himself but must be in the hands of a third party.

5.23 The latest reform makes considerable amendments in the sphere of diligence on the dependence to the Debtors (Scotland) Act 1987. Essentially the law as it stands in present times reflects the practice of the Scottish courts in the years prior to the statutory reform. A warrant for diligence by arrestment on the dependence may be sought either at the commencement of or during the proceedings.[58] If a warrant is sought at the commencement of the action the court may grant the interim order without a hearing, as a matter of the presiding judge's discretion. To exercise that discretion the court needs to be persuaded that: the creditor has a *prima facie* case *(fumus boni iuris)*;[59] that there is a real and substantial risk that enforcement of any decree in favour of the creditor would be defeated or prejudiced by reason of (i) the debtor being insolvent or verging on insolvency, or (ii) the likelihood of the debtor removing, disposing of, burdening, concealing, or otherwise dealing with all or some of the debtor's assets if a warrant is not granted (*periculum in mora*);[60]and that it is reasonable to grant the warrant.[61] Furthermore, and enhancing the provisional character of the arrestment on the dependence, it is established that if the proceedings on the merits are not served within a 21-day period beginning with the day on which the arrestment is executed, the arrestment on the dependence shall cease to have effect.[62]

[56] *The Clan Line Steamers Ltd v The Earl of Douglas Steamship Co* 1913 SC 967 (IH (1 Div)). It is probably the diligence most practitioners turn to in the first place (E Baijal, 'The Bankruptcy and Diligence etc (Scotland) Act 2007: The New Jewel in the Creditor's Crown' (2007) 9 *Scots Law Times* (Legislative Comment) 55, 57.

[57] See Richard Aird, 'The Scottish Arrestment and the English Freezing Order' (2002) 51 *International and Comparative Law Quarterly* 155.

[58] s 15D of the Debtors (Scotland) Act 1987, as amended.

[59] s 15E(1) of the Debtors (Scotland) Act 1987, as amended.

[60] s 15E(2) of the Debtors (Scotland) Act 1987, as amended.

[61] s 15E(3) of the Debtors (Scotland) Act 1987, as amended.

[62] s 15G of the Debtors (Scotland) Act 1987, as amended.

Arrestment of a ship on the dependence. Arrestment of a ship on the dependence is rather different from arrestment on the dependence in general Scots law. However, and most importantly, the requirements in relation to the granting of the warrant as referred to in the previous paragraph also apply in relation to the arrestment of a ship on the dependence. **5.24**

Arrestment of a ship on the dependence is a diligence against the ship itself and is eventually made good by a process of sale. There may be arrestment of a ship on the dependence of an Admiralty action *in personam* involving: (i) claims included in section 47(2)(p)–(s) of the Administration of Justice Act 1956 when the result is pecuniary; (ii) claims included in section 47(2)(b) for loss of life or personal injury; (iii) use or hire of a ship; (iv) carriage of goods (agreement); (v) carriage of goods (loss or damage); (vi) general average; (vii) towage; (viii) pilotage; (ix) supplies; (x) construction, repair, or equipment of a ship; (xi) liability for dock charges or dues. **5.25**

Only one ship (the ship concerned or a sister ship) per action may be arrested on the dependence.[63] Contrary to the Admiralty arrestment *in rem*, arrestment on the dependence is competent but not an essential incident of an Admiralty action *in personam*. Unlike arrestment *in rem*, arrestment of ships on the dependence in Scots law does not found jurisdiction; it does not display a jurisdictional function at all. If jurisdiction is to be found upon arrestment an 'arrestment to found jurisdiction' needs to be served in addition to the 'arrestment on the dependence'. **5.26**

Arrestment to Found Jurisdiction

In addition to the three kinds of arrestment of ships mentioned above, a ship can be arrested under Scots traditional law to found jurisdiction (the so-called arrestment *ad fundandam jurisdictionem*). This peculiar means of establishing jurisdiction is not technically a provisional and protective measure. Arrestment to found jurisdiction does not prevent the ship from sailing (no protective function) and does not establish a *nexus*[64] with the property arrested (no security function); the effects of this kind of arrestment in the case of ships as well as in the case of any other kind of movable property of the defender, are solely *fundandae causa* (jurisdictional function) and are examined in Chapter 7. **5.27**

[63] Administration of Justice Act 1956, s 47(1). See also *Interatlantic (Namibia) (Ptr) Okeasnki Ribolov Ltd (The Afala)* [1995] 2 Lloyd's Rep. 286 (OH).

[64] Stewart, *Treatise on the Law of Diligence* (1898) 269; *North v Stewart* (1890) 17 R 60 (HL); D Maxwell, *The Practice of the Court of Session* (Edinburgh, Scottish Courts Administration, 1980) 387; *Fraser-Johnston Engineering Co v Jeffs* ((1920) 2 Lloyd's Rep 33 (IH (1 Div)); ARG McMillan, *Scottish Maritime Practice* (1926) 10; *Mill v Fides* 1982 SLT 147 (OH).

V. CONSISTENCY WITH THE INTERNATIONAL CONVENTIONS

5.28 Article 1(2) of the 1952 and 1999 International Arrest Conventions contain an autonomous definition of arrest of ships as formed by various parts: (i) what is arrest (the detention of a ship; the detention or restriction on removal of a ship); (ii) how is it effected (judicial process; order of a court); (iii) what is its purpose (to secure a maritime claim); (iv) what is excluded from the scope of the legal category in the Conventions (the seizure of a ship in execution or satisfaction of a judgment or other enforceable instrument). Furthermore, Article 6(2) of the 1952 International Arrest Convention leaves procedural issues related to the arrest of ships to the law of the *forum arresti*. In the following paragraphs the consistency of the arrestment of ships as practised in Scotland with such an autonomous definition is scrutinized.

(i) Arrest Means Physical Detention of a Ship

5.29 Except for arrestment to found jurisdiction in Scots law, all the other types of arrestment mentioned above prevent the ship from sailing; and in that sense fit within the Conventions' categorization. The phrase 'restriction on removal' added in the 1999 International Arrest Convention does not present any difference as far as current Scots law is concerned.

(ii) Arrest is a Judicial Remedy

5.30 In relation to the way of effecting ship arrestment in Scotland, alignment with the Conventions provisions was not straightforward before the latest law reform in this field. Article 1(2) of both international Conventions refers to the detention of a ship by judicial process and Articles 4 and 2, respectively, provide that a ship 'may only be arrested [or released from arrest] under the authority of a court [or of the appropriate judicial authority] of the State party in which the arrest is made [effected]'. Under Scots law, not so long ago[65] warrant for diligence on the dependence was granted as a matter of right without judicial consideration; the 'judicial authority' intervention was limited to an order of the clerk of courts. Currently

[65] Before the implementation of the European Convention on Human Rights into Scots law. See *Karl Construction Ltd v Palisade Properties Plc* 2002 SC 270 (OH).

judicial intervention is mandatory.[66] Hence, in present times warrants to arrest on the dependence have become judicial acts.[67]

(iii) Arrest is a Provisional Measure; it is Not Seizure in Execution

As examined above, arrestment of ships can be used in Scots law before a court has reached a decision on the merits of a maritime claim; arrestment in execution is also available, but it has been deliberately left outside the characterization of arrest of ships in the international Conventions.[68] **5.31**

(iv) Arrest is a Measure intended to 'Secure a Maritime Claim'

In Scots law a clear distinction is made between arrestments of the ship (on the dependence or *in rem*) which place a *nexus* on the arrested ship and arrestments of the ship which has no such effect (as in the case of arrestment *ad fundandam jurisdictionem*).[69] Arrestments of the ship *in rem* to secure non-pecuniary claims are somehow in between these two categories from the point of view of the security function of arrest. As outlined earlier in this chapter,[70] this kind of arrestment is distinctive in terms of nature and functions. Nevertheless, this restricted class of statutory arrestment relating to issues concerned with ownership of and interest in ships can be considered as within the autonomous definition of arrest of ships in the international Arrest Conventions. Interpreting the different provisions of the Conventions consistently imply recognizing that when Art 1(2) refers to the arrest of ships as a measure 'to secure a maritime claim' this includes the kind of provisional and protective measure 'to secure the *res*' related to claims involving a proprietary right on the ship. It should not be understood too restrictively as referring exclusively to measures intended 'to secure payment of the eventual judgment' but the interpretation should be inclusive enough to accommodate the arrest of ships in relation to all the claims listed in Article 1(1) of the same Conventions. **5.32**

[66] See Bankruptcy and Diligence etc (Scotland) Act 2007, Pt 6 (Diligence on the Dependence).

[67] See Rules of the Court of Session 1994, as amended, Ch 16 (Service, intimation and diligence), para 16.13 (Arrestment of ships and arrestment *in rem* of cargo on board ship). See further discussion of the judicial intervention in this context in paras 5.35–5.40 below.

[68] Arrest/arrestment in execution is beyond the scope of this book since it has been expressly excluded from the international framework (Art 1(2) 1952 and 1999 International Arrest Conventions).

[69] Maher and Rodger, *Civil Jurisdiction in the Scottish Courts* (2010) 335.

[70] See paras 5.18–5.21 above.

1. Arrestment of Ships as a Provisional Measure

5.33 The 'provisional' character of arrest of ships is related to its temporary condition and to its supportive nature to the case on the merits. Due to these features provisional measures are generally discretionary, and can always be recalled under the provision of alternative security.

Arrestment *in rem* to Enforce a Maritime Lien

5.34 In the case of arrestment *in rem* to enforce a maritime lien, arrestment is currently a legal right rather than a discretionary remedy in Scots law. There are no differences in this regard to English law.[71]

Arrestment *in rem* or in the dependence when there is no maritime lien at stake

5.35 As outlined earlier in this chapter, in Scotland, except for arrestment *in rem* to enforce a maritime lien, Admiralty arrestment is part of the general framework of diligences in security (protective measures), and may be used on the dependence of an action *in personam* (as a provisional measure). Until recently, authority to use diligence on the dependence in an action *in personam* was given more or less automatically.[72] This state of affairs was considered by the Scottish Law Commission discussion paper *Diligence on the Dependence and Admiralty Arrestments 1989*[73] and the *Report on Diligence on the Dependence and Admiralty Arrestments* mentioned above, where judicial discretion was recommended for the grant of a warrant for arrestment of a ship on the dependence of an action *in personam*, or a warrant for arrestment *in rem* securing a decree of specific implement in an Admiralty action *in personam* in relation to a non-pecuniary claim. It was also recommended there that arrestment *in rem* in an Admiralty action *in rem* to enforce a maritime lien should receive a different treatment since in those cases the arrest is the only method of making good the lien. It was considered that judicial discretion would be out of place in those cases

[71] See Ch 4, para 4.41 above.

[72] G Maher, 'Diligence on the Dependence: Principles for Reform' [1998] *Juridical Review* 188. Nonetheless, well before the statutory law reform in this sphere, the summons needed to show a 'colourable case', ie 'some intelligible and discernible cause of action', to permit the arrestment of a ship on the dependence (G Maher and DJ Cusine, *The Law and Practice of Diligence* (Edinburgh, Butterworths, 1990) 96; *West Cumberland Farmers Ltd v Ellon Hinengo Ltd* 1988 SLT 294 (OH); *Clipper Shipping Co Ltd v San Vicente Partners* 1989 SLT 204 (OH)).

[73] Scottish Law Commission, *Diligence on the Dependence and Admiralty Arrestments* (Scot Law Com DP No 84, December 1989).

and, accordingly, a warrant for arrestment *in rem* should continue to be available to the maritime lien-holder as of right.[74]

Furthermore, the Scottish Law Commission analysed the situation in the light of Protocol 1 (right to property, education, and free elections) of the European Convention on Human Rights (ECHR).[75] Two decisions of the Scottish courts, the cases of *Karl Construction Ltd v Palisade Properties Plc*[76] and *Advocate General for Scotland v Taylor*[77] affirmed that the way in which diligence on the dependence was then available in Scots law infringed Article 1 of Protocol 1 of the ECHR because of a disproportionate interference with the debtor's property rights. **5.36**

According to *Karl*, four conditions needed to be satisfied before diligence on the dependence could be compatible with Article 1 of Protocol 1 of the ECHR: the creditor needed to show a *prima facie* case (*fumus boni iuris*) and a specific need for diligence on the dependence (*periculum in mora*); there should be a hearing before a judge (due process); and the creditor must be liable to pay damages for losses of the debtor should the action fail. **5.37**

Taylor[78] provided a more limited analysis of the issues. In contradiction to *Karl*, the court held in *Taylor* that a hearing was not necessary, and all that was needed was for the decision on the application for permission to use diligence to be made by a judge. The creditor needed to show only a *prima facie* case and there was no need to show *periculum in mora*. However, it raised the issue of proportionality; the use of such diligence would require it to be proportionate to the claim being made. *Taylor* clearly establishes just as low a minimum as required for compatibility with the ECHR. As such it was subject to academic criticism.[79] **5.38**

Since the decisions in *Karl* and *Taylor* and because of the differences between them, practice in the courts did not develop in a consistent way. This led to uncertainty and unfairness. The Bankruptcy and Diligence etc (Scotland) Act 2007 enacted to modernize the law of diligence more generally in Scots law, tackles the issue by applying a specific test in order to get **5.39**

[74] Scottish Law Commission, *Report on Diligence on the Dependence and Admiralty Arrestments* (Scot Law Com No 164, 1998), para 1.10.

[75] The European Convention on Human Rights and Fundamental Freedoms signed in Rome on 4 November 1950.

[76] *Karl Construction Ltd v Palisade Properties Plc* 2002 Session Cases 270.

[77] *Advocate General for Scotland v Taylor* 2003 *Scots Law Times* 1340.

[78] *Advocate General for Scotland v Taylor* 2003 *Scots Law Times* 1340.

[79] G Maher, 'Diligence on the Dependence: Reform Needed' (2004) 27 *Scots Law Times* (news) 167.

permission to use diligence on the dependence.[80] According to it the creditor must have a *prima facie* case (*fumus boni iuris*) and satisfy the court that there is a specific need to use diligence (*periculum in mora*). The court will need to be satisfied that it is reasonable in all the circumstances that permission is given and in making the decision consider whether the debtor is insolvent or verging on insolvency, or likely by removal or disposal of his assets to defeat or prejudice enforcement of any decree (*periculum in mora*). It is intended that there will be a hearing in every case, except where the court is satisfied that there is an urgent need to act before intimation of the claim document[81] (the need for the so-called 'surprise effect' of *ex parte* warrants). In order to strike the balance between the rights of the debtor and the creditor the court may limit the sum secured, the limit being set by reference to a formula.[82]

5.40 This judicial discretion applies to arrestment of ships with the only exception of the arrestment of ships *in rem* to enforcement maritime liens; that is, even arrestment *in rem* to secure non pecuniary claims should be affected by the new legislation on diligence on the dependence.[83]

5.41 Accordingly, in present times Scots law is in line with the internationally recognized standards in the field, except for one thing: if proportionality is to be achieved the court should have discretion to ask for a cross-undertaking in damages since the creditor must be liable to pay damages for losses of the debtor should the action fail. Further discussion of this issue is offered in the following paragraphs.

No Cross-undertaking in Damages

5.42 In the 1952 International Arrest Convention the issue of cross-undertakings is left to the law of the *forum arresti*, whereas the 1999 International Arrest Convention expressly empowers courts with discretionary powers in this regard.[84] According to Scots law, Scottish courts have the power to order counter security, caution, or consignation in Scots law terms, though it is rarely invoked and virtually unknown in the modern practice of

[80] For an account of the milestones of the reform process, see Maher, 'Diligence on the Dependence: Reform Needed' (2004).

[81] See Debtors (Scotland) Act 1987, s 15, Pt 1A (Diligence on the Dependence) ss 15E (Grant of Warrant without a Hearing) as introduced by Bankruptcy and Diligence etc (Scotland) Act 2007, Pt 6, s 169.

[82] Ibid, ss 15H (Sum Attached by Arrestment on Dependence) as introduced by Bankruptcy and Diligence etc (Scotland) Act 2007, Pt 6, s 169.

[83] Scottish Law Commission, *Report on Diligence on the Dependence and Admiralty Arrestments* (Scot Law Com No 164, 1998) 131.

[84] 1999 International Arrest Convention, Art 6.

arrestment of ships in Scotland.[85] The current rule in Scots law, which applies with regard to diligence more generally and not limited to Admiralty arrestment, is that a litigant using diligence on the dependence is generally not liable for loss which has been caused if his claim should eventually prove to be unfounded; unless malice or want of probable cause can be proven, which is extremely difficult.[86]

As explained in the Scottish Law Commission *Report on Diligence on the Dependence and Admiralty Arrestments*,[87] a requirement for a pursuer to provide a cross-undertaking in damages is difficult to reconcile with the pursuer's entitlement to obtain a warrant for diligence on the dependence as of right (which was the position of Scots law until recently, but this has already changed); and with the rule that he is not liable for damages merely because the action in question turns out to be unsuccessful. In that sense, the caution could only be required to secure against damages for diligence which is wrongful, ie unlawful.[88] **5.43**

The first circumstance given as a justification for the lack of this requirement (entitlement as of right) has already changed in Scots law.[89] In relation to compensation for wrongful arrest, the Scottish Law Commission in its *Report* recommended that the pursuer should be liable in damages to the defender not only in the case of the warrant being wrongful (wrongfully obtained or executed) but also when it was unreasonable for the pursuer to apply for that warrant.[90] The Scottish Executive in its consultation paper entitled *The Enforcement of Civil Obligations in Scotland*[91] expressed its intention to apply the Commission's recommendation[92] in relation to liability of the pursuer equally to Admiralty arrestment on the dependence as to diligence on the dependence more generally. However, in the following paragraph of the same document it was affirmed: 'In line with the Executive's intentions for diligence on the dependence generally, it is not intended to provide for the provision of security by the pursuer, as a **5.44**

[85] MacLean, 'Ship Arrest in Scotland' (2010) 580.

[86] Maher, 'Diligence on the dependence: reform needed' (2004) 167.

[87] Scottish Law Commission, *Report on Diligence on the Dependence and Admiralty Arrestments* (Scot Law Com No 164, 1998) 42 at para 3.65.

[88] Ibid.

[89] See Debtors (Scotland) Act 1987, s 15, Pt 1A (Diligence on the Dependence) as amended.

[90] Scottish Law Commission, *Report on Diligence on the Dependence and Admiralty Arrestments* (Scot Law Com No 164, 1998), Recommendation 6, para 3.63.

[91] Scottish Executive, *Enforcement of Civil Obligations in Scotland: A Consultation Document* (April 2002).

[92] Scottish Law Commission, *Report on Diligence on the Dependence and Admiralty Arrestments* (Scot Law Com No 164, 1998), Recommendation 6, paras 5.51–5.56.

condition of the grant of a warrant to arrest, or the maintaining of an arrestment of a vessel once executed.'[93] No reasons were given to justify such a dogmatic position which is indeed inconsistent with the Scottish Law Commission finding that if their recommendation on liability of the pursuer was to be adopted there would be much greater scope for caution or consignation[94] (cross-undertaking in damages).

5.45 Particularly in the case of arrestment of ships, the Scottish Law Commission suggested that there may even be cases 'where the competency of the diligence is in doubt, e.g. where a ship sought to be arrested on the dependence belongs to the defender, and warrant (if granted at all) has to be granted forthwith because speed is essential in the circumstances. In such a case, it may be useful for the court to require the arrester to find caution.'[95] Moreover, in this respect there is no issue of consistency with the 1952 International Arrest Convention since the issue is expressly left to the law of the *forum arresti* under Article 6(1).

5.46 The justification might be that there is no need for reform, since the Scottish courts already have such power.[96] Nevertheless, as mentioned above, in modern Scottish practice, a cross-undertaking in damages offered by the arresting pursuer is unheard of in the field of diligence on the dependence more generally as well as in the field of Admiralty arrestment; even when in theory it may be competent.[97] Yet, Recommendation 62 of the Scottish Law Commission *Report* advocated for liability for wrongful or unjustified diligence and the empowerment of courts, as a condition for granting warrant for an Admiralty arrestment *in rem* or in the dependence, to request caution or consignation to the pursuer, ie to require the pursuer to provide security for any loss which may be incurred by another party to the action or any other interested party, as a direct result of the arrestment having been wrongful or unjustified.

5.47 In the case of Admiralty arrestment on the dependence and *in rem* to secure non-pecuniary claims the test should be higher than in the case of

[93] Scottish Executive, *Enforcement of Civil Obligations in Scotland: A Consultation Document* (April 2002), para 5.78.

[94] Scottish Law Commission, *Report on Diligence on the Dependence and Admiralty Arrestments* (Scot Law Com No 164, 1998), para 3.67.

[95] Ibid.

[96] Scottish Law Commission, *Report on Diligence on the Dependence and Admiralty Arrestments* (Scot Law Com No 164, 1998) 43, Recommendation 7, para 3.71. This position was further corroborated in *Observations of the Scottish Law Commission on the International Convention on Arrest of Ships* 1999, 13–14.

[97] Scottish Law Commission, *Report on Diligence on the Dependence and Admiralty Arrestments* (Scot Law Com No 164, 1998) 136.

arrestment *in rem* to enforce a maritime lien since in the later case the pursuer has no choice but to arrest to make good his right in security. In such cases reasonableness is the Scottish Law Commission's preferred criterion.[98]

It is indeed regrettable that these recommendations were not adopted in the new Act.[99] Nothing was mentioned in the relevant provisions[100] about the power of the court to request a cross-undertaking in damages. This is inconsistent with the reforms introduced by the Act which makes arrestment on the dependence a discretionary diligence; and collides with the 'balance of convenience' between pursuer and defender; a paramount consideration in the field of provisional and protective measures so as to prevent misuse. **5.48**

In the field of arrest of ships the issue certainly raises difficult questions in terms of policy, as the disagreements (in fact the inability to reach an agreement) in respect of liability for wrongful arrest in the preparation of the two international Arrest Conventions denote.[101] The main argument against reform seems to have been that Scots law should not be different from English law in this regard because the difference could enhance 'forum shopping', affecting negatively Admiralty litigation in Scotland.[102] In the 2002 consultation paper referred to above the Scottish Executive made it clear that Scotland should not be a less favourable jurisdiction within which to arrest than others.[103] This is a strong policy argument; indeed, it is here submitted that it is the kind of argument that English legislators would have been very ready to consider if the case was **5.49**

[98] Scottish Law Commission, *Report on Diligence on the Dependence and Admiralty Arrestments* (Scot Law Com No 164, 1998) 139.

[99] The issue was raised in the context of diligence on the dependence in general, and in the context of arrestment of ships particularly (Scottish Law Commission, *Report on Diligence on the Dependence and Admiralty Arrestments* (Scot Law Com No 164,1998) paras 3.64–3.71 and 7.111–7.124 respectively).

[100] See Debtors (Scotland) Act 1987, s 15, Pt 1A (Diligence on the Dependence) ss 15E (Grant of Warrant without a Hearing) and F (Hearing on Application) as introduced by Bankruptcy and Diligence etc (Scotland) Act 2007, Pt 6, s 169.

[101] The 1952 International Arrest Convention leaves the whole issue to the law of the *forum arresti*. The 1999 International Arrest Convention confers on the court where arrest has been effected the power to impose a cross-undertaking in damages.

[102] In that sense, the risk is that litigants might prefer to litigate in England in order to take advantage of the absence of any judicial power to order counter-security there. On the same line of thought, pursuers in Scottish admiralty actions should not be under a significant disadvantage compared with claimants in England, see Scottish Law Commission, *Report on Diligence on the Dependence and Admiralty Arrestments* (Scot Law Com No 164, 1998) 138.

[103] Scottish Executive, *Enforcement of Civil Obligations in Scotland: A Consultation Document* (April 2002), para 5.70.

the opposite. The problem here lies in the fact that English law is arguably inadequate in this matter[104] and by following such pattern Scots law misses the opportunity to bring itself into line with internationally accepted standards as now contained in the 1999 International Arrest Convention.

Proportionality

5.50 The issue of proportionality in terms of the availability of repeated arrestment of the same ship, and on the arrestment of two or more ships, on the dependence of the same action (or to secure the same claim) has raised difficulties within Scotland. Before the entry into force of the Administration of Justice Act 1956 there were no formal limits in Scots law on the number of ships owned by the defender which could be competently arrested on the dependence of an action for payment.[105]

5.51 The leading case on how the right has been limited by the 1956 Act is *Interatlantic (Namibia) (Pty) Ltd v Okeanski Ribolov Ltd*.[106] This dictum, following the English dictum in *The Banco*,[107] held that the purpose of the 1956 Act was to incorporate into Scots law the provisions of the 1952 International Arrest Convention and its general policy against multiple or repeated arrestment for the same claim. The 2007 Act, taking into consideration the Scottish Law Commission recommendation,[108] further clarifies the issue and provides that a creditor in Admiralty action may, on cause shown, obtain a warrant to re-arrest a ship, or arrest a sister ship, on the dependence of that action.[109] This is consistent with Article 3(1) of the 1952 International Arrest Convention.

[104] *Centro Latino Americano de Commercio Exterior SA v Owners of the Kommunar (The Kommunar) (No 3))* [1997] 1 Lloyds Rep 22, 33 (QBD (Admlty)) (Colman J).

[105] Scottish Law Commission, *Report on Diligence on the Dependence and Admiralty Arrestments* (Scot Law Com No 164, 1998) 134. In *Sheaf Steamship Co v Compania Transmediterranea* (1930) SC 660, the Court of Session held that, while Scots Admiralty law may be the same as English Admiralty law, the law on remedies and procedure was not the same.

[106] *Interatlantic (Namibia) (Pty) Ltd v Okeanski Ribolov Ltd* 1996 SLT 819 (OH).

[107] *Owners of the Monte Ulia v Owners of the Banco (The Banco)* [1971] 1 Lloyd's Rep 49 (CA); see also *Gatoil International Inc v Arkwright-Boston Manufacturers Mutual Insurance Co (The Sandrina)* [1985] 1 Lloyd's Rep 181 (HL) (Lord Keith of Kinkel).

[108] Scottish Law Commission, *Report on Diligence on the Dependence and Admiralty Arrestments* (Scot Law Com No 164, 1998) Recommendation 61, 135–6.

[109] Bankruptcy and Diligence (Scotland) Act 2007, Sch 4 introduced by s 197(7)(3)(1)(B).

2. Arrestment of Ships as a Protective Measure

In the 1999 International Arrest Convention, Article 3(3) provides that the arrest of a ship which is not owned by the person liable for the claim shall be permissible only if, under the law of the State where the arrest is applied for, a judgment in respect of that claim can be enforced against that ship by judicial or forced sale of that ship. It was presumed that 'this is a question of national law which is not expected to have a significant impact in common law countries'.[110] On the contrary, Scots law, where the property of a third party is not generally affected to satisfy the debts of another, has been modified in respect of arrestment of ships against demise charterers to allow judicial sale of the ship in those cases. In line with the 1999 International Arrest Convention the latest reform allows the pursuer in an Admiralty action against a demise charterer to be entitled to complete diligence by judicial sale of a ship which has been arrested on the dependence of the action. The sale is competent even though the ship is owned by a third party.[111] This is a fundamental departure from traditional Scots law but brings Scots law into conformity with the international trends and with the position in England. **5.52**

VI. CONCLUSIONS

While it is often assumed that Scots law will always follow English law in Admiralty matters,[112] this Chapter has shown that this statement is not altogether true.[113] And in the sphere of arrest/arrestment of ships, it is particularly inaccurate. The differences are historical and conceptual. Most of the historical differences were already shown in Chapter 2. As far as the conceptual ones, the main difference is that Admiralty arrestment in Scots **5.53**

[110] R Shaw and N Gaskell, 'Arrest Convention 1999' [1999] *Lloyds Maritime and Commercial Law Quarterly* 1, 10.

[111] See Administration of Justice Act 1956, Ch 46, s 47E (Sale of a ship arrested on the dependence of an action against demise charterer) as introduced by Sch 4 to the Bankruptcy and Diligence (Scotland) Act 2007.

[112] *Boettcher v Carron Co* 1861 23 D 322; *Currie v McKnight* [1897] AC 97 (HL); *SS Blaimore Co Ltd v Macredie* (1898) 25 R (HL) 57, 59; *Clydesdale Bank Ltd v Walker & Bain* 1926 SC 72, 82; *The Goring* [1988] 1 AC 831 (HL) 853.

[113] As recognized by the Scottish Law Commission, *Diligence on the Dependence and Admiralty Arrestments* (Scot Law Com DP No 84, 1989) 'There is no comprehensive, systematic and authoritative comparison of the two systems of Admiralty law on which alone a sound generalisation could be based' (206), statement affirmed by Gretton in 'Diligence' *The Laws of Scotland, Stair Memorial Encyclopaedia*, vol 8, para 322.

law forms part of the general law of diligence that has no English counterpart. This has, in turn, advantages and disadvantages on both sides of the borders. Having a conceptual framework helps to understand the different functions and effects of the measure; however, these general concepts were not crafted to meet the needs of maritime commerce; conversely, that can be said about ship arrest as developed in English law.

5.54 Scots law has always recognized the difference between arrestment and action *in rem*, and the enactment of the 1952 International Arrest Convention in a self-contained section of the Administration of Justice Act 1956 for Scotland has not blurred that distinction. Scots law has all the possibilities, and makes a clearer distinction between the different types of arrestment of ships available to the claimant in Scotland. It could be said that it is not just a coincidence that a mixed legal system understands better the complexities of a mixed legal institution,[114] but maybe this would be too presumptuous. Indeed, Scots law continues to struggle with certain key features of modern day commercial reality, eg cross-undertakings, and it is unfortunate that policy considerations have gotten in the way here.

[114] V Ruiz Abou-Nigm, 'The Arrest of Ships as a Mixed Legal Institution', Conference paper, 2010 Society of Legal Scholars Conference (Southampton, September 2010).

Part II

The Arrest of Ships in Private International Law

6

Arrest of Ships, Security, and Applicable Law

I. INTRODUCTION

As examined throughout this book,[1] the arrest of ships serves several functions. The 'security'[2] function refers to arrest as a method of securing a maritime claim by safeguarding a certain asset (the ship) against which **6.01**

[1] For an overview of the three functions of arrest of ships see Ch 1, paras 1.21–1.29 above; see also Ch 7, paras 7.06–7.09 below for an analysis of the jurisdictional function in the context of private international law and Ch 8, paras 8.06–8.10 below for an analysis of the protective function of arrest of ships in the context of judicial cooperation between states.

[2] It is necessary to distinguish from the outset of this chapter the concept of security in this context from the radically different and unconnected concept of 'maritime security' in the public international law sense. The latter relates to safety at sea. The aspect of security for claims this

the final award or judgment can be enforced, ultimately ensuring the availability of the judicial sale of the ship.[3] It can be defined as the availability of the *res* for satisfaction of a judgment.

6.02 The security function of arrest of ships has been considered as its most relevant one.[4] On this basis the argument is that the ultimate *ratio* of arrest of ships as a legal institution is to give the creditor the chance to create a right in security over the ship, and in turn, that possibility puts pressure on the debtor in order to provide alternative security[5] to prevent the arrest of the ship or to allow it to be released, and ultimately, to comply with the eventual judgment; that is actually what makes it so effective.[6]

6.03 Security rights play a very important economic role and a well-developed legal framework in this field is vital in terms of economic growth. The right to enforce security rights in case of debtor default is recognized generally, but the nature and extent of the rights which arrest confers on the arrester vary significantly in different legal systems. Variations in this regard do not only arise between different legal systems, but within one legal system, between the different types of arrest of ships available therein.

6.04 The main question in this regard is whether the arrest itself creates a right in security different from the preference originated by the cause of action. Hence, two different issues arise in relation to the arrest of ships and security: on the one hand, there is the right in security that the arrest itself may create in certain circumstances, and, on the other hand, there is the ancient device of the maritime lien, ie a right of preference attracted by certain types of maritime claims. This chapter analyses these two different issues from the private international lawyer's perspective.

book is concerned with is, in Scots law terms, the *nexus* created by the arrestment as an effect of diligence, ie the judicial right in security that the arrest/arrestment confers on the creditor over the ship. For an examination of 'maritime securities' in Scots law more generally see JAG Lowe, 'Maritime Securities' *The Laws of Scotland, Stair Memorial Encyclopaedia*, vol 20, 118.

[3] DC Jackson, *Enforcement of Maritime Claims* (4th edn, London, LLP, 2005) 427. In English law a court may not order a judicial sale unless the ship is under arrest; see *The Wexford* (1883) 13 PD 10.

[4] JJ Álvarez Rubio, *Derecho Marítimo y Derecho Internacional Privado, Problemas básicos* (Vitoria-Gasteiz, Servicio Central de Publicaciones del Gobierno Vasco, 2000) 102.

[5] In most legal systems the arrest of the ship may be prevented, or the release of the ship from arrest may be obtained, by the provision of alternative security, most commonly through the provision of a contractual guarantee by a bank or a letter of undertaking to pay such amount as may be ordered by a court from a Protection and Indemnity (P&I) Club or insurance company, and less commonly through payment into court. It is within the courts' power to specify what the form of alternative security should be; see Civil Procedure Rules 1998, r 61.5(10). For a detailed analysis of security alternative to the arrest of the ship, see Jackson, *Enforcement of Maritime Claims* (2005) 427 *et seq*, paras 15.127–15.141.

[6] Álvarez Rubio, *Derecho Marítimo y Derecho Internacional Privado* (2000) 102.

6.05 In line with the international Conventions on the topic, at present in English and in Scots law the right to arrest does not depend on the existence of a maritime lien,[7] but is available for a broader but closed list of maritime claims. However, in English law, the link between arrest and maritime liens still explains the most salient features of the law on arrest of ships, particularly in relation to its security function.

6.06 In English and Scots law, maritime liens attach only to a restrictive group of maritime claims, namely, seamen's wages, master's wages, and disbursements, salvage, damage caused by a ship, and the bonds of bottomry and respondentia.[8] These 'traditional maritime liens' enjoy priority when confronted with other causes of action, notably mortgages, therefore, a maritime lienee is generally among the first to be satisfied when various competing actions exist against the ship. On the contrary, it is established in English and Scots law that, for example, claims for 'necessaries'[9] do not attract a maritime lien. Conversely, in the United States and in some civil law jurisdictions, including Member States of the European Union, certain maritime claims which are not within the 'traditional maritime claims' of English and Scots law, such as claims for necessaries, cargo damage, and general average, give rise to maritime liens or rights of preference.

6.07 Applicable law issues will often arise when the court has to determine the distribution of the court fund. If there has been an effectual arrest of a ship, and the ship has not been released by the provision of alternative security,

[7] Nonetheless, in the opinion of Jackson, in English law the availability of arrest does depend on the existence of a lien, if not maritime, statutory, but always a lien (Jackson, *Enforcement of Maritime Claims* (2005) 395). The English term 'maritime lien' strictly corresponds to a maritime hypothec in traditional Scots law; however, due to the internationalism that the English term has acquired through international Conventions in the field, Scots law has recognized by statue the usage of the English term in order to indicate a hypothec over a ship, cargo, or other maritime property; ie a non-possessory real right of security in a ship, cargo, or other maritime property (see Administration of Justice Act 1956, Ch 46, s 48(2), as amended by Sch 4 to the Bankruptcy and Diligence etc (Scotland) Act 2007 in force from 1 July 2010).

[8] Bonds of bottomry and respondentia were already considered obsolete at the end of the first quarter of the twentieth century, yet, the Administration of Justice Act 1956 provided that a claim arising out of bottomry is within Admiralty Jurisdiction, and the Supreme Court Act 1981 (now renamed as Senior Courts Act 1981 by the Constitutional Reform Act 2005, s 59 and Sch 11 in force 1 October 2009) which has taken the place of the former Act as far as England repeats the provision. See *The Conet* [1965] 1 Lloyd's Rep 195, PDAD.

[9] In this context the concept of 'necessaries' has been defined as to include 'those items or services which a prudent owner or master would deem to be reasonably required to facilitate the use of the ship, save her from danger and enable her to perform those acts currently demanded of her' (Elijah E Jhirad, Alexander Sann et al, *Benedict on Admiralty* (7th rev edn, New York, M Bender, 1975). A lien arisen as a result of the provision of necessaries is generally known as a contractual lien.

the applicable law issue will arise *after* the ship has been arrested and sold by judicial sale—at the stage when that court has to determine how the distribution of the proceeds is to be made—in the cases where the maritime claim of the arrester (or any other party with a proprietary interest on the ship that has taken part in the proceedings) attracts a privilege of a certain status under the governing law[10] but it does not do so in the same way under the law of the *forum arresti*.[11] In this context private international law has a primary role to play, and in present times a sound conflict-of-laws rule is paramount to achieve a good case management on the merits.

6.08 Therefore, in the present chapter, after looking at the security function of arrest of ships from the private international lawyer's perspective, some of the applicable law issues connected with it will be addressed, namely, the applicable law to the existence and qualification of maritime liens broadly considered, and the applicable law to the question of priorities of such security rights.[12]

II. THE SECURITY FUNCTION OF ARREST OF SHIPS

6.09 A right in security[13] is a

> [R]ight which a creditor may hold for ensuring payment or satisfaction of his debt, distinct from and in addition to his right of action and execution against the debtor under the latter's personal obligation.[14]

[10] The governing law is the law which governs the subject-matter of an action.

[11] The law of the *forum arresti* is the domestic law of the country where the ship has been arrested.

[12] It may be argued that the conflict of laws issues studied in this chapter do not really relate to arrest as a provisional and protective measure, since the matter arises at a later stage, at a moment in time where the provisional arrest has resulted in more permanent effects (as opposed to temporary ones) through judicial sale. Notwithstanding, the applicable law issue in this sphere affects the security function of arrest of ships as a provisional and protective measure in the first place, therefore, its revision is germane in the context of this book. It should also be noted that the analysis is focused on the examination of maritime liens, since it is in this field where, from the private international lawyer's perspective, the situation is still confusing, not only in English and Scots law but more extendedly (see Martin Davies, 'Choice of Law and U.S. Maritime Liens' (2009) 83 *Tulane Law Review* 1435). Conversely, registered mortgages are recognized practically world-wide and governed by the law of the country of registration.

[13] *Pignus utriusque gratia datur, et debitoris, quo magis ei pecunia crederetur, et creditoris, quo magius ei in tuto sit creditum* (*Institutiones Justiniani* iii.xiv 4).

[14] WM Gloag and JW Irvine, *Law of Rights in Security, Heritable and Moveable: including Cautionary Obligations* (Edinburgh, Green, 1897) 2.

Rights in security can be divided into express rights (agreement), tacit rights (implied by law), and judicial rights (diligence/protective measures). This threefold division can be exemplified in the case of ships as: (i) ship mortgage (express); (ii) maritime lien/maritime hypothec (tacit); (iii) ship arrest/arrestment (judicial). 6.10

In comparative law, largely, the claimant who has arrested a ship will be treated as a secured creditor in the distribution of the sale proceeds. The question is whether such preference is previous, concurrent, or consequential upon arrest; in other words, whether the security derives from the cause of action (a preferential debt, or a claim to which a maritime lien attaches), or is created by the arrest (maritime claims attracting a right to proceed *in rem*, sometimes named statutory liens in English law). Does the effectual arrest constitute or crystallize the right in security? The answer is 'it depends' on the applicable law.[15] 6.11

1. The Civil Law Approach

Arrest, Embargo, and Seizure of Ships

In civil law systems there are generally three different institutions that could come eventually under a broad conception of arrest of ships; the differences between them lie in the security function of arrest of ships as displayed by each of them. These three types of measure, namely, arrest, *embargo*, and seizure of ships have been distinguished by Herbert,[16] Fresnedo,[17] and Aguirre.[18] In this conception, arrest is viewed as a provisional measure whose only effect is to situate the ship in a particular jurisdiction, and prevent it from sailing, in most cases in order to enforce a previous right or to make possible the adoption of a concurrent or subsequent protective measure, the latter being the one that provides security 6.12

[15] A certain consideration of the governing law (German law) was given to this issue by Langton J in *Smith v Owners of the SS Zigurds (The Zigurds)* (1932) 43 Lloyd's Rep 156, PDAD. Yet, after such consideration, German law was disregarded, on the grounds that it was a matter of German procedural law (and not substantive law); and it was for English procedural law to determine priorities.

[16] R Herbert and C Fresnedo de Aguirre, 'El Arresto de Buques y el Principio de Jurisdicción más Próxima' [1993] *Revista de Transporte y Seguros* 158.

[17] Ibid; C Fresnedo de Aguirre, 'Embargo de Buques como Medida Cautelar en el Derecho Internacional Privado Uruguayo' (1997) 14 *Anuario de Derecho Marítimo* 385.

[18] F Aguirre Ramírez, 'Embargo y Arresto de Buques en Uruguay' [2005] *Revista de Transporte y Seguros* 275. Uruguay has not ratified the international Conventions in the field but nevertheless Herbert, Fresnedo, and Aguirre do consider the provisions of the Arrest Conventions in order to formulate such distinctions; thus, it is possible to apply their examination more generally to civil law systems where the arrest of ships displays the same functions.

for the result of the pending or imminent proceedings.[19] Hence, the arrest of the ship is not by itself a means of security but the mechanism to obtain or enforce such security. Consequently, the priorities that constitute part of such security do not crystallize upon the arrest but are created by a previous (maritime lien), concurrent (seizure), or subsequent right (embargo) made possible or enforced through the arrest.

6.13 Differently, an embargo[20] (civilian concept meaning in general terms a prohibition to sell) is a protective measure that by itself guarantees the result of a pending or imminent proceeding. It provides the embargo-holder a priority against future encumbrances and any other future rights (*in rem* or *in personam*) constituted on the ship. It is usually an encumbrance that needs to be registered in order to be enforceable. In most legal systems, to grant an embargo the ship must have been arrested first; nevertheless, sometimes it is possible to register such encumbrance without the ship's prohibition to sail.[21]

6.14 In turn, seizure (*secuestro*) is usually either an interim measure of protection, or a measure in execution of a judgment, that implies the loss of possession of the ship by the owner. Generally, it is the way of making the embargo effective.

6.15 There are differences also in the availability of such measures depending on whom the proceedings have been against or are to be brought. Embargo and seizure are available to the claimant only in the case of the owner being the defendant. By contrast, arrest is also available against the charterer. This evidences that the security function of arrest of ships goes beyond the relationship between claimant and defendant and strikes heavily on the effects of the arrest of ships with regard to third parties.

2. The Approach in English and in Scots Law

Arrest of Ships to Enforce Maritime Liens and Arrest of Ships Based upon Statutory Rights *in rem*

6.16 In common law systems, these differences present themselves between arrest of ships to enforce maritime liens and arrest of ships based upon

[19] Herbert and Fresnedo de Aguirre, 'El Arresto de Buques y el Principio de Jurisdicción más Próxima' [1993].

[20] The 1952 International Arrest Convention has been translated into Spanish as *Convenio sobre unificación de ciertas reglas relativas al* embargo *preventivo de buques*.

[21] For instance, the so-called 'ship-register arrest' in Danish law, whereby the warrant of arrest is not executed on the ship but is only endorsed in the ship's register (see Berlingieri, *Berlingieri on Arrest of Ships* (London, Informa, 2006) 24).

statutory rights to initiate an *in rem* claim (statutory liens). Technically, in English law the security function is not displayed by the arrest of the ship but by the issuing of an *in rem* claim. In the words of Jackson, 'arrest, when used, is simply an early step ensuring physical retention of an asset'.[22] In Scots law, the effects of the security function of arrest differ depending on the type of arrestment, namely, arrestment of ships *in rem* in an action *in rem* (maritime liens); arrestment of ships *in rem* in an action *in personam* (non-pecuniary obligations); and arrestment of ships on the dependence of an action *in personam* (all the other admiralty claims). In the framework of the action *in rem*, in English law as well as in Scots law, arrest of ships is connected to a lien which a claim enforceable by such an action attracts.[23] Hence, in the following paragraphs the applicable law issues concerning maritime liens are explained and analysed.

III. THE APPLICABLE LAW PROBLEMS

Different legal systems have different understanding of the aims and objectives of private international law. Nonetheless, there is universal consensus as to its difficulty.[24] The most extended conception, that of English and Scots law as well as most civilian systems, is that the subject includes the study of jurisdiction, the applicable law, and the recognition and enforcement of foreign judgments. **6.17**

The following paragraphs deal with one of these germane concerns of private international law: that of the applicable law in relation to the security function of arrest of ships in English and in Scots law. In general terms, though Scots domestic law differs substantially from English municipal law, yet there is no such difference as to their principles of private international law,[25] particularly in relation to the applicable law to maritime liens. **6.18**

[22] Jackson, *Enforcement of Maritime Claims* (2005) 404.

[23] Ibid.

[24] Particularly in England '... the cases decided in the field have been heavily influenced by policy considerations, national pride, and local economic impact of the decisions that must be made. The case law is often inconsistent, with the reasoning underlying many decisions appearing to be an almost ad hoc quality. The unpredictability of the law in this area has from time to time been judicially noted ...' (G Bowtle and K McGuinness, *The Law of Ship Mortgages* (London, LLP, 2001) 237).

[25] See Elizabeth B Crawford and Janeen M Carruthers, *International Private Law in Scotland*, para 2-04. See also JJ Fawcett and JM Carruthers, *Cheshire, North & Fawcett Private International Law* (Oxford, 14th edn, OUP, 2008) 10. Scots *international private law* falls within the scope of 'Scots private law' in the interpretation given by the Scotland Act 1998 (s 126(4)(a)), hence in

6.19 The dilemma that gives rise to private international law as a legal discipline is created by the confrontation between a world divided into different legal systems (each one with a defined territorial application), and private legal relations that go beyond frontiers. In this context the aim of conflict of law rules is to provide juridical continuity to legal relations across national borders;[26] ie the dynamic objective at the centre of concern of private international law in this sphere is the validity of legal relations across the discontinuity of legal orders.[27]

6.20 There are at least three conflict-of-laws questions a court needs to answer when adjudicating a dispute that involves a foreign maritime lien. The first one is what legal system(s) governs the claimant's cause of action, ie the underlying claim that attracts a maritime lien. Once determined, this law (or these laws, if *dépeçage*[28] is necessary and possible) constitutes the law applicable to the underlying claim, ie the governing law.

6.21 In relation to this first question, if, for example, the cause of action involves a contract the court will look into the conflict of laws system of the forum to determine the applicable law; in English and in Scots law as well as in all the other legal systems of the European Union, contractual matters[29] are governed by Regulation (EC) 593/2008 of the European Parliament and of the Council of 17 June 2008 on the law applicable to contractual obligations (Rome I).[30] This Regulation provides a system of conflict-of-law rules applicable to most contractual matters.[31] If the cause of action is based on a non-contractual obligation then the conflict rules to follow by the courts in England and in Scotland are the ones embodied in Regulation (EC) 864/2007 of the European Parliament and of the Council of 11 July 2007

this field legislative competence pertains to the Scottish Parliament except for the private international law aspects of reserved matters (s 29(3) of the same Act) that are reserved to the Westminster Parliament.

[26] See R Herbert in D Opertti Badán (ed), *Objeto y Método en el Derecho Internacional Privado* (2nd edn, Montevideo, Fundación de Cultura Universitaria, 1990) 93–118.

[27] Ibid, 100.

[28] *Dépeçage* refers to the application of the laws of different States to different issues in the same case. The doctrine of *dépeçage* is used as a device that may solve complex private international law problems. See Willis LM Reese, '*Dépeçage*: A Common Phenomenon in the Choice of Law' (1973) 73 *Columbia Law Review* 58. See also Symeon C Symeonides, 'The American Revolution and the European Evolution in Choice of Law: Reciprocal Lessons' (2008) 82 *Tulane Law Review* 1782.

[29] For contracts concluded after 17 December 2009.

[30] OJ L 177 of 4.7.2008.

[31] OJ L 199 of 31.7.2007. For the material scope of application of the Regulation see Art 1; for the scope of the law applicable see Art 12.

on the law applicable to non-contractual obligations (Rome II).[32] A maritime claim, whether contractual or non-contractual, if it attracts a maritime lien it raises proprietary issues and this may generate the possibility of using *dépeçage*, ie different laws (from two different jurisdictions) may be applicable as the governing law to different aspects of the claim. It may be that the substantive claim as the wholesale issue has to be analysed into two separate sub-issues referable to different laws.[33]

Once the law applicable to the cause of action (the governing law) has been determined according to the conflict-of-law rules of the forum, the court is faced with further issues to decide; these involve the characterization[34] of maritime liens. If that court is confronted with a maritime claim that under its applicable law attracts a certain privilege but it does not under the law of the *forum arresti*, that court has two fundamental decisions to take. The court must, first, decide whether or not to recognize that foreign privilege (right of preference) regardless of the fact that a corresponding claim arising within the court's own territorial jurisdiction may not attract a similar preference. Secondly, if the court recognizes the existence of the foreign right, it must then decide how to rank that right of preference in the distribution of the sale proceeds. These controversial issues are connected to the characterization of maritime liens (as substantive rights or procedural remedies) and this characterization is the one that generates real difficulties in practice; hence, these issues are the ones discussed in the following paragraphs.[35] It may be argued that these two applicable law problems (the law applicable to the existence of the maritime lien and the law applicable to the ranking of the maritime claim) are so intermingled that the decision process of the court should not be split in the two steps mentioned above; the distinction matters only as a methodological approach to the study of the problem. The discussion that follows examines this argument. **6.22**

[32] For the material scope of application of the Regulation see Art 1; for the scope of the law applicable see Art 15. The latter provides that the scope of the applicable law encompasses virtually all issues likely to arise in tort litigation, including the basis and extent of liability; the grounds for exemption from liability; any limitation of liability and any division of liability; the existence, the nature, and the assessment of damage or the remedy claimed; injunctive relief; the proper beneficiaries of the right to claim damages, and its transferability or heritability; and the extinction or prescription of the obligation (statutes of limitation).

[33] Fawcett and Carruthers, *Chesire, North & Fawcett, Private International Law* (2008) 54.

[34] For the concept of 'characterization' in private international law, see Ch 3, para 3.25 above.

[35] See paras 6.23–6.80 below.

1. Two Faces of the Same Coin: Existence and Ranking of Rights of Preference

6.23 Traditionally, in private international law studies these two applicable law issues, the applicable law governing the existence of the preferential right of the creditor and the applicable law governing the ranking of maritime claims, have merited separate examination. Yet, in the case of maritime liens, it is submitted, in opposition to traditional authority, that they should not be governed by different laws.

6.24 However, most legal systems split the characterization of maritime liens into two categories, substance and procedure, or right and remedy, and provide for two different conflict rules, invariably deciding all questions of ranking according to the law of the forum.[36] It has been argued that it remains critical to identify the two categories for characterization purposes.[37]

6.25 This book proposes a different and fresh approach to the issue. It is submitted that a fragmented approach to the characterization of maritime liens jeopardizes the legal validity of this type of preferential rights across national borders, the ultimate aim of private international law in this sphere.[38]

[36] See J Asser, *Maritime Liens and Mortgages in the Conflicts of Laws* (Gothenburg, Gothenburg School of Economics and Business Administration Publications, 1963).

[37] Jackson, *Enforcement of Maritime Claims* (2005) 682. See the decision of the Court of Appeal in *The Colorado* (1923) 14 Lloyd's Rep 251, a decision where it was recognized that the existence of the right (as opposed to the remedy) should be determined according to the governing law. Even though the distinction was drawn therein for the case at hand, the submission of priorities to the law of the forum was supported upon previous cases where such distinction had failed to be drawn, and where the right (and not only the remedy) were examined under the loop of the law of the forum (see Scrutton LJ referring to *The Milford*, Swabey 362 and *The Tagus* [1903] P 44 at 255). Yet, Briggs seems to be of the opinion that it is possible to eliminate this distinction '… where lines of demarcation, or of characterization, can be eliminated without substantial cost, it is good that they should be. The line which separates right from final remedy is one which could usefully be eliminated, with the result that the *lex causae* would prevail generally …' (A Briggs, 'Conflict of Laws and Commercial Remedies' in A Burrows and E Peel (eds), *Commercial Remedies: Current Issues and Problems* (Oxford, OUP, 2003) 286).

[38] See Didier Opertti Badán, *Exhorto y Embargo de Bienes Extranjeros* (Montevideo, Amalio M Fernández, 1976) 327. In different words, Briggs acknowledges that in the sphere of commercial remedies '… the coherence of results is conducive to the doing of practical justice …' (Briggs, 'Conflict of Laws and Commercial Remedies' (2003) 286).

IV. MARITIME LIENS IN THE CONFLICT OF LAWS[39]

1. Maritime Liens: Generalities

A lien is a form of security interest in property which arises by operation of law. As such, it is accessory to a situation which has a legal character of its own (contract, tort/delict).[40] The concept of lien is applied widely in English and Scots law and responds mainly to two different concepts: the common law lien (possessory lien or 'right of retention') and the equitable lien. One of the main differences between these two is that the first depends on possession and arises usually out of a contract of services, whereas the latter disregards possession and arises by implication of law, and is lost when a sale of the *res* to a bona fide purchaser is performed. **6.26**

However, a 'maritime lien' is a distinctive legal institution:[41] it does not depend on possession and it 'travels' with the *res*; it is not registered anywhere; and is independent of notice. In the words of Thomas, 'maritime liens are secret and invisible'.[42] **6.27**

In English law there is a further distinction between traditional maritime liens, and 'statutory liens' (or right to proceed *in rem*); the concept of lien is so intermingled with ship arrest (as the only way to enforce maritime and 'statutory' liens), and the *in rem* claim (the framework in which such enforcement takes place) that they often get confused with one another.[43] In the words of Sir John Jervis, the maritime lien 'is inchoate from the **6.28**

[39] Two very well-known scholars have enlightened this field, J Asser, *Maritime Liens and Mortgages in the Conflicts of Laws* (Gothenburg, Gothenburg School of Economics and Business Administration Publications, 1963) and W Tetley, 'Maritime Liens in the Conflict of Laws' in JAR Nafziger and SC Symeonides (eds), *Law and Justice in a Multistate World: Essays in Honor of Arthur T. von Mehren* (Ardsley, NY, Transnational Publishers, 2002) 439. See also Davies, 'Choice of Law and US Maritime Liens' (2009).

[40] The illustration of Jackson is clarifying: 'A seaman to whom wages are due has a lien—to enforce his contractual right' (Jackson, *Enforcement of Maritime Claims* (2005) 460).

[41] Two monographs have particularly informed the theme of 'maritime liens', see G Price, *The Law of Maritime Liens* (London, Sweet & Maxwell, 1940) and DR Thomas, *Maritime Liens* (London, Stevens, 1980). For later developments see J Brown, 'The Extinction of Maritime Liens' (2003) 3 LMCLQ 361; N Hutton, 'The Origin, Development, and Future of Maritime Liens and the Action *in rem*' (2003) 28 *Tulane maritime law journal* 81; P K Mukherjee, 'The Law of Maritime Liens and Conflict of Laws' (2003) 9 JIML 545; RP Hayden and KC Leland, 'The Uniquenes of Admiralty and Maritime Law: The Unique Nature of Maritime Liens' (2005) 79 *Tulane Law Review* 1227. For the particular issues discussed in this chapter, see Davies, 'Choice of Law and U.S. Maritime Liens' (2009) 1435.

[42] Thomas, *Maritime Liens* (1980) 4.

[43] For instance in G Bowtle and K McGuinness, *The Law of Ship Mortgages* (London, LLP, 2001) 119 a maritime lien is defined as 'the right of a person who has a claim against the ship

moment the claim or privilege attaches, and when carried into effect by legal process by a proceeding *in rem*, relates back to the period when it first attached'.[44]

6.29 Story was the first to use the term 'maritime lien' in the North American case *The Nestor*.[45] In a few words, a maritime lien can be defined as a maritime privilege[46] which gives the privilege-holder a right on the ship and freight of a property kind. As has been stated in *The Tolten*,[47] the lien travels with the ship into whoever's possession it may come and has a certain ranking with other maritime liens, all of which take priority over mortgages. This right arises with the claim without registration or other formalities.[48]

6.30 In English law, its first comprehensive definition appeared in *Daniel Harmer v William Errington Bell and Others* (*The Bold Buccleugh*).[49] However, there is no statutory definition of 'maritime lien' in English law. In the words of Jackson, 'they are interests of prime importance and of no inconsiderable uncertainty'.[50]

6.31 'Maritime lien' is an Anglo-American term. In Scots law the institution is named as a 'maritime hypothec'. However, due to the use of the expression 'maritime lien' in English law and in international Conventions, this expression was adopted in Scots law, even when it was not strictly accurate; hence, giving rise to confusion. For the sake of harmonization the issue has been clarified by statute: in Scots law a 'maritime lien' means a hypothec over a ship, cargo, or other maritime property.[51]

to arrest the ship and, if the claim is not paid, to have the ship sold by the court and the claim paid from the sale proceeds'.

[44] [1851] 7 Moo PC 267, 284. The definition has been cited in various cases since then, eg *The Halley* [1867] LR 2 PC 193; *The Feronia* [1868] LR 2 A&E 65; *The Charles Amelia* [1868] LR 2 A&E 330; *The Beldis* [1936] P 51; *The Tolten* [1946] P 135.

[45] (1831) 18 Fed Cas 9 (Case No 10, 126) 11 (CC D Me 1831).

[46] Even though the 'maritime lien' is a common law institution there are similar ways of granting a preference in civil law systems, generally as 'preferential debts' or 'privileges'.

[47] [1946] P 226 242.

[48] Tetley, 'Maritime Liens in the Conflict of Laws' (2002) 442.

[49] [1851] 7 Moo PC 267 (Sir John Jervis).

[50] Jackson, *Enforcement of Maritime Claims* (2005) 459.

[51] See Administration of Justice Act 1956, Ch 46, s 48(2), as amended by Sch 4 to the Bankruptcy and Diligence etc (Scotland) Act 2007 in force since 1 July 2010: 'In this Act and in any other enactment (including an Act of the Scottish Parliament and any enactment comprised in subordinate legislation under such an Act) "maritime lien" means a hypothec over a ship cargo or other maritime property.'

2. Applicable Law Governing Rights of Preference

First and foremost, it has to be taken as the starting assumption that the issue of applicable law governing rights of preference[52] is indeed a very difficult and complex[53] one. It is primarily a matter of characterization, and particularly, the main decision to be taken is whether a maritime lien or similar right of preference is a procedural remedy governed by the law of the forum or, on the contrary, should be regarded as a substantive right and therefore subject to the governing law. The distinction has a very practical consequence: taking into consideration that the lists of claims which give rise to rights of preference do vary quite radically from country to country, the question of which legal system is to determine the existence of such rights is vital in practice.[54] **6.32**

Arguably, the applicable law issues in this sphere are the reflection of a real conflict of interests between the ship financing sector and ship operators. This explains the limited success of the harmonization efforts in this area of the law,[55] as well as the opposed views as to the characterization (and its consequences) of maritime liens. Mortgagees are the natural competitors of maritime lienees and this is reflected in the case-law referred to in this part of the discussion. However, it should be stated that the analysis of this book is focused on the examination of maritime liens rather than mortgages, since it is in relation to the former where the applicable law problems present themselves more frequently.[56] Conversely, registered **6.33**

[52] 'Preferential debts', 'privileges', 'maritime lien', 'maritime hypothec' are not necessarily identical or interchangeable concepts; 'rights of preference' is the preferred concept bearing in mind the importance of characterization in private international law and the need to undertake such process in as broad an internationalist spirit as possible, as acknowledged by Mance LJ in *Raiffeisen Zentralbank Osterreich AG v Five Star General Trading LLC (The Mount I)* [2001] 1 Lloyd's Rep 597, CA, paras 26–27.

[53] In the opinion of Davies the complexity stems from the need to understand both Admiralty procedure and conflict of laws principles, see Davies, 'Choice of Law and US Maritime Liens' (2009) 1435.

[54] DR Thomas, *Maritime liens* (London, Stevens, 1980) 320–1. From *Louis Castrique v William Imrie and W.J. Tomlinson* [1869–70] LR 4, HL 414 to *Andromeda Marine SA v O W Bunker & Trading A/S* [2006] WL 1078890, QBD (Comm Ct) there is a large number of cases decided in England and in Scotland on the topic.

[55] The main criticism levelled at the principles of the 1926 International Convention for the Unification of Certain Rules Relating to Maritime Liens and Mortgages in force since 2 June 1931 is directed at Art 2(5) according to which the liens referred to in that paragraph, namely liens for claims resulting, inter alia, from contracts entered into by the master for the purpose of preserving the ship or continuing the voyage, take precedence over mortgages (Asser, *Maritime Liens and Mortgages in the Conflicts of Laws* (1963) 29).

[56] See eg *Oceanconnect UK Ltd v Angara Maritime Ltd* [2010] EWCA Civ 1050.

mortgages are recognized practically world-wide and governed by the law of the country of registration.

The Law of the Forum Approach

6.34 In this context, the forum-centred methodology is construed upon a positivistic approach that considers a judge as an instrument of the legislative will and as such a way to apply forum policies.[57] The law of the forum approach represents the most extreme and possibly the simplest solution to the applicable law issues hereby examined.[58] In the field of maritime liens its application has been justified in various ways, some of which are outlined as follows.

6.35 One way of applying the law of the forum in this sphere is to adopt as a connecting factor the place where the ship is situated, and consider it as governed by the *lex rei sitae*. According to this approach, the ship is fixed by arrest to the territorial jurisdiction of the court and therefore the law of the forum is applied as the governing law.[59] Another way of enhancing the role of the law of the forum, as traditionally done in English private international law, is through the application of the 'substance and procedure rule'. It is with this 'escape device'[60] that the examination in this chapter is more concerned. A radically different approach, with similar results, is the exclusion of foreign law via the 'international public policy' (*ordre public*) of the forum.[61] Nonetheless, none of these theories are applied by the courts in a pure form; practically, courts strive to find a formula which in their opinion, and according to its own private international law rules, leads to the fairest solution in each case.

6.36 As a conflict of laws approach, the law of the forum can be regarded as the main territorial predilection common to all times,[62] that can be traced back

[57] Carl Georg von Wächter, 'Über die Collision der Privatrechtgesetze verschiedener Staaten' (1841) 24 *Archiv für die Civilistische Praxis* 230.

[58] Asser, *Maritime Liens and Mortgages in the Conflicts of Laws* (1963) 14.

[59] *The Tagus* [1903] P 44, PDAD.

[60] By 'escape device' reference is made to private international law 'tools' such as the use of *renvoi* or the application of the exception of *ordre public*, amongst others. The 'escape clauses' in the words of Symeonides if carefully crafted 'can remedy many of the deficiencies of bad rules, as well as provide a needed safety valve in the application of even good rules to unanticipated exceptional cases' see Symeonides, 'The American Revolution and the European Evolution in Choice of Law: Reciprocal Lessons' (2008) 1773.

[61] As done, for instance, traditionally, in France and Belgium (Asser, *Maritime Liens and Mortgages in the Conflicts of Laws* (1963) 14).

[62] Juenger referred to it as 'the twentieth century unilateralism' (FK Juenger, *Choice of Law and Multistate Justice* (Dordrecht, Martinus Nijhoff, 1993) 34).

to the unilateralists of the sixteenth century. D'Argentre assumed that courts should normally apply their own law, whereas foreign rules of decision were relevant only in exceptional cases.[63] Wächter[64] adopted a similar position. Modern scholars such as Currie[65] and Ehrenzweig[66] have also acknowledged the law of the forum approach.

In English law, one of the arguments advanced for the remission of maritime liens to the law of the forum in the 1960s was that it should not be possible '... to enlarge the jurisdiction to benefit the foreign claimants when English claimants have no similar benefits conferred upon them'.[67] This line of argument is very old in private international law. It was already advanced by Jitta who acknowledged that a judge cannot give to a legal relation a character different to that given to it by his national law.[68] Yet, in modern times the benefits of the law of the forum approach have been also exalted for avoiding the difficulty and expense of proving foreign law.[69] In this view, the practical convenience of the law of the forum approach over the multilateral method of law-selection as conceived by Savigny[70] is apparent. As explained by Juenger, there are various reasons why a non-choice rule such as the law of the forum is simpler to most conflict approaches: one of the main reasons is that in practice what courts apply as foreign law is often a 'bad replica of the foreign law itself'.[71] **6.37**

However, one of the problems of the law of the forum approach is that it is one-sided: it benefits only those litigants who are in the position to take the best out of 'forum shopping' opportunities.[72] Particularly, in relation to issues such as the ones examined in this chapter, the 'first' *in rem* claimant would then be 'shopping' for the court that concedes the best security and priority to their cause of action. This position would certainly favour that first claimant but not necessarily the other claimants that 'often feel forced **6.38**

[63] Currie, *Selected Essays on the Conflict of Laws* (1963) 183.

[64] Wächter, 'Über die Collision der Privatrechtgesetze verschiedener Staaten' (1841) 230.

[65] Currie, *Selected Essays on the Conflict of Laws* (1963).

[66] AA Ehrenzweig, *Private International Law: A Comparative Treatise on American International Conflicts of Law, Including the Law of Admiralty* (Leyden, Oceana, 1967).

[67] *The Acrux (No 3)* [1965] 1 Lloyd's Rep 565, PDAD 573 (Hewson J).

[68] DJ Jitta, *La méthode du droit international privé* (The Hague, Belinfante, 1890) 198.

[69] R Fentiman, *Foreign Law in English Courts: Pleading, Proof and Choice of Law* (Oxford, OUP, 1998) 2.

[70] FC von Savigny, *Private International Law and the Retrospective Operation of Statutes. A Treatise on the Conflict of Laws and the Limits of their Operation in Respect of Place and Time* (tr W Guthrie, 2nd edn, Edinburgh, Clark, 1880).

[71] Juenger, *Choice of Law and Multistate Justice* (1993) 162. For the complex issue of the application of foreign law see also Fentiman, *Foreign Law in English Courts* (1998); S Geeroms, *Foreign Law in Civil Litigation: A Comparative and Functional Analysis* (Oxford, OUP, 2004).

[72] Juenger, *Choice of Law and Multistate Justice* (1993) 162.

to bring their claims in the same court for fear of losing their rightful security and priority'.[73]

The Law of the Forum Approach to Maritime Liens in English Law: A Thing of the Past

6.39 In times gone by the principal authorities[74] on the applicable law to maritime liens in English case-law were *The Milford*,[75] *The Tagus*,[76] *Hills Dry Docks & Engineering Co Ltd v Colorado (The Colorado)*,[77] *Smith v Owners of the SS Zigurds (The Zigurds)*,[78] and *Casa Nazionale Della Previdenza Marinara v the proceeds of the sale of the Italian Steamship Acrux (The Acrux)*.[79] Except for *The Colorado*, where the right was recognized by reference to the governing law (French law) but the ranking (priorities) was governed by the law of the *forum arresti*, the common feature of all the other decisions is the submission of the 'assimilated-to-maritime-lien-right' to the law of the *forum arresti*. In *The Milford* via characterizing it as a question of remedy and not of contract at all; in *The Tagus*, applying the law of the forum as the governing law, using as the connecting factor the territorial location of the *res (lex rei sitae)*; in *The Zigurds* via posing the question as one of priorities (remedial) rather than connected to the existence of the right;[80] and finally in *The Acrux*,[81] even though under Italian law the claim would have been considered as a maritime lien, it was remarked that no maritime lien existed under English law and, therefore, (*obiter*) the Italian maritime lien would have not been recognized under English law. Such observation was grounded on a strict 'law of the forum characterization' considering only the narrow scope of the domestic law category and adding that without legislative intervention there could be no extension of those categories.

6.40 In *Bankers Trust International v Todd Shipyards Corp (The Halcyon Isle)*,[82] the Privy Council, in a three-to-two decision reversing the Singapore Court of Appeal, refused to recognize the status of maritime liens to any claims which differed from the six 'traditional' maritime liens in English law.

[73] Davies, 'Choice of Law and US Maritime Liens' (2009) 1435.

[74] Thomas, *Maritime Liens* (1980) 322–9.

[75] [1858] Swab 362, HCA.

[76] [1903] P 44, PDAD.

[77] [1923] P 102, CA.

[78] *Smith v Owners of the SS Zigurds (The Zigurds)* (1932) 43 Lloyd's Rep 156, PDAD.

[79] *Casa Nazionale Della Previdenza Marinara v the proceeds of the sale of the Italian Steamship Acrux (The Acrux No 3)* [1965] 1 Lloyd's Rep 565, PDAD.

[80] *The Zigurds* (1932) Langton J.

[81] Hewson J.

[82] *Bankers Trust International v Todd Shipyards Corp (The Halcyon Isle)* [1980] 2 Lloyd's Rep 325, PC (Sing).

The majority decision was based on the notion that maritime liens, in the conflict of laws, are procedural remedies rather than substantive rights.[83]

As a result, the ship-repairer's claim ranked below that of the mortgagee, because the repairman's claim, which according to its governing law (US law) attracted a maritime lien, did not so attract according to English law. In English law the claim was secured merely by a statutory right *in rem* which did not 'travel' with the ship and which ranked after the mortgage. **6.41**

The dissenting position, on the contrary, citing various precedents, and in particular the English decision in *The Colorado*[84] observed that: **6.42**

> A maritime lien is a right of property given by way of security for a maritime claim. If the Admiralty court has, as in the present case, jurisdiction to entertain the claim, it will not disregard the lien. A maritime lien validly conferred by the *lex loci* is as much part of the claim as is a mortgage similarly valid by the *lex loci*. ... It would be a denial of history and principle, in the present chaos of the law of the sea governing the recognition and priority of maritime liens and mortgages, to refuse the aid of private international law.[85]

Thus, they argued that the governing law of the foreign maritime lien merited recognition, even if English law denied maritime lien status to the equivalent claim arising in England. Commentators on the whole prefer the minority position.[86] And that is in tune with current international practice in this sphere.[87]

It is submitted, though, that the approach of the majority in *The Halcyon Isle*, as discredited as it is now, may be a result of the fact that maritime liens (substantive rights) are necessarily given effect through an action *in rem* (procedural) and in turn this has generated such an amalgamation of the substantive and procedural aspects of the claim that the fusion is indeed a source of confusion. However, most probably, the characterization of maritime liens as procedural is also an 'escape device' used to avoid the application of the governing law and to apply the law of the forum instead. In any case, despite the reasons or excuses to regard maritime **6.43**

[83] Speaking for the majority Lord Diplock held that maritime liens involve '... rights that are procedural or remedial only and accordingly the question whether a particular class of claim gives rise to a maritime lien or not [is] one to be determined by English law as the law of the forum', ibid, 331.

[84] *Hills Dry Docks & Engineering Co Ltd v Colorado* [1923] P 102, CA.

[85] [1980] 2 Lloyd's Rep 325 (PC (Sing)) 339 (Lord Salmon and Lord Scarman).

[86] Fawcett and Carruthers, *Chesire, North & Fawcett, Private International Law* (2008) 94; Lord Collins of Mapesbury (ed), *Dicey, Morris and Collins on the Conflict of Laws* (14th edn, London, Sweet & Maxwell, 2006) 191.

[87] See eg *Oceanconnect UK Ltd v Angara Maritime Ltd* [2010] EWCA Civ 1050.

liens as procedural rather than substantive, it seems that the arbitrary line has already been moved. Leading commentators and international practice coincide in affirming that 'the existence and quantification of each creditor's claim is of course a matter for the *lex causae* of the claim'.[88]

The Governing Law Approach

6.44 Some sources suggest that before 1835[89] certain kinds of maritime liens, particularly liens for necessaries, were recognized in English and Scots law according to the governing law, applicable to the substance of the case at hand.[90] Yet, as mentioned above, decisions since then have not consistently followed this line.[91]

6.45 Doubtless, the decision of the Court of Appeal in *The Colorado*[92] represented a break-through in the treatment of the issue. Scott LJ in *The Tolten*[93] supported also the opinion that a maritime lien represents a substantive right. In his words the consequences of a lien are 'indubitably a rule of substantive law in admiralty'.[94]

The Scots Law Approach

6.46 There is not in this field much difference between English and Scots law, arguably due to the 'reception'[95] of English jurisprudence in this area of

[88] Collins (ed), *Dicey, Morris and Collins on the Conflict of Laws* (2006) 191; Fawcett and Carruthers, *Chesire, North & Fawcett, Private International Law* (2008) 93.

[89] *William Hodges v Jacob Sims (The Neptune)* [1835] 3 Kn PC 94.

[90] 'By the law of some foreign countries a person who supplies necessaries has a lien upon the ship, and at one time he could maintain such a suit in England; but in 1835 it was decided in the case of *William Hodges v Jacob Sims (The Neptune)* [1835] 3 Kn PC 94 that the Admiralty Court had no jurisdiction to try such a case, and that the material or necessaries man could only bring an action against the owner and not against the ship' Lord Dewar (OH) in *Constant v Klompus* [1912] 2 SLT 62.

[91] *Bankers Trust International v Todd Shipyards Corp (The Halcyon Isle)* [1980] 2 Lloyd's Rep 325, PC (Sing).

[92] [1923] P 102, CA.

[93] [1946] P 135, 159.

[94] [1946] P 135, 145.

[95] *Currie v McKnight* [1897] AC 97 (Lord Watson): 'From the earliest times the Courts of Scotland exercising jurisdiction in Admiralty causes have disregarded the municipal rules of Scottish law and have invariably professed to administer the law and customs of the sea generally prevailing among maritime states. In later times with the growth of British shipping the Admiralty law of England has gradually acquired predominance and resort has seldom been had to the laws of other States for the guidance of the Courts.' The 'reception' of English law in Scotland has merited academic consideration in present times, see para 6.47 below.

Scots law. In *The Baltic*,[96] Lord Dewar understood the question for decision before him as to whether the pursuer, a mortgagee, had a preferable claim to the proceeds of the judicial sale of the ship in virtue of his mortgage, or whether the competing defender was to be preferred in virtue of an alleged maritime lien (based upon coals supplied and cash advanced to the master of *The Baltic* when she was lying at the port of Copenhagen). In present times it could be argued that the issue for decision was a question of priorities; indeed it was—as it always is—a question of existence *and* priority of the foreign privilege; even though this decision, as so many other decisions of that time, earlier, and later ones, have not drawn a distinction between the substance of the right and the question of priorities.[97]

According to the law of Denmark (the governing law) the coal supplier had a preferential claim. Nevertheless, Lord Dewar disregarded the application of the law of Denmark and after consideration of Scottish and English authorities[98] applied what he understood was the law of Scotland at that moment in time, submitting the issue to the law of the forum. He explained his reasoning in the following terms: '... the only question is whether, according to the law of Scotland, the compearing defender has a maritime lien for the necessaries he supplied and the cash he advanced to the master of the "Baltic" '.[99] Based on the settled principle of Admiralty law as administered in England where the 'material man' has no maritime lien for necessaries, he concluded that the defender did not have a maritime lien. He did not find anything in the Scottish authorities or doctrine to suggest that there was any peculiarity in the law of Scotland which distinguished it from the Admiralty law of England. On the contrary, he found authorities to point to the assimilation of both legal systems in this branch of jurisprudence.[100] **6.47**

The similarities between English and Scots law on the determination of the applicable law to maritime liens are incontestable. Nonetheless, the conflict rule in Scots international private law could reflect the clearer distinction in Scots law between the arrestment of ships and maritime hypothec/liens. In this sense, it is submitted that there are no justifications in Scots international private law to examine foreign preferential claims under the loop of the law of the forum. Arguably, there are not justifications in English law either; but in Scots law, where a maritime hypothec/lien is clearly a substantive right, and the action *in rem* (the procedural aspect) is **6.48**

[96] *Constant v Klompus* 1912 2 SLT 62, OH (Lord Dewar).

[97] Because in fact there is none; the distinction itself is just a fallacious way of dealing with the issue with a view to applying the *law of the forum*.

[98] *Mecca* [1895] P 95, *Clark v Bowring & Co* 1908 SC 1168 and *The Tagus* [1903] P 44.

[99] *Constant v Klompus* 1912 2 SLT 62, OH (Lord Dewar).

[100] *Hay v Le Neve* (1824) 2 Sh App 395; *Boettcher v Carron Co* (1861) 23 D 322.

not so inextricably linked with the substantive right, there is no explanation for treating foreign maritime liens as procedural; therefore, there has never been any reason to follow the law of the forum approach of English private international law in this regard.

6.49 Even though the issue is strikingly complex, it is suggested that the position of Scots international private law in this sphere could be regarded as a way of 'reception',[101] a form of legal development considered to be a fundamentally disruptive force in all legal systems;[102] 'when one body of law is overwhelmed by another because of the intervention of powerful cultural and political forces the mixture that often results can be very much worse, not better, than the law drawn from a single tradition that was replaced'.[103]

6.50 In general terms, it has been argued that it is time that reception of English law at the expense of the civil law came to an end in Scotland.[104] It is here submitted that the issue at hand offers a great opportunity for such a change. In Scots law the arrestment of ships, on the one hand, and the maritime hypothec on the other, are always kept, conceptually, independent from each other, ie the substantive right and the way to enforce it, are distinct clear-cut categories. This represents a difference in the functionality of arrestment of ships as compared to English law, ie a warrant of arrestment to found jurisdiction and a warrant to arrest on the dependence are not necessarily connected to a maritime lien, and are not by themselves sufficient to effect a lien on a ship which has been arrested under either of these warrants; a warrant for arrestment *in rem* is necessary if it is desired to effect a maritime lien over a ship.[105] It is regrettable, then, that this difference has not had an impact on the understanding of applicable law issues to maritime hypothec/liens and its ranking in Scots international private law, probably because English case-law has been followed.

[101] 'Reception as a form of legal development requires that lawyers replace their own law, or a part of it, with a foreign body of law' (R Evan-Jones, 'Mixed Legal Systems, Scotland and the Unification of Private Law in Europe' in JM Smits (ed), *The Contribution of Mixed Legal Systems to European Private Law* (Antwerp, Intersentia, 2001) 44). Lord Deward in *The Baltic* concluded his judgment quoting the words of Lord Watson in *Currie v McKnight* [1897] AC 97: '... In later times, with the growth of British shipping, the Admiralty law of England has gradually acquired predominance, and resort has seldom been had to the laws of other States for the guidance of the Courts.'

[102] Evan-Jones, 'Mixed Legal Systems, Scotland and the Unification of Private Law in Europe' (2001) 45.

[103] Ibid, 44.

[104] On the reception of English law in Scots law see, inter alia, Hector L McQueen, 'Scots and English Law: The Case of Contract' (2001) 54 *Current Legal Problems* 205; R. Evans-Jones, 'Receptions of Law, Mixed Legal Systems and the Myth of the Genius of Scots Private Law' (1998) 114 LQR 228.

[105] *Mill v Fildes* [1982] SLT 147.

Notwithstanding the foregoing, arguably, in Scots law the submission to the law of the forum in this sphere has not been justified on a fallacious distinction between substance and procedure but on application of the law of the forum as the governing law. In the 1950s Donaldson[106] affirmed that in Scots conflict rules, as regards proprietary rights over ships situated in Scotland, Scots law as the *lex situs* should give way to the governing law in special circumstances. Scots law has long disliked fallacious applications of the law, thus, the 'substance and procedure rule' in the English fashion would fit uneasily in the Scottish legal tradition. In the words of Lord Reid '… During early stages of the development of a legal system legal fictions have been invaluable … But in this day and age I dislike them intensely. Why should we tell lies when the truth will serve our purpose equally well if only we give a little care to the formulation of our principles …'.[107] **6.51**

3. Applicable Law Governing the Ranking of Maritime Claims

As mentioned at the beginning of this chapter, conflicts of ranking between maritime claims usually arise between maritime lienees *inter se* and between them and holders of other kinds of security interests on the ship, such as maritime charges or mortgages. The order in which maritime claims rank varies from country to country and public policy considerations are usually at stake. Furthermore, the effect of the security function of arrest as such deserves consideration in this context. An illustration will probably show the extent of the problem better. **6.52**

An Illustration of the Applicable Law Problems: *England v United States*

The traditional ranking of maritime claims[108] in English case-law is on the whole as follows:[109] (1) special legislative rights;[110] (2) court costs eg costs **6.53**

[106] A Donaldson, 'Some Conflict Rules of Scots Law' (1953) 39 *Problems of Public and Private International Law Transactions of the Grotius Society* 145, 175.

[107] (1968) 54 *Proceedings of the British Academy* 189, 200 as quoted by Scot Law Com No 164 (1998) 186.

[108] It is outside the scope of this book to examine the general problems of priority matters and to engage with the full spectrum of maritime and non-maritime security interests that may be enforceable against the ship. The analysis of priorities in this chapter is very limited and is referred to inasmuch as necessary to illustrate the applicable law problems and the effect of characterizing maritime liens and the priorities they entail as procedural for the purposes of selecting the applicable law. For a comprehensive discussion of priorities in this sphere, see Jackson, *Enforcement of Maritime Claims* (2005) ch 23.

[109] Tetley, 'Maritime Liens in the Conflict of Laws' (2002) 445.

[110] *The Sea Spray* [1907] P 133; *The Charger* [1966] 1 Lloyd's Rep 670; *The Blitz* [1992] 2 Lloyd's Rep 441.

of arrest,[111] *custodia legis*, and judicial sale; (3) 'traditional' maritime liens (arising out of salvage, collision, master's and seamen's wages and master's disbursements); (4) ship registered mortgages; (5) statutory rights *in rem* (necessaries: bunkers, repairs, supplies, towage, etc). However, questions of priority are not capable of being compartmentalized in the form of strict rules of ranking.[112]

6.54 Liens arising out of tort/delict will normally have precedence over contractual liens, but apparently rank *pari passu* among themselves.[113] Salvage is usually treated as a contractual lien, but is given a priority not only amongst contractual liens but also against damage liens if the salvage has preserved the *res*.[114]

6.55 It is within the discretionary powers of English courts to organize priorities purporting to do justice to all in the case at hand, having regard to considerations of equity and public policy. Such discretion is very broad, and judges face the difficult task of analysing the relevant authorities in the light of the particular features of each case. Thomas explains that 'the Admiralty and Appellate Courts have adopted a broad discretionary approach with rival claims ranked by reference to considerations of equity, public policy and commercial expediency, with the ultimate aim of doing that which is just in the circumstances of the case'.[115] That discretion has resulted in the advancement of multiple criteria, and as a consequence, in the 'chaos of the law of the sea governing the recognition and priority of maritime liens' that Lord Salmon and Lord Scarman mentioned in *The Halcyon Isle*.[116] However, the court's discretion is vital in this sphere and

[111] Admiralty Marshal's costs and expenses and the arrester's costs in the creation of the fund (in that order) take priority over maritime liens (Jackson, *Enforcement of Maritime Claims* (2005) 563).

[112] D Steel, J (Admlty Ct) in *The Ruta* [2000] 1 Lloyd's Rep 359.

[113] MC Meston, 'Admiralty' *Stair Memorial Encyclopaedia*, vol 1, para 413.

[114] Ibid.

[115] Thomas, *Maritime Liens* (1980) 418.

[116] [1980] 2 Lloyd's Rep 325 (PC (Sing)) 339. Nevertheless, there are several hints. First, judges have had regard to considerations such as the voluntary or involuntary nature of a lien. In that sense a damage lienee's interest should be protected first if considered against a voluntary right holder because the latter may consider all the possible risks and decide what is most advisable for his own interest where the person suffering the damage has no option (*The Aline* [1839] 1 W Rob 111). In the words of Mr Justice Gorell Barnes 'it is clear that liens arising ex delicto take precedence over prior liens arising ex contractu' (*The Veritas* [1901] P 304). Secondly, the availability of alternative security has been taken into account in several cases, to prioritize those lienees who have no other means of making good their rights (*The Aline* [1839] 1 W Rob 111; *The Chimera* [1852] 11 LT 113 (Dr Lushington); *The Linda Flor* [1857] Swab 309 (Dr Lushington); *The Duna* [1861] 5 LT 217; *The Ruta* [2000] 1 Lloyd's Rep 359 (Mr JD Steel)). Thirdly, the preservation of the fund (the *res*) has also been considered,

this book proposes a particular role for such powers in the context of the conflict of laws problems in this field later on in this chapter.[117]

By comparison, the United States has its own original ranking system which is different from the rest of the world. Under the US system the priorities in maritime claims are as follows:[118] **6.56**

(1) special legislative rights;
(2) *custodia legis* and court costs;
(3) preferred maritime liens:
   (a) wages of master and crew (including maintenance and cure),
   (b) salvage (including contract salvage) and general average (cargo against the ship)
   (c) maritime torts (eg collision), including personal injury and death, property damage, and cargo tort liens;
   (d) longshoremen (individuals, not stevedore company),
   (e) US contract maritime liens (necessaries) entered into before the filing of a US preferred mortgage. This includes repairs, supply of bunkers, supplies, stevedores, towage, contract cargo damage liens, and charterer's liens etc (and also including statutory maritime liens, eg for civil penalties);
(4) preferred US ship mortgage liens, as of the date of filing, as well as preferred ship mortgages on foreign ships whose mortgages have been guaranteed under Title XI of the Merchant Marine Act 1936;[119]
(5) US contract liens (necessaries) arising after the filing of the US preferred ship mortgage;
(6) foreign ship mortgages;
(7) US contract liens (other than necessaries) (eg contract cargo damage liens and charterers liens);
(8) unregistered mortgages and perfected non-maritime liens (including tax liens and other Government claims which are subordinate to maritime liens), state chattel mortgages and liens and liens for maritime attachment, and foreign contract liens, eg UK statutory rights *in rem*.

ie a salvage lienee should have priority as the salvage services had preserved the ship (*The Lyrma* [1978] 2 Lloyd's Rep 30 (Mr J Brandon)). Finally, considerations of public policy as well as commercial expediency have always mattered.

[117] See para 6.68 below.

[118] It must be stated that it is not possible to provide an exhaustive and definitive ranking of maritime liens in US law. This ranking of liens has been taken from Tetley, 'Maritime Liens in the Conflict of Laws' (2002) 445–6 and the reference should be understood as an illustration only of the applicable law issues involved.

[119] 46 US Code App ss 1101 *et seq* at ss 1271 *et seq*.

6.57 The problem arises if a maritime claim attracting a lien according to its governing law, being the latter US law, is to be ranked in English or Scottish courts according to the law of the forum; in those cases it is difficult to see how the policies of any of the two legal systems connected to the claim would be advanced. The solution needs to be workable, reasonable, but most importantly it needs to be fair. It is important to take into account that very often the maritime lienee is forced to enforce the security right against the ship in a certain forum, not necessarily the one he would have chosen, because another creditor has arrested and sold the ship in that particular country.[120]

Uniform Solutions: International Conventions

6.58 To solve this problem international Conventions have attempted to create a uniform framework in this field. There are three international Conventions on the topic: the 1926 International Convention for the Unification of Certain Rules Relating to Maritime Liens and Mortgages,[121] the 1967 International Convention for the Unification of Certain Rules Relating to Maritime Liens and Mortgages,[122] and the 1993 International Convention on Maritime Liens and Mortgages.[123] The 1967 Convention never entered into force. None of them has been ratified by the United Kingdom, despite the fact that the United Kingdom is a signatory of the 1926 Convention.

1926 International Convention for the Unification of Certain Rules Relating to Maritime Liens and Mortgages

6.59 The order of priorities of maritime claims is established in Article 2 of the Convention. According to it, the ranking is as follows:

(1) cost of preserving ship in *custodia legis* (eg court costs and Marshall's expenses) and judicial sale costs;
(2) immediately arising salvage and general average claims;
(3) master and crew wages;
(4) salvage and general average claims;
(5) damage and personal injury claims;

[120] Davies, 'Choice of Law and US Maritime Liens' (2009) 1435.

[121] The 1926 International Convention for the Unification of Certain Rules Relating to Maritime Liens and Mortgages (Brussels, 10 April 1926) in force since 2 June 1931.

[122] The 1967 International Convention for the Unification of Certain Rules Relating to Maritime Liens and Mortgages (Brussels, 27 May 1967).

[123] International Convention on Maritime Liens and Mortgages 1993 (Geneva, 6 May 1993). For a detailed exposition on the three international Conventions, see Jackson, *Enforcement of Maritime Claims* (2005) 509–16.

(6) master's disbursements or necessaries provided, *inter alia*, the ship is away from her home port and the contracts were necessary for the preservation of the ship or the continuation of the voyage;
(7) registered mortgages;
(8) other claims.

This Convention is the only one to recognize a lien for necessaries. In turn, Articles 5 and 6 establish that, apart from claims for salvage and general average, claims arising immediately out of the last voyage have priority over claims of the same kind arising out of earlier voyages. That is the well-known rule[124] about liens that rank *inter se* in inverse order of effectual attachment; the theory being that the latest services rendered tend to preserve the ship.[125] Many civilian countries (including, in the European Union, Belgium, Estonia, France, Hungary, Italy, Luxembourg, Poland, Portugal, Romania and, Spain[126]) are party to that Convention. **6.60**

1967 International Convention for the Unification of Certain Rules Relating to Maritime Liens and Mortgages

This Convention never entered into force. Its order of priorities is established in Article 4 of the Convention. The principal changes with respect to the previous Convention as to the creation of maritime liens are: the abolition of master's disbursement claims; the broadening of 'collision claims'; and the exclusion of claims involving nuclear activities. Maritime liens are given priority over mortgages and any other liens created by a state, and the order of priorities between maritime liens themselves is specified by Article 5 of the Convention. **6.61**

1993 International Convention on Maritime Liens and Mortgages

The latest international Convention on the issue entered into force on 5 September 2004. Basically, it maintains the structure of the previous Conventions providing for the order of ranking in its Articles 5, 6, and 7. It alters the order in the case of port dues and salvage claims, which are taken down in the first case and up in the second, and it suppresses the ship-repairer's lien (in its place Article 7 of the 1993 Maritime Liens and Mortgages Convention provides that a ship-repairer may be entitled to a **6.62**

[124] G Price, 'The Priority of Maritime Liens' (1942) 24 *Journal of Comparative Legislation and International Law* 1, 38–40; MC Meston, 'Admiralty', *The Laws of Scotland, Stair Memorial Encyclopaedia*, vol 1, 197, para 413.

[125] Asser, *Maritime Liens and Mortgages in the Conflicts of Laws* (1963) 25. This theory has been also reflected in the 1993 Maritime Liens and Mortgages Convention, Art 5(4) in relation to maritime liens securing claims for reward for the salvage of the ship.

[126] Spain is also a party to the 1993 Maritime Lien and Mortgages Convention.

right of retention (possessory lien) according to the law of the State where the ship was reconstructed or repaired).

6.63 The numbers of claims which rank above mortgages have been reduced compared to the previous Conventions in order to stimulate ship financing operations. States are allowed to create privileges for other claims in their national law, but those claims rank after claims which have been secured by a mortgage.[127]

6.64 In relation to its scope of application the 1993 Maritime Liens and Mortgages Convention establishes that the Convention should apply 'to all seagoing vessels registered in a State Party or in a State which is not a State Party, provided that the latter's vessels are subject to the jurisdiction of the State Party'.[128]

6.65 Bearing in mind that financing by means of credits granted by banks and other financial institutions became an increasingly important feature of maritime commerce; and that learned authors and national courts of all maritime nations have been trying to find a solution to this conflict of laws,[129] it is somehow puzzling that these Conventions appear to have such limited success.

The Conflicts Solution in English and Scots Law

6.66 In English and Scots law, as no uniform international Convention in this field has been adopted in these legal systems, a conflict-of-laws rule is necessary to determine which is the law governing the order of priorities of maritime claims. The settled principle under English private international law is grounded on the assumption that priorities form no part of the transaction under which a creditor has acquired his right; it is remedial—extrinsic—and therefore subject to the law of the forum.[130] It is suggested

[127] Amongst the European Union only Estonia and Spain are States party to this Convention (CMI Yearbook 2009, 551).

[128] 1993 Maritime Liens and Mortgages Convention, Art 13.

[129] Asser, *Maritime Liens and Mortgages in the Conflict of Laws* (1963) 13.

[130] *Pardo v Bingham* [1868] LR 6 Eq 485, Ct Ch; *Re Melbourn (No 1)* [1870] 6 Ch App 64, CA Ch; *Hills Dry Docks & Engineering Co Ltd v Colorado (The Colorado)* [1923] P 102, CA '... But the right of priority forms no part of the contract. It is extrinsic, and is rather a personal privilege dependent on the law of the place where the property lies, and where the Court sits which is to decide the cause' (Bankes J) at 107.

that this is an axiom that, applying Cook's thesis,[131] 'shows that some imaginary line has been arbitrarily taken as a boundary'.[132]

As expressed in 1935 by Mendelssohn,[133] the English conception of characterization of certain issues as remedial is closely knit with the whole of English private international law as a system. In the opinion of English leading commentators, the distinction between right and remedy, parallel to the distinction between substance and procedure, is an eternal truth of every system of private international law.[134] Following that, preferences depend on the law of the country where the remedy is sought.[135] **6.67**

Scottish courts will normally follow English sources in this respect, which, however, differ among themselves.[136] In the case of *Clark v Bowring & Co*[137] it was held that the law of Scotland only could be applied in determining the ranking of claims on a British ship locally situated in Scotland. The same opinion was held in *Clark and Another v Hine and Others*.[138] The latter case involved a maritime lien obtained under the law of New York which the lienees tried to make good in Scotland. The judgment stated that 'as I can only apply our own law in determining the ranking of claims on a British ship locally situated in Scotland, they must be treated as unsecured creditors of the bankrupt owner'.[139] **6.68**

The Law of the Forum 'as an Arbiter'[140]

The most understandable argument in favour of the application of the law of the forum as a conflict of laws rule for the issue of priorities is that the law of the forum provides a clear solution for the cases where different competing rights in security, created under different legal systems, seek to be enforced against the sale proceeds of the same *res*. As already mentioned, the law of the forum approach is surely the simplest solution, **6.69**

[131] WW Cook, '"Substance" and "Procedure" in the Conflict of Laws' (1933) 42 *Yale Law Journal* 333.

[132] GN Lewis, *The Anatomy of Science* (1926) referred by Cook, ' "Substance" and "Procedure" in the Conflict of Laws' (1933) 333.

[133] A Mendelssohn Bartholdy, 'Delimitation of Right and Remedy in the Cases of Conflict of Laws' (1935) *The British Yearbook of International Law* 20, 23.

[134] Fawcett and Carruthers, *Chesire, North & Fawcett, Private International Law* (2008) 75.

[135] Ibid.

[136] Scottish Law Commission, *Report on Diligence on the Dependence and Admiralty Arrestments* (Scot Law Com No 164, March 1998) 176.

[137] 1908 SC 1168.

[138] (1908) 15 SLT 914, OH.

[139] Lord Salvesen at 915.

[140] Jackson, *Enforcement of Maritime Claims* (2005) 683.

but is it the only workable one? Is it reasonable? Is it the fairest? It is here submitted that the answer to the last three questions is 'no'. The traditional law of the forum approach hardly advances the legal validity of the substantive rights across national borders, ie the juridical continuity of legal relations internationally and, furthermore, it enhances the undesirable consequences of 'forum shopping'.[141]

6.70 On the one hand, when the governing law of the competing rights is the same or where even if they are different they lead to the same result, there is no justification for applying the order of priorities of the law of the forum.[142] On the other hand, even in the cases where there is a real conflict because of differences in the ranking of the relevant governing laws, the priorities should be organized to try to accommodate the ranking of the different legal systems significantly connected to the case according to their respective underlying policies.[143] Otherwise, '... the policies, purposes, and values embodied in a state's law can be adversely affected when that law is not applied to a case the law was intended to reach'.[144] Thus, it is suggested that flexibility in this sphere is preferable to an uncritical allocation of the issue of priorities to the law of the forum. As recognized by leading British private international law academics, '[n]either justice nor convenience is promoted by rigid adherence to any one principle; it is preferable that the various principles should fit the needs of the different legal relations ...'.[145]

[141] Already in the early 1900s pursuers/claimants and also defenders/defendants considered where to litigate in terms of the impact of the applicable law to the possible outcome. In *Clark and Another v Hine and Others* (1908) it was considered that '... the defenders have an obvious interest in resisting a judicial sale, for if the vessel was to go to an American port they would be able to enforce their alleged lien against her there ...' (L Salvesen, 915). Later on in the 1920s, when still 'forum shopping' was far from being named as such, claimants considered their possibilities in such terms, as a result of the application of the law of the forum to the order of priorities, instead of the governing law. See *The Colorado* (1923) 14 Lloyd's Law Rep 251 (CA). 'The repairers evidently thought now that they would have been better off if instead of bringing their action in England they had allowed the ship to proceed to her home port in France and had instituted an action there' at p 252.

[142] See Jackson, *Enforcement of Maritime Claims* (2005) 682. See also Crawford and Carruthers, *International Private Law in Scotland* (2006) 201 '... [t]here is room for a little unease here. If all claims arise under the same law, perhaps the forum should defer to that law ...'.

[143] In English private international law 'regard will be had to the policy objectives of choice of law rules', see Fawcett and Carruthers, *Chesire, North & Fawcett, Private International Law* (2008) 37.

[144] Symeonides, 'The American Revolution and the European Evolution in Choice of Law: Reciprocal Lessons' (2008) 82 *Tulane Law Review* 5, 1787.

[145] Fawcett and Carruthers, *Chesire, North & Fawcett, Private International Law* (2008) 37.

6.71 The suggestion of Jackson,[146] that the law of the forum has a claim to govern only as an arbiter, applies to this kind of situation. As mentioned earlier in this chapter,[147] courts have discretionary powers in the adjudication of priorities and this is vital for the ends of justice in the context of the conflict of laws problems being discussed. These discretionary powers could be used in determining the conflict of laws in this sphere to balance the interests of not only the private parties to the claim but also the policies underpinning the different applicable laws that are substantially connected to the claim.[148] That is, trying to accommodate foreign and forum policies as much as possible in accord with the expectations of the parties for the interest of justice. The contention that this proposal would affect certainty and predictability, such valuable concepts for commercial parties,[149] should not be overestimated. English courts have praised themselves for being readily concerned with the fair and just result of the case at hand rather than with certainty and predictability as abstract values.[150] The type of situation described in the previous paragraphs provides a further opportunity to continue to adopt that attitude with a view to favour a good overall management of the case.

6.72 The traditional fragmented approach to the characterization of maritime liens, and its division into right and remedy for the sake of applicable law issues connected to them, favoured by the majority,[151] has various downsides. It can lead to bizarre results, such as the outcome in *The Atlantis Two*.[152]

[146] Jackson, *Enforcement of Maritime Claims* (2005) 683.

[147] See para 6.52 above.

[148] Symeonides is of the opinion that 'an analysis that fails to take into account the adverse consequences of a choice-of-law decision on state interests is presumptively deficient', Symeonides, 'The American Revolution and the European Evolution in Choice of Law: Reciprocal Lessons' (2008) 1788.

[149] Certainty and predictability are also core values in the process of Europeanization of private international law and the European rules on applicable law as well as the case law of the European Court of Justice in the field of private international law have always emphasized these values.

[150] See Fawcett and Carruthers, *Chesire, North & Fawcett, Private International Law* (2008) 37: 'The instinct of the English lawyer is to test a proposed rule by its practical bearing on normal human activities and expectations. It is by this method that in his opinion the purpose of law, which at bottom is to promote justice and convenience can best be furthered. He is nothing if not an empiricist and a pragmatist.'

[151] It has to be recognized that most legal systems, even those recognizing the substantive nature of a maritime lien—such as US and Canadian law—distinguish between the lien (the substantive right, therefore governed by the governing law) and the priority it entails (a procedural remedy, thus established according to the law of the forum). Commenting on US law, Davies considers the connection between the existence of the maritime lien and the governing law as axiomatic (Davies, 'Choice of Law and US Maritime Liens' (2009) 1438).

[152] [1999] 170 FTR 1.

In that case the courts of Vancouver recognized a US maritime lien in favour of a sub-charterer for breach of the charter-party. The court further recognized that if the priorities were to be determined according to the governing law, the sub-charterer's lien would rank behind the prior registered mortgage. However, the court held that priorities were to be determined according to the law of the forum, and under Canadian law the maritime lien of the sub-charterer ranked ahead of the mortgagee. Hence, the sub-charterer received a higher priority in Canada, according to its law of the forum, than it would have received under the governing law.

6.73 A similar situation (with a similar outcome) was faced by Hill J in *The Colorado*[153] in the 1920s, affirmed by the Court of Appeal.[154] In that case, applying the law of the forum to the order of priorities led to the foreign claimant being benefited in a way that he would have not if the issue was submitted to the governing law, since according to English law (the law of the forum), the mortgagee had priority over the necessaries men. Hill J decided, via characterization of the French mortgage based on the law of the forum, that the French mortgagee was to rank with priority over the ship-repairers of Cardiff. Yet, by French law the rights of the mortgagee were of quite a different character compared to the ones of an English mortgagee (the Court of Appeal assimilated them to the rights of a maritime lien holder). The French mortgagee under French law had no right to take possession or to sell the ship, and his rights were postponed to those of the necessaries men. Hence, these cases show that the law of the forum as a conflicts rule, even when it is a simple and workable solution for the issue of priorities, does not fulfil the ends of justice and severely affects the legal validity of substantive rights across frontiers, somehow disregarding the main purpose of any private international law system.

The law of the flag approach

6.74 Traditionally the law of the flag has enjoyed a particular status in private international law issues of a maritime nature. Due to the particular kind of *res* that a ship constitutes, it can be assimilated to the law of the domicile of a person or to the law of the incorporation in the case of a company. There are various examples in comparative law of the application of the law of the flag as the conflict of laws rule that determines the applicable law to maritime liens in national legal systems.[155]

[153] (1922) 13 Lloyd's Law Rep 474.

[154] (1923) 14 Lloyd's Law Rep 251, CA.

[155] Amongst them is the Netherlands 1993 Conflict of Maritime Laws Act, Art 3(2); see W Tetley, *International Conflict of Laws: Common, Civil and Maritime* (Montreal, Blais, 1994) 1069. According to it the law of the ship's registry (flag) governs the question of whether a maritime claim is protected by a lien, as well as the scope and consequences of such a lien,

In the latest international Convention on Maritime Liens and Mortgages[156] the law of the ship's place of registration governs the ranking of registered mortgages, 'hypothecques', or charges as between themselves and, without prejudice to the provisions of the Convention, their effect with regard to third parties. As such securities are effective only if they comply with the law of the place of registration of the ship, the conflict of laws rule in order to assert the law applicable to their recognition and to the ranking between themselves is perfectly coherent. However, this strong connection with the law of the flag existing in the case of registered securities is missing in the case of maritime liens that are *per se* non-registrable.[157] **6.75**

Following that, why should the law of the flag be more decisive than the law of the place where the contract was made if the maritime lien attaches to a contractual claim; or the law of the place where the tort/delict was committed if the maritime lien originated in tort/delict? The answer is not **6.76**

except for the ranking which is subjected to The Netherlands law. Another example is Art 9 of the 1958 Greek Code of Private Maritime Law which requires that the law of the ship's flag determine everything related to proprietary rights over ships. Interestingly, and differently from the case of The Netherlands, this provision has been interpreted by commentators as governing not only the recognition of the existence of the foreign lien but also the ranking of foreign maritime claims; see AM Antapassis, *Les Codes maritimes Grecs* (Paris, Librairie Générale, 1983) 114. See the text in English by TB Karatzas and NP Ready, *The Greek Code of Private Maritime Law* (The Hague, Martinus Nijhoff, 1982) 6. A third example is the Swedish Maritime Code 1994 (similar codes were adopted the same year by Denmark, Finland, and Norway) according to which Swedish law governs maritime liens on Swedish-registered ships when the lien or right is invoked in Sweden (Swedish Maritime Code, ch 3, s 51) (see the Swedish and English text (Stockholm, Juristförlaget, 1995)); in the case of foreign ships the effect of a maritime lien is determined by the law of the ship's registry. As far as priorities, foreign maritime liens rank after any maritime lien or right of retention provided for in ch 3 of the Code, and after any hypothec (ship mortgage). The order of priorities in that ch 3 complies generally with the Maritime Liens and Mortgages Convention 1967 (that never entered into force). Furthermore, the Maritime Procedure Code of Panama provides for a conflict of law rule that establishes that in the case of maritime liens the applicable substantive law is that of the flag of the ship's registry (Tetley, *International Conflict of Laws* (1994) 175–224). This rule received consideration in English jurisprudence in *Berliner Bank AG v C Czarnikow Sugar Ltd (The Rama)* [1996] 2 Lloyd's Rep 281, QBD (Admlty).

[156] International Convention on Maritime Liens and Mortgages 1993 (Geneva, 6 May 1993) in force since 5 September 2004.

[157] As far as the registrable character of arrest as such, the Maritime Liens and Mortgages Conventions are silent; the issue is left to national law. For example, in French law, Art 93 of the decree of 27 October 1967 provides that the arrest (*saisie*) is not effective *vis-à-vis* third parties prior to its registration in a special register (see *Ste Transunt v Baudoin Lefevre and Others (The Patrick Victor)* [1982] DMF 420). However, R Rodière in *Le Navire* (Paris, Dalloz, 1980) 255 states that the arrest of ships when granted as a provisional measure (*saisie conservatoire*) is not registrable; Berlingieri disapproves of that interpretation (Berlingieri, *Arrest of Ships* (2006) 133). In Spain and Italy the arrest of ships (*embargo preventivo/secuestro conservativo*) is also registrable.

connected only to the law applicable to the existence of maritime liens but it is also connected to the issue of priorities of maritime claims. Hence, it is necessary to approach these two faces of the same coin coherently and cohesively.

6.77 The benefits of the law of the flag as the relevant '"adjudicating" law'[158] is that it provides one foreseeable answer for the frequent cases where there is a question of priority between two contractual liens, and these proprietary interests are subject to different governing laws, which in turn produce different results in terms of the final outcome. This position is supported by a large tradition of commentators, that despite different justifications, see in the selection of the law of the flag a conflicts rule that tends towards the greatest uniformity, and finally that is the most equitable to creditors who can foresee the applicable law to which their lien will be subject.[159] It is indeed difficult to find a counter-argument for such a proposition since this conflict rule is the only one in this sphere that could provide uniformity of decision. That is why, following the internationally accepted link between a ship and the country of her flag for registered securities, it has been strongly argued that all issues of property in a ship should be referred to the law of the flag—unless, of course, an international Convention such as the 1993 Maritime Liens and Mortgages Convention applies to the case.[160]

6.78 Nevertheless, looking at the reality of ship registration systems, and bearing in mind that many ships nowadays fly flags of convenience,[161] adopting such a connecting factor could be regarded as anachronistic and the fear is that, even when providing uniformity and foreseeability, applicable law issues connected to maritime liens could end up being governed by the law of a legal system totally unconnected to the case. Frequently there is no significant connection between the country of registry and the owners, operators, and insurers of ships.[162]

[158] Jackson, *Enforcement of Maritime Claims* (2005) 718.

[159] Nonetheless, this theory has been rarely followed in judicial practice (Asser, *Maritime Liens and Mortgages in the Conflicts of Laws* (1963) 16).

[160] Jackson, *Enforcement of Maritime Claims* (2005) 718, para 26.179.

[161] A ship is said to be flying a flag of convenience (FOC) when it flies the flag of a country other than the country of ownership. There are various factors that could motivate a shipowner's decision to 'flag out'. However, it is generally understood that there should be a genuine link between the real owner of a ship and the flag that she flies. On flags of convenience, see HE Anderson, 'The Nationality of Ships and Flags of Convenience: Economics, Politics, and Alternatives' (1996) 21 *Tulane Maritime Law Journal* 139.

[162] On the law of the flag generally in conflicts of maritime law, see W Tetley, *International Conflict of Laws: Common, Civil and Maritime* (Montreal, Blais, 1994) 175–224.

In summary, it has to be assumed rather than circumvented that conflict-of-laws rules in this sphere are unable to provide a simple and fair solution hence an international uniform solution imposes itself. Yet again, the international harmonization efforts have not really succeeded in this complex area of the law. **6.79**

V. THE ROLE OF THE SECURITY FUNCTION OF ARREST OF SHIPS IN THE RANKING OF MARITIME CLAIMS

In contrast to the issue of priorities, the effect of the security function of arrest of ships in the ranking of maritime claims is a matter inherently procedural, therefore, to be governed by the law of the forum, unless there was international unification of procedural rules in this regard. **6.80**

1. International Conventions

The 1952 International Arrest Convention deals with the right to arrest but, apart from the declaration that nothing in the Convention creates a right of action, it is silent as to the consequences of the arrest on the property rights of persons interested in the ship.[163] The 1999 International Arrest Convention limits the right to arrest in certain circumstances to claims that can be enforced against the ship by judicial sale,[164] in that sense connecting the provisional and security functions of the arrest of a ship and establishing somehow that the arrest itself is a means of securing the claim. In turn, the Maritime Liens and Mortgages Conventions of 1926, 1967, and 1993 deal with maritime liens and rights of retention; they refer to arrest only in the context of maritime liens and mortgages, and assume that such causes of action carry with it the right to arrest; however, they do not deal with the right in security created by the arrest as such. **6.81**

During the preparation of the 1952 International Arrest Convention the French and the British delegates at the Diplomatic Conference expressly objected to create a link between this Convention and the 1926 Maritime Liens and Mortgages Convention, and attempts to move forward in the discussion of this issue were unsuccessful.[165] A new opportunity arose in the preparatory work undertaken pursuant to the 1999 International **6.82**

[163] Jackson, *Enforcement of Maritime Claims* (2005) 402.

[164] Article 3(3) International Convention on the Arrest of Ships 1999.

[165] The *travaux préparatoires* of the International Convention for the Unification of Certain Rules Relating to the Arrest of Sea-Going Ships 10 May 1952 (CMI 1997).

Arrest Convention where, even though account was taken of the fact that in some countries an arrest not only prevents the physical removal of the ship but also results in a prohibition against disposal of the ship by sale or otherwise, the Conference still did not find it reasonable to include such a requirement in the definition of arrest.[166]

6.83 It is indeed regrettable that currently the international Arrest Conventions and the Maritime Liens and Mortgages Conventions do not enhance one another in this sphere.[167] The present state of affairs of 'chaotic inconsequence' in this area of the law[168] would certainly improve if it was possible to rely on coherent and consistent international standards for the different aspects of the international enforcement of maritime claims.

2. English Law

6.84 In English domestic law the priority afforded by the *in rem* claim, or the right to proceed[169] *in rem*, depends on the nature of the cause of action, eg whether it encumbers a maritime lien, or a mere statutory right *in rem*, or derives from a mortgage or other charge of the same nature; it depends on the nature of the substantive right, as outlined below.

Arrest *in rem* to Enforce Maritime liens

6.85 When ship arrest is granted to enforce a maritime lien the priority derives from the maritime lien and not from the arrest; this means that once the ship is arrested, the security function goes back in time to the moment where the lien attached, namely the moment the cause of action originated.

[166] The *travaux préparatoires* of the 1999 International Arrest Convention (F Berlingieri, *Arrest of Ships* (2006) 526–8) (Report of the CMI on Art 1(2), para 29).

[167] In fact, when the 1952 International Arrest Convention entered into force more than 50 years ago, it did enhance the 1926 Maritime Liens and Mortgages Convention by filling the gap the latter left in the enforcement of liens and mortgages; see JM Kriz 'Ship Mortgages, Maritime Liens, and Their Enforcement: The Brussels Conventions of 1926 and 1952. Part Two' (1964) 1 *Duke Law Journal* 70.

[168] In *The Halcyon Isle* [1980] 2 Lloyd's Rep 325 the dissenting opinion held that private international law had an important role to play in 'the present chaos of the law of the sea governing the recognition and priority of maritime liens and mortgages' (Lord Salmon and Lord Scarman 339).

[169] Very often this right to proceed *in rem*, ie this procedural right, is mentioned as 'this right *in rem*', confusing the procedural nature of quasi *in rem* actions with the substantive feature of rights *in rem*.

Arrest *in rem* to Enforce Statutory Rights *in rem*

So far as the statutory rights *in rem* are concerned, the security effect crystallizes on the property from the time of the issue of the *in rem* claim form. This was established in *The Monica S*[170] where Brandon J pointed that 'It seems to me that it would be strange if a statutory right of action *in rem* only become effective, as against a subsequent change of ownership of the res, upon arrest of the res, and yet, by the same statute, as conferred the right of action, arrest was in many cases prohibited.'[171] It has been argued that policy considerations must have been determinant in this decision, which has remained unchallenged since 1967.[172] **6.86**

Consequently, it seems that in English law the position of a secured creditor in relation to maritime claims not secured by a maritime lien arise from the issuance of an *in rem* claim form and not from arrest. However, this was not always the case. In *The Henrich Bjorn*,[173] the charge created upon the ship based on 'statutory liens' (right to proceed *in rem*) in favour of the claimant, was held to accrue from the time of the arrest of the ship. Nonetheless, in present times it is the issuance of an *in rem* claim form (and not the effectual arrest) that creates a security which cannot be defeated by insolvency and is available only for maritime claims.[174] It will only be defeated by a maritime claim having greater priority.[175] In that sense, arrest does not create a right in security as defined earlier in this chapter, at least not a right that is distinct from, and in addition to, the right of action. **6.87**

3. Scots Law

In Scots law the latest statutory enactment relating to Admiralty actions and the arrestment of ships provides for a general rule of ranking of arrestments on the sale of a ship chartered by demise[176] and specific rules of **6.88**

[170] [1967] 2 Lloyd's Rep 113 (PDAD).

[171] Ibid at 131.

[172] A Mandaraka-Sheppard, *Modern Maritime Law and Risk Management* (2nd edn, London, Informa, 2009) 71–2.

[173] *The Northcote v Owners of the Henrich Bjorn (The Henrich Bjorn)* (1885) LR 10 PD 44 (CA).

[174] This is to be contrasted with the obtaining of security by means of a freezing order (formerly *Mareva* injunction) in English law. A freezing order does not create *nexus* (in Scots law terms), merely preserves a fund against which execution may be taken which in fact is liable to be defeated by insolvency process or by a prior execution creditor.

[175] N Meeson, *Admiralty Jurisdiction and Practice* (3rd edn, London, LLP, 2003) 17.

[176] Bankruptcy and Diligence etc (Scotland) Act 2007, asp 3 (Scottish Act), Sch 4 Modifications and Enactments relating to Admiralty Actions and the Arrestment of Ships, s 47F.

ranking if a ship is arrested on the dependence of an Admiralty action against the demise charterer of the ship and after the arrestment the owner of the ship's estate is sequestrated or it is wound up (if the owner is a company).[177] The general rule provided for in this enactment establishes that in any ranking process relating to the proceeds of sale of a ship, an arrestment of the ship executed before the sale by a creditor of the owner of the ship shall rank in preference over any arrestment of the ship executed on the dependence of an Admiralty action against the demise charterer of the ship.[178]

6.89 Furthermore, some insight may be thrown into the particular effects of arrestment of ships from the general law of diligence as analysed in the following paragraphs.

Litigiosity[179] and *Nexus* in Scots Law

6.90 There have been two approaches to the effects of arrestment in general in Scots law: the prohibition theory and the attachment theory.[180] These theories can be easily applied to the arrestment of ships in Scots law and to the arrest of ships as an institution more broadly. The prohibition theory considers arrestment as a mere prohibition upon the arrestee from parting with the arrested subject (and in that sense coinciding with the nature of arrest as understood by Herbert, Fresnedo, and Aguirre[181]). In turn, the attachment theory regards arrestment as being not only a prohibition but also laying a *nexus* (right in security) on the subject arrested (thus constituting an *embargo* in the opinion of the authors mentioned above).

[177] s 47 G, Bankruptcy and Diligence etc (Scotland) Act 2007, Sch 4.

[178] s 47 F, Bankruptcy and Diligence etc (Scotland) Act 2007, Sch 4.

[179] Litigiosity in Scots law refers to a tacit prohibition of alienation to the disappointment of an action, or of diligence, the direct object of which is to obtain possession, or to acquire the property of a particular subject, or to attach it in security of debt. It has to be borne in mind that the principle of litigiosity in this sphere of Scots law may be undergoing reconsideration; notably, the 'fictional litigiosity theory' as understood by Erskine (Institute 111, 6, 19) has been severely rejected by the Scottish Law Commission in its *Report on Diligence on the Dependence and Admiralty Arrestments* (Scot Law Com No 164 (1998) 187, para 9.23). There the Scottish Law Commission argued that '... the fictional litigiosity theory of the arrester's preference should be abandoned and replaced by properly formulated principles. In our view however it would be preferable if this result were to be achieved by judicial development of the law rather than by legislation ...'. Litigiosity was then considered as an out-of-date doctrine in the sense that it represents a 'mere personal prohibition against the arrestee parting with the arrested property having no effect in competitions with third parties' (ibid, 184, para 9.14).

[180] GL Gretton,'Diligence', *The Laws of Scotland, Stair Memorial Encyclopaedia*, vol 8, para 285.

[181] For the analysis of these authors see paras 6.12–6.14 above.

In the case of arrestment of ships this *nexus* is a *nexus realis*,[182] ie a *jus in re aliena* (a right acquired by one over a thing belonging to another).[183]

6.91 As Gretton explains, from the times of Stair these theories have been in the field of diligence in Scots law producing inconsistent *dicta*; some decisions reflect one theory, some the other.[184] As a consequence, there is no settled conceptual framework in which the law can be developed.[185] Seemingly, the attachment theory has gained more acceptance; the particular rules which depend on the prohibition theory are currently regarded as inconsistent.[186]

6.92 In terms of specific effects both theories agree that arrestment results in *litigiosity*; but the prohibition theory holds that arrestment does not lay a nexus in addition to *litigiosity*.[187] Bell, when considering the effects of arrestment in security more generally, called it an 'embargo upon a man's floating capital, his goods and his money';[188] that could be interpreted as arrestment creating not only *litigiosity* but also *nexus*.[189] Hence, it seems that in modern Scots law arrestment as a form of diligence, excluding thus arrestment to found jurisdiction, creates a *nexus* (attachment[190]) which

[182] Dicta have not been consistent to answer the question whether arrestment gives rise to a *nexus realis*. For an affirmative answer see *Inglis v Robertson and Baxter* [1898] 25 R, 70 at 73 (HL) per Lord Watson. On the contrary view, Stewart's statement that arrestment of itself gives no real right (p 125) sits uneasily with his advocacy of the attachment theory; following Stewart, arrestment has been held to give no real right in several Scottish dicta; see Gretton, 'Diligence', *The Laws of Scotland, Stair Memorial Encyclopaedia*, vol 8, para 285.

[183] [1897] *The Ripon City* P 226 per Gorell Barnes J (242).

[184] Gretton, 'Diligence', *The Laws of Scotland, Stair Memorial Encyclopaedia*, vol 8, para 285.

[185] Gretton argues that 'In the whole law of diligence, this failure to develop a coherent doctrine as to the effect of arrestment is probably the most remarkable and most inexcusable. The fault is perhaps lightened by being spread over many centuries' (Gretton, 'Diligence', *The Laws of Scotland, Stair Memorial Encyclopaedia*, vol 8, para 285).

[186] Gretton, ibid.

[187] Ibid.

[188] GJ Bell, *Commentaries on the Law of Scotland and on the Principles of Mercantile Jurisprudence*, vol 2 (7th edn, Edinburgh, T&T Clark, 1870; reprint Edinburgh, Butterworths, 1990) 66.

[189] Gretton, 'Diligence', *The Laws of Scotland, Stair Memorial Encyclopaedia*, vol 8, para 116.

[190] AJ Sim, 'The Receiver and Effectually Executed Diligence' (1984) *Scots Law Times* (News) 25 '... in modern Scots law ... the orthodox view has been that an arrestment effects a true attachment—and so can be regarded as a diligence executed on property—with certain important and defined effects which cannot be explained on the principle of litigiosity ...' (at 28). Notwithstanding, the principle of litigiosity is still being used by Scottish courts; see *Iona Hotels Ltd v Craig* 1990 SC 330, IH (1 Div) 334–6, arguably, in the opinion of the Scottish Law Commission, failing to take account of the way in which the law on the effect of arrestments has developed since the eighteenth century (Scot Law Com No 164 (1998) 184, para 9.17).

gives a preference to the creditor over acts of the debtor and of the competing creditor.[191]

Arrestment on the dependence in an Admiralty action in personam

6.93 According to the foregoing discussion on the effects of arrestment in the general law of diligence, an arrestment of a ship on the dependence creates a preference for the arrester which will be recognized and enforced in subsequent rankings of creditors. Seemingly ranking after 'traditional' maritime hypothecs and ship mortgages even though there are no modern authorities.[192]

Arrestment *in rem* in an Admiralty action *in rem* to enforce a maritime lien

6.94 As well as in English law, when a warrant of arrestment is obtained in order to enforce a maritime lien, it is the maritime lien (in Scots law terms, hypothec) that constitutes the security and not the arrestment as such.

Arrestment *in rem* in an Admiralty action in personam to enforce a statutory right *in rem*

6.95 The arrestment *in rem*[193] under a cause of action listed in section 47(2), paragraphs (p)–(s) of the Administration of Justice Act 1956 (non-pecuniary claims) does not have any effect on the ranking of creditors, or in competition with bona fide purchasers or mortgagees, or generally on the substantive rights of parties, other than rights to interim possession.[194]

Arrestment to found jurisdiction

6.96 The arrestment to found jurisdiction creates no *nexus* with the ship arrested. Thus, no security function is ever displayed by this kind of arrestment alone.

[191] Scot Law Com No 164 (1998) 186. Note, however, the position of Gretton who considers that viewing arrestment as an attachment rather than a mere prohibition is not always true (Gretton, 'Diligence', *The Laws of Scotland, Stair Memorial Encyclopaedia*, vol 8, para 286). Arrestment to found jurisdiction is indeed an example of an arrestment that it is not an attachment.

[192] Lowe, 'Maritime Securities', *The Laws of Scotland, Stair Memorial Encyclopaedia*, vol 20, paras 273–315.

[193] According to s 47(3)(b) the arrestment is *in rem* if the result of the cause of action in (p)–(s) of s 47(2) is non-pecuniary.

[194] Scot Law Com No 164 (1998) 131.

That is the reason why it is usually applied for together with a warrant for arrestment on the dependence.

VI. AT THE CROSSROADS: SUBSTANCE/PROCEDURE AND RIGHT/REMEDY IN PRIVATE INTERNATIONAL LAW

The decision as to where to draw the line between substance and procedure, and right and remedy in a certain legal system, is to decide on how far to take the law of the forum approach within it. In most systems of private international law there is an axiomatic rule: procedural issues are governed by the law of the forum whereas substantive matters are subject to the governing law. It has been proclaimed as 'the most inveterate doctrine of the conflict of laws'.[195] But when it comes to the point where it is necessary to decide what is procedure or remedy, as opposed to substance or right, things become doubtful and subject to 'acrimonious controversy'.[196] **6.97**

The distinction became established in medieval times. In the thirteenth century in a case before Parisian courts, the defendant alleged an excuse for non-appearance purporting that the 'custom of Normandy' allowed it. However, the defence was rejected on the ground that the matter was procedural (*de processu causae*) and was therefore governed by the law of the forum.[197] The following century the post-glossators, Bartolus and Baldus, **6.98**

[195] EH Ailes, 'Substance and Procedure in the Conflict of Laws' (1940–41) 39 *Michigan Law Review* 392 '... It is perhaps the most inveterate doctrine of the conflict of laws that all questions of procedure in a given instance are governed by the law of the forum, or the law of the court invoked, regardless of the law under which the substantive rights of the parties accrued. For seven centuries, at least, courts and lawyers have broadly stated or assumed to be axiomatic the rule that substantive rights are fixed and immutable whilst the procedural devices by which such rights may be vindicated and enforced depend solely upon the law of the forum'.

[196] Mendelssohn Bartholdy, 'Delimitation of Right and Remedy in the Cases of Conflict of Laws' (1935) 33. The distinction between substance and procedure within private international law has been the object of numerous studies since the early twentieth century until present times. See, eg, Cook, '"Substance" and "Procedure" in the Conflict of Laws' (1933) 333; Ailes, 'Substance and Procedure in the Conflict of Laws' (1940–41) 39 *Michigan Law Review* 392; JM Carruthers, 'Substance and Procedure in the Conflict of Laws: A Continuing Debate in Relation to Damages' (2004) 53 ICLQ 691; G Panagopoulos, 'Substance and Procedure in Private International Law' (2005) 1 *Journal of Private International Law* 69.

[197] [1265] Les Olim, I, Ed Beugnot, 1839, 630 as cited by Ailes, 'Substance and Procedure in the Conflict of Laws' (1940–41) 397.

clearly laid down the same distinction.[198] Following them the forthcoming centuries took the rule as a settled axiom.

6.99 The rule has been of particular influence in common law systems, notably in English private international law. In 1896 Dicey expressed that '... English lawyers give the widest possible extension to the meaning of the term "procedure". The expression as interpreted by our judges includes all legal remedies, and everything connected with the enforcement of a right'.[199] Arguably, the rationale behind such an expansive notion of procedure is that in English law this rule operates as an 'escape device'[200] in terms of the functioning of private international law, thus, helping courts to achieve a fair judgment.[201] Yet, the line between substance and procedure has been consistently drawn to avoid the impact of foreign law.[202]

6.100 Cook explained the issue in the following terms:

> if we admit that the 'substantive' shades off by imperceptible degrees into the 'procedural', and that the 'line' between them does not 'exist', to be discovered merely by logic and analysis, but is rather to be drawn as best to carry out our purpose, we see that our problem resolves itself substantially into this: How far can the court of the forum go in applying the rules taken from the foreign system of law without unduly hindering or inconveniencing itself?[203]

In this respect Arden LJ confirmed that '... when in the conflict of laws, the court says that a particular issue is one of procedure rather than substance, the court is really saying that it cannot, for whatever reason, apply the relevant foreign law to that issue'.[204]

6.101 This approach has been repeatedly criticized. Lorenzen,[205] in a letter written to Ailes in 1929, concluded that the terms 'substance' and 'procedure' have

[198] Bartolus de Saxoferrato (1313–57), *Commentarius in Codicem Iustinianum: 'de summa trinitate' glossa 'quod si Bononiensis'* (Lyon 1521). His writings have been translated into English by JH Beale, *A Treatise on the Conflict of Laws*, vol 1 (Cambridge, MA, Harvard University Press, 1916). For Baldus de Ubaldis (1327–1400), disciple of Bartolus, see A Lainé, *Introduction au Droit International Privé*, vol 1 (Paris, F Pichon, 1888/92) 121.

[199] AV Dicey, *A Digest of the Law of England with Reference to the Conflict of Laws* (London, Stevens, 1896) 712.

[200] This term is meant to point to private international law 'tools' such as the use of *renvoi* or the application of the exception of *ordre public*, amongst others.

[201] In *Chaplin v Boys* [1969] 2 Lloyd's Rep 487 (HL) the 'substance and procedure rule' was described as a tool which '... in skilful hands ... can be powerful and effective' (Lord Wilberforce).

[202] As for a relatively recent example, even if outside international shipping litigation, see *Harding v Wealands* [2006] UKHL 32, [2006] All ER (D) 40.

[203] Cook, '"Substance" and "Procedure" in the Conflict of Laws' (1933) 343–4.

[204] *Harding v Wealands* [2005] 1 All ER 415, 437.

[205] EG Lorenzen (ed), *Cases on Conflict of Laws* (St Paul, West Publishing, 1937).

no inherent meaning and that, for the purposes of conflict of laws, the only issue that matters is that the created rights are enforced in every court. He admitted only two exceptions to this main rule: when the local judicial machinery would be obstructed thereby (for inherently procedural matters), or if the enforcement or recognition of such rights 'would be shocking to the local community'[206] (*ordre public* exception). On the same line, Chamberlayne went further expressing that '... the distinction between substantive and procedural law is artificial and illusory. In essence, there is none. The remedy and the predetermined machinery, so far as the litigant has a recognized claim to use it, are legally speaking, part of the right itself ... '.[207]

Scottish courts have been more restrictive with the 'substance and procedure' device;[208] arguably, showing the internationalist spirit that has characterized Scots international private law. In present times Carruthers[209] puts the issue under discussion in terms of self-restraint and self-promotion of the forum, arguing in favour of the former '... for the whole foundation of the conflict of laws requires that a court should restrict the field of its own procedure and be prepared to follow as far as possible the foreign substantive law ...'.[210] **6.102**

The modern doctrinal approach (as opposed to the jurisprudential one),[211] thus, is to ascribe a natural meaning to the terms substance and procedure,[212] limiting the scope of 'procedural' to those issues strictly necessary to conduct court proceedings.[213] In Panagopoulos' words, 'matters of procedure are concerned with manners, whereas matters of substance are concerned **6.103**

[206] Ailes, 'Substance and Procedure in the Conflict of Laws' (1940–41).

[207] CF Chamberlayne, AW Blakemore, and DC Moore, *Handbook on the Law of Evidence* (Albany, NY, M Bender, 1919) 171, 1911 as cited by Ailes, 'Substance and Procedure in the Conflict of Laws' (1940–41) 394.

[208] AE Anton, *Private International Law* (Edinburgh, Green, 1967) 542; AE Anton and P Beaumont, *Private International Law* (2nd edn, Edinburgh, Green, 1990) 743. In the latter (1990) it was '... not as yet clear how far this approach will be developed ...' (743).

[209] Carruthers, 'Substance and Procedure in the Conflict of Laws: A Continuing Debate in Relation to Damages' (2004) '... Self-promotion on the part of any forum foments reluctance to concede that foreign rules are substantive, and encourage litigants to indulge in the vice of forum shopping. Self-restraint, on the other hand, fosters willingness to characterize foreign rules as substantive and, in turn, to apply those rules unless to do so would be impractical or impossible or offensive to the forum's public policy ...' (710).

[210] AH Robertson, *Characterization in the Conflict of Laws* (Cambridge, MA, Harvard University Press, 1950) 247 as cited by Carruthers, 'Substance and Procedure in the Conflict of Laws: A Continuing Debate in relation to Damages' (2004) 695.

[211] *Harding v Wealands* [2006] UKHL 32.

[212] Panagopoulos, 'Substance and Procedure in Private International Law' (2005) 70.

[213] [1991] *McKain v Miller* 174 CLR 1, 27 (HCA) per Mason CJ.

with matters'.[214] Doubtless, the original rationale behind the distinction, and its consequential rule that procedural matters are governed by the law of the forum, is to 'avoid imposing upon a court foreign legal machinery with which it is unfamiliar'.[215] Since under this modern approach the scope of 'procedural' is therefore reduced to a considerable extent, specific areas have been the object of recent development (eg in the sphere of limitation of actions, considered as a 'prelude of things to come'[216]) and some other areas, such as the field of remedies, are presently being tested.[217]

6.104 Surprisingly, the distinction between right and remedy in private international law has not deserved the same scholarly attention as its corollary, substance and procedure, despite its relevancy as far as characterization is concerned. After Mendelssohn Bartholdy's[218] analysis in 1935, which is actually more concerned with characterization (qualification), there is hardly any other well-known study of the topic. However, some studies devoted to the analysis of the distinction between substance and procedure in private international law give consideration to this issue.[219] Notably, the question appears repeatedly in case-law.[220]

6.105 Traditionally, there have been two main approaches: the 'traditionalist' and the 'realist'. For the traditionalist the difference is axiomatic, and is seen as a useful device for the administration of justice; by contrast, for the realist the distinction is not well grounded, and in some cases is even inconvenient for it 'involves a denial of right which is the more reprehensible in that it purports to rest upon a "mere" denial of "remedy"'.[221]

6.106 The traditional approach has received considerable support since the distinction became established in medieval times.[222] Yet, it is here submitted

[214] Panagopoulos, 'Substance and Procedure in Private International Law' (2005) 71.

[215] Thomas, *Maritime Liens* (1980) 322.

[216] Panagopoulos, 'Substance and Procedure in Private International Law' (2005) 70.

[217] Ibid, 77.

[218] Mendelssohn Bartholdy, 'Delimitation of Right and Remedy in the Cases of Conflict of Laws' (1935).

[219] See Cook, '"Substance" and "Procedure" in the Conflict of Laws' (1933) 341 '... if ... we examine into the distinction between "substantive law" and "remedial and procedural law" as that distinction is involved in legal problems, we find that this distinction is drawn for a number of different purposes, each involving its own social, economic or political problems'.

[220] See eg *Kendrick v Burnett* (1897) 25 R 82 (Lord Kinnear) 90 '... The rule that whatever belongs to the remedy is to be determined by the *lexi fori* ... depends upon the distinction between questions as to the constitution of obligations and questions as to the mode in which they are to be enforced'; *Naftalin v LMS Railway* 1933 SLT 193 (Lord Murray) 200; see also DM Walker, *The Law of Civil Remedies in Scotland* (Edinburgh, Green, 1974) 19.

[221] Ailes, 'Substance and Procedure in the Conflict of Laws' (1940–41) 394.

[222] Ibid, 396.

that in the case of maritime liens the realist approach is to be preferred since it is actually a field where to deny the remedy means to deny the right. This approach has been recently supported by commentators.[223] Panagopoulos argues that, on the one hand, remedies are certainly not norms ruling on the manner in which the court's proceedings should be conducted and, therefore, should not be seen as inherently procedural. On the other hand, the remedy is an integral part of the right being enforced, actually affecting its existence and scope, therefore, it should be characterized as substantive.[224] Jackson is also of the opinion that the issue of priorities in the case of maritime liens should be submitted to the same law governing the existence of the security right.[225]

In this modern (realist) conception, therefore, there is no place to consider maritime liens as procedural; moreover, there is no place either to consider the priorities they imply as remedial. Consequently, neither the right nor the priorities intrinsically adjudged to the right should be considered procedural under the modern loop of private international law. Both right and priority are inherently substantive and should coherently be subject to the governing law. **6.107**

In *McElroy v McAllister*[226] C Thomson LJ stated: **6.108**

> ... matters of 'remedy', being truly matters of procedure and not of substantive right, fall to be dealt with according to the law of the forum. There are sound reasons for this attitude. So far as remedy is concerned the reasons are practical, though the line between what is a matter of remedy, and what is substantive right may be difficult to draw....[227]

The inconvenience of the fragmentation into right and remedy for private international law purposes has been examined by Briggs.[228] In his opinion '... there should be no line which separates right from remedy in the conflict of laws, or, to put it another way, the remedial rules of the governing law should apply in an English court unless it would be contrary to public **6.109**

[223] See Panagopoulos, 'Substance and Procedure in Private International Law' (2005) 77.

[224] Ibid, 78.

[225] Jackson, *Enforcement of Maritime Claims* (2005) 681–2. In his opinion 'Any reference of priority to the law of the forum assumes that questions of the substance or nature of a right (which should be a matter for the law governing its creation) and priority of the right as against other rights are distinct issues. But, on the contrary, priority may be dictated by the nature ... To distinguish nature and priority is to draw a distinction inherently inconsistent with the whole framework of which the two aspects are part', para 26.36; '... it is artificial to refer the connected issues of priority and substance to different laws', para 26.37.

[226] 1949 SC 110, IH (Ct of 7 Judges)).

[227] Ibid at 117.

[228] Briggs, 'Conflict of Laws and Commercial Remedies' (2003) 274.

policy to do so, at which point the nearest English equivalent should apply instead …'.[229] Outside private international law, it has been observed that '… right and remedy are indissolubly connected and correlated … it is as idle to ask whether the court vindicates the suitor's substantive right or gives a suitor a procedural remedy as to ask whether thought is a mental or a cerebral process'.[230] Leading commentators, however, along with traditional authority, still affirm that in general terms the question of priorities is a remedial matter for the law of the forum.[231] Nonetheless, '… the principle that priorities are governed by the *lex fori* is not, however, a universal one'.[232] It looks as if the door is being left open to future developments of the law in this regard. The change of characterization on 'limitation of actions'[233] within English and Scots[234] private international law shows how feasible it is to change from one category to the other, and in reality how arbitrary the boundaries are. Hopefully, this change could gradually lead to a better general understanding of maritime liens as the preferential rights they are, and consequently, to re-align the distinction between right and remedy in the future, as to allow for the intrinsic issue of priorities to be subject also to the governing law.

VII. CONCLUSIONS

6.110 As mentioned in the introduction to this book, arrest of ships benefits both creditors and ship-owners.[235] Yet, when it comes to applicable law issues connected to it, the conflict of interests in the adjacent field of security

[229] Ibid, 277–8.

[230] *Chase Manhattan Bank NA v Israel-British Bank (London)* [1981] Ch 105, 124.

[231] Fawcett and Carruthers, *Chesire, North & Fawcett, Private International Law* (2008) 92.

[232] Collins (ed), *Dicey, Morris and Collins on the Conflict of Laws* (2006) 191.

[233] Nowadays the Foreign Limitation Periods Act 1984 provides that time-bar provisions are subject to the governing law and not English law unless the latter is the governing law. This welcomed modification attuned with the general modification in English private international law of contracts after the adoption of the 1980 Rome Convention on the applicable law to contractual obligations (currently replaced by Reg Rome I) helps to harmonize characterization of statutes of limitation within Europe as substantive (Fawcett and Carruthers, *Chesire, North & Fawcett, Private International Law* (2008) 81). Nevertheless, English law on limitation will still apply if the application of the governing law is contrary to public policy; see A Briggs, *The Conflict of Laws* (Oxford, OUP, 2002) 38.

[234] A similar process occurred in Scots law; see the Scottish Law Commission Report on Prescription and the Limitation of Actions—Report on Personal Injuries Actions and Private International Law Questions (Scot Law Com No 74 (1983)); DM Walker, *The Law of Prescription and Limitation of Actions in Scotland* (6th edn, Edinburgh, Green, 2002).

[235] It may be argued that also in this sense arrest of ships has, functionally, the characteristics of a right in security. Already in the *Corpus Juris Civilis* it was established that *Pignus*

interests in ships makes it very difficult to strike a balance acceptable to the shipping community as a whole. In the current international legal environment creditors are exposed to the risk of not having their security rights recognized or not having their priority respected and therefore the overall cost of transactions increases.[236] Therefore, harmonization of the law in this field remains paramount. Nonetheless, even though a first step towards uniformity has been achieved with the entry into force of the 1993 Maritime Liens and Mortgages Convention in 2004, in present times, conflict-of-laws rules are far from being redundant.[237]

6.111 A fragmented approach to the characterization of maritime liens in private international law, either through the distinction between substance and procedure or right and remedy, should be resisted.[238] When a given 'procedural' question is treated differently in the different legal systems connected to a certain private international law case (ie as 'procedural' for the law of the forum and as 'substantive' for the governing law) the outcome of the case in terms of applicable law will probably differ depending on the chosen forum. This result may end up defeating the policies of the different legal systems significantly connected to the case.

6.112 The law of the forum approach should be avoided; in the twenty-first century a lienee should not be in a position of having his claim substantially satisfied or entirely shut out, depending upon the legal system of the

utriusque gratia datur, et debitoris, quo magis ei pecunia crederetur, et creditoris, quo magius ei in tuto sit creditum (A security is given for the benefit of both parties: of the debtor in that he can borrow more readily, and of the creditor in that his loan is safer). *Institutiones Book III, Tit. XIV* translated in TL Mears, *Analysis of M. Ortolan's Institutes of Justinian: Including the History and Generalization of Roman Law* (London, Stevens, 1876). Even though this definition describes security rights given by agreement, in the case of ships the rationale behind the common benefit encompasses all three kinds of security rights mentioned in para 6.10 above.

236 For the detrimental effect that the current legal environment has in relation to security rights more generally, particularly in the European Union, see M Cristina di Luigi, 'Divergences of Security and Property Law in the European Union: The Need for Action' (2008) *Journal of Business Law* 526.

237 Arguably, even if the 1993 Maritime Liens and Mortgages Convention achieves greater success, a good conflict of laws rule will always be needed to supplement the Conventional system. For the supplementary role of private international law in substantive unification, see C Fresnedo de Aguirre and V Ruiz, 'El Derecho Marítimo y El Derecho Internacional Privado' [2005] 22 *Anuario de Derecho Maritimo* 189.

238 See PBH Birks, 'Rights, Wrongs and Remedies' (2000) 20 *Oxford Journal of Legal Studies* 1, arguing that 'the habit of thinking of the law in terms of wrongs and remedies encourages a malignant, criminal model of the civil law', what he calls 'discretionary remedialism'; a 'model where "rights" dissolve'. Indeed, if the distinction is applied for the purposes of characterization (and consequently the determination of the applicable law) to maritime liens, the right does dissolve.

jurisdiction in which the ship is arrested and sold.[239] Moreover, an appropriate conflict rule cannot be based on the fallacy that the maritime lien/hypothec is a procedural aspect of the maritime claim and therefore governed by the law of the forum.[240] The traditional law of the forum approach in the English fashion has for a long time been a minority position considering other maritime courts around the world, where the trend has been to define a maritime lien as a substantive right and, consequently, subject to the governing law.[241]

6.113 Against this background, the far-reaching concept of 'procedure' in English law as to cover the existence of maritime liens should be seen as a thing of the past. The modern doctrinal approach is consistent in asserting that the characterization of certain aspects of a claim as 'procedural' should be restricted to matters directly related to the conduct of court proceedings. Matters that affect the existence, scope, and enforceability of the rights themselves, are inherently substantive, therefore, should be left to the governing law.[242]

6.114 Furthermore, it is inconvenient to refer the connected issues of existence and ranking of maritime liens to different laws; it could lead to incoherencies that would neither advance the policies underlying the governing law nor the law of the forum. Using the same illustration as throughout this chapter, if, for example,[243] a US lien ranked following the English priority system it will probably not advance the rationale underlying either US law or English law, therefore jeopardizing the juridical continuity of the legal relations and disregarding the rationale of the foreign system of priorities. Jackson suggests that 'a priority issue necessarily poses a proprietary issue and the whole should be considered as a matter of substance'.[244]

6.115 Time is ripe for the re-examination of private international law rules in this sphere. It is submitted that the ranking of the governing law should be considered unless there are such circumstances amounting to an application of the public policy exception, grounded on international public

[239] JM Kriz, 'Comment' (1955) 64 *Yale Law Journal* 878, 893.

[240] For the same opinion, see Tetley, *Maritime Liens and Claims* (2nd edn, Montreal, Blais, 1998) 7.

[241] Thomas, *Maritime Liens* (1980) 23.

[242] Jackson, *Enforcement of Maritime Claims* (2005) 681–2.

[243] In the United States there are a considerable number of maritime liens which are organized according to priorities; in English law there is a restricted range of maritime liens with no clear-cut system of priorities. The priority order is determined on a case-by-case basis and it is related to the relation between the different types of lien (Jackson, *Enforcement of Maritime Claims* (2005) 682).

[244] Jackson, *Enforcement of Maritime Claims* (2005) 683.

policy issues, which is a well-recognised justification in modern private international law for disregarding the application of the governing law.

Finally, as far as the role of the security function of arrest of ships in the distribution of the sale's proceeds is concerned, there is no uniform framework for the law to develop; neither in national, international, nor regional law. This carries the uncertainty of the effect of arrest on third-party proprietary interests.[245] This is certainly an area that needs further clarification and uniformity for the sake of predictability and legal certainty in the sphere of ship-financing transactions. It is submitted that, in present times, this is a fertile field for unification of procedural law. At the *Comité Maritime International* Conference held in Amsterdam in 1949 pursuant to the adoption of the 1952 International Arrest Convention, the British representative, Mr Cyril Miller, affirmed that it was quite '… impossible to attempt, and indeed undesirable, to unify the law of procedure …'.[246] Fortunately, 60 years later the international community is beginning not to think the same way.[247] **6.116**

[245] Jackson, *Enforcement of Maritime Claims* (2005) 404.

[246] Berlingieri, *Berlingieri on Arrest of Ships* (2006) 6.

[247] See eg the American Law Institute/Unidroit Principles of Transnational Civil Procedure adopted in 2004 (2004) 4 *Uniform Law Review* 758–809. In the particular field of international security interests see the Unidroit Convention on Mobile Equipment (Cape Town Convention) in force since 30 March 2006.

7

Arrest of Ships and Jurisdiction

I. INTRODUCTION

7.01 Ship-related businessmen have always been particularly affected by jurisdictional issues since shipping by its very nature involves contacts with various countries, their laws, and their adjudicatory powers. Some of the most fiercely contested conflicts of jurisdiction take place in shipping litigation and much effort and resources are devoted to solve the jurisdictional dispute—which in many cases becomes much more important than the subject-matter itself.[1] The arrest of ships plays an important role in

[1] In *Spiliada Maritime Corp v Cansulex Ltd (The Spiliada)* [1987] AC 460 (HL) it was made clear by Staughton J (as he then was) at first instance that the decision as to the appropriate forum will put one party or the other into a stronger negotiating position. The same reasoning

that conflict of jurisdictions, insofar as jurisdiction on the merits based on the arrest of the ship within the jurisdiction is an established jurisdictional basis under some national legal systems and under international Conventions.

In the current scenario of international commercial litigation in Europe,[2] it is generally accepted that a court is entitled to exercise jurisdiction on the merits of a claim if it is a forum with which the dispute or the parties to the dispute have a substantial connection. And one of the main duties of private international law in the field of jurisdiction is to identify what constitutes a substantial connection with the forum across the whole range of private international law categories. Furthermore, a court is entitled to exercise jurisdiction even if it does not have a substantial connection with the dispute or the parties to the dispute for the sole purpose of granting interim relief in support of foreign proceedings. The latter type of jurisdiction is referred to throughout this book as 'ancillary jurisdiction' as different to the court exercising jurisdiction in the main proceedings that is the one referred to as exercising 'jurisdiction on the merits'. **7.02**

Therefore, two main themes arise in connection with jurisdiction and the arrest of ships. On the one hand, the jurisdictional function of arrest, that is, the arrest of the ship in a certain country as creating a substantial connection with the forum of that country for the purpose of grounding jurisdiction on the merits. In relation to this issue, this chapter is concerned with the position of the *forum arresti* in the international Conventions and, as in the 1952 International Arrest Convention[3] the issue is left, to a certain extent, to the law of the *forum arresti*, specifically to its position in English and Scots law. Moreover, due to the Europeanization of private international law affecting the way this issue is looked at by English and **7.03**

was followed in *Golden Ocean Assurance and World Mariner Shipping SA v Martin (The Goldean Mariner)* [1989] 2 Lloyd's Rep 390 (QBD (Comm)). Moreover, the jurisdictional issue has become a prime concern within the European judicial area due to the 'court first seized' rule (Art 27) of Council Regulation (EC) No 44/2001 of 22 December 2000 on Jurisdiction and the Recognition and Enforcement of Judgments in Civil and Commercial Matters (Brussels I Reg) [2001] OJ L/12/3; see Jonathan Harris, 'Understanding the English Response to the Europeanisation of Private International Law' (2008) 4 *Journal of Private International Law* 347 at 371.

[2] Even though a certain connection with the forum is a universally recognized criterion, it is not necessarily universal that such connection needs to be substantial; see eg the 'minimum contacts plus reasonableness' criterion in the US personal jurisdictional law (Guangjian Tu, 'Finding a Proper Nexus for Constructing Specific (Special) Jurisdiction Regarding Commercial Contract and Tort Cases: A Comparative Study of the US and European Approaches' (2009) 5 *Journal of Private International Law* 243 at 266.

[3] International Convention for the Unification of Certain Rules Relating to the Arrest of Sea-Going Ships, signed in Brussels on 10 May 1952, in force since 24 February 1956.

Scots law within the European judicial area, this chapter looks also at the positioning of *forum arresti* in the European jurisdictional scheme, ie the so-called Brussels regime.[4] On the other hand, the distinction between 'jurisdiction on the merits' based upon arrest and jurisdiction to arrest for the sole purpose of granting interim relief, ie 'ancillary jurisdiction', becomes paramount in this context. In English law, this distinction whilst clear in principle is jeopardized by the intrinsic connection between arrest of ships and the *in rem* claim.[5] The exercise of ancillary jurisdiction is only outlined in this chapter. The subject-matter is indeed more related to judicial cooperation than to direct jurisdiction which is why its analysis is left to Chapter 8.[6]

7.04 Thus, the main task of this chapter is to examine the jurisdictional function of the arrest of ships to unravel the foundations of the *forum arresti* principle. The aim is to scrutinize the nexus that justifies the exercise of jurisdiction on the merits as a consequence of the arrest of ships, with a view towards enhancing its legitimacy.[7]

II. THE JURISDICTIONAL FUNCTION OF THE ARREST OF SHIPS

7.05 The jurisdictional function of the arrest of ships has long-standing foundations. The impact of English law on its development is remarkable: due to the fact that English law recognized such jurisdictional ground, in the preparatory work pursuant to the adoption of the 1952 International Arrest Convention, the international community thought that it was wiser for the other countries—in the absence of any hope of the English abandonment of such basis—to opt for allowing themselves as well to be competent on such a basis with certain limitations.[8] In turn, the English approach is a

[4] When reference is made to the 'Brussels regime' or the 'European jurisdictional scheme' or similar, the author is referring to all texts dealing with jurisdiction and the recognition and enforcement of judgments in civil and commercial matters, adopted in the framework of the European integration.

[5] This intrinsic connection is analysed in Ch 4 above.

[6] See Ch 8, paras 8.11–8.33.

[7] In the European judicial area, this issue has been identified as an unanswered question by Schlosser in B Hess, T Pfeiffer, and P Schlosser, *Report on the Application of Regulation Brussels I in the Member States* (Study JLS/C4/2005/03) (hereafter the *Heidelberg Report*) in the following terms: 'The question remains whether the *forum arresti* is really justified in intra-European relationships, even if limited to the arrest of ships', para 310.

[8] L Franck, *The travaux préparatoires of the International Convention for the Unification of Certain Rules of Law with Respect to Collision between Vessels, 23 September 1910, and of the International Convention for the Unification of Certain Rules Relating to the Arrest of Sea-Going Ships, 10 May 1952* (Antwerpen, CMI 1997) 399 ('Do you think that our English friends can

consequence of the inherent link between arrest and the *in rem* claim (the old action *in rem*). It is possible to argue that if English law would have not recognized the *forum arresti* when the first international convention on the arrest of ships was adopted, it is doubtful that *forum arresti* would have become an internationally accepted jurisdictional ground.[9]

This jurisdictional ground, despite the fact it has been for long part of the law of the 'great maritime nations',[10] has not been free from criticism. Already in 1902, during the *Comité Maritime International* Conference held in Hamburg, where preliminary work pursuant to the 1910 Collision Convention[11] was undertaken, several opinions were submitted against the *forum arresti* as a jurisdictional basis for the merits of the dispute. The two main arguments against it in those days were: first, that this jurisdictional basis could result in the infinite multiplication of courts that may have jurisdiction to address a particular dispute;[12] secondly, it was argued that this excessive extension of jurisdiction came from the lack of distinction between jurisdiction on the merits and jurisdiction for the sole purpose of granting interim relief.[13] **7.06**

This lack of distinction, reflecting the lack of distinction between the different functions of arrest of ships, was, and still is, an important source of misunderstandings. Admittedly, the extended practice is to allow for the arrest of a ship as a provisional and protective measure as broadly as possible.[14] However, to establish jurisdiction on the merits upon arrest is a completely different question. **7.07**

Another distinction was also missing in those days. Those who were against arrest of ships as a jurisdictional basis for the merits of the dispute argued that the only jurisdictional basis for such purpose should be **7.08**

seize our ships and judge our business in London without reciprocity? ...' (trans by the author)). Paradoxically, in present times it is not the arrest of the ship but the service of the *in rem* claim form that displays the jurisdictional function in English law.

[9] It may be possible to suggest that the common law creativity usually finds its way to gain international acceptance. See para 7.78 below for reflections on this issue in relation to *forum non conveniens* in the current panorama of international litigation in Europe.

[10] Franck, The *travaux préparatoires* (1997) 398.

[11] The International Convention on Certain Rules Concerning Civil Jurisdiction in Matters of Collision signed at Brussels on 10 May 1952.

[12] M Autran, *The travaux préparatoires of the International Convention for the Unification of Certain Rules of Law with Respect to Collision between Vessels, 23 September 1910, and of the International Convention for the Unification of Certain Rules Relating to the Arrest of Sea-Going Ships, 10 May 1952* (Antwerpen, CMI 1997) 398.

[13] Ibid.

[14] See Schlosser in the *Heidelberg Report*, 'maritime law has always been rather favourable to the provisional seizure of seagoing vessels subject to security to be given for release', para 294.

the domicile or habitual residence of the defendant;[15] doubtless, they did not consider the distinction between general and special (specific) jurisdictional bases.[16]

1. Bases of Jurisdiction

7.09 In the sphere of international commercial litigation, a jurisdictional basis is the link between a certain forum and a certain international dispute. In principle, that connection contributes to establishing the level of appropriateness[17] of the *fora* of that particular country to hear the merits of that particular international dispute.[18] Bases for assuming adjudicatory jurisdiction rest on different kinds of relationships between the forum and the dispute, or the forum and the parties to the dispute. The strength of these links vary from minimal, ie defendant's transitory presence in the forum's territorial jurisdiction, to a strong concern of the forum, ie when the action has a real and substantial connection with the forum's state, based either on its relationship with the parties or the dispute. The internationally recognized criterion in present times is that, in most cases, the stronger the connection the more appropriate the forum is to adjudicate the merits of that particular dispute.

7.10 Fernández Arroyo recognizes several reasons and interests generally related to the attribution of international jurisdiction. He also identifies different kinds of arguments that underpin the distribution of jurisdiction internationally.[19] Amongst the reasons and interests, he mentions the necessary connection between the forum and the dispute; the domicile of the defendant as the paradigm of reasonable jurisdictional basis; party

[15] Autran, *The travaux préparatoires* (1997) 398.

[16] Interestingly, as early as in 1930 a plea of *forum non conveniens* was sustained in a Scottish court against jurisdiction based on the arrestment of a ship to found jurisdiction (Scottish jurisdiction, Dumbarton) in favour of the court of the domicile of the defendant (Spain) in *Sheaf Steamship Co Ltd v Compania Trasmediterranea* (1930) 36 Lloyd's Rep 197 (IH (2 Div)).

[17] In English law the assessment of the appropriateness of a certain forum in international civil and commercial litigation is not limited to the consideration of the jurisdictional basis but includes several other factors such as the availability of witnesses, the governing law, the residence or place of business of the parties (*Spiliada Maritime Corp v Cansulex Ltd (The Spiliada)* [1987] AC 460).

[18] Depending on the emphasis given, this appropriateness of the forum is referred to with notions such as 'the natural forum', or 'the forum in which the case might be suitably tried in the interests of the parties and for the ends of justice', or 'the forum with which the action had its most real and substantial connection'. Other views in this regard include concepts such as reasonableness and proximity.

[19] See Diego P Fernández Arroyo, *Compétence exclusive et compétence exorbitante dans les relations privées internationales, Recueil des cours*, vol 323, 2006 (Leiden, Martinus Nijhoff, 2008) Ch 1.

autonomy; the right of access to justice; the rights of the defendant; and non-discrimination considerations. In relation to the different arguments that support different jurisdictional theories, he identifies political and economic arguments such as State sovereignty, State interests and the good administration of justice; legal arguments related to the will of the parties, such as the freedom of the parties in relation to private international law relationships and the tendency to forum shopping, and the need to protect certain weaker parties. Moreover, he distinguishes legal arguments based on the interest of the different legal systems, such as legal certainty and predictability and the need of coherence within a certain jurisdictional regime. Furthermore, he recognizes arguments based on practical considerations in the international sphere, such as the efficiency of judgments and the need to avoid the multiplication of proceedings.[20]

Jurisdictional bases have been divided into three categories in the private international law arena: 'consensual' jurisdiction; 'connected' jurisdiction; and 'universal' jurisdiction.[21] In turn, four different strands of the 'connected' bases have been distinguished, ie exclusive, general, special, and protective jurisdiction.[22] Without entering into detail as to the different categories, it is clear that *forum arresti* in the case of ships is a case of 'connected' jurisdiction, that in turn it is neither exclusive nor protective.[23] Thus, the general and special categories call for examination. **7.11**

General and Special Jurisdiction

This classification was first coined by von Mehren and Trautman in a very influential essay more than 40 years ago.[24] These American scholars distinguished, on the one hand, jurisdictional grounds based on the relationship between the forum and the person or persons whose legal rights are to be affected (general jurisdiction) and, on the other hand, jurisdictional grounds based on the relationship between the forum and the dispute **7.12**

[20] Ibid.

[21] JD Hill, 'The Exercise of Jurisdiction in Private International Law' in P Capps, M Evans, and S Konstadinidis (eds), *Asserting Jurisdiction: International and European Legal Perspectives* (Oxford, Hart, 2003) 39 at 49.

[22] Ibid.

[23] Protective jurisdictional bases are those adopted to achieve a better balance between the parties favouring the weak party connected with the *forum*. Examples of protective *fora* are jurisdictional bases related to consumer contracts, employment contracts, and to incapable and maintenance creditors; see DP Fernández Arroyo, 'Exorbitant and Exclusive Grounds of Jurisdiction in European Private International Law: Will They Ever Survive' in *Festschrift für Erik Jayme* (Munich, Sellier, 2004) 169 at 171.

[24] AT von Mehren and DT Trautman, 'Jurisdiction to Adjudicate: A Suggested Analysis' (1966) 79 *Harvard Law Review* 1121.

(special jurisdiction).[25] In their opinion, the universal assertion that the claimant should sue the defendant where the latter is located[26] (the habitual residence of the defendant being the connecting factor) is the only internationally acceptable one in terms of general jurisdiction.[27] However, many legal systems do consider other jurisdictional bases that are also general—even if not all of them have such extended international acceptance—such as the defendant's nationality, and personal connections such as domicile, habitual residence, or nationality of the claimant. None of them, not even the widest accepted defendant's domicile,[28] is free from criticism.[29]

7.13 In international commercial litigation in Europe,[30] the other category—special bases of jurisdiction—includes the jurisdictional grounds based on an objective link between the forum and the dispute, such as 'the place of performance of the obligation in question' in matters relating to a contract,[31] 'the place where the harmful event occurred or may occur' for tort/delict claims,[32] or the place where the *res* is situated for jurisdiction regarding proceedings concerning rights *in rem* in relation to immovable/heritable property.[33] A court exercising special jurisdiction 'may adjudicate only disputes which are related to the particular connecting factor on which jurisdiction is based'.[34] It is clear that modern trends tend to elaborate more and more special jurisdictional bases.

7.14 Party autonomy can also be considered as a source of special jurisdiction: even though it is related to the will of the parties and not necessarily to a certain connection between the forum and the dispute, the agreement of the parties determines the scope of competence of the agreed jurisdiction; hence, the chosen court may adjudicate only disputes that are within that

[25] LI de Winter, 'Excessive Jurisdiction in Private International Law' (1968) 17 *International and Comparative Law Quarterly* 717 at 718. Note that in US private international law special jurisdiction is known as 'specific jurisdiction'; however, since this book is concerned mainly with the relevance of this concept in the European judicial area the term used in Brussels I, ie special jurisdiction (Art 5), is the one used throughout this book.

[26] Following the well-known Latin maxim *actor sequitur forum rei*.

[27] de Winter, 'Excessive Jurisdiction in Private International Law' (1968) 718.

[28] The domicile of the defendant has been considered as the paradigm in terms of the reasonableness of a forum; see Fernández Arroyo, *Compétence exclusive et compétence exorbitante dans les relations privées internationales* (2008) 44–6.

[29] DP Fernández Arroyo (ed), *Derecho Internacional Privado de los Estados de Mercosur* (Buenos Aires, Zavalia, 2003) 157.

[30] Cf with the current US scenario, see Tu, 'Finding a Proper Nexus for Constructing Specific (Special) Jurisdiction Regarding Commercial Contract and Tort Cases: A Comparative Study of the US and European Approaches' (2009) 243.

[31] Article 5.1 Brussels I Reg.

[32] Article 5.3 Brussels I Reg.

[33] Art 22.1 Brussels I Reg.

[34] Hill, 'The Exercise of Jurisdiction in Private International Law' (2003) 52.

competence attributed to the court by the choice of court agreement.[35] It is clear that party autonomy is the brightest star in the jurisdictional constellation above Europe and beyond, and the latest developments,[36] with a few exceptions,[37] so confirm.

The arrest of ships—even though included in the broadest 'general' category of 'seizure of the defendant's asset within the territory'—has survived the re-examination of jurisdictional bases in the European judicial area, as a basis of 'special jurisdiction', limited to a close list of maritime claims, via the *lex specialis* provision now included in Article 71 of Brussels I.[38] Article 71 provides that Brussels I 'shall not affect any conventions to which the Member States are parties and which in relation to particular matters, govern jurisdiction or the recognition or enforcement of judgments'.[39] However, seizure of the defendant's (other) assets within the territory (of the forum's country) is nowadays considered to be an exorbitant jurisdictional ground.[40] Hence, the legitimacy of *forum arresti* in the case of arrest of ships is still questioned.[41] **7.15**

[35] Richard Fentiman, *International Commercial Litigation* (Oxford, OUP, 2010) para 8.03.

[36] The European Union has acceded to the 2005 Hague Convention on Choice of Court Agreements on behalf of all the Member States. However, in relation to the matters considered in this book note the maritime exceptions on the referred Hague Convention. On the latter issue see Craig Forrest, 'The Hague Convention on Choice of Court Agreements: The Maritime Exceptions' (2009) 5 *Journal of Private International Law* 491.

[37] See the severely criticized decision of the European Court of Justice in *Allianz SpA v West Tankers Inc* [2009] ECR I-663. This decision might hopefully in the future be recalled as an exception, even though it did not surprise commentators when it was delivered. Following the European Parliament non-legislative resolution (7 September 2010) on the Brussels I review, it seems that there might be light at the end of the tunnel (see European Parliament document reference T7-0304/2010, para (M) favouring the state of affairs prior to the *West Tankers* decision). On the implications of the *West Tankers* decision see, inter alia, Patrizio Santomauro, 'Sense and Sensibility: Reviewing *West Tankers* and Dealing with its Implications in the Wake of the Reform of EC Regulation 44/2001' (2010) 6 *Journal of Private International Law* 281.

[38] Formerly Art 57 of the Brussels Convention and of the original Lugano Covention (Convention on jurisdiction and the enforcement of judgments in civil and commercial matters, signed in Lugano, 16 September 1988); Art 67 of the new Lugano Convention (2007 Lugano Convention) entered into force between the Member States of the European Union (including Denmark) and Norway on 1 January 2010. The 2007 Lugano Convention entered into force in Switzerland on 1 January 2011.

[39] Article 71.1 Brussels I Reg.

[40] Exorbitant rules are prohibited by Art 3.2 Brussels I Reg. This provision explicitly provides for the non-applicability of the rules of national jurisdiction as set out in Annex I to the Reg against defendants domiciled in a Member State. These 'unreasonable' bases remain of use in the intra-European litigation scenario for the sole purpose of granting provisional measures in support of foreign proceedings, making it clear in the European scheme the distinctive function of jurisdictional grounds to adjudicate the case on the merits as different from ancillary jurisdiction to grant interim relief.

[41] See *Heidelberg Report*, para 310.

Excessive or Exorbitant Jurisdiction

7.16 It is difficult to give a clear definition of what constitutes an excessive or exorbitant jurisdictional basis.[42] Fernández Arroyo provides a negative definition and describes exorbitance as lack of reasonableness.[43] In general terms it can be said that when the balance between the interests of the claimant(s) and the defendant(s) is not even, and one or the other is put in such a position close to a practical denial of justice, the situation is unacceptable from an international point of view.[44] Hence, if a judgment is rendered in such conditions in a certain forum it should not be recognized and enforced abroad. Certainly, this kind of explanation is related to the fact that international jurisdiction is not a goal in itself but it is a way of ensuring juridical continuity to international legal relations.[45]

7.17 Traditionally, there have been clear cases of exorbitant jurisdictional bases in many legal systems. The most well-known examples include the nationality of the claimant,[46] the presence of the non-resident defendant's assets within the jurisdiction,[47] the domicile of the claimant,[48] and arrestment of movables belonging to non-residents as in the Scottish rules of jurisdiction. All of these jurisdictional grounds as bases of general jurisdiction met with disapproval as considered excessive or exorbitant. In the European Union jurisdictional regime, these excessive jurisdictions have been all re-examined, and excluded from the European jurisdictional scheme now embodied in the Brussels I Regulation.[49]

[42] See, among others, KH Nadelmann, 'Jurisdictionally Improper Fora in Treaties on Recognition of Judgements: The Common Market Draft' (1967) *Columbia Law Review* 995; de Winter, 'Excessive Jurisdiction in Private International Law' (1968) 712; FAP Mann, *The Doctrine of Jurisdiction in International Law* (1964) 111 *Recueil des Cours* 1; KA Russell, 'Exorbitant Jurisdiction and Enforcement of Judgements: The Brussels System as an Impetus for the United States Action' [1993] *Syracuse Journal of International Law and Commerce* 2.

[43] Fernández Arroyo, 'Exorbitant and Exclusive Grounds of Jurisdiction in European Private International Law' (2004) 170; *Compétence exclusive et compétence exorbitante dans les relations privées internationales* (2008) Ch 3.

[44] Particularly in Europe that situation would be contrary to Art 6 of the European Convention on Human Rights (ECHR). On the impact of the ECHR in private international law issues see JJ Fawcett, 'The Impact of Article 6 (1) of the ECHR on Private International Law' (2007) 56 *International and Comparative Law Quarterly* 1.

[45] For the concept of juridical continuity see Ch 1, paras 1.32–1.35 above. In the European judicial area this idea permeates the whole of the Brussels regime as its overall objective is to promote the free movement of judicial decisions.

[46] For example Art 14 of the French Civil Code.

[47] For example Art 23 of the German Code of Civil Procedure and Art 99 of Austrian Court Jurisdiction Act.

[48] For example Art 126(3) of the Dutch Code of Civil Procedure.

[49] Annex I to the Brussels I Reg. The list of exorbitant grounds of jurisdiction included therein is not exhaustive.

III. *FORUM ARRESTI*: THE PROBLEMS

When scrutinizing the scenario where the *forum arresti* has an important role to play, several perennial problems of international commercial litigation more generally which have a particular incidence in shipping litigation come to the surface. These problems are addressed in the following paragraphs. **7.18**

1. The Different Perspective in International Shipping Litigation: The Balance between Principles and Practicalities

The reasonableness of a certain jurisdictional basis in international commercial litigation needs to be judged not only from the point of view of the defendant but also the claimant. In the law of procedure all over the world and throughout the ages the traditional rule *actor sequitur forum rei*, ie the defendant must be sued at the courts of his domicile, is the leading principle of general jurisdiction, both domestic and international. This is doubtless reasonable and fair and is set to protect the defendant. However, the trouble and expense involved in pursuing judicial proceedings in a foreign court are always burdensome, so the position of the claimant is also worth contemplating. The costs of instituting proceedings as well as defending an action in a foreign court are always considerable: therefore there are certain issues to examine in international litigation that are not present when selecting an objective jurisdictional ground for the purpose of domestic litigation. As expressed already 40 years ago, 'the position of a claimant in international cases is already far from enviable owing to the fact that even if he gets judgment against the defendant in his own country, it will usually be difficult to make this judgment effective. So at least his interest in being provided with an accessible jurisdiction should not be entirely neglected.'[50] **7.19**

As in most issues in law (and in life), it is a matter of balance of convenience. One thing is not to neglect the burden of the claimant and a very different one is to argue, as it has been done,[51] under the umbrella of the claimant's convenience, the supremacy of certain *fora* when it comes to **7.20**

[50] de Winter, 'Excessive Jurisdiction in Private International Law' (1968) 717.

[51] See Sir W Phillimore in *The travaux préparatoires* (1997) 400. Fortunately this *mentalité* has been changing. A quarter of a century after Philimore's opinion, Lord Reid recognized that 'There was a time when it could reasonably be said that our system of administration of justice though expensive and elaborate was superior to that in most other countries. But today we must admit that as a general rule there is no injustice in telling a plaintiff that he

Admiralty disputes. This is not acceptable in present times. Even when it is possible to agree that for assessing the balance of convenience between the claimant and the defendant practical considerations should be taken into account, these considerations should not go as far as to consider one forum better equipped than others because of its own 'greatness'.[52]

7.21 Furthermore, it has been argued that jurisdictional issues in private international law have become too dominated by practicalities related to cost and convenience, and that also the proper division of competence between States is being left aside.[53] Hill stresses that, as a matter of principle, 'unless the parties have expressly or impliedly chosen the forum in question, the exercise of jurisdiction is not legitimate if the dispute does not have some territorial connection with that forum'.[54]

7.22 It is here submitted that it is also important to recognize that international adjudication of jurisdiction has not an aim of its own but constitutes a way of assuring juridical continuity to international legal relations across national borders.[55] Therefore, practical consequences are important ones; and it is necessary to find the right balance between principles and practicalities. As practical as it may be that the ship (or alternative security given[56]) is already within the jurisdiction of the adjudicating court, this justifies the convenience of *forum arresti* for the specific causes of action ultimately involving the ship. That is to say, in relation to cases where the claim attracts a right in security against the ship (maritime lien), or where the ship is the asset securing enforcement of the judgment, or in relation to claims where the *res* needs to be preserved until the merits of the case are settled,[57] the *forum arresti* represents a reasonable special jurisdictional ground.

should go back to his own courts' in *Owners of the Atlantic Star v Owners of the Bona Spes (The Altantic Star and The Bona Spes)* [1974] AC 436.

[52] Phillimore in *The travaux préparatoires* (1997) 400. As Lord Reid recognized in *The Atlantic Star and The Bona Spes* (above), there was a time 'when inhabitants of this island felt an innate superiority over those unfortunate enough to belong to other races' (*The Atlantic Star* [1974] AC 436).

[53] Hill, 'The Exercise of Jurisdiction in Private International Law' (2003) 45–8.

[54] Ibid.

[55] On this point see Ch 1 above.

[56] Article 1 of the 1952 Collision Convention.

[57] These three different 'types' of arrest of ships are distinguished in Scots law; see Ch 5, paras 5.14–5.25 above. The distinction is also drawn in this study in relation to ship arrest in English law based on their different functions, see Ch 4, paras 4.19–4.30 above. Favouring the courts of the place where the asset is physically located at the time that the court becomes seized, for causes of action involving title, possession, or control of the ship, is recognized as sound by a leading English private international law commentator in the context of the revision of the Brussels I Reg. See Andrew Dickinson, Brussels I Review-Online Focus Group,

2. Forum Shipping, Forum Shopping

Another factor that needs to be considered in this context is that in international litigation the availability of concurrent jurisdictions is a commonplace occurrence,[58] and as a consequence of that, and to a certain extent, 'forum shopping' becomes unavoidable.[59] Particularly in relation to shipping litigation, it is often the case that the courts of more than one country will be able to exercise jurisdiction over a particular dispute. It is intrinsic to the international legal relations generated by the shipping industry to have substantial connections with more than one forum. And in these cases most legal systems allow the claimant a choice of forum. The problem arising out of this permission is that two parties to a dispute may bring similar proceedings in different jurisdictions; or even more troublesome, that the same party could present the same claim in more than one forum. The potential problems generated by parallel proceedings in certain circumstances are tackled in different ways in jurisdictional systems. The approach to these problems in the context of civil and commercial litigation is particularly different in common law systems and in civil law ones.[60] **7.23**

Thus, the availability of concurrent jurisdictions has always been a matter of special concern in shipping cases where there will invariably be a number of potential *fora* whose jurisdictional rules would permit the dispute to be entertained. Ship-related businessmen have always been vulnerable to parallel litigation because of the nature of their business which takes them from forum to forum, making maritime claims 'particularly vulnerable to "forum shopping"'[61] and rendering every port an 'Admiralty emporium'.[62] Hence, maritime law is a particular area where in relation to many causes of action the jurisdiction of the court of a given country is prescribed by international Conventions to which that country is a signatory. In this context, *forum arresti* should be seen as a private international law device created as an attempt to circumvent the problems associated with parallel **7.24**

8 June 2009 available at http://conflictoflaws.net/2009/brussels-i-review-online-focus-group/ (last visited 10 November 2010).

[58] Fernández Arroyo distinguishes between normal and abusive concurrence in this context, see Fernández Arroyo, *Compétence exclusive et compétence exorbitante dans les relations privées internationales* (2008) 38.

[59] R. Geimer, *Internationales Zivilprozeßrecht* (5th edn, Cologne, Dr Otto Schmidt KG, 2005) 862.

[60] As to the approach to this issue in the Brussels jurisdictional regime see paras 7.34–7.35; in Scots law see paras 7.68–7.70; in English law see paras 7.82–7.84.

[61] *DSV Silo und Verwaltungsgesellschaft mbH v Owners of the Sennar (The Sennar) (No 2)* [1985] 1 Lloyd's Rep 521 (HL) (Lord Diplock).

[62] *The Atlantic Star* [1974] AC 436 (Lord Simon of Glaisdale).

proceedings in the shipping litigation arena in particular.[63] It is a device crafted with the needs of the shipping industry in mind; that is why *forum arresti* as provided for in the international Arrest Conventions is a clear example of a specialized provision, and, in the context of the Brussels regime, it should be given priority due to its specificity. A key principle underlying the solutions coined by such Conventions is the principle of territorial proximity examined in the following paragraphs.

3. Territorial Proximity: The Underpinning of *Forum Arresti*

7.25 In the context of jurisdiction for the sole purpose of granting interim relief, ie ancillary jurisdiction, the possibility to arrest a ship in a certain jurisdiction to support the proceedings on the merits in another jurisdiction has been justified in some legal systems through the territorial proximity principle,[64] based on the territorial proximity between the forum and the ship.[65] In the European judicial area this territorial connection in the sphere of ancillary jurisdiction is not expressly mentioned in the provisions relating to provisional, including protective measures of the Brussels I Regulation[66] but in *Van Uden Maritime BV v Firma Deco Line*[67] the European Court of Justice held that a 'real connecting link' between the subject-matter of the measure sought and the territorial jurisdiction of the court granting them was necessary for a court to exercise ancillary jurisdiction in support of foreign proceedings.[68] The following paragraphs explore

[63] This submission is further discussed at para 7.111 below.

[64] It is important to distinguish this principle as underpinning ancillary jurisdiction for the sole purpose of granting interim relief from the more general principle of proximity (meaning a close connection between the forum and the dispute or the parties to the dispute) as the underpinning of jurisdiction on the merits. In relation to the latter see P Lagarde, *Le principe de proximité dans le droit international privé contemporain* (1986) 196 *Recueil des Cours* 9, 131–2. See also Fernández Arroyo, *Compétence exclusive et compétence exorbitante dans les relations privées internationales* (2008) 42.

[65] For an analysis of this principle in relation to the arrest of ships in Uruguayan law see C Fresnedo de Aguirre and R Herbert, 'El Arresto de Buques y el Principio de Jurisdicción mas Próxima' [1993] *Revista de Transporte y Seguros* 158.

[66] Article 31 of the Brussels I Reg in its present form. Note that the particular provisions dealing with provisional, including protective measures in the Brussels I Reg, have been subject to amendments in the recently published European Commission Proposal for a Regulation of the European Parliament and of the Council on jurisdiction and the recognition and enforcement of judgments in civil and commercial matters (Recast) 14.12.2010 (COM (2010) 748/3 (hereafter 'the EU Commission Proposal').

[67] *Van Uden Maritime BV v Firma Deco Line* Case C-391/95 [1998] ECR I-7091.

[68] In the context of the revision of the Brussels I Reg, the *Heidelberg Report* and the European Commission Green Paper seemed sceptical as to the legal basis for this requirement. This is further discussed in the context of ancillary jurisdiction in Ch 8 below.

whether territoriality is also underpinning direct jurisdiction on the merits based on the arrest of the ship.

The international jurisdiction to adjudicate is a direct consequence of the international jurisdiction to legislate which in turn is derived from State sovereignty.[69] Consequently, since sovereignty is territorial in character, the public international law impact on civil jurisdiction has remained firmly rooted in territoriality.[70] As a rule, jurisdiction extends and is limited to everybody and everything within the sovereign's territory. In 1834 Story[71] maintained that every nation possesses an exclusive sovereignty and jurisdiction within its own territory.[72] As a result, a defendant was not subject to the jurisdiction unless he had been served with process within the jurisdiction or had voluntarily submitted to it. In turn, jurisdiction *in rem* could not be exercised over a *res* unless it was situated within the forum. **7.26**

A century later Cook[73] purported to free the common law from what he considered the misleading notion of territoriality and associated theories.[74] He demonstrated that Story's theory was defective in that Story accepted that jurisdiction *in rem* and jurisdiction *in personam* could be exercised independently. Cook, on the contrary, understood that to exercise jurisdiction over a *res* within the forum necessarily involved the exercise of some jurisdiction over persons claiming an interest in it.[75] **7.27**

More recently, the strictly territorial character of the doctrine of international jurisdiction has been loosening up particularly in the commercial sphere. It has been suggested that the application of the territorial **7.28**

[69] FAP Mann, 'The Doctrine of International Jurisdiction Revisited After 20 Years' (1984) 186 *Recueil des Cours* 9 at 51.

[70] Ibid.

[71] J Story, *Commentaries on the Conflict of Laws* (Boston, Hilliard, Gray & Co, 1834).

[72] In his view it would be 'wholly incompatible with the equality and exclusiveness of the sovereignty of all nations, that any one nation should be at liberty to regulate either persons or things not within its own territory', MM Bigelow, *Story's Commentaries on the Conflict of Laws* (8th edn, Boston, Little, Brown, 1883) 20.

[73] WW Cook, *The Logical and Legal Bases of Conflict of Laws* (Cambridge, MA, Harvard University Press, 1942).

[74] Michael Pryles, 'The Basis of Adjudicatory Competence in Private International Law' (1972) 21 *International and Comparative Law Quarterly* 62.

[75] Cook, *The Logical and Legal Bases of Conflict of Laws* (1942) 62 'Legal rights cannot exist independently of legal persons and when a court exercised jurisdiction over a thing it necessarily affected the rights of persons interested in that thing. Thus if a court exercised *in rem* jurisdiction over a *res* and persons claiming some interest in the *res* were outside the jurisdiction, the court was doing what Story said could not be done—binding persons not resident in the forum.' Cf with the analysis of the nature of the action *in rem* in English law as developed in the nineteenth century in Ch 2, particularly paras 2.36–2.38 above; see also Ch 4, paras 4.09–4.11 above as to this issue in modern English law.

principle is likely to lead to jurisdiction being exercised on insubstantial connections, and therefore to a high incidence of parallel and related proceedings.[76] Reasonableness,[77] fairness, and substantial contacts with the forum, have dominated the supplementary connections.

7.29 Notwithstanding the foregoing, *forum arresti* in the case of arrest of ships as a special jurisdictional ground shows that in certain scenarios, particularly the ones involving certain types of assets, jurisdiction remains firmly rooted in territoriality. Both in the case of jurisdiction on the merits and in the context of ancillary jurisdiction, the territorial proximity with the ship operate as the link. However, this link operates differently in both scenarios.[78] In the case of jurisdiction on the merits, territoriality should not be understood as an abstract underpinning based on the sovereignty of the state but—as the previous paragraphs have attempted to show—on practical considerations. In this distinctive field of law, that of shipping litigation, certain practicalities gain vital importance due to the fact that in most cases the ship is the only asset of the defendant, and as a movable tangible asset it can become elusive. This practical advantage as the underpinning of a jurisdictional ground fits easier into certain kinds of jurisdictional paradigms than in others. The following paragraphs aim to assess the fitness of *forum arresti* in the European regime, in Scots law, and in English law.

IV. DIFFERENT PARADIGMS OF INTERNATIONAL JURISDICTION

7.30 In the context of the Europeanization of private international law the uneasy relationship between the common law tradition and the civilian pattern of European Regulations is more often than not explained in terms of a clash of mentalities.[79] Hence, in an attempt to explain how the jurisdictional function of arrest of ships is perceived by the European regime, Scots and English law, respectively, the overview of these different

[76] Hill,'The Exercise of Jurisdiction in Private International Law' (2003) 61.

[77] Reasonableness has been evaluated as a strong principle in the elaboration and interpretation of jurisdictional rules in Europe; see Fernández Arroyo,'Exorbitant and Exclusive Grounds of Jurisdiction in European Private International Law' (2004) 173; *Compétence exclusive et compétence exorbitante dans les relations privées internationales* (2008) 42.

[78] For further analysis of how territoriality operates in the case of arrest of ships in one jurisdiction to support the proceedings in another jurisdiction, see Ch 8, paras 8.34–8.37 below.

[79] See eg Harris, 'Understanding the English Response to the Europeanisation of Private International Law' (2008) 352.

paradigms of international civil and commercial jurisdiction become enlightening.

A paradigmatic account 'must be painted with a broad brush',[80] details within each system are neglected; the aim is to draw a picture that is not necessarily complete but comprehensive enough to discuss the central concern of this book. Hence, a selective outline of the relevant features of each paradigm is offered and some material peculiarities are highlighted. Paradigmatic differences are very important in practice. These differences in *mentalité*[81] (mentality) define the inner structure of a legal system and the approach taken to the decision-making process in the field, and by comparing different ones unrecognized similarities and differences come to the surface and may help to unravel larger knots. **7.31**

1. The European Paradigm of Jurisdiction[82]

The Brussels regime is modeled on a civilian system as far as jurisdiction is concerned.[83] General jurisdiction is based on the defendant's domicile.[84] In addition, the regime recognizes choice of court agreements[85] (party autonomy) and submission to the jurisdiction[86] as forms of prorogation of jurisdiction, and special jurisdictional grounds based on a close link between the court and the claim.[87] Following that, the European regime has battled against exorbitant *fora* and has banished entirely from the application amongst the Member States the use of certain controversial jurisdictional bases insofar as to the exercise of jurisdiction on the merits.[88] **7.32**

[80] R Michaels, 'Two Paradigms of Jurisdiction' (2006) 27 *Michigan Journal of International Law* 1026.

[81] See HP Glenn, 'Legal Cultures and Legal Traditions' in M van Hoecke (ed) *Epistemology and Methodology of Comparative Law* (Oxford, Hart, 2004) 7.

[82] There is an enormous wealth of legal literature on this theme and it would be impossible to even try to refer to them without running the risk of not mentioning the most relevant ones.

[83] Council Regulation (EC) 44/2001 of 22 December 2000 on Jurisdiction and the Recognition and Enforcement of Judgments in Civil and Commercial Matters, [2001] Art 2, OJ L/12/3 (hereafter 'Brussels I Reg').

[84] Article 2 Brussels I Reg.

[85] Article 23 Brussels I Reg.

[86] Article 24 Brussels I Reg.

[87] Article 5 Brussels I Reg.

[88] Article 3 (2) Brussels I Reg. As far as the United Kingdom is concerned, three jurisdictional bases are expressly excluded from the European regime in Annex 1 to the Brussels I Reg. Rules which enable jurisdiction to be founded on (a) the document instituting the proceedings having been served on the defendant during his temporary presence in the United Kingdom, or (b) the presence within the United Kingdom of property belonging to

7.33 In terms of legal technique the civilian approach seeks to resolve jurisdictional problems through an integrated framework of hard-and-fast rules. The role of judicial discretion has so far been very limited.[89] Oversimplifying it, this civilian model includes restrictive jurisdictional grounds but jurisdiction on such grounds needs to be exercised by the courts, and there is hardly any room to stay proceedings when the court is internationally competent to hear the merits as far as the defendant is domiciled in a Member State.[90] The system is based on narrowly defined bases of jurisdiction, which a claimant is entitled to invoke as of right.

7.34 In terms of priorities, in the case of parallel proceedings between the same parties and in relation to the same cause of action, the system in its present form gives automatic precedence to the court first seized.[91] A clear ranking of principles is established where the aim to avoid parallel proceedings is above all other considerations. No explicit precedence *inter se* amongst the different categories of jurisdictional grounds is established except for the case of protective *fora*[92] and exclusive jurisdiction.[93] This regime has the advantage of simplicity but the disadvantage of inflexibility.

7.35 The Brussels I Regulation does not prioritize general over special jurisdictional grounds or vice versa. Article 2 (general jurisdictional ground-domicile of the defendant) and Article 3 (possibility to sue elsewhere under special rules) are linked with a 'may'. The claimant 'may' opt at his best interest. It could be argued that this parity in treatment is what concurrent jurisdiction is all about. Furthermore, Fernández Arroyo submits that a choice like this one, between reasonable *fora*, represents in most

the defendant, or (c) the seizure by the claimant of property situated in the United Kingdom. Noteworthy, these include arrestment to found jurisdiction in Scots law under (b) and (c). For this particular type of arrestment in the case of ships, see further paras 7.57–7.67 below; see also Ch 5, para 5.26 above.

[89] However, this could be changing. See in the context of the revision of the Brussels I Reg, the European Parliament Resolution of 7 September 2010, para 14 in relation to *forum non conveniens*. However, the EU Commission Proposal is much more conservative in this regard, allowing discretion only in cases involving disputes on the same subject matter and between the same parties which are pending before the courts in the EU and in a third country. A court of a Member State can exceptionally stay proceedings if a non-EU court was seized first and it is expected to decide within a reasonable time and the decision will be capable of recognition and enforcement in that Member State (proposed Art 34) (See EU doc COM (2010) 748/3, 14.12.2010).

[90] *Owusu v Jackson* [2005] QB 801 (Case C-281/02) (ECJ).

[91] Articles 27–30 Brussels I Reg.

[92] Articles 8-14; 15; 18 Brussels I Reg.

[93] Article 22 Brussels I Reg.

cases a strengthening of the right of access to justice.[94] A prioritization would amount to subsidiary rather than concurrent jurisdictional grounds. However, certain precedence in case of parallel litigation does not necessarily mean subsidiarity as a corollary. The claimant would still be able to opt, and, in principle, all the concurrent jurisdictional grounds (ie all the reasonable/non-abusive concurrent jurisdictional grounds) would be available to him. Yet, it is here suggested, that in the case of parallel proceedings, a certain order of precedence amongst jurisdictional grounds, favouring specificity, could provide an alternative solution to that of the court first seized. The latter is certainly unfair in various ways and causes too many disruptions in the system (eg the so-called 'Italian torpedo' litigation tactic, a technique used to delay proceedings by abusing the rule provided for in Article 27 of the Brussels I Regulation).[95]

Another essential component of the European paradigm is the mutual trust principle and as such it permeates all the issues mentioned above. The principle is based on the assumption that the courts of the Member States are equally competent to adjudicate jurisdiction according to the Regulation. The trilogy of private international law cases heard by the European Court of Justice, *Erich Gasser v Misat*,[96] *Turner v Grovit*,[97] and *Owusu v Jackson*[98] leave room for little doubt in this regard.[99] Following that it has been held that European jurisdictional thinking is 'international'; what matters is the relation between nations.[100] **7.36**

Legal certainty is also at the heart of the Regulation. The interest of the parties are sought to be protected via the predictability achieved by the **7.37**

[94] Fernández Arroyo, *Compétence exclusive et compétence exorbitante dans les relations privées internationales* (2008) 64.

[95] In this regard the EU Commission Proposal (EU doc COM (2010) 748/3, 14.12.2010) aims to improve this situation by prescribing a time-limit for the court first seised to decide on its jurisdiction. In addition, the amendment introduced in the proposed Art 29.2 provides for an exchange of information between the courts seized of the same matter.

[96] *Erich Gasser v Misat* [2005] 1 QB 1 (Case C-116/02) (ECJ).

[97] *Turner v Grovit* [2005] 1 AC 101 (Case C-159/02) (ECJ).

[98] *Owusu v Jackson* [2005] QB 801 (Case C-281/02) (ECJ). However, as the decision in *Choudhary v Bhatter* [2009] EWCA Civ 1176 demonstrates, where possible, English courts have sought to interpret *Owusu* restrictively and find practical ways in which to mitigate the effect of Brussels I Reg's strict rules.

[99] The reaction of English lawyers to these ECJ decisions has been to reassert the role of the common law as much as possible trying to limit the impact of these decisions in the sphere of international commercial litigation; see amongst others Harris, 'Understanding the English Response to the Europeanisation of Private International Law' (2008) 381.

[100] Michaels 'Two Paradigms of Jurisdiction' (2006) 1049.

regime.[101] Furthermore, the ultimate goal of promoting the good functioning of the internal market constitutes the justification of the private international law competence of the European Union in jurisdictional issues[102] and this also permeates the vision of the European regime.

The *lex specialis* Provision

7.38 Notwithstanding the foregoing analysis, the European regime gives way to other international Conventions where further special bases of jurisdiction have been recognized. The purpose of the *lex specialis* provision of the Brussels I Regulation is to 'ensure compliance with the rules on jurisdiction laid down by specialized Conventions, since in enacting those rules account was taken of the specific features of the matters to which they relate [specificity]'.[103]

7.39 This is particularly the situation in respect of jurisdiction based on the arrest of ships in the terms of Article 7 of the 1952 International Arrest Convention, and Article 1 of the 1952 Collision Convention[104] where the *forum arresti* acquires jurisdiction on the merits in certain specific circumstances. This is an example of a jurisdictional basis that, even though excluded from the European regime in general, has been preserved for the case of ships, according to the *lex specialis* provision (Article 71 of Brussels I Regulation)[105] of the European regime.

7.40 The particular case of jurisdiction based on the arrest of ships was considered during the preparatory work pursuant to the accession of the United Kingdom, Ireland, and Denmark to the Brussels Convention 1968 (Accession Convention 1978).[106] The possibility of introducing a special

[101] The main aim of the Regulation was to facilitate the sound administration of justice by making rules on jurisdiction highly predictable (Recitals 11 and 12 of Brussels I Reg). See also in the EU Commission Proposal (EU doc COM (2010) 748/3, 14.12.2010) the (new) Recital 12, where legal certainty and predictability are connected with the possibility of the defendant to foresee the possibility of being sued before a particular court.

[102] Article 81 of the Treaty on the Functioning of the European Union (OJ C 115, 9.5.2008).

[103] *Maciej Rataj (The Tatry)* [1995] (Case C 406/92) 1 Lloyd's Rep 302 (ECJ).

[104] In relation to the 1952 Collision Convention the Court of Appeal in *The Po* [1991] 2 Lloyd's Rep 206 (CA) was content to uphold substantive jurisdiction under the latter on the basis that the claimant had complied with the Convention and English law.

[105] The functioning of Art 71 Brussels I Reg has been specially addressed in the Brussels I review (see *Heidelberg* Report, paras 139–145), however, Art 71 has not been subject to any material amendments in the EU Commission Proposal (EU doc COM (2010) 748/3, 14.12.2010).

[106] Convention on Jurisdiction and the Recognition and Enforcement of Judgments in Civil and Commercial Matters signed in Brussels on 27 September 1968. Applicable in the United Kingdom pursuant to the Council Convention on the accession of the Kingdom of

part in the Convention in order to 'protect' Admiralty jurisdiction as exercised particularly in the United Kingdom and Ireland was considered.[107] Schlosser remarked then that 'it would have been inappropriate to limit the exercise of admiralty jurisdiction to the basis of jurisdiction included in the 1968 Convention in its original form. If a ship is arrested in a State because of an internationally recognized maritime claim, it would be unreasonable to expect the creditor to seek a decision on his claim before the courts of the ship-owner's domicile.'[108] However, more recently Schlosser has questioned whether *forum arresti* is really justified in intra-European relationships, even if limited to the arrest of ships.[109] Again, the issue seems to be related to measuring the practical advantages of a jurisdictional ground against its fitness in the principled jurisdictional scheme that the European Union has crafted.

At the time of the Accession Convention 1978, the common understanding was that the United Kingdom would have suffered an unacceptable loss of jurisdiction if a special provision[110] had not been introduced. No wonder the story of *forum arresti* would have been very different if the United Kingdom had not won this battle at that point in time. **7.41**

Even Member States which are not parties to the 'convention on a particular matter' (specialized Convention) must recognize and enforce decisions given by courts which have jurisdiction only under the specialized Convention.[111] For jurisdiction to be based on arrest of ships within Europe, ie for the *forum arresti* to be operative within the European regime through the *lex specialis* provision, actual arrest must have been made under the circumstances provided for in Article 7 of the 1952 International Arrest **7.42**

Denmark, Ireland, and the United Kingdom of Great Britain and Northern Ireland to the Convention on jurisdiction and the enforcement of judgments in civil and commercial matters and to the Protocol on its interpretation by the Court of Justice (Accession Convention), signed in Brussels on 9 October 1978, 78/884/EEC.

[107] P Schlosser, 'Official Report on the Association of the Kingdom of Denmark Ireland and the United Kingdom of Great Britain and Northern Ireland to the Convention on Jurisdiction and the Enforcement of Judgments in Civil and Commercial Matters' (1979) OJ C/59/140.

[108] Ibid. The issue went far enough to consider a special section dealing with admiralty jurisdiction; see H Gaudemet-Tallon, *Les Conventions de Bruxelles et de Lugano Competence Internationale, reconnaissance et execution des jugements en Europe* (Paris, Librairie générale de droit et de jurisprudence, 1993) 155. Finally this proposal was dropped and instead a Joint Declaration urging the then Community States to accede to the 'most important of all the Conventions on maritime law, namely the Brussels Convention of 10 May 1952' was signed in Luxemburg on 9 October 1978.

[109] Schlosser in the *Heidelberg Report*, para 310.

[110] Article 57.2 of the Brussels Convention was amended by Art 25.2 of the 1978 Accession Convention in a way which clarified the priority of specialized Conventions.

[111] Article71.2 Brussels I Reg.

Convention. Security for the claim provided *in lieu* of arrest is not sufficient to found jurisdiction in the case of the 1952 International Arrest Convention.[112] Nonetheless, security for the claim provided *in lieu* of arrest is sufficient to found jurisdiction in collision cases if the priority provision gives place to Article 1 of the 1952 Collision Convention.[113] Hence *forum arresti* has taken on an enhanced importance in Europe.

7.43 The operational issues in relation to the *lex specialis* provision are various and complex enough to have been left open to judicial and doctrinal development.[114] As far as the interaction between the specialized Conventions provisions and the Brussels jurisdictional regime it seems that whether the rules of the specialized Convention override, are additional to, or are alternative to the Regulation depends on the specialized Convention.[115] During the life-time of the Brussels Convention Schlosser was of the opinion that the *lex specialis* provision of the Convention meant that the special provisions on jurisdiction contained in special Conventions were to be regarded as if they were provisions of the European regime themselves;[116] this meant to subsume the special jurisdictional ground under the much broader scheme provided for by the European regime.

7.44 Similarly in the maritime sphere, Jackson is of the opinion that the 'special laws'[117] providing for specific heads of jurisdiction in particular matters are to be read together[118] with the Regulation in relation to jurisdictional grounds. He emphasizes that the 1952 International Arrest Convention

[112] *Owners of Cargo Lately Laden on Board the Deichland v Owners and/or Demise Charterers of the Deichland (The Deichland)* [1990] 1 QB 361 (CA) 370; *The Tatry* [1995] 1 Lloyd's Rep 302 (ECJ); cf *The Anna H* [1995] 1 Lloyd's Rep 11 (CA).

[113] *Owners of the Bowditch v Owners of the Po (The Po)* [1991] 2 Lloyd's Rep 206 (CA).

[114] P Schlosser, *Schlosser Report* OJ C 59 [5.3.1979], para 240.

[115] DC Jackson, *Enforcement of Maritime Claims* (4th edn, London, LLP, 2005) 156; *Schlosser Report* (1979), para 240. In the *Jenard Report* to the Brussels Convention (OJ C/59 [5.3.1979]) it was highlighted that the rules of jurisdiction laid down in the special Conventions have been dictated by particular considerations relating to the matters of which they treat (at p 60). On this issue see the criticism to the decision of the ECJ in *The Tatry* (Case C 406/92) [1995] 1 Lloyd's Rep 302 by Beaumont on the grounds that Art 57 of the Brussels Convention was therein construed too narrowly. In his opinion, it had the 'the effect of distorting the Arrest Convention by adding a rigid lis pendens rule that was not provided for by the drafters of that Convention' (P Beaumont, 'European Court of Justice and Jurisdiction and Enforcement of Judgments in Civil and Commercial Matters' (1997) 46 *International and Comparative Law Quarterly* 205 at 211).

[116] *Schlosser Report* (1979), para 240.

[117] Jackson, *Enforcement of Maritime Claims* (2005) 155.

[118] This methodology was advanced by the opinion of the Advocate-General, Mr Tesauro in the ECJ case *Maciej Rataj (The Tatry)* (Case C 406/92) [1995] 1 Lloyd's Rep 302 (ECJ).

'forms an important part of the Brussels jurisdiction framework'.[119] The great majority of the Member States of the European Union are parties to it and this enables 'maintaining of jurisdiction in relation to maritime claims based on arrest of seagoing ships while removing any general jurisdiction based on seizure or arrest of property'.[120]

An alleged clash between Article 7 of the 1952 International Arrest Convention and Article 17 of the then Brussels Convention (currently Article 23 of the Brussels I Regulation) arose in *The Bergen (No 1)*.[121] The claim involved a jurisdiction and choice-of-law clause in a bill of lading providing for disputes to be decided where the carrier had his principal place of business (Germany) under the law of such country. The relevant ship was served and arrested in England. Under English domestic law and therefore under Article 7(1) of the 1952 International Arrest Convention, the English Courts had jurisdiction to determine the claim on the merits. The core of the problem was whether the forum selection clause of the bill of lading invalidated the jurisdiction of the *forum arresti*. The dictum upheld the jurisdiction of the English Court based on the arrest of the ship within English territorial jurisdiction as recognized in English domestic law.[122] The main argument was centred on the priority of Article 7 of the 1952 International Arrest Convention over the rules of the Brussels jurisdictional system; based on specificity, the dictum favoured the former over the latter. **7.45**

In this context, it is regrettable that the decision in *The Bergen (No 1)* referred to above did not apply Article 7 of the 1952 International Arrest Convention as a whole, where in fact choice-of-court agreements are expressly recognized (Article 7(3)),[123] and where the interpretation of Article 7 as a whole should have led to the conclusion that if a forum other than the *forum arresti* has been agreed by the parties, the arresting court is fully competent to exercise ancillary jurisdiction (for the purpose of the arrest as security), but, for the merits of the case the arresting court would limit itself to establishing a time limit to bring the claim to the agreed forum. **7.46**

Article 7(3) of the 1952 International Arrest Convention reads 'If the parties have agreed to submit the dispute to the jurisdiction of a particular **7.47**

119 Jackson, *Enforcement of Maritime Claims* (2005) 159.

120 Ibid.

121 *The Bergen (No 1)* [1997] 1 Lloyd's Rep 380 (QBD (Admlty)).

122 *The Bergen (No 1)* [1997] 1 Lloyd's Rep 380 (QBD (Admlty)). See also *The Linda* [1988] 1 Lloyd's Rep 175.

123 In *Siamar v Spedimex* [1990] ILPr 266 the Italian Supreme Court assessed the validity of a choice of court agreement in accordance with Art 7(3) of the 1952 International Arrest Convention in an action on the merits under the Convention.

Court other than that within whose jurisdiction the arrest was made or to arbitration, the Court or other appropriate judicial authority within whose jurisdiction the arrest was made may fix the time within which the claimant shall bring proceedings.' This last sentence should be interpreted as the time within which the claimant shall bring proceedings *to the agreed court*. The ambiguity of Article 7(3) has been remedied in the 1999 International Arrest Convention, where it is made clear in Article 7(1) that the *forum arresti* has jurisdiction on the merits, 'unless the parties validly agree or have validly agreed to submit the dispute to a court of another State which accepts jurisdiction, or to arbitration'.[124]

7.48 It seems clear that the purpose of the *lex specialis* provision of the Brussels regime is to ensure compliance with the rules of jurisdiction laid down by specialized Conventions;[125] and in the case of arrest of ships that means with the rules of jurisdiction of the 1952 International Arrest Convention as a whole, not only with the rule laid down in Article 7(1).

7.49 In present times, however, there seems to be a consensus as to the need to limit the scope of application of Article 71 of the Brussels I Regulation.[126] The current position of the ECJ is that account need to be taken not only to the wording of Article 71 of Brussels I (the *lex specialis* provision) but also 'the context in which Article 71 occurred and the objectives pursued by the Regulation'.[127] Taking that into account, jurisdictional rules of specialized Conventions 'applied provided that they were highly predictable, facilitated the sound administration of justice and enabled the risk of concurrent proceedings to be minimized and that they ensured ... the free movement of judgments in civil and commercial matters and mutual trust in the administration of justice in the European Union (*favor executionis*)'.[128] Seemingly, this is the latest test to be passed for a jurisdictional ground in a specialized Convention to be able to 'survive' under the current Brussels regime. It is here submitted that not only Article 7 of the 1952 International Arrest Convention fulfils the required criteria but also that Article 7 of the 1999 International Arrest Convention passes this test as well.[129]

124 Article 7(1) 1999 International Arrest Convention.

125 A Briggs, 'The Brussels Convention Tames the Arrest Convention' [1995] *Lloyd's Maritime and Commercial Law Quarterly* 161.

126 *Heidelberg Report*, para 145.

127 *TNT Express Nederland BV v AXA Versicherung AG*, Case C-533/08 of 4 May 2010, [2010] ILPr 35 at para 44. See also paras 32 *et seq* of the opinion of Advocate General Juliane Kokott delivered on 28 January 2010 in connection with this case.

128 Ibid at para 56.

129 This submission is discussed in paras 7.107–7.114 below.

Moreover, it has been expressed that since the purpose of the *lex specialis* provision is to maintain the level of harmonization achieved through international Conventions in specific matters 'only the special links listed in [the 1952 International Arrest Convention] Article 7(1) under (a) to (f) prevail over the provisions of the Jurisdiction Convention [now the Brussels I Regulation], while when jurisdiction is based on the domestic rules of the country in which the arrest is made the provisions of the [then] Jurisdiction Convention remain wholly operative'.[130] **7.50**

This restrictive interpretation has been favoured by Berlingieri who is of the opinion that the first sentence of Article 7(1) of the 1952 International Arrest Convention—recourse to the law of the forum—as a conflicts rule—should be a reference to the European scheme provisions themselves as the law of the forum (a special kind of *renvoi*).[131] In other words, the aim of the *lex specialis* provision of the European regime is not to interfere with the harmonization achieved amongst the Member States in jurisdictional issues in specific matters. And the level of harmonization achieved in relation to the jurisdictional function of the arrest of ships in the 1952 International Arrest Convention, is evidenced in the particular cases mentioned in (a)–(f) in Article 7(1).[132] Further discussion on the interface between the 1952 International Arrest Convention and the Brussels jurisdictional scheme is offered later in this chapter.[133] **7.51**

[130] A Philip, 'Maritime Jurisdiction in the EEC' [1977] *Nordisk Tidss-Krift for internationale ret* 121; see also JP Verheul, 'The Convention Relating to the Arrest of Seagoing Ships of 1952: Some Questions' [1983] *Netherlands International Law Review* 383 at 386.

[131] 'The first sentence of Art 7 (1) pursuant to which the courts of the country in which the arrest is made have jurisdiction on the merits if such jurisdiction is granted by the *lex fori* has the nature of a rule of private international law. The consequence is that if the country where the arrest is made is a party to the Jurisdiction Convention [now the Brussels I Regulation] its provisions shall apply except for the special links set out in art 7 (1)' (F Berlingieri, *Berlingieri on The Arrest of Ships* (London, Informa, 2006) 279).

[132] Article 7(1) of the 1952 International Arrest Convention reads: 'The courts of the country in which the arrest was made shall have jurisdiction to determine the case upon its merits if the domestic law of the country in which the arrest is made gives jurisdiction to such courts or in any of the following cases namely: (a) if the claimant has his habitual residence or principal place of business in the country in which the arrest was made; (b) if the claim arose in the country in which the arrest was made; (c) if the claim concerns the voyage of the ship during which the arrest was made; (d) if the claim arose out of a collision or in circumstances covered by Article 13 of the International Convention for the unification of certain rules of law with respect to collisions between vessels, signed at Brussels on 23 September 1910; (e) if the claim is for salvage; (f) if the claim is upon a mortgage or hypothecation of the ship arrested.'

[133] See paras 7.107–7.111 below.

7.52 In *Ladgroup Ltd v Euroeast Lines SA*[134] it was held that the (then) Brussels Convention and Schedule 8 to the Civil Jurisdiction and Judgments Act 1982 (giving effect to that Convention in the United Kingdom) left unaffected the pre-existing law of Scotland in Admiralty causes where arrestment to found jurisdiction[135] provided a basis for jurisdiction.[136] This turns the focus to Scots law and the way jurisdictional issues are perceived by this outstanding mixed legal system.

2. The Scottish Paradigm of Jurisdiction

7.53 The Scottish rules of jurisdiction are set out in Part III of and Schedule 8 to the Civil Jurisdiction and Judgments 1982 Act. These rules are of general application in patrimonial matters where neither the European scheme nor the scheme for allocation within the United Kingdom applies.[137] These general rules are not to affect 'the operation of any enactment which confers jurisdiction on a Scottish court in respect of a specific subject-matter or specific grounds' (s 21(1)). This rule has the same aim as the *lex specialis* provision inserted in the European regime. It has been argued that a more far-reaching solution should be adopted to eliminate exorbitant jurisdictional bases—like arrestment to found jurisdiction—and to use the provisions of the Brussels regime to resolve all jurisdictional disputes.[138]

[134] *Ladgroup Ltd v Euroeast Lines SA* 1997 SLT 916 (OH).

[135] The situation of arrestment of ships to found jurisdiction in Scots law is complex. On the one hand, the 1952 International Arrest Convention does not apply to this kind of arrestment of ships, which is subject to the rules on arrestment to found jurisdiction generally (see Maher and Rodger, *Civil Jurisdiction in the Scottish Courts* (2010) 335). On the other hand, arrestment to found jurisdiction as a general jurisdictional ground has been banned from the European and intra-UK jurisdictional schemes. Hence, if Art 7 of the 1952 International Arrest Convention applies by virtue of Art 71 of the Brussels I Reg, it seems inconsistent with the purposes of the European jurisdictional system as a whole to understand the remission to the law of the forum in Art 7 as applicable in this context as a remission to a jurisdictional ground that has expressly been excluded from the system. See further discussion of this peculiar jurisdictional ground of Scots law in paras 7.59–7.69 below.

[136] 1997 SLT 916 (OH), Lord Prosser.

[137] The scheme for allocation of jurisdiction within the United Kingdom is not addressed in this book. For a monographic study of private international law issues in the intra-UK scheme, including jurisdictional issues, see Kirsty J Hood, *Conflict of Laws within the UK* (Oxford, OUP, 2007).

[138] AE Anton and P Beaumont, *Civil Jurisdiction in Scotland* (2nd edn, Edinburgh, Green, 1995) 21.

The Scottish Dual Formula of *forum arresti–forum non conveniens*

Interestingly, the Scottish jurisdictional system has traditionally counted on, on the one hand, a broad jurisdictional basis such as arrestment to found jurisdiction (as a general jurisdictional basis; and not limited to the arrestment of ships) and, on the other hand, a device to adjust it: *forum non conveniens*. The two make sense in terms of the other. That is why *forum arresti* does not fit so easily in legal systems that do not provide for a device to contain it and *forum non conveniens* is seen as jeopardizing legal certainty in jurisdictional systems that do not contemplate broad jurisdictional bases.[139] **7.54**

The Scottish jurisdiction based on arrestment used to be primarily a common law one.[140] However, in relation to the arrestment of ships, since the implementation of the 1952 International Arrest Convention in the United Kingdom and, moreover, since the entry into force of the Civil Jurisdiction and Judgments Act 1982, the special jurisdiction based on the arrestment of ships derives from a sequence of statutory provisions. **7.55**

The Scottish arrestment jurisdiction in Admiralty actions is expressly excluded from Schedule 8 to the Civil Jurisdiction and Judgments Act 1982. Section 21(1)(b) provides that Schedule 8 does not apply to the proceedings listed in Schedule 9. In turn Schedule 9(6) provides for the exclusion of certain Admiralty causes, inter alia, '[A]dmiralty causes insofar as the jurisdiction is based on arrestment *in rem* or *ad fundandam jurisdictionem* of a ship cargo or freight'. This exclusion follows a similar provision in Schedule 5(7) concerning 'Certain Admiralty proceedings in Scotland'. And its justification (and the different treatment compared to Admiralty jurisdiction in England) obeys the fact that in England the arrest of ships is based on statutory provisions implementing the 1952 International Arrest Convention. Proceedings therefore brought under these provisions would be excluded by the operation of the provision included in Schedule 5(6) (proceedings under certain Conventions). **7.56**

[139] In view of the current state of affairs with relation to the review of the Brussels I Reg and bearing in mind that discretion is finding its way into the system, even if in fairly self-contained scenarios, this could lead the way to the adoption of the 1999 International Arrest Convention by the European Union, since, if the proposed amendment is adopted, the framework system would have incorporated already the device to control the broader jurisdictional ground; therefore the 1999 International Arrest Convention would represent 'pure specificity' rather than the introduction of 'new' discretionary powers.

[140] Currently, Maher and Rodger draw a distinction between arrestment as a ground of jurisdiction (to be determined mostly by reference to the 1982 Act) and as a form of procedure (governed by the common law rules); see Maher and Rodger, *Civil Jurisdiction in the Scottish Courts* (2010) 110.

7.57 In turn, the Civil Jurisdiction and Judgments Act 1982 provides in section 20(1) that Schedule 8 has effect to determine in what circumstances a person may be sued in civil proceedings in the Court of Session or in the sheriff court. Notwithstanding, section 21 establishes that Schedule 8 does not affect: (a) the operation of any enactment which confers jurisdiction on a Scottish court in respect of a specific subject-matter on specific grounds; (b) without prejudice to the foregoing generality, the jurisdiction of any court in respect of any matter mentioned in Schedule 9.

7.58 In Scots law, arrestment of a ship does not necessarily found jurisdiction. Indeed, arrestment of a ship on the dependence as such does not; neither does an arrestment *in rem* in an action *in personam*. Only in an action *in rem* an arrestment *in rem* founds jurisdiction.[141] Apart from the latter case, an arrestment to found jurisdiction needs to be ordered together with the warrant of arrestment of a ship on the dependence, or an arrestment *in rem* in an action *in personam*, to found the jurisdiction of the Scottish courts.

Arrestment to Found Jurisdiction

7.59 'There is perhaps no more curious doctrine in any legal system than the Scottish form of arrestment *ad fundandam jurisdictionem*, namely the procedure by which jurisdiction is established over a foreigner by arresting such of his goods as are situated in this country.'[142] This type of arrestment to found jurisdiction, also known as arrestment *jurisdictionis fundandae causa*, originated as a practice displaying the security and the jurisdictional function of arrestment. It existed as part of the *lex mercatoria* and was applied as early as the thirteenth century by the *pie-poudre* Courts which sat in the great fairs which were held in England.[143] Its origins are inherently linked with commerce, transport, and foreigners as these three relate with each other. It was certainly followed at a very early date in the Admiralty Court of Scotland.[144] However, the original conception was already entirely departed from by the end of the nineteenth century.[145]

7.60 Since then[146] it is solely a means of establishing jurisdiction against a defender that would otherwise not be subject to the Scottish courts on the

141 Civil Jurisdiction and Judgments Act 1982, Sch 5[7] and Sch 9[6]; Maher and Rodger, *Civil Jurisdiction in the Scottish Courts* (2010) 334.

142 ARG McMillan, 'The Theory of Arrestment *ad fundandam jurisdictionem*' (1922) *Scots Law Times* (News) 89.

143 McMillan,'The Theory of Arrestment *ad fundandam jurisdictionem*' (1922) 89.

144 Ibid.

145 *Guthrie v Brunsgaard Kjosterud & Co* (1896) 3 SLT 265 (IH (1 Div)).

146 *Fraser Johnston Engineering Co Ltd v Jeffs* (1920) 2 Lloyd's Rep 33 (IH (1 Div)).

basis of the presence[147] within Scotland of moveable assets.[148] Already in the 1920s this jurisdictional ground was criticized as running counter to one of the main planks of Scots law, namely, *actor sequitur forum rei.*[149] McMillan argued that it was merely a legal fiction and as such not conforming with either the principles of the *lex mercatoria* from which it originated or to those of the civil law on which the law of Scotland is founded.[150] Furthermore, he suggested that as a matter of principle it should be discarded entirely as a useless and indefensible theory, or the theory should be restored to its original substantial form as displayed in the *lex mercatoria.* None of these has happened and arrestment to found jurisdiction continues to be a peculiarity of modern Scots law.[151]

Arrestment to found jurisdiction confers jurisdiction upon the Court of Session and the sheriff court of the place where the goods are located.[152] Subject to a few exceptions,[153] arrestment to found jurisdiction may not be executed where the defender is domiciled in the United Kingdom or a European Union State.[154] However, rule 2(8) of Schedule 8 to the Civil Jurisdiction and Judgments Act 1982 has preserved this jurisdictional ground for extra-UK and extra-EU cases. The Maxwell Committee,[155] **7.61**

[147] Already in 1896 Lord McLaren described its main features in the following terms '… [a]rrestment jurisdictionis fundandae causa does not attach the property arrested. … It seems to me merely to attest the fact that the ship is at the time within the jurisdiction and that notice has been given that it is the intention of the person using the diligence to raise an action founding on the jurisdiction which results from the property being within the country. … No disability is imposed upon the owner of the ship, and the master is put under no obligation to make the ship forthcoming. … [t]he action should fall if the party who had used the diligence had not followed up the arrestment within a reasonable time' (*Guthrie v Burnsgaard Kjosterud & Co* (1896)).

[148] GL Gretton, 'Diligence', *The Laws of Scotland, Stair Memorial Encyclopaedia,* Vol 8, para 249.

[149] McMillan,'The Theory of Arrestment *ad fundandam jurisdictionem*'(1922) 89.

[150] Ibid.

[151] As such, and particularly for the case of arrestment of ships against demise charterers, its competence has been recently provided for in Scots law; see Administration of Justice Act, Ch 46, s 47H (Arrestment to Found Jurisdiction in Action against Demise Charterer) as introduced by Sch 4 to the Bankruptcy and Diligence etc (Scotland) Act 2007 in force since 1 July 2010.

[152] Rules of the Court of Session 1994, as amended; Sheriff Courts (Scotland) Act 1907, as amended.

[153] The exceptions are: (a) in an action of reparation arising out of the collision or manoeuvring of ships or non-compliance with ship collision regulations under s 45 of the Administration of Justice Act 1956; and (b) in an Admiralty cause where the defender is domiciled in the United Kingdom or elsewhere except another European Union State.

[154] Arrestment to found jurisdiction is nowadays regarded as internationally unacceptable as an exorbitant ground of jurisdiction in non-maritime cases, and it is precluded within Europe by the Brussels I Reg. See paras 7.17–7.18 above.

[155] *Report of the Scottish Committee on Jurisdiction and Enforcement* (1980) HMSO, Edinburgh (Chairman: the Hon Lord Maxwell) (the *Maxwell Report*), para 13.164.

despite the general acknowledgement of the fact that this jurisdictional basis is exorbitant, considered that it was appropriate to retain it in relation to persons against whom there may be no other ground of jurisdiction to convene them to the Scottish Courts.[156]

7.62 In times gone by, the rationale of arrestment to found jurisdiction was that the pursuer has got hold of something that would satisfy a judgment in his favour.[157] In modern times, arrestment of movables to found jurisdiction has lost that function and is used instead along with an arrestment on the dependence of an action.[158] It has been described as '... an anomalous procedure which should be strictly looked at and should not be extended ...'.[159] It may be argued that, the rationale behind, on the one hand, jurisdiction based on presence of moveable assets within Scotland and, on the other hand, jurisdiction based on the arrest/arrestment of a ship as understood in modern times, is different. As explained in previous paragraphs, the latter is justifiable in terms of the proximity principle; the former was originally based on commercial needs.[160]

7.63 Functionally, the differences are also considerable. Arrestment to found jurisdiction 'renders the foreign owner liable to be convened in a process issuing from the Court of Session at the instance of the arrester for recovery of a personal debt'; 'but [differently from arrest of ships as provided for in the international Conventions] it does not necessarily guarantee that the subject arrested will remain within the jurisdiction'.[161] This general

[156] In this context the comments of Fernández Arroyo merit consideration '... European States should not be proud of keeping in their legislation certain criteria against which they have clearly objected. It is impossible to understand that, what is considered unacceptable in European (Brussels and Lugano) and world (Hague) transactions can be tolerable in other cases. With a fundamental right [such as the access to justice] the double standard is completely unacceptable' (Fernández Arroyo, 'Exorbitant and Exclusive Grounds of Jurisdiction in European Private International Law' (2004) 186).

[157] *Union Electric Co Ltd v Holman & Co* 1913 SC 954 at 957 (IH (1 Div) CS) (Lord President).

[158] G Maher and DJ Cusine, *The Law and Practice of Diligence* (Edinburgh, Butterworths, 1990) 104.

[159] *Stenhouse London Ltd v Allwright* 1972 SLT 255 (IH (2 Div)) 258 (LJ-C Grant). Cf *Leggat Brothers v Gray* 1908 SC 67 (IH (1 Div)) 72; *Alexander Ward & Co v Samyang Navigation Co Ltd* [1975] 2 Lloyd's Rep 1 (HL) (Lord Kilbrandon).

[160] In medieval times this type of arrestment was the only effective method of subjecting itinerant merchants to the local jurisdiction of the territory within which they might at the time be situated (McMillan, 'The Theory of Arrestment *ad fundandam jurisdictionem*' (1922) 89).

[161] *Mill v Fildes* [1982] SLT 147 (OH).

jurisdictional basis has always been subject to the right of the court to decline jurisdiction on the principle of *forum non conveniens*.[162]

Arrestment of Ships to Found Jurisdiction

The jurisdiction based on the arrestment of ships is provided for in the Sheriff Courts (Scotland) Act 1907, Chapter 51, section 6(c): 'Any action competent in the sheriff court may be brought within the jurisdiction ... [w]here the defender is a person not otherwise subject to the jurisdiction of the courts of Scotland, and a ship or vessel of which he is owner or part owner or master, ..., have been arrested within the jurisdiction.' Looking at this provision alone it seems that jurisdiction based on arrestment of a ship is thereby established as a general jurisdictional ground. However, this has to be read in conjunction with the provisions mentioned above of the Administration of Justice Act 1956, Chapter 46, Part V (Admiralty Jurisdiction and Arrestment of Ships in Scotland), section 47. Following that, jurisdiction based on the arrestment of ships in Scotland, despite arrestment being a general jurisdictional basis according to the 1907 Act, has become a special ground of jurisdiction regarding Admiralty actions by the operation of the 1956 Act. **7.64**

To consider jurisdiction based on the arrestment of ships in Scotland as a special jurisdictional basis is indeed indispensable for its survival under the European regime. Only 'special' heads of jurisdiction can survive under the *lex specialis* provision of the Brussels regime. And even then, there is the more restrictive interpretation mentioned above[163] that considers the survival of *forum arresti* through the *lex specialis* provision limited to the particular circumstances in which this jurisdictional basis is recognized in Article 7 of the 1952 International Arrest Convention regardless of the law of the *forum arresti*; namely, if the claimant has (a) his habitual residence or principal place of business, or (b) the claim arose, in the country in which the arrest was made; (c) if the claim has arisen during the voyage of the ship during which the arrest was made; or in cases of (d) collision, (e) salvage, (f) mortgage or hypothecation. **7.65**

In terms of its functional analysis, in modern times, it seems that the only operative function of arrestment to found jurisdiction is the jurisdictional one. However, the jurisdictional function is not consequential upon arrest as it is in the case of arrestment *in rem* but consequential upon the ship being fixed in Scotland; hence, the sole purpose and effect of an arrestment **7.66**

[162] In present times as especially provided for in s 22(1) of the Civil Jurisdiction and Judgments Act 1982.

[163] See para 7.52 above.

to found jurisdiction is to fix the locality of the subjects arrested in Scotland.

7.67 As in modern practice, arrestment to found jurisdiction and arrestment on the dependence can be sought simultaneously,[164] the protective and security functions are displayed together with the jurisdictional one by virtue of one warrant, though technically arrestment to found jurisdiction precedes any other kind of measure in a certain action, since it is its pivotal ground in terms of the court assuming jurisdiction.[165]

7.68 Even though the general rule in Scots law is that the subjects arrested must belong to the debtor in the capacity in which he is being sued,[166] section 47H of the Administration of Justice Act 1956 as introduced by Schedule 4 to the Bankruptcy and Diligence (Scotland) Act 2007, has the effect that where a pursuer wishes to raise an action against a demise charterer to enforce a claim listed in section 47(2) but the demise charterer is not within the jurisdiction of the court, the pursuer can arrest the ship under demise charter (providing it is within the court's territorial jurisdiction) to found jurisdiction for the action and allow it to be heard by that court.

Forum non conveniens

7.69 *Forum non conveniens* is also a doctrine of general application in Scots law.[167] In *Sim v Robinow*[168] Lord Kinnear in a widely quoted passage explained that 'the plea can never be sustained unless the court is satisfied that there is some other tribunal, having competent jurisdiction, in which the case may be tried more suitably for the interest of all the parties and for the ends of justice'.[169] It was confirmed for the first time by the House of Lords in *Societé du Gaz de Paris v La Societé Anonyme de Navigation*

[164] Rules of the Court of Session 1994, Ch 16 [16.15] as amended.

[165] *Societé du Gaz de Paris v La Societé Anonyme de Navigation 'Les Armateurs Francais'* [1925] 23 Lloyd's Rep 209 (HL).

[166] Anton and Beaumont, *Private International Law* (1990) 190.

[167] *Forum non conveniens* has been particularly preserved during the process of law reform that radically changed the law of Civil Jurisdiction in Scotland. The Civil Jurisdiction and Judgments Act 1982, which entered into force in 1987, has a supplementary provision that specially establishes: '(1) Nothing in Schedule 8 [Civil Jurisdiction in Scotland] shall prevent a court from declining jurisdiction on the ground of *forum non conveniens*'. The doctrine has successfully developed in the United States; see among the leading cases *Canada Malting Co Ltd v Paterson Steamships Ltd* [1932] 285 US 413; and later, in England. For a survey of the development of the doctrine in other jurisdictions see DJB Svantesson, 'In Defence of the Doctrine of Forum Non Conveniens' (2005) *Hong Kong Law Journal* 395.

[168] [1892] 19 R 665.

[169] Ibid at 668.

'Les Armateurs Francais' where Lord Sumner put the rule rather differently in the following words,

> ... the court has to consider how best the ends of justice in the case in question and on facts before it, so far as they can be measured in advance, can be respectively ascertained and served.... The object in the words *'non conveniens'* ... is to find that forum which is the more suitable for the ends of justice, and which is preferable because pursuit of litigation in that forum is more likely to secure the ends of justice.[170]

The doctrine took various tags when it first appeared: *forum non conveniens*, *forum conveniens* and *forum non competens*. The earliest cases identified as the origins of the doctrine date from the 1830s.

In *Brown's Trs v Palmer*[171] an arrestment was used against funds in Scotland **7.70**
owed to an executor under a will executed under English law in India who had remained in India and was subject to the jurisdiction of the courts there. The Scottish decision held, without referring to the doctrine by name, that the arrestment was not a sufficient authority to found the jurisdiction of the Scottish courts to hear the case.[172]

In *Tulloch v William*[173] the first decree (judgment) to use the expression **7.71**
forum competens appeared; surprisingly, it was a case found on a jurisdictional ground other than arrestment. In *Longworth v Hope*[174] the doctrine was developed a step further; in that case Lord Deas said that even though the question raised in the case had been named as *forum competens* or *forum non competens*, the plea was really not that the forum was incompetent but that the other forum ought to be preferred. A year later Lord Justice Clerk Inglis in *Clements v Macaulay*[175] asserted that for the ends of justice the case may more suitably be tried elsewhere; from then on the plea was labelled *forum non conveniens* and it was in that form that it reached *Sim v Robinow*,[176] where Lord Kinnear[177] made the doctrine 'fit for export'[178] providing the world with a valuable device to secure the ends of justice; and particularly, to contain far-reaching general jurisdictional bases.

[170] [1925] 23 Lloyd's Rep 209 (HL) 213.
[171] (1830) 9 S 224.
[172] On the same line see *Macmaster v Macmaster* (1833) 11 S 685, cf *Peters v Martin* (1825) 4 S 108.
[173] (1846) 8 D 657.
[174] (1865) 3 M 1049.
[175] (1866) 4 M 583.
[176] (1892) 19 R 665.
[177] Ibid at 668.
[178] Lord Hope of Craighead, 'Forum non conveniens: where next?' Conference Paper, Journal of Private International Law Conference 2007, Birmingham 26 June 2007, 4. (1830) 9 S 224.

7.72 *Forum non conveniens* was first exported to the United States, then to England and many other common law legal systems. Currently, transposition and cross-fertilization are undoubtedly happening between the legal systems of the European Union and it is to be hoped that in the near future this valuable private international law device finds its way also into the European jurisdictional scheme. This turns the focus to English law and the way English lawyers think about jurisdiction.

3. The English Paradigm of Jurisdiction

7.73 English thinking about jurisdiction is dramatically different from the European paradigm.[179] English law is a system in which the judge rather than the academic is the major evolutionary force,[180] since precedent rather than doctrine is a source of law.[181] Long-established rules include a wide range of jurisdictional bases. These rules are shaped by judicial discretion:[182] value-based judgments; tailor-made solutions crafted to meet individual circumstances; judicial discretion has been idiosyncratic since Henry II.[183] All these concepts do not form part of the European vogue.

7.74 It is generally acknowledged that the exercise of jurisdiction in maritime matters plays a far greater role in England than elsewhere in the United Kingdom or the rest of Europe. The English jurisdictional trends in Admiralty have spread worldwide through the international Conventions where such approach to jurisdiction has been taken into account, remarkably, in the 1952 and 1999 International Arrest Conventions. The fact that the English Admiralty Court 'is one of the most famous and historic courts in the world'[184] constitutes also part of the English paradigm. The welfare of England is ultimately at stake.[185] Therefore, trying to keep its leadership

[179] In the words of Harris, English common law rules of jurisdiction 'are of a diametrically opposed nature' to the European regime. See Harris, 'Understanding the English Response to the Europeanisation of Private International Law' (2008) 352.

[180] In the words of leading private international law academics, English law 'is not scientifically founded on the reasoning of jurists, but it is beaten out on the anvil of experience', JJ Fawcett and JM Carruthers, *Cheshire, North & Fawcett Private International Law* (14th edn, Oxford, OUP, 2008) 37.

[181] R Evan-Jones, 'Mixed Legal Systems, Scotland and the Unification of Private Law in Europe' in JM Smits (ed), *The Contribution of Mixed Legal Systems to European Private Law* (Antwerp, Intersentia, 2001) 42–3.

[182] *Spiliada Maritime Corp v Cansulex Ltd* [1987] AC 460.

[183] Lord J Mance, 'Is Europe Aiming to Civilise the Common Law?' The Chancery Bar Lecture, 27 March 2006.

[184] *The Atlantic Star* [1974] AC 436 (Lord Simon of Glaisdale).

[185] Arguably, policy considerations are paramount in every legal system. For example in Scots law the jurisdiction *rationae rei situs* was extended to personal obligations attaching

as a centre for international shipping litigation could be regarded as the 'public interest' attained in every decision on the matter. This leadership is almost incontestable and is used[186] by English courts both positively and negatively with the respective doctrines of *forum conveniens* and *forum non conveniens*. These doctrines, together with the powers of case management[187] (seeking to prevent waste and to promote the expediency of the litigation process) are the heart of English courts' inherent discretion in the jurisdictional sphere. *Forum non conveniens*, as many other private international law devices, is not good or bad in itself but it depends on the context where and how it is used. Clearly *forum non conveniens* is not the panacea in every scenario;[188] but as Harris explains case management powers are a 'flexible weapon' and 'it shows the inclination of the English courts to adopt flexible structures that are at odds with the more certain but also more rigid rules of the Brussels I Regulation'.[189]

Several Schemes under One Paradigm

In present times, there are several different jurisdictional schemes in England, ie the 'traditional' rules of jurisdiction, the European jurisdictional regime (including the Lugano Convention), and the intra-UK jurisdictional system. The complexity that derives from these different schemes in shipping litigation in England has even prompted the suggestion that an Admiralty Code is necessary in English law.[190] **7.75**

movables unconnected therewith to encourage the commerce of the country (see *Societé du Gaz de Paris v La Societé Anonyme de Navigation 'Les Armateurs Francais'* [1925] 23 Lloyd's Rep 209 (HL) (Lord Sumner)).

[186] Judges and commentators agree in that the 'Admiralty court is a court to which suitors from a range of maritime countries have been accustomed or content to resort. No chauvinism is involved in recognizing as a fact that it has been at the choice of many ship owners from other countries that Admiralty cases have been brought in the English Admiralty Court' (*The Atlantic Star* [1974] AC 436 (HL) (Lord Morris of Borth-y-Gest)). These kinds of arguments have motivated the most critical reactions from non-English lawyers and scholars, who do indeed see chauvinism. Nonetheless, it is a fact that the exercise of jurisdiction in maritime matters has traditionally played a far greater role in the United Kingdom than elsewhere, as recognized by Schlosser, *Schlosser Report* (1979), para 121.

[187] The importance of case management has been recognized particularly in the sphere of international shipping litigation by the *Heidelberg Report*, para 277.

[188] There are examples in the field of torts where the use of *forum non conveniens* has prevented the access to justice by victims of accidents linked to industrial activities in the country of the parent corporate defendant, see Horatia Muir-Watt, 'Reshaping Private International Law in a Changing World' Guest Editorial, ConflictofLaws.net, 2 April 2008.

[189] Harris, 'Understanding the English Response to the Europeanisation of Private International Law' (2008) 393.

[190] Jackson, *Enforcement of Maritime Claims* (2005) 7.

7.76 The critical issue is whether the existence of radically different jurisdictional regimes, as the Brussels regime on the one hand and traditional English rules on jurisdiction on the other hand represent, is desirable in English law inasmuch as international civil and commercial litigation is concerned, or whether the Scottish approach—that is a more general revision of jurisdictional grounds in general, even outside the European framework—is preferable or defensible.[191] Jackson, looking particularly into maritime jurisdiction, has put forward the related question of whether English maritime jurisdiction should fit into Europe or vice-versa.[192]

7.77 It is clear that the coexistence of dramatically different schemes of jurisdiction under one legal system generates difficulties. Naturally, English judges when applying the European jurisdictional regime crave the discretionary powers that they have under the English traditional rules. In turn, they try to limit as much as possible the influence of the former[193] and to expand as much as possible the scope of application of the latter. The results are double-sided: on the one hand, the European harmonization of private international law becomes more problematic as it is more easily resisted by English judges and commentators;[194]on the other hand, it seems that this 'resistance' could be having its own impact in the referred process of Europeanization[195] (cross-fertilization?) and arguably the outcome could be a greater mixture of the common law and the civil law traditions.

'The Flexibility and Ingenuity of the Common Law'[196]

7.78 In terms of legal technique, as discretion has such a central role in English traditional rules of jurisdiction it results in unavoidable litigation

[191] The current situation may change considerably if the EU Commission Proposal as published in EU doc COM (2010) 748/3 on 14.12.2010 is adopted. The Proposal extends the Regulation's jurisdiction rules to third country defendants. See proposed (new) Recital 14.

[192] DC Jackson, 'Fitting English Maritime Jurisdiction into Europe—or vice versa? [2001] *Lloyd's Maritime and Commercial Law Quarterly* 219; 232.

[193] See eg *Choudhary v Bhatter* [2009] EWCA Civ 1176 how English courts have sought to interpret *Owusu* restrictively and find practical ways to limit its impact.

[194] Harris, 'Understanding the English Response to the Europeanisation of Private International Law' (2008); TC Hartley, 'The European Union and the Systematic Dismantling of the Common Law of Conflict of Laws' (2005) 54 *International and Comparative Law Quarterly* 813.

[195] See in the context of the review of Brussels I Reg the recognition of *forum non conveniens* in the European Parliament Resolution of 7 September 2010, para 14.

[196] See Harris, 'the natural tendency of many English lawyers is to try and salvage something from the situation [the ECJ judgments on jurisdiction which restrict the role of the common law] by drawing upon the flexibility and ingenuity of the common law' in 'Understanding the English Response to the Europeanisation of Private International Law' (2008) 381.

on jurisdictional points. Uncertainty is therefore an inherent component of the traditional English rules on jurisdiction.[197] It is understood that even though uniformity and certainty are loadable values they should not be applied at any cost; the fair decision in the individual case is what ultimately matters most.

At its heart, the English approach to jurisdiction pursues the protection of the rights of the parties to the dispute. This has been referred to as '[t]he English instinct to protect the commercial needs of the parties'.[198] Arguably, this flexibility usually brings about the use of efficient methods to deal with the case at hand in a way that results in most cases in expediency and a better overall management of the case. **7.79**

Certainly England, 'the metropolis of the common law',[199] has always been pragmatic and empirical when it came to the production of a just and fair result and this type of attitude has enhanced the position of the English courts, and particularly London, as an internationally recognized centre for international commercial litigation. This consideration also forms part of the English paradigm of jurisdiction. **7.80**

In terms of priorities, the common law approach initially considers all the relevant connecting factors equally. The circumstances of the particular case will result in a certain factor having more relevance than the others but there are no definite rules to be drawn in general. Another fundamental difference between the European and the English (and indeed also the Scottish) paradigms of jurisdiction is the right to decline to exercise jurisdiction.[200] **7.81**

Forum conveniens

Forum conveniens plays an essential role in the assumption of jurisdiction by the English courts.[201]In English traditional rules, jurisdiction can be based on presence of the defendant within the jurisdiction; submission of the defendant to the English courts; or permission to serve the claim form **7.82**

[197] Hill,'The Exercise of Jurisdiction in Private International Law' (2003) 58.

[198] Harris, 'Understanding the English Response to the Europeanisation of Private International Law' (2008) 373.

[199] Symeon C Symeonides, 'The American Revolution and the European Evolution in Choice of Law: Reciprocal Lessons' (2008) 82 *Tulane Law Review* 8.

[200] On declining jurisdiction see JJ Fawcett (ed), *Declining Jurisdiction in Private International Law* (Oxford, Clarendon, 1995).

[201] Practice Direction B to Part 6 of the Civil Procedure Rules, para 3(1) includes detailed provisions for service out of the jurisdiction; one of the requirements therein is that the claimant must demonstrate that England is the proper place for trial.

out of the jurisdiction.[202] The latter is exercised based on discretion.[203] Hence, when permission to serve out of the jurisdiction is needed, English courts exercise discretionary powers aiming for the litigation to take place in the forum that is most suitable, expedient, and cost-effective. In this context, *forum conveniens* refers to the criterion for exercising this discretion in favour of the English courts jurisdiction only where England is clearly the most appropriate forum 'for the interests of all the parties and the ends of justice'.[204] This rationale underpins also the discretion to stay proceedings on the basis of *forum non conveniens* after the service of a claim form.[205]

7.83 This has not always been like that. In the past English courts were insensitive to arguments to the effect that proceedings in England would be inconvenient or inappropriate for the factual circumstances of the case,[206] even in cases involving international parallel proceedings.[207] This dramatic change of approach has been described by Lord Diplock in *The Abidin Daver*,[208] as judicial chauvinism giving way to judicial comity and, in turn, to the recognition and development of the Scottish legal doctrine of *forum non conveniens*.[209] The path towards this new vision of the exercise of jurisdiction was not free from encumbrances. The House of Lords in its three-to-two decision in *The Atlantic Star*[210] showed the resistance at the time to open the door to its neighbour's doctrine.[211]

[202] For an authoritative analysis of the English traditional rules on jurisdiction, see JJ Fawcett and JM Carruthers, *Cheshire, North & Fawcett Private International Law* (14th edn, Oxford, OUP, 2008) Ch 12.

[203] Civil Procedure Rules 1998, rr 6.36 and 6.37 and supplementary Practice Direction.

[204] Lord Goff in *Spiliada Maritime Corp v Cansulex Ltd (The Spiliada)* [1987] AC 460 said that this was the fundamental principle underlying the exercise of discretion in this field.

[205] Ibid.

[206] See the significant change in this regard in *Vishva Abha* [1990] 2 Lloyd's Rep 312 (QBD (Admlty)); *Caltex Singapore v BP Shipping* [1996] 1 Lloyd's Rep 286 (QBD (Admlty)); *Caspian v Bouygues* [1997] 2 Lloyd's Rep 533 (CA); *Owners of the Herceg Novi v Owners of the Ming Galaxy* [1998] 2 Lloyd's Rep 454 (CA); *The Kapitan Shvetsov* [1998] 1 Lloyd's Rep 199 (CA (HK)).

[207] It is in this sphere where the greatest changes in the English paradigm have taken place as of late. It used to be the case that parallel litigation in the international sphere was considered inconvenient in English law only when it was vexatious or oppressive, and it was not considered vexatious to bring an action in more than one country where there were substantial reasons of benefits to the claimant. In the words of Jessel M R '… if there are substantial reasons to induce him [the claimant] to bring the two actions, why should we deprive him of that right? ...' (*Peruvian Guano Company v Bockwoldt* (1883) LR 23 Ch D 225 (CA)). In that sense, the inbalance between the parties was not particularly linked to one specific jurisdictional ground but it was embedded in the whole system, which was notoriously claimant-orientated.

[208] *Owners of the Las Mercedes v Owners of the Abidin Daver* [1984] 1 Lloyd's Rep 339 (HL).

[209] *The Abidin Daver* [1984] 1 Lloyd's Rep 339 (HL) 203.

[210] *The Atlantic Star* [1974] AC 436 (HL).

[211] It was held by Lord Reid that in re the plea of *forum non conveniens* that even though it was desirable to diminish remaining differences between the law of the sister countries

More than 35 years later, *forum non conveniens* is at the heart of the English common law of jurisdiction enabling a court to stay proceedings commenced in England at the behest of the defendant who can demonstrate that the natural forum for the litigation lies in a foreign court.[212] **7.84**

Forum arresti?

In England a ship can be arrested whenever the claimant has the right to initiate an action *in rem* against the ship. The English implementation of the 1952 International Arrest Convention, through the reform in the Administration of Justice Act 1956 of the internal jurisdictional rules of the Admiralty Court, up to a certain extent served different purposes from that of the Convention itself.[213] In plain contradiction to the Convention, the jurisdictional rules established in English law make arrest dependent on assertion of merits jurisdiction *in rem*. Hence, there is no *forum arresti* strictly recognized under English jurisdictional rules. The link between arrest and action *in rem* does not make arrest a jurisdictional basis but, instead, the basis is service of an *in rem* claim form.[214] The paradox cannot be overestimated. The legal system that spread the *forum arresti* and fought for it in the international sphere does not exactly provide for it in a plain sailing way! Following the foregoing, jurisdiction on the merits is previous to the arrest of the ship in English law instead of consequent upon arrest as it is in the international Conventions. **7.85**

(England and Scotland) ... 'I am not at all satisfied that it would be proper for this House to make such a fundamental change [by accepting the application of the plea in English law] or that it is necessary or desirable', *The Atlantic Star* [1974] AC 436.

212 See Harris, 'Understanding the English Response to the Europeanisation of Private International Law' (2008) 353.

213 Nicholas Gaskell and Richard Shaw, 'The Arrest Convention 1999' [1999] *Lloyd's Maritime and Commercial Law Quarterly* 2.

214 Jurisdiction for the arrest as an interim measure of protection, and jurisdiction for the merits of the dispute, have been clearly distinguished in England since *Mike Trading and Transport Ltd v R Pagnan & Fratelli (The Lisboa)* (1980) 2 Lloyd's Rep 546 (CA). In that case Lord Denning MR made it clear that proceedings to obtain security were separable from proceedings to establish liability and, therefore, even when—as it was the case—there was an exclusive choice of forum as to the merits, this would not invalidate the jurisdiction of the *forum arresti* as to the arrest of the ship; bearing in mind that the purpose of the latter was to obtain security. The decision is fully consistent with Art 7(3) of the 1952 International Arrest Convention.

V. *FORUM ARRESTI*: THE INTERNATIONAL SOLUTIONS

7.86 The approach taken in the international Conventions dealing with the arrest of ships indicate that when arrest is considered as a jurisdictional ground it should be a basis of special jurisdiction only; the availability of arrest is always limited to a certain category of 'maritime claims', therefore, in the international Conventions, no issue of general jurisdiction ever arises.

7.87 Jurisdiction for the arrest is expressly distinguished from jurisdiction on the merits of the claim. Article 7 of both international Arrest Conventions of 1952 and 1999 is apparent in this regard. The first paragraph deals with direct jurisdiction; the rest of the Article's provisions deals with arrest in the context of judicial cooperation.

7.88 Under the 1952 International Arrest Convention the jurisdictional function of arrest of ships arises (in the provided circumstances) upon effective arrest; there is no jurisdiction based on alternative security—differently from the 1952 Collision Convention.[215] This has been changed in the 1999 International Arrest Convention where the jurisdictional function operates if 'an arrest has been effected or security provided to obtain the release of the ship'. The *Comité Maritime International* had proposed a deeper change, so as to allow security 'to avoid arrest' to operate as a jurisdictional ground as much as effectual arrest and security to release the ship from arrest.[216] However, this proposal was faced with strong opposition at the Diplomatic Conference in Geneva;[217] hence, only security given to

[215] Article 1(b) of the Collision (Civil Jurisdiction) Convention 1952 reads: '(1) An action for collision occurring between seagoing vessels, or between seagoing vessels and inland navigation craft, can only be introduced: (b) [b]efore the Court of the place where arrest has been effected of the defendant ship or of any other ship belonging to the defendant which can be lawfully arrested, *or where arrest could have been effected and bail or other security has been furnished*' [emphasis added].

[216] Paragraph 1 of Art 7 of the Draft prepared by the *Comité Maritime International* International Sub-Committee read: 'The courts of the State in which an arrest has been made or security given to avoid arrest or obtain the release of the ship shall have jurisdiction to determine the case upon its merits …' (see *The travaux préparatoires* of the 1999 Arrest Convention in F Berlingieri, *Berlingieri on Arrest of Ships* (2006) 633). The definite drafting deleted the mention to 'security to avoid arrest'. Clearly the English view on that issue is that alternative security in lieu of arrest should found jurisdiction as much as effectual arrest. On that line, Art 36 (transitory provisions) of the Accession Convention 1978, pursuant to the accession of Denmark, Ireland, and the United Kingdom to the Brussels Convention, took such broader view into a black letter—though transitory—provision (Jackson, *Enforcement of Maritime Claims* (2005) 161).

[217] The *travaux préparatoires* of the 1999 International Arrest Convention shows not only that there was no unanimous opinion as to this matter but also the strong opposition of

release the ship from arrest can be counted towards establishing jurisdiction on the merits in the 1999 International Arrest Convention.

1. The 1952 International Arrest Convention

Already at the beginning of the twentieth century the question whether the courts of the country in which the arrest is made should have jurisdiction to determine the case upon its merits was one of the most seriously discussed ones, and the divided opinions did present a problem in the preparatory works pursuant to the 1952 International Arrest Convention.[218] The common law approach to jurisdiction had historically recognized arrest of ships as a means of obtaining jurisdiction, whilst civil law systems had not. However, the division was not a clear-cut one between common law and civil law traditions but between particular legal systems. The legal systems of the United States, Scotland, the Netherlands, Belgium, and England contemplated arrest as a jurisdictional ground on the merits, while the ones of France and Italy clearly did not. The 'compromise'[219] solution was to allow jurisdiction based on arrest in a limited number of cases. These limited number of cases were chosen following two different private international law methodological veins: first, the admittance of the law of the forum so as to allow legal systems (such as English and Scottish ones) providing for jurisdiction based on the arrest of the ship to keep it; and secondly, the identification of particular connecting factors[220] which constituted the 'substantive' link between the forum and the dispute. The result is Article 7(1) of the 1952 International Arrest Convention. **7.89**

Article 7(1) of the 1952 International Arrest Convention identifies six different connecting factors. The first two are cumulative connecting factors, ie two factual circumstances need to be present in order to constitute a **7.90**

Spain, supported amongst others by France and Italy, as to the inclusion of wording allowing for security given to prevent arrest as a jurisdictional ground (see Proceedings of the Main Committee at the Diplomatic Conference held in Geneva, 5 March 1999 in F Berlingieri, *Berlingieri on Arrest of Ships* (2006) 638–43).

[218] In the *Comité Maritime International* International Sub-Committee Meeting in Antwerp in 1951 it created a situation which would have meant the dropping of the Convention altogether; see *The travaux préparatoires of the International Convention for the Unification of Certain Rules of Law with Respect to Collision between Vessels, 23 September 1910, and of the International Convention for the Unification of Certain Rules Relating to the Arrest of Sea-Going Ships, 10 May 1952* (Antwerpen, CMI 1997) 414.

[219] This 'compromise' is criticized by P Chauveau, *Traité de Droit Maritime* (Paris, Librairies Techniques, 1958), para 246.

[220] For a detailed analysis of the individual connecting factors in relation to the way they operate insofar as certain maritime claims, see Berlingieri, *Berlingieri on the Arrest of Ships* (2006) 282–90.

'substantial' connection with the forum. These two cumulative connecting factors are (a) the habitual residence or principal place of business of the claimant, and (b) the place where the claim arose, if that happens to be-and this is the second factual circumstance applicable to both connecting factors—in the country in which the arrest was made.

7.91 Article 7(1) reads:

> The Courts of the country in which the arrest was made shall have jurisdiction to determine the case upon its merits: If the domestic law of the country in which the arrest is made gives jurisdiction to such Courts or in any of the following cases namely: (a) if the claimant has his habitual residence or principal place of business in the country in which the arrest was made; (b) if the claim arose in the country in which the arrest was made; (c) if the claim concerns the voyage of the ship during which the arrest was made; (d) if the claim arose out of a collision or in circumstances covered by Article 13 of the International Convention for the unification of certain rules of law with respect to collisions between vessels, signed at Brussels on 23rd September 1910; (e) if the claim is for salvage; (f) if the claim is upon a mortgage or hypothecation of the ship arrested. (2) If the Court within whose jurisdiction the ship was arrested has not jurisdiction to decide upon the merits, the bail or other security given in accordance with article 5 to procure the release of the ship shall specifically provide that it is given as security for the satisfaction of any judgment which may eventually be pronounced by a Court having jurisdiction so to decide; and the Court or other appropriate judicial authority of the country in which the arrest is made shall fix the time within which the claimant shall bring an action before a Court having such jurisdiction. (3) If the parties have agreed to submit the dispute to the jurisdiction of a particular Court other than that within whose jurisdiction the arrest was made or to arbitration, the Court or other appropriate judicial authority within whose jurisdiction the arrest was made may fix the time within which the claimant shall bring proceedings. (4) If, in any of the cases mentioned in the two preceding paragraphs, the action or proceedings are not brought within the time so fixed, the defendant may apply for the release of the ship or of the bail or other security. (5) This Article shall not apply in cases covered by the provisions of the revised Rhine Navigation Convention of 17 October 1868.

7.92 Connecting factors such as the habitual residence or principal place of business of the claimant, as related to the claimant rather than the defendant, are in modern times excluded from the 'white list' of acceptable jurisdictional bases. In the European Union arena, Schlosser says that 'the black list' of jurisdictional bases is 'so to speak the confessions of sins made by the member states'.[221] During the preliminary work pursuant to the adoption of the 1952 International Arrest Convention, the Italian and the Yugoslavian delegations strongly opposed the inclusion of such

[221] P Schlosser, 'Jurisdiction in International Litigation–The Issue of Human Rights in Relation to National Law and to the Brussels Convention' (1991) *Rivista di diritto internazionale* 5.

jurisdictional bases, alleging that they did not represent a close connection between the claim and the *forum*.[222] Nowadays they could be easily labelled as exorbitant; however, as discussed previously in this chapter,[223] there is no intrinsic reason why a relational theory should focus only on the defendant. The habitual residence or principal place of business of the claimant are the only connecting factors of a personal nature as opposed to the other relevant connecting factors that are related to the dispute—rather than related to the parties to the dispute.

The third jurisdictional link is constituted by a connecting factor peculiar to the arrest of ships: if the claim has arisen during the voyage of the ship during which the arrest was made. Finally, the last three 'substantial' connections are related to the nature of the claim in cases of collision, salvage, mortgage, or hypothecation of the ship. **7.93**

In practice, the results of this 'compromise' solution have not provided the degree of harmonization intended when it was adopted. Since common law countries (notably England) retained their system and civil law countries could only avail themselves of arrest as a ground for acquiring jurisdiction in respect of certain claims with no specific reason, the solution has furthered the imbalance between the different countries.[224] Furthermore, it is here submitted, from a technical point of view, that the particular connecting factors chosen add unnecessary complexity to the determination of jurisdictional grounds in the field. As most of these links provided for in Article 7(1) are factual circumstances combined with legal concepts such as, for example, habitual residence and principal place of business, the process of establishing jurisdiction on the merits gets cumbersome; and, as the *Comité Maritime International* recognized in 1994, there are no reasons to justify such added difficulty.[225] **7.94**

2. The 1999 International Arrest Convention

In this sphere there are several modifications in the new Convention. The new regime moves forward to a plain recognition of the jurisdictional power of the *forum arresti*, without any conditions, and not subject to its recognition by national laws. Moreover, the new Convention recognizes party autonomy (choice of forum agreements or arbitration agreements), **7.95**

[222] *Comité Maritime International* (CMI) Conferences (1947–51) (CMI Amberes 1951) 190.

[223] See para 7.19 above.

[224] The CMI evaluated the results of the 'compromise' solution as non-satisfactory, JIGE Seventh Session, 5–9 December 1994, Report-Anex I; JIGE Ninth Session, 2–6 December 1996, Report-Anex II (Berlingieri, *Berlingieri on Arrest of Ships* (2006) 635).

[225] Ibid, JIGE Seventh Session, 5–9 December 1994, Report-Anex I.

as the main jurisdictional basis taking priority over the jurisdiction of the *forum arresti*.[226]

7.96 Doubtless the 1999 International Arrest Convention is in line with the latest trends in jurisdictional issues in the international sphere. Article 7 of the Convention sets out

> 1. The Courts of the State in which an arrest has been effected or security provided to obtain the release of a ship shall have jurisdiction to determine the case upon its merits, unless the parties validly agree or have validly agreed to submit the dispute to a Court of another State which accepts jurisdiction, or to arbitration. 2. Nonetheless, the provisions of paragraph 1 of this article, the Courts of the State in which an arrest has been effected, or security provided to obtain the release of the ship, may refuse to exercise that jurisdiction where that refusal is permitted by the law of that State and a Court of another State accepts jurisdiction. 3. In cases where a Court of the State where an arrest has been effected or security provided to obtain the release of the ship (a) does not have jurisdiction to determine the case upon its merits; or (b) has refused to exercise jurisdiction in accordance with the provisions of paragraph 2 of this article, such Court may, and upon request shall, order a period of time within which the claimant shall bring proceedings before a competent Court or arbitral tribunal.

7.97 The plain recognition of the *forum arresti* could be seen as advancement of its legitimacy as a jurisdictional basis. However, the reasons for such a recognition eliminating the conditions set out in the 1952 International Arrest Convention had to do with practicalities rather than abstract considerations. It was perceived as a drawback to uniformity to allow for different jurisdictional systems depending on the different national laws of the contracting parties.[227] Bearing in mind that eliminating the *forum arresti* was not acceptable as a way of unification, the only possibility was to recognize it in general terms. This does not necessarily represent evolution of juridical thinking but it is another reflection of the importance that practicalities have in admiralty jurisdiction.

7.98 Another novelty of the new Convention is the inclusion of discretionary powers in the exercise of jurisdiction by the courts if such discretion is recognized by the law of the *forum arresti*, for example, in cases where the jurisdictional rules of the law of the *forum arresti* permit the courts to decline jurisdiction based on the doctrine of *forum non conveniens*.[228]

[226] Cf this with the decision in *The Bergen (No 1)* [1997] 1 Lloyd's Rep 380 (QBD (Admlty)).

[227] Francesco Berlingieri, opinion shared with the author at interview held in Genoa, Italy on 22 May 2006.

[228] Article 7(2) of the 1999 International Arrest Convention reads: 'Notwithstanding the provisions of paragraph 1 of this article, the courts of the State in which an arrest has been

This permission, however, operates under a further condition: that a court of another State accepts jurisdiction. To a certain extent, this represents the adoption of the Scottish dual formula of *forum arresti–forum non conveniens* in the field of arrest of ships. This home-grown Scottish doctrine crafted and named by judges and practitioners:[229] *forum non conveniens*, arose to contain a broad general jurisdictional basis available in Scots law at the time, namely, arrestment to found jurisdiction.[230] If this potentially excessive jurisdictional ground would have not existed in Scots law the doctrine of *forum non conveniens* may never have emerged.[231] Following that, it may be argued that it is indeed the incorporation of this dual formula in the 1999 International Arrest Convention that really represents advancement at the international level; not because it has been taken from Scots law as a system of 'genius'[232] but because a far-reaching jurisdictional ground such as *forum arresti* has been combined with its natural correlative.[233] In that sense it may be argued that the formula advanced in this Convention represents 'the golden mean between the competing values of certainty and flexibility'.[234]However, Article 7(2) of the 1999 International Arrest Convention authorizes states parties to decline jurisdiction only 'where that refusal is permitted by the law of that State' therefore the issue is left to the law of the *forum arresti*.

Allegedly Member States of the European Union are prevented from ratifying individually the 1999 International Arrest Convention due to the fact that it contains jurisdictional provisions which would affect the rules contained in the Brussels I Regulation. Ratification/accession hence stays **7.99**

effected, or security provided to obtain the release of the ship, may refuse to exercise that jurisdiction where that refusal is permitted by the law of that State and a court of another State accepts jurisdiction.'

[229] Lord Hope of Craighead (HL), 'Forum non conveniens: where next?'(2007).

[230] Ibid.

[231] Ibid.

[232] R Evan-Jones,'Mixed Legal Systems, Scotland and the Unification of Private Law in Europe' in JM Smits (ed), *The Contribution of Mixed Legal Systems to European Private Law* (Antwerp, Intersentia, 2001) 44; 'Receptions of Law, Mixed Legal Systems and the Myth of the Genius of Scots Private Law' (1998) 114 *Law Quarterly Review* 228. For other views of the 'genius' of Scots law, see A Rodger, 'Thinking About Scots Law' (1996) 1 *Edinburgh Law Review* 3; JM Thomson, 'Legal change and Scots private law', in J Cairns and O Robinson (eds), *Critical Studies in Ancient Law. Comparative Law and Legal History: Essays in Honour of Alan Watson* (Oxford, Hart, 2001) 379.

[233] See Lord Hope of Craighead (HL), 'Forum non conveniens: where next?' (2007).

[234] Symeonides, 'The American Revolution and the European Evolution in Choice of Law: Reciprocal Lessons' (2008) 36.

with the European Union as a whole.[235] In the current context of the review of the functioning of the Brussels regime, where the impact of Article 71 (the *lex specialis* provision) has been addressed and its advantages seem to continue to be more profitable than detrimental, the accession of the European Union to the 1999 International Arrest Convention should be seriously considered as a way forward to promote jurisdictional uniformity and a level playing field in the European area of justice. If that happens, it is to be hoped that the dual formula *forum arresti–forum non conveniens* follows the fostering path that *forum arresti* has taken via the *lex specialis* provision thus helping to consolidate a well-balanced special jurisdictional scheme for maritime claims in the European regime.

VI. *FORUM ARRESTI* AS A COOPERATIVE JURISDICTIONAL BASIS

7.100 English and Scottish practitioners, judges, and commentators might well be surprised that at the beginning of the twenty-first century somebody has considered that legitimating of the *forum arresti* in the case of ships was necessary in a book on the topic. However, if the one making that assessment is originally formed in a civil law system, the surprise disappears.A good example of the general 'distaste' of civil lawyers for jurisdictional rules based on the arrest/arrestment of the ship may be found in the opinion of the Advocate-General in the European Court of Justice decision in *The Tatry*.[236] He expressed that the jurisdiction available under the 1952 International Arrest Convention was 'fortuitous', 'a matter of chance', and certainly encouraging 'forum shopping'. 'An unexpected assessment, one may think, of the provisions of an international Convention.'[237] Yet, it is not an uncommon opinion amongst civil lawyers. Hence, following the main discussion in this chapter the remaining paragraphs aim at providing a synthesis of the advantages of *forum arresti* as a jurisdictional basis.

[235] The ECJ has established the principle that where common rules have been adopted the Member States no longer have the right to act individually, or even collectively, to undertake obligations with non-member countries to affect those rules. In such case the EU also has exclusive competence to conclude international agreements (ECJ opinion issued on 7 February 2006, <http://curia.europa.int>). However, Spain acceded to the 1999 International Arrest Convention on 7 June 2002.

[236] *Maciej Rataj (The Tatry)* (Case C-406/92) [1995] 1 Lloyd's Rep 302 (ECJ) (Advocate General Mr G Tesauro, opinion of 13 July 1994).

[237] A Briggs, 'The Brussels Convention Tames the Arrest Convention' Case and Comment *The Tatry* [1995] *Lloyd's Maritime and Commercial Law Quarterly* 161, 163.

1. *Forum Arresti*: A Special Jurisdictional Basis

7.101 In terms of legal technique, determining the most convenient jurisdiction in cases of concurrent jurisdiction is a difficult task of private international law. In most cases the courts involved will be internationally competent to hear the merits due to a close connection between the forum and the parties, or the forum and the dispute. Which one should prevail requires a horizontal comparison between those connections. Doubtless, this is a field where no definite answers have been found yet, and further research in this sphere would go far beyond the scope of analysis of this book. Notwithstanding, it may be argued that the distinction between general and special jurisdiction coined by the professors of Harvard[238] more than 40 years ago, that has been so influential in the development of jurisdictional theory in private international law in the United States, should be promoted to the highest degree in Europe.

7.102 The usefulness of a special jurisdictional basis in the case of ships has been recognized by a leading English private international law commentator in the context of the review of the Brussels I Regulation. Dickinson suggests that '[a]n additional rule of special jurisdiction for cases concerning title, possession or control of tangible moveable assets (favouring the courts of the place where the asset is physically located at the time the court becomes seized) would potentially be valuable, particularly in cases involving ships and aircraft'.[239] In line with this suggestion, the recently proposed amendments to the Brussels I Regulation, with a view to improving the practical functioning of jurisdiction rules, include a provision creating a jurisdictional ground for claims involving rights *in rem* at the place where movable assets are located.[240] This could certainly be seen as enhancing the suitability of *forum arresti* in the case of the arrest of ships.

7.103 Upon this background, it is possible to say that *forum arresti* in the case of arrest of ships is suitable as a special basis of jurisdiction. As such, its practical advantage is blatant: the presence of the defendant's asset (generally its only or main asset[241]) in the forum makes the enforcement of the eventual judgment more expedient. At this stage of evolution of international judicial cooperation where recognition and enforcement of foreign

[238] See para 7.12 above.

[239] See Andrew Dickinson's post of 8 June 2009 in relation to 'Rules of special jurisdiction' in ConflictofLaws.net 'Brussels I Review-Online Focus Group' available at http://conflictoflaws.net/2009/brussels-i-review-online-focus-group/> (last visited 10 November 2010).

[240] See EU Commission Proposal, para 3.1.6 and proposed Art 5.3.

[241] Very often a shipping company sets up a separate subsidiary company to own each ship.

judgments—especially *ad extra* integrated areas—is not as straightforward as might be desired, this obvious advantage should not be underestimated. By contrast, it is difficult to find technical arguments in favour of the *forum arresti* as a general jurisdictional basis.

7.104 The reason for arguing in favour of fostering special jurisdictions over general ones is supportable from a private international law perspective, ie a forum seized because it is related to the subject-matter of the case has a closer link to the dispute than a forum that has been seized because the defendant is domiciled or habitually resident within its territory. Jurisdiction should be based on the proximity between the forum and the dispute.[242] Fernández Arroyo ascertains that 'the general acceptance of a certain jurisdictional basis has a lot to do with the essential or principal character that the elements taken into account hold in the legal relationship'.[243] In this sense, it may be argued that when jurisdiction is linked to the dispute (special) instead of to the parties (general), the elements taken into account are germane to the particular legal relation and not only to one of the parties. Indeed, specificity in terms of jurisdiction is recognized in several international instruments and certainly is the *raison de être* of the *lex specialis* provision of Article 71 of the Brussels I Regulation.[244]

2. *Forum Arresti*: A Cooperative Forum

7.105 The latest dicta seem to indicate that in the opinion of the European Court of Justice the *lex specialis* provision of the Brussels I Regulation allows for a special jurisdictional basis to operate only if such special jurisdictional basis is, first, highly predictable, secondly, it facilitates the sound administration of justice, thirdly, it enables the risk of concurrent proceedings to be minimized, and finally, it ensures the free movement of judgments and mutual trust in the European Union.[245] These requirements are interpretative of Article 71 and are yet to be developed by further case-law. As the case is not connected particularly with *forum arresti* one needs to be cautious in any generalization. However, if those requirements were to be confirmed as of general application in relation to the *lex specialis* provision,

[242] Lagarde, *Le principe de proximité dans le droit international privé contemporain* (1986) 131–2.

[243] Fernández Arroyo,'Exorbitant and Exclusive Grounds of Jurisdiction in European Private International Law' (2004) 170.

[244] The 1952 International Arrest Convention has been recognized as being a 'convention on a particular matter' in terms of the *lex specialis* provision (See *Schlosser Report* [1979] OJ C 59/71, para 238 note 59).

[245] Criteria as set by the ECJ in the decision in *TNT Express Nederland BV v AXA Versicherung AG*, Case C-533/08 of 4 May 2010, [2010] ILPr 35 at para 56.

it is here submitted that *forum arresti* in the case of ships passes that added test (not included in the wording of Article 71 but 'added' by a contextual interpretation of such Article by the ECJ).[246] The following paragraphs explain that submission in greater detail.

It is Highly Predictable

Forum arresti in the case of the arrest of ships forms part of the European jurisdictional framework since the Accession Convention 1978. Most EU Member States are parties to the 1952 International Arrest Convention, hence, when it comes to the adjudication of jurisdiction on the merits once the ship has been arrested in a certain jurisdiction, the assumption of jurisdiction by the *forum arresti* comes as no surprise. In that sense, it has been sustained that *forum arresti* constitutes a general trend in international procedural maritime law and that it is justified in terms of convenience, derived from the essentially movable nature of the ship.[247] Hence, the assumption of jurisdiction by the courts of the country where the ship has been arrested is as such highly predictable. In other words, when a ship is entering the ports of a particular country it is reasonably foreseeable for the shipowner, the demise charterer, or any other person who might be a defendant in a maritime claim connected to that ship, that if the ship is arrested in that country, jurisdiction on the merits of the claim may follow in that jurisdiction as a consequence of the arrest. **7.106**

It Facilitates the Sound Administration of Justice

A ship is elusive and the shipping management chain makes her more so. **7.107** The commercial management of ships places peculiar problems on those faced with an unpaid debt incurred in the course of shipping. In addition to the inherent mobility of ships as the main (and so frequently unique) asset of the debtor, there is the unawareness from the point of view of the creditor, to some extent, of whom he is doing business with and where the counterparty can be reached. The arrest of ships with the several functions discussed throughout this book attempts to make sure that some particular maritime claims can be secured by the accessibility to a provisional and protective measure while awaiting judgment, at the same time making sure that this security does not slip away. This is achieved through physical and legal obstacles being placed on the owner's or user's right to

[246] See para 7.49 above.

[247] Herbert and Fresnedo de Aguirre, 'El Arresto de Buques y el Principio de Jurisdicción mas Próxima' [1993] 167.

employ the ship. If the procedure simultaneously serves the purpose of establishing jurisdiction on the merits, it certainly facilitates the sound administration of justice.

It Enables the Risk of Concurrent Proceedings to be Minimized

7.108 The frequent allegation that *forum arresti* increases the chances of 'forum shopping' deserves consideration in this context. It is submitted that the comments of Lord Reid in *The Atlantic Star*[248] are sound. He said 'I would not regard a foreigner who arrests a ship in England as necessarily forum shopping. The right to arrest a ship is an ancient and often necessary right. Not only may there be difficulty otherwise in establishing jurisdiction in an appropriate forum, but the arrest gives to the arrester what may be a very necessary security.'[249] If the arrest of ships displays its three functions (ie the jurisdictional, the security, and the protective function) at once in the same jurisdiction that enables the risk of concurrent proceedings to be minimized.

The Adoption of the 1999 Arrest Convention Would Enhance the Mutual Trust Principle in the European Union

7.109 The issue of extraterritorial enforcement hardly arises in connection with the arrest of ships. Nevertheless, the mutual trust principle would be enhanced if the European Union accedes to the 1999 International Arrest Convention. This would represent the availability of a cooperative jurisdictional ground for shipping litigation to every Member State regardless of their different domestic laws. Hence, one of the difficulties shown in the review of Brussels I (the difficulty in application of Article 71 of Brussels I due to the fact that different Member States are parties to different specialized conventions) would disappear. This is not to be underestimated considering the importance of the international Arrest Conventions in maritime litigation.[250] Thus, the adoption of the 1999 International Arrest Convention would allow Member States to be in an equal position in this regard, and this undoubtedly also implies that, if the need for extraterritorial recognition arises, that equal position would favour the free movement

[248] *The Altantic Star* [1973] 2 Lloyd's Rep 197 (HL) 201.

[249] Ibid.

[250] See the Joint Declaration signed in Luxembourg on 9 October 1978 urging the [then] Community States to accede to the 'most important of all the Conventions on maritime law, namely the Brussels Convention of 10 May 1952 [the 1952 International Arrest Convention]'.

of judicial decisions in line with the principle of mutual recognition, ie the mutual trust principle in the European area of justice.

As the foregoing discussion illustrates, it is possible to affirm that *forum arresti* based on the arrest/arrestment of a ship as a jurisdictional basis is not exorbitant but cooperative.[251] It does not jeopardize the balance between the parties; it does not favour one party particularly linked with the forum. The element taken into account to determine competence is essential to the legal relation, it is not merely accidental[252] (and in that sense arrest/arrestment of a ship differs from the arrestment of movables as a general jurisdictional basis in Scots traditional law). Its recognition in the international Conventions guarantees that the reasonableness standard has been passed, ie agreement has been achieved on the convenience of the criterion. This feature is not enough by itself but it is to be considered as one of the tests to determine the legitimacy of a jurisdictional basis. **7.110**

The adoption of the 1999 International Arrest Convention by the European Union could represent, therefore, the availability of such a cooperative device to every Member State of the Union. Moreover, under Article 267 of the Treaty of Functioning of the European Union (TFEU) the Court of Justice has jurisdiction to interpret international Conventions to which the European Union itself has become a party in accordance with the procedure laid down in Article 218 TFEU. This could represent the sought after advancement of uniformity in the international law on the arrest of ships,[253] at least in Europe. **7.111**

[251] Schlosser in the *Heidelberg Report* comments on the suggestion of The Netherlands Maritime and Transport Law Association that expressed that 'a provision similar to Article 7 of the Arrest Convention 1999' should be adopted in the revision of Brussels I. The main argument of this suggestion is centred on the highly valued tradition of the *forum arresti* in shipping matters (Study JLS/C4/2005/03 137).

[252] The lack of such link between the element taken into account and the legal relationship has been considered as a criterion for defining an exorbitant jurisdictional basis, see Fernández Arroyo, 'Exorbitant and Exclusive Grounds of Jurisdiction in European Private International Law' (2004) 171.

[253] See the favourable position of leading academics in the field soon after the 1999 International Arrest Convention was adopted in Nicholas Gaskell and Richard Shaw, 'The Arrest Convention 1999' [1999] *Lloyd's Maritime and Commercial Law Quarterly* 1. They predicted that despite the advantages of the Convention it was unlikely that a legislative opportunity for adopting the Convention in England could be found in the immediate future (at p 11).

VII. CONCLUSIONS

7.112 The main task of this chapter was to provide an assessment of the exercise of jurisdiction as a consequence of the arrest of ships. And the main question to be answered was whether arrest constituted a sufficient connection with the forum so as to justify the assumption of direct jurisdiction by that forum in the absence of any other relevant connections. In light of all the foregoing, the answer is negative when it comes to general jurisdiction and positive when analysed as a special jurisdictional ground for certain types of maritime claims. It follows from the discussion in the body of this chapter that the widest held opinion is that in terms of general jurisdiction the domicile or habitual residence of the defendant is 'the rule'. No arguments can be found to justify arrest of a ship as a general jurisdictional ground (or to treat a ship as domiciled where it can be found[254]) and to maintain *forum arresti* as a general jurisdictional basis denotes a non-balanced system. However, combining a general jurisdictional basis such as the defendant's domicile as an alternative to party autonomy with a thoughtful scheme of special jurisdictions should avoid a clash between the interests of the claimant and those of the defendant.[255]

7.113 The different paradigms of jurisdiction in which the arrest of ships as a legal institution has developed its jurisdictional function have diverse standards to be considered when determining the legitimacy of a particular jurisdictional basis. Nevertheless, with its survival as a special jurisdictional ground for maritime claims in the European regime, a further merger has taken place in the long chain of amalgamations that have crafted the arrest of ships as the contemporary institution that pertains to the common law and the civil law, somehow building up a bridge amongst these traditions.

7.114 The ideal would be to envisage and create an internationally acceptable system that would find a middle point between the common law and the civilian approach to international jurisdiction; one in which a hybrid system which mixes hard-and-fast rules and discretion would work for the benefit of all. In the international sphere the issues are yet in a state as to

[254] Phillimore in the *travaux préparatoires* to the 1952 International Arrest Convention (CMI 1997) 400.

[255] Already more than 40 years ago it was suggested that what was paramount for a real solution of the problem of exorbitant jurisdictions in international litigation was '... a well thought out and well balanced system of specific jurisdictions: jurisdictions which are closely linked with the legal relationship from which the action arises ...' (de Winter, 'Excessive Jurisdiction in Private International Law' (1968) 719).

find universally accepted answers to what is an ideal jurisdictional system in international litigation.[256] However, at the time of writing there are reasons to be optimistic that such hybrid system is feasible and achievable.[257]

Furthermore, it is suggested that the *forum non conveniens* battle is not yet lost in the EU jurisdictional scheme. And the solutions advanced by the 1999 International Arrest Convention in this sphere could promote the well-deserved recognition of this paradigmatic jurisdictional device, the British *forum non conveniens,* at least in the particular context of shipping litigation. **7.115**

Therefore, other steps towards further achievements in this area need to be taken to prepare the arena for the future. One of these steps that seems to be already consolidated in private international law is the distinction between, on the one hand, ancillary jurisdiction for the purposes of interim relief and, on the other hand, jurisdiction on the merits. The 1952 International Arrest Convention has been a pioneer in fostering that distinction. This study turns to its analysis in the following chapter. **7.116**

[256] The original failure of the Hague Conference in Private International Law in achieving a comprehensive Convention on Jurisdiction and Foreign Judgments in Civil and Commercial Matters so demonstrates.

[257] In the context of the review of the Brussels I Reg, it has been suggested by the European Parliament in the Resolution of 7 September 2010 that the Hague Conference project on an international judgments convention should be revived (para 15). Furthermore, the proposed extension of the Brussels I Reg to third country defendants and the introduction—albeit limited—of discretionary powers to decline jurisdiction in certain circumstances may make the Brussels I Reg if so amended a model of such hybrid system.

8

Arrest of Ships, Judicial Cooperation, and The Recognition and Enforcement of Foreign Judgments

I. INTRODUCTION

8.01 This chapter is concerned with the third domain germane to private international law: the recognition and enforcement of foreign judgments. As it has been acknowledged from the very beginning of this book, the arrest of ships can be said to be a truly private international law institution.[1] Its main rationale is to provide a useful device for international commerce and to compensate for the difficulty of enforcing judgments abroad.

[1] See Ch 2, para 2.01 above.

Therefore, the relation between the arrest of ships and the enforcement of foreign judgments is inherent to the legal institution itself. In turn, the recognition and enforcement of foreign judgments should be looked at from the standpoint of international judicial cooperation.[2] It is in this broader sphere that the arrest of ships as a provisional and protective measure plays a key role in maritime litigation. This takes the analysis to the field of the ancillary jurisdiction that is sometimes exercised by the courts in one country for the sole purpose of granting interim relief to support proceedings on the merits in another country. The issues that the arrest of ships raises in relation to the exercise of this ancillary jurisdiction and in relation to the recognition and enforcement of foreign judgments are the main concerns of this chapter.

The distinction between jurisdiction on the merits and jurisdiction for the sole purpose of granting provisional measures (hereafter 'ancillary jurisdiction'[3]) becomes paramount in this context. Certainly, in the field of provisional and protective measures in the international arena, judicial cooperation between the courts of the different States involved is vital. On this matter, it is important to acknowledge the latest developments in European law to further develop the European area of justice, the aim of which is to provide a framework in which Member States' courts can facilitate the administration of justice by courts of other Member States without interfering in the determination of rights and obligations by the courts of other Member States.[4] **8.02**

International judicial cooperation in this field is two-fold. On the one hand, a court that has no jurisdiction to hear the merits of a case can still exercise jurisdiction for the sole purpose of granting provisional and **8.03**

[2] The need to improve communications between courts of the EU Member States has been recognized by the European Parliament non-legislative resolution (7 September 2010) on the Brussels I review and it has been reflected in the wording of the European Commission Proposal for a Regulation of the European Parliament and of the Council on jurisdiction and the recognition and enforcement of judgments in civil and commercial matters (Recast) 14.12.2010 (COM (2010) 748/3 (hereafter 'the EU Commission Proposal').

[3] In *Crédit Suisse Fides Trust v Cuoghi* [1998] 1 QB 818, Millett J commenting on Art 24 of the Lugano Convention referred to the exercise of jurisdiction for the sole purpose of granting provisional measures as 'ancillary jurisdiction' at 827. The use of this term has been adopted by the author to refer to jurisdiction in this sphere, also in V Ruiz Abou-Nigm, 'Ancillary Jurisdiction for Interim Measures of Protection in Support of Cross-Border Litigation' (2005) 4 *Uniform Law Review* 759. The expression is used also in this context by leading English private international law commentators, see JJ Fawcett and JM Carruthers, *Cheshire, North & Fawcett Private International Law* (14th edn, Oxford, OUP, 2008) 319.

[4] See new Art 31 as included in the EU Commission Proposal for amendments to the Brussels I Reg.

protective measures in support of foreign proceedings or arbitration.[5] The 1952 International Arrest Convention has been a pioneer in fostering this possibility in the field of arrest of ships.[6] Furthermore, the Europeanization of private international law has brought further advancement of the distinction more generally into English and Scots law. There is a clear distinction between jurisdiction on the merits and jurisdiction for the purposes of interim relief in the European jurisdictional scheme, introduced first by the original Brussels and Lugano Conventions, and currently established in (EC) Regulation 44/2001 on jurisdiction and the recognition and enforcement of foreign judgments (Brussels I Regulation)[7] and in the Lugano II (2007) Convention.[8]

8.04 On the other hand, there is the recognition and enforcement of foreign judgments rendered in connection with the provisional and protective measures granted to support the foreign proceedings on the merits. The supportive character of the provisional measure is the most effective in the case of arrest of ships if the eventual foreign judgment is going to be enforceable against the ship or the security given to release the ship from arrest. As the arrest of a ship is essentially a territorial provisional and protective measure, in the context of the 1952 International Arrest Convention and according to the European jurisdictional scheme, [9] the core question in practice is whether the judgment on the merits of the maritime claim will be recognized and enforced in the legal system where the ship has been arrested or alternative security provided to prevent or release the ship from the arrest. If the answer to this question is negative the effectiveness of arrest as an interim measure of protection in support of foreign proceedings is severely jeopardized. This issue was at the centre of the discussion in the *travaux préparatoires* of the 1999 International Arrest

[5] Note that in the context of the review of Brussels I the EU Commission Proposal prevents the free circulation within the European area of justice of measures ordered by a court other than the one having jurisdiction on the substance. According to the Proposal the effect of these measures should be limited to the territory of the Member State where they were granted (see Proposal, para 3.1.5.).

[6] Article 7(2) of the International Convention for the Unification of Certain Rules Relating to the Arrest of Sea-Going Ships, signed in Brussels 10 May 1952.

[7] Regulation (EC) No 44/2001 on jurisdiction and the recognition and enforcement of judgments in civil and commercial matters ([16.1.2001] OJ L12/1).

[8] See Council Decision 2009/430/EC of 27 November 2008 concerning the conclusion of the Convention on jurisdiction and the recognition and enforcement of judgments in civil and commercial matters ([10.6.2009] OJ L147/1).

[9] When reference is made to the 'European jurisdictional scheme' or the 'Brussels regime' or similar, the author is referring to all texts dealing with jurisdiction and the recognition and enforcement of judgments in civil and commercial matters, adopted in the framework of the European integration.

Convention, and the results clearly reinforce the protective function of arrest and its provisional character, as allegedly the decision on its adoption by the European countries does not depend on the will of individual Member States but rests with the European Union,[10] the issue is examined in the light of the relevant provisions of the European regime.

Against this background, this chapter starts by continuing to examine the protective function of arrest of ships. The effectiveness of such function, to a certain extent, depends on the availability of jurisdiction for the sole purpose of interim relief in the relevant legal system. Jurisdiction for the sole purpose of interim relief is therefore defined and examined in this chapter in connection with the arrest of ships, in national, international, and European law. The consideration of the proximity principle as the foundation of the departure from general principles of international jurisdiction in the sphere of interim relief is reviewed. Finally, the specific problems connected to indirect jurisdiction, ie the recognition and enforcement of foreign judgments, is also looked at in the national, international, and regional frameworks. Bearing in mind the Europeanization of private international law, and the benefits that the 1999 International Arrest Convention could bring to the European countries, in terms of legal certainty and further harmonization in the field, this chapter addresses the consistency between the current European regime of international jurisdiction and the jurisdiction and recognition and enforcement provisions of the 1999 International Arrest Convention, in view of the possible adoption of the latter by the European Union. **8.05**

II. THE PROTECTIVE FUNCTION OF ARREST OF SHIPS

In the first chapter of this book it was submitted[11] that it is the speed with which the defendant's main asset—the ship—could leave the jurisdiction that the arrest of ships is primarily trying to counteract. It should be added that in the current scenario of international judicial cooperation this protective function is not limited to one forum particularly connected to the **8.06**

[10] The ECJ has established the principle that where common rules have been adopted the Member States no longer have the right acting individually, or even collectively, to undertake obligations with non-member countries to affect those rules. In such case the EU also has exclusive competence to conclude international agreements (ECJ opinion issued on 7 February 2006 <http://curia.europa.eu>). However, Spain acceded to the 1999 International Arrest Convention on 7 June 2002.

[11] See Ch 1, para 1.03 above.

dispute but could be exercised by any jurisdiction that provides for the arrest of ships in its legal system, at least in Europe. This is a direct consequence of characterizing arrest of ships as a provisional and protective measure, and as such within the definition of 'provisional, including protective measures' of Article 31 of the Brussels I Regulation in its present form. According to the case-law of the European Court of Justice these measures are the ones 'intended to preserve a factual or legal situation so as to safeguard rights the recognition of which is sought elsewhere from the court having jurisdiction as to the substance of the matter'.[12] However, in the State parties to the 1952 International Arrest Convention this function can only be displayed by the arrest of ships in relation to a closed list of maritime claims and cannot be displayed for non-maritime claims.

8.07 As a protective measure the arrest of a ship needs to be most frequently granted as an *ex parte* measure, ie without notice to the defendant, as measures of this kind would be rendered meaningless if the defendant debtor had to be informed that the ship is going to be arrested. The practical utility of *ex parte* provisional measure implies, however, certain limitations when it comes to the recognition and enforcement of such measures in the international sphere.[13] However, in the case of arrest of ships, since it is primarily a territorial measure that is usually granted by the courts of the jurisdiction where the measure is to take effect, this rarely represents a problem.

8.08 In English law, ship arrest and interim relief are treated distinctly. The judicial discretion to grant interim relief is provided for in section 25 of the Civil Jurisdiction and Judgments Act 1982. These provisions apply, for instance, to the granting of freezing orders.[14] Arrest of maritime property is excluded from that framework and it can only be applied for in the framework of an *in rem* claim. Arguably this approach, as opposed to the

[12] Case C-394/07, *Reichert v Dresdner Bank (No 2)* [1992] ECR I-2149, para 34.

[13] However, if the amendments to the Brussels I Reg included in the EU Commission Proposal crystallize as part of the Brussels scheme, even if granted *ex parte*, provisional, including protective measure granted by a court having jurisdiction on the merits of the case, would be able to be fully recognized and enforced within the European area of justice, albeit subject to certain conditions and limitations.

[14] The relation between the arrest of ships as a private international law category in the international Arrest Conventions and the English freezing order involving a ship is somehow unsettled in English law. See Ch 4, paras 4.31–4.35 above. In the preliminary work pursuant to the 1999 International Arrest Convention, the UK delegation expressed that a discussion was under way in England on whether it would be desirable for the *Mareva* injunction (as it was then called) to be covered by the definition of 'arrest'. See the *travaux préparatoires* of the 1999 International Arrest Convention, Ninth Session 2–6 December 1996, as included in F Berlingieri, *Berlingieri on Arrest of Ships* (London, Informa, 2006) 527.

approach taken in Scotland, where arrestment of ships is part of the more general framework of diligence,[15] favours the particular needs of maritime commerce. Furthermore, this claimant-orientated policy of treating ship arrest as a legal entitlement in the framework of the action *in rem*, even if the action is pursued only to secure a claim on the merits in another jurisdiction or in arbitration, could be seen as a means of protecting England as one of the world leaders of maritime litigation.

Notwithstanding these arguments, as explained in detail in Chapter 4, it is here submitted that this calls out for reform. In English law, the protective function of arrest of ships is jeopardized, even though, in general, ancillary jurisdiction in the international litigation scenario is dealt with by English law in a far-reaching manner. In contrast to civil law jurisdictions, and to Scots law, there are no possibilities in England to arrest a ship as an interim measure of protection in an action *in personam*.[16] By and large, recent reforms in English civil procedure reveal a remarkable convergence between the common law and the civil law.[17] However, it is regrettable that such convergence has left the arrest of ships aside and another opportunity[18] has been missed to bring the law on the arrest of ships into line with the latest trends in the field of provisional and protective measures. **8.09**

The considerable advantage of Scots law as compared to English law is that in the case of arrestment of ships it is not necessary to initiate substantive proceedings if the arrestment is sought as a provisional and protective measure in support of foreign proceedings or arbitration. Certainly, **8.10**

[15] See Ch 5 paras 5.07 to 5.13.

[16] Since the creation of the *Mareva* injunctions, those freezing orders are the ones available *in personam* in the maritime sphere, as well as in civil and commercial cases in general. The freezing order is another example of the common law ingenuity. Created by Lord Denning in *Nippon Yusen Kaisha v Karageorgis* [1975] 2 Lloyd's Rep 137 and *Mareva Compañia Naviera SA v International Bulk Carriers SA* [1975] 2 Lloyd's Rep 509. In these two cases Lord Denning took recourse to a discretionary power vested in the High Court under s 45 of the Supreme Court of Judicature Act 1925. At present, the jurisdiction of the English courts to grant a freezing order derives from the Senior Courts Act 1981 (s 37(1) and (3)) and is set out in the Civil Procedure Rules 1998, r 25(1 (f) along with interim measures of protection.

[17] R Stürner, 'Anglo-American and Continental Civil Procedure: The English Reform as a Model for Further Harmonization?' in M Andenas, N Andrews, and R Nazzini (eds), *The Future of Transnational Civil Litigation, English Responses to the ALI/UNIDROIT Draft Principles and Rules of Transnational Civil Procedure* (London, BIICL, 2004) 11.

[18] Jackson shows chronologically how English law has missed several opportunities to bring Admiralty jurisdiction into line with the 1952 International Arrest Convention (DC Jackson, *Enforcement of Maritime Claims* (London, LLP, 2005) 5–7). In his opinion, in the significant latest developments of civil procedure in English law 'nothing has changed in relation to the various fundamental and confused aspects of the approach to enforcement of maritime claims in English law' at 7. He stresses that the 1999 International Arrest Convention represents a further opportunity for a comprehensive framework change.

Scots law represents in this regard a more balanced system. The relevant provisions[19] do provide in a plain and straightforward fashion for ancillary jurisdiction, ie jurisdiction that is exercised with the sole purpose of granting provisional, including protective, measures to support foreign proceedings or arbitration.[20]

III. ANCILLARY JURISDICTION

1. The Concept of Ancillary Jurisdiction[21]

8.11 Ancillary jurisdiction in this context could be defined as the jurisdictional basis upon which interim relief is granted to support proceedings on the merits sought in another jurisdiction or in arbitration. A court exercising ancillary jurisdiction is not in the same position as the court hearing the merits. The former court's function is a limited one, and is intended to be supportive only.[22] National, regional, and international law provide for ancillary jurisdiction based on different considerations such as the location of the assets or the person affected by the order, or more openly the availability of different types of provisional protection in different jurisdictions.[23] Regardless of the fact that a given court might not have jurisdiction to hear the merits of the case, that court is still empowered to grant provisional and protective measures in certain circumstances in support of foreign proceedings or arbitration. Most frequently in international commercial litigation, the ancillary court's competence is a matter of sheer practical necessity.

[19] Sections 27 and 28 Civil Jurisdiction and Judgments Act 1982.

[20] Note that the law of diligence more generally, and admiralty arrestment in particular, have been the object of recent law reform in Scotland. See Pt 14 of and Sch 4 (Admiralty actions and the Arrestment of Ships) to the Bankruptcy and Diligence etc (Scotland) Act 2007 that came into force on 1 July 2010 (Bankruptcy and Diligence etc (Scotland) Act 2007 (Commencement No 6 and Savings) Order 2010/249 (Scottish SI)).

[21] See V Ruiz Abou-Nigm, 'Ancillary Jurisdiction for Interim Measures of Protection in Support of Cross-Border Litigation' (2005) 759.

[22] A Johnson, 'Interim Measures under the Draft Principles and Rules of Transnational Civil Procedure: Some Reflections from the English Perspective' in BIICL (ed), *The Future of Transnational Litigation, English Responses to the ALI/Unidroit Draft Principles and Rules of Transnational Civil Procedure* (London, BIICL, 2004) 112–13.

[23] In the context of the revision of the Brussels I Reg in Europe it has been acknowledged by Profs B Hess, T Pfeiffer, and P Schlosser, *Report on the Application of Regulation Brussels I in the Member States* (Study JLS/C4/2005/03) (the *Heidelberg Report*) that '"Provisional" forum shopping is not systematically to be discouraged' (para 777).

When the arrest of a ship is ordered by a court exercising ancillary jurisdiction, the granting of the measure is in itself the way of cooperating with the proceedings abroad, and in most cases no issue of recognition or enforcement of the provisional measures arises,[24] since the measure is ordered where it is meant to take effect. **8.12**

In some legal instruments, namely, the Inter-American Convention on Execution of Preventive Measures,[25] this kind of international judicial cooperation is meant to be exceptional and it is justified by territorial proximity in matters of urgency.[26] In this Convention, the main ground for justifying the departure from the general principles of international jurisdiction is the maximum efficiency of the protective measure. The arrest of ships is generally taken as the clearest example: if the ship is in a certain port of a jurisdiction that is not internationally competent to hear the merits, for just a few days or hours, it would be useless to request its arrest before the court internationally competent, because the entire proceedings (requesting the measure from the court deciding on the merits and waiting for that court to forward it—complying with all the formalities—to the court of enforcement) would take too long, and the ship would be out of the jurisdiction before the measure could be enforced against her. In those cases 'urgent competence' is justified.[27] In this conception, therefore, this jurisdictional basis is exceptional; the court seized on the merits retains absolute control of the case management;[28] a certain time is usually allowed to initiate the case if it has not already been initiated; and last but not least, measures taken are always territorial in nature. **8.13**

[24] The issues related to the extraterritorial effect of provisional and protective measures are complex. They usually do not arise in the case of arrest of ships since the latter is essentially a territorial measure.

[25] Inter-American Convention on Execution of Preventive Measures (Montevideo, 1979) adopted under the auspices of the Organization of American States (OAS).

[26] Urgency has been considered relevant in this sphere also by the English Arbitration Act 1996, s 44(1)(2)(e). See also Andrew Dickinson, 'Provisional Measures in the "Brussels I" Review—Disturbing the Status Quo?' (2010) IPRax 203 at 213. Urgency is a condition for granting provisional, including protective, measures in Art 20 of the Regulation (EC) No 2201/2003 concerning jurisdiction and the recognition and enforcement of judgments in matrimonial matters and the matters of parental responsibility [23.12.2003] OJ L338, 1 (Brussels II*bis* Reg).

[27] For an analysis of this *competencia de urgencia* in the Inter-American system, see DP Fernández Arroyo (ed), *Derecho Internacional Privado de los Estados de Mercosur* (Buenos Aires, Zavalia, 2003) 537.

[28] Case management is also a relevant aspect taken into account in English jurisdictional rules on the basis that 'complex international litigation can be more effectively handled if proceedings in different jurisdictions are effectively co-ordinated to reduce waste and irreconcilable judgments', see Harris, 'Understanding the English Response to the Europeanisation of Private International Law' (2008) 4 *Journal of Private International Law* 347 at 391.

2. The European Framework

8.14 Interestingly, the European regime has so far taken a radically different approach to that of the Inter-American Convention to the subject-matter of ancillary jurisdiction. The text of Article 31 of the Brussels I Regulation in its present form provides for completely detached-from-merits jurisdiction in the case of provisional, including protective measures, without further conditions. However, certain limitations have been established by the case-law of the European Court of Justice.[29] Provisional measures in the current European regime can be ordered either by the court having jurisdiction on the merits or by a court exercising ancillary jurisdiction. And no urgency requirement is imposed by the scheme in its present form for a court to assume jurisdiction for the sole purpose of granting interim relief.

8.15 Several questions have arisen with regard to this provision since it was first included in the Brussels Convention on jurisdiction. Some of these issues have been highlighted by different jurisdictions in the current process of review of the functioning of the Brussels I Regulation. In relation to the particular focus of this chapter, it is interesting to note that as there is no jurisdictional ground specially mentioned in terms of ancillary jurisdiction,[30] all heads of jurisdiction could be used in this regard, even exorbitant jurisdictional bases that have been banned in the sphere of jurisdiction on the merits. The possibility to take recourse to national jurisdictional grounds including exorbitant jurisdictional bases, has generated over the life of the Brussels regime real concern about the role of former Article 24 of the Brussels Convention and current Article 31 of the Brussels I Regulation. It has been suggested that this provision has the potential to undermine the objectives pursued by the scheme, enabling circumvention of its core provisions.[31] In the opinion of learned authors the provision 'creates a non-uniform landscape in which it is not possible for litigants to determine on the basis of the Regulation alone whether a particular court is competent to

[29] See Case 143/78, *De Cavel v De Cavel I* [1979] ECR 1055 and Case 120/79, *De Cavel v De Cavel II* [1980] ECR 731; Case 125/79, *Denilauler v Couchet Frères* [1980] ECR 1553; Case C-261/90, *Reichert v Dresdner Bank II* [1992] ECR I-2149; Case C-391/95, *Van Uden Maritime BV v Firma Deco Line* [1998] ECR I-7091; Case C-99/96, *Mietz v Intership Yachting Sneek BV* [1999] ECR I-2277; Case C-80/00, *Italian Leather SpA v WECO Polstermöbel GmbH* [2002] ECR I-4995; and Case C-104/03, *St Paul Dairy Industries NV v Unibel Exser BVBA* [2005] ECR I-3481.

[30] This is another difference with the model used by the Inter-American Convention since territorial proximity is therein the only jurisdictional ground that justifies the departure from general principles of international jurisdiction.

[31] Dickinson, 'Provisional Measures in the "Brussels I" Review-Disturbing the Status Quo? (2010) 6 *Journal of Private International Law* 530.

grant provisional measures'.[32] This has been seen as a circumstance that jeopardizes coordination and makes international judicial cooperation more difficult.[33] Furthermore, it has been submitted that this provision enables the requested court to decline jurisdiction on the grounds of the 'inexpediency' of the measure to safeguard the rights it purports to protect.[34]

However, in the opinion of Mann this different approach to ancillary jurisdiction as compared to jurisdiction on the merits is perfectly compatible with a well-balanced jurisdictional system. He stressed in this field that, for example, general principles of public and private international law 'have never had any objection against protective measures in the country in which the debtor's property is located, even if neither party has any other connection with it'.[35] In the European jurisdictional scheme these considerations are particularly relevant in the case of arrest of ships, ie a measure relating to a specific asset within a particular Member State where the courts of the place where the ship is located are the best placed to grant or refuse the arrest, being the only courts capable of exercising direct control over the execution of the measure and any other dealings in connection with it. **8.16**

Arguably, in the case of the arrest of ships in the States parties to the 1952 International Arrest Convention, the basis for granting the arrest of a ship exercising ancillary jurisdiction does not need to be found in national law since it is expressly provided for in the Convention. In that sense it could be claimed that the effect of Article 71 of the Brussels I Regulation (the *lex specialis* provision examined in Chapter 7[36]) covers not only direct jurisdiction to hear the merits, but also the exercise of ancillary jurisdiction if so provided by a specialized Convention. This broad interpretation is fully consistent with the approach of the European scheme to ancillary jurisdiction more generally. **8.17**

In the Brussels regime in its present form, the availability and the requirements concerning provisional, including protective, measures are for the most part left to the law of the forum granting the provisional measure.[37] **8.18**

[32] Ibid at 520.

[33] B Hess, *Study No. JAI/A3/2002/02 on European Enforcement,* prepared for the EU Commission by the Institute of Foreign, Private International and Comparative Law of the University of Heidelberg (2003) General Report 132–3.

[34] FJ Garcimartin Alferez, *El régimen de las medidas cautelares en el comercio internacional* (Madrid, McGraw-Hill, 1996) 109.

[35] FAP Mann, *The Doctrine of International Jurisdiction Revisited After 20 Years* 186 *Recueil des Cours* 9 (1984) 58.

[36] See Ch 7, paras 7.38–7.52 and 7.107–7.111 above.

[37] This is also different in the Inter-American Convention on Execution of Preventive Measures (CIDIP II Montevideo 1979) where the final word as regards the appropriateness or inappropriateness of the measure lies exclusively with the court of the main proceedings

The Real Connecting Link

8.19 In the *Van Uden* case the European Court of Justice developed the distinction between the powers of a court exercising merits jurisdiction according to the Brussels scheme and a court exercising its power to order provisional measures in support of proceeding on the merits in another court. Certain limitations were introduced by this dictum requiring the existence of a 'real connecting link' between the subject-matter of the measures sought and the territorial jurisdiction of the court granting the measure. Since this requirement was introduced by the European Court of Justice in the *Van Uden*[38] case, much has been discussed about the convenience of such requirement. It has been suggested that it may provide 'a manageable (ie sufficiently flexible to reflect the variety of measures available and of the circumstances in which courts may be asked to grant them) outer limit upon the exercise of national rules of jurisdiction and procedure under Article 31'.[39] However, the case for diminishing this requirement introduced by the *Van Uden* case into a factor for consideration in the court's discretion when exercising ancillary jurisdiction seems to be the prevailing doctrinal position in present times.[40]

3. England (Sections 25 and 26 of the Civil Jurisdiction and Judgments Act 1982)

8.20 The legitimacy of ancillary jurisdiction in the case of the arrest of ships was recognized in English law even before the Civil Jurisdiction and Judgments Act 1982 entered into force. In *The Lisboa*[41] a bill of lading included a choice of court agreement designating London as the competent jurisdiction. The claimant's ship, *The Lisboa*, was on a voyage from Buenos Aires (Argentina) to Chioggia (Italy), with a cargo of wheat owned by the defendant. During the voyage the vessel broke down off Tunisia and was towed to Chioggia, and the cargo-owners claimed a large amount for towage expenses. They raised legal proceedings in Venice in breach of the jurisdiction clause in the bill of lading, and the court of Venice authorized the

which must be informed promptly of any such measure granted by the court exercising ancillary jurisdiction (Art 10).

[38] *Van Uden Maritime BV v Firma Deco Line* [1998] ECR I-7091; Case C -99/96.

[39] Dickinson, 'Provisional Measures in the "Brussels I" Review-Disturbing the Status Quo?' (2010) 6 *Journal of Private International Law* 546. See also the suggestion of the *Heidelberg Report*, para 783.

[40] Ibid. However, note that the new Art 36 (an adaptation of current Art 31) included in the EU Commission Proposal does not make any reference to the real connecting link nor does the Proposal as a whole.

[41] [1980] 2 Lloyd's Rep 546 (CA).

arrest of the ship. The ship-owners then sued in England for damages for the unlawful arrest of the vessel in breach of the exclusive jurisdiction clause, and furthermore, the cargo-owners raised proceedings in England on the merits of the case claiming that the vessel was unseaworthy. The ship-owners applied for an injunction to restrain the cargo-owners from proceeding with the arrest of the ship. The Court of Appeal reached a unanimous decision rejecting the grant of an injunction. Lord Denning MR invoked the 'maritime law of the world' in order to reach a fair and just result in this case. He expressed: '… by the maritime law of the world, the power of arrest should be, and is, available to a creditor—exercising it in good faith in respect of a maritime claim—wherever the ship is found—even though the merits of the dispute have to be decided by a Court in another country or by an arbitration tribunal in another country'.[42]

Section 25(1) of the Civil Jurisdiction and Judgments Act 1982 was enacted **8.21** in order to give effect to Article 24 of the Brussels Convention, but it has been amended[43] and since 1997[44] it has applied in relation to proceedings worldwide; with sections 25 and 26 of the Civil Jurisdiction and Judgments Act 1982 a serious gap in English procedural law was filled.[45] The scope of application of section 25 is very broad[46] and the statute itself provides for a discretion allowance in order to contain it, via the so called 'expediency test'. According to the latter, the court may refuse to grant the relief if, in the opinion of the court, the fact that the court has no jurisdiction to hear the merits of the case makes it inexpedient for the court to grant it.[47] Yet, as examined in Chapter 4, arrest of property is expressly excluded from the scope of application of section 25[48] and it is regulated by section 26 of the same Act[49]

[42] At 549–50.

[43] Civil Jurisdiction and Judgments Act 1982, s 3, Sch 2 [12]; SI 2001/3929, Sch 2, Pt IV [10].

[44] SI 1997/302.

[45] L Collins (ed), *Dicey, Morris and Collins on the Conflict of Laws* (14th edn, London, Sweet & Maxwell, 2006) 215.

[46] However, s 25 cannot be used in support of arbitration. See *ETI Euro Telecom International NV v Republic of Bolivia* [2008] EWCA Civ 880.

[47] L Collins (ed), *Dicey, Morris and Collins on the Conflict of Laws* (2006) 218; see *Crédit Suisse Fides Trust SA v Cuoghi* [1998] QB 818 (CA).

[48] Section 25 (7).

[49] Section 26(1) 'Where in England and Wales or Northern Ireland a court stays or dismisses Admiralty proceedings on the ground that the dispute in question should be submitted to the determination of the courts of another part of the United Kingdom or of an overseas country, the court may, if in those proceedings property has been arrested or bail or other security has been given to prevent or obtain release from arrest—(a) order that the property arrested be retained as security for the satisfaction of any award or judgment which—(i) is given in respect of the dispute in the legal proceedings in favour of which those proceedings are stayed or dismissed; and—(ii) is enforceable in England and Wales or, as the case may be, in Northern Ireland; or—(b) order that the stay or dismissal of those proceedings be

and section 11 of the Arbitration Act 1996.[50] In turn, these provisions are similar to Article 7(2) of the 1952 International Arrest Convention.[51]

8.22 Section 26 of the Civil Jurisdiction and Judgments Act 1982 authorizes the starting of proceedings *in rem* for the sole purpose of obtaining security in support of substantive proceedings to be heard in a foreign court. There is an important difference in relation to the discretion that the English courts have in the case of the arrest of ships in this framework of ancillary jurisdiction as compared to the framework of the 'true' action *in rem*. If arrest of the ship is requested under section 26 of the Civil Jurisdiction and Judgment Act for the sole purpose of interim relief, the court is empowered with discretion not to grant the measure; whereas, as it was examined in Chapter 4,[52] when arrest is requested in the 'truly' framework of the action *in rem* it is considered to be an entitlement of the maritime claimant as a matter of right.

8.23 In accordance with the provisions of section 26 of the Civil Jurisdiction and Judgments Act mentioned above, a claimant who successfully uses the *in rem* procedure to secure its claim is not thereby obliged to have the substantive claim heard by the Admiralty Court. It may apply to stay the substantive proceedings, in the same manner as this possibility is open to the defendant. Where a stay is ordered, the relevant procedural rules[53] provide for the continuance of any arrest or the maintenance of any security, unless the court orders otherwise. The Court should follow one of two options when faced with this kind of case. Under subsection (1)(a) it can order the retention of the arrested property as security; alternatively, under subsection (1)(b) the court can make the stay conditional on the provision of alternative security. The latter option is not available to the Court when the defendant is entitled to a mandatory stay.[54]

conditional on the provision of equivalent security for the satisfaction of any such award of judgment'.

[50] See *Kallang Shipping SA Panama v AXA Assurances Senegal (The Kallang)* [2008] EWHC 2761 (Comm).

[51] In *The Nordglimt* [1987] 2 Lloyd's Rep 470 (QBD (Admlty)) it was held that s 26 of the 1982 Act should be construed in accordance to the provisions of the 1952 International Arrest Convention; it was also held that s 26 applied where the foreign proceedings or arbitration had already been commenced at the time of the institution of the proceedings in England. See also *The Jalamatsya* [1987] 2 Lloyd's Rep 164 (QBD (Admlty)).

[52] See Ch 4, paras 4.41–4.45 above.

[53] Civil Procedure Rules 1998 (SI 1998/3132), Pt 61.12.

[54] The defendant is entitled to a mandatory stay where the parties have agreed to submit their disputes to arbitration (Arbitration Act 1996, s 9) or where they have concluded a choice-of-court agreement in favour of the courts of a Member State of the European regime. The same would apply if the English court is under a duty to decline jurisdiction,

This provision is a partial, fallacious, and intricate solution to the issue of ancillary jurisdiction in the field of arrest of ships. It undermines the distinction between ancillary jurisdiction and jurisdiction on the merits, making arrest available only after initiating the substantive claim. Consequently, the jurisdictional and the protective functions of arrest get intermingled and, most importantly, English law neither clearly complies with the international obligations assumed under the 1952 International Arrest Convention, nor provides a basis for ancillary jurisdiction in the case of arrest of ships. **8.24**

Particularly in the case of choice-of-court agreements or arbitration agreements, that clearly provide for a jurisdiction different from that where the arrest is being pursued, the procedure for the claimant should be distinctive enough so as not to be understood as an infringement of the agreements, not only according to English law but elsewhere. To be forced to initiate proceedings on the merits against such clauses, followed by the need to apply for them to be stayed afterwards, confirms what Jackson has called the 'schizophrenic'[55] approach to maritime claims in English law. To put it in the words of Lord Reid, '... [w]hy should we tell lies when the truth will serve our purpose equally well if only we give a little care to the formulation of our principles?'[56] Furthermore, this mechanism might not achieve the speed and secrecy which is often necessary to make protective remedies effective. **8.25**

4. Scotland (Sections 27 and 28 of the Civil Jurisdiction and Judgments Act 1982)

Article 24 of the Brussels Convention was given effect in Scots law by sections 27 and 28 of the Civil Jurisdiction and Judgments Act 1982. According to section 27 the Court of Session may grant a warrant for the arrestment of any assets situated in Scotland where proceedings have been commenced elsewhere. Originally this jurisdiction was limited to foreign proceedings instituted in other parts of the United Kingdom or in another Member State **8.26**

where proceedings have been commenced first in another State of such scheme (Art 27 Brussels I Reg).

[55] Jackson, *Enforcement of Maritime Claims* (2005) 240.

[56] '... During early stages of the development of a legal system legal fictions have been invaluable ... But in this day and age I dislike them intensely. Why should we tell lies when the truth will serve our purpose equally well if only we give a little care to the formulation of our principles ...' ((1968) 54 *Proceedings of the British Academy* 189, 200 as quoted by Scot Law Com No 164 (1998) 186).

of the European Union;[57] however, by virtue of the Civil Jurisdiction and Judgments Act 1982 (Provisional and Protective Measures) (Scotland) Order 1997[58] this jurisdiction is currently exercisable in relation to proceedings worldwide. Under these provisions the Court of Session can grant warrant of arrestment only where the foreign proceedings have already been commenced.[59] It is not clear why Scots law is so restrictive in this area.[60]

8.27 An area of concern highlighted by Maher is the role that the European Court of Justice has in relation to the exercise of ancillary jurisdiction of the Scottish courts. The underlying principles of any decision of the European Court must be given effect whenever the Scottish courts are interpreting a provision of the Brussels regime,[61] and this duty applies to questions of interpreting sections 27 and 28 of the 1982 Act. The issue is whether Scottish courts would or should apply the European case-law to actions involving these provisions but which are outside the scope of the European regime. Maher argues that the courts should as far as possible apply the principles advanced by European Court of Justice decisions even in these types of cases with a view to achieve general consistency of approach to these provisions.[62] In view of the more general process of Europeanization of private international law, Maher's submission is to be supported. Applying different standards within and outside the European judicial area is not justified. Moreover, it can be argued that general consistency of approach improves the functioning of the European regime in the international legal order.[63]

8.28 As well as in English law in this context, in Scots law pursuers under section 27 are not entitled to arrestment as of right.[64] In *Clipper Shipping Co v San Vicente Partners*[65] it was held that the court had power to refuse to grant a warrant under that section on the ground that granting it would be oppressive.[66] At present this is consistent with what was examined in

[57] G Maher and DJ Cusine, *The Law and Practice of Diligence* (Edinburgh, Butterworths, 1990) 87; G Maher, 'Provisional and Protective Measures in Respect of Foreign Proceedings' (1998) *Scots Law Times* (News) 225.

[58] SI 1997/2780.

[59] Maher, 'Provisional and Protective Measures in Respect of Foreign Proceedings' (1998) 226; H Raulus, 'Questionnaire on Provisional Measures: Scottish Report' in B Hess, *Study No JAI/A3/2002/02 on European Enforcement*, prepared for the EU Commission by the Institute of Foreign, Private International and Comparative Law of the University of Heidelberg.

[60] Maher, ibid.

[61] Civil Jurisdiction and Judgments Act 1982, s 3(1).

[62] Maher, 'Provisional and Protective Measures in Respect of Foreign Proceedings' (1998) 227.

[63] Improving the functioning of the Brussels I Reg in the international legal order is one of the aims of the EU Commission Proposal for amendments to it. See para 3.1.2. (2010) (COM) 748/8.

[64] *Stancroft Securities Ltd v McDowall* 1990 SC 274(IH (2 Div)).

[65] 1989 SLT 204 (OH).

[66] Maher and Cusine, *The Law and Practice of Diligence* (1990) 88.

Chapter 5,[67] insofar as in Scots law the competency of arrestment of a ship on the dependence relies upon there being a 'colourable case' (a good arguable case) set out in the pleadings, and this applies also in the context of ancillary jurisdiction.[68] In *Motordrift A/S v Trachem*[69] arrestment was used on the dependence of an action related to a contract providing for the merits of the case to be subject to arbitration in England. It was correctly held that the arbitration agreement did not oust the jurisdiction of the Scottish courts for the purposes of interim relief.

5. The International Arrest Conventions

It is evident from the discussions undertaken during the preliminary work pursuant to the 1952 International Arrest Convention that the issue of ancillary jurisdiction for interim measures of protection was far from being developed at the time.[70] Nevertheless, Article 7 of the Convention clearly distinguishes between jurisdiction on the merits (in its paragraph 1), and arrest as a provisional and protective measure in support of foreign proceedings or arbitration (paragraphs 2 to 4). Reflecting the legal development in the field of interim relief, ancillary jurisdiction is furthered in the 1999 International Arrest Convention in Article 2(3).[71] **8.29**

IV. INTERNATIONAL JUDICIAL COOPERATION

Not infrequently, 'international comity'[72] or 'judicial comity',[73] are resorted to in order to justify international judicial cooperation. However, it is here submitted that these concepts are deeply rooted in sovereignty-related **8.30**

[67] See Ch 5, paras 5.35–5.41 above.

[68] Maher and Cusine, *The Law and Practice of Diligence* (1990) 88.

[69] 1982 SLT 127 (OH); see also *Svenska Petroleum AB v HOR Ltd* 1986 SLT 513 (IH (1 Div)); *Mendok BV v Cumberland Maritime Corpn* 1989 SLT 192 (OH).

[70] M Clunet, The *travaux préparatoires* of the International Convention for the Unification of Certain Rules of Law With Respect to Collision between Vessels, 23 September 1910 and of the International Convention for the Unification of Certain Rules Relating to the Arrest of Sea-Going Ships, 10 May 1952 (*Comité Maritime International (CMI)* 1997) 400–1.

[71] 'A ship may be arrested for the purpose of obtaining security notwithstanding that, by virtue of a jurisdiction clause or arbitration clause in any relevant contract, or otherwise, the maritime claim in respect of which the arrest is effected is to be adjudicated in a State other than the State where the arrest is effected, or is to be arbitrated, or is to be adjudicated subject to the law of another State.'

[72] For an analysis of comity in the context of private international law see, inter alia, Richard Fentiman, *International Commercial Litigation* (Oxford, OUP, 2010) paras 15.78–15.95.

[73] See eg A Johnson, 'Interim Measures under the Draft Principles and Rules of Transnational Civil Procedure' (2004) 112–13. Under principles of comity, courts of one jurisdiction give

ideas and, therefore, outdated. Even as long as 30 years ago, the sovereignty concept was rejected as an argument for disallowing extraterritorial enforcement of the attachment of assets.[74] Today, rather than resting on comity, certain judicial cooperation instruments rest expressly on reciprocity.[75] However, reciprocity has also been criticized in this arena;[76] it is found to reduce the scope for cooperation and to be devoid of meaning as a criterion, since litigants rather than countries are the ones concerned in international civil and commercial litigation. Furthermore, and taken to extremes, reciprocity could amount to a denial of justice, just what international judicial cooperation is trying to avoid.[77] Therefore, neither comity nor reciprocity should be indispensable *prima facie* for the recognition and enforcement of foreign judgments.[78] Both concepts, by establishing a territorial limit to justice, would only protect the evasive defendant rather than the national sovereignty they seemingly purport to advance.

8.31 International judicial cooperation is an autonomous concept *per se* and there is no need to justify it by having recourse to any other concept. It is an 'imperative factual concept' which does not need further underpinnings.[79] The EU Commission Proposal[80] for amendments to the Brussels I Regulation seems to recognize the importance of judicial cooperation in the sphere of interim relief. The proposed new Article 31 expressly mentions that 'the

effect to the judicial decisions of other jurisdictions, not as a matter of obligation but out of deference and respect.

[74] Opertti Badán, *Exhortos y Embargo de Bienes Extranjeros. Medios de Cooperación Judicial Internacional* (1976) 322; FK Juenger, *Selected Essays on the Conflict of Laws* (New York, Transnational Publishers, 2001) 319.

[75] For example, the Foreign Judgments (Reciprocal Enforcement) Act 1933, s 9; Civil Jurisdiction and Judgments Act 1982; arguably the Brussels regime also rests on reciprocity; see N Andrews, 'Provisional and Protective Measures: Towards a Uniform Protective Order in Civil Matters' [2001] *Uniform Law Review* 932.

[76] In Uruguay, reciprocity has been eliminated as a criterion in the case of enforcement and recognition of foreign judgments (E Tellechea Bergman, *La dimensión judicial del caso privado internacional en el ámbito regional* (Montevideo, FCU, 2002) 67).

[77] D Opertti Badán, *Exhortos y Embargo de Bienes Extranjeros. Medios de Cooperación Judicial Internacional* (1976) 55.

[78] Reciprocity could only be justified, for example, in the battle against exorbitant *fora*. Fernández Arroyo suggests that States should avail themselves of certain 'protection' in terms of reciprocity, ie in addition to prohibit its own exorbitant *fora* adopt a common legal regime about it, in which it would be clearly stated that legal decisions from any State in the world based on exorbitant jurisdiction shall not be recognised nor executed therein (Fernández Arroyo, 'Exorbitant and Exclusive Grounds of Jurisdiction in European Private International Law: Will They Ever Survive' (2004) 186).

[79] Opertti Badán, *Exhortos y Embargo de Bienes Extranjeros. Medios de Cooperación Judicial Internacional* (1976) 56–7.

[80] EU Commission Proposal (COM (2010) 748.

courts concerned shall cooperate in order to ensure proper coordination between the proceedings as to the substance and the provisional relief'.[81]

1. The Principle of Territorial Proximity Revisited

Already in 1926 McMillan considered that where there was reason to believe that the ship will have sailed before the measure could be enforced against her, it might 'be expeditious to proceed in the Sheriff Court of the sheriffdom within which the vessel is situated'.[82] Even though this reasoning concerned the distribution of domestic Scottish jurisdiction, rather than international jurisdiction, it is clear that the rationale is generally also sound. Indeed, it has brought about the adoption of the principle of territorial proximity in the field of interim relief more extendedly. Such principle has been adopted in the international arena by the Inter-American Convention on Execution of Preventive Measures.[83] As such it is known in Inter-American Spanish legal parlance as *principio de jurisdicción más próxima*, referring to its underlying rationale: it is manifest that territorial proximity in cases of urgency constitutes the only ground for the exception to the general rule on international jurisdiction based on a substantial connection between the case and the forum. Interestingly enough, this underlying rationale can be seen also in the provision concerning provisional, including protective, measures in the Brussels II*bis* Regulation.[84] **8.32**

The underpinnings of the principle of territorial proximity can be found in the earliest work of Opertti Badán, who outlined his ideas on the issue in 1965.[85] Already then, he submitted that a time would come where the **8.33**

[81] EU Commission Proposal (COM (2010) 748, new Art 31.

[82] ARG McMillan, *Scottish Maritime Practice* (Edinburgh, Hodge, 1926) 12.

[83] Inter-American Convention on Execution of Preventive Measures (Montevideo, CIDIP II, 1979). See para 8.13 above. Article 10 of this Convention authorizes the courts of the State Parties to 'order and execute all preventive or urgent measures of a territorial nature whose purpose is to guarantee the result of a pending or potential suit' regardless of which is the court competent as to the merits if the asset or the person to whom the measure is addressed is located within the territory of the court granting the order. And '[i]f the case is pending the court that ordered the measure shall immediately inform the judge or court of the principal proceedings. If proceedings have not been instituted the judge or court that ordered the measure shall set a date by which the petitioner must appear in court to assert his rights: he must abide by the final judgment on them rendered by the judge competent in the international sphere in any of the States Parties.'

[84] Article 20, para 1.

[85] Analysing in particular the case of an embargo on foreign assets, he suggested that to submit the enforcement of embargoes (when granted as interim measures of protection) to the prior verification as to the international jurisdiction on the merits by the court enforcing the measure on its territory would not only be a technical error but a mistake in practical terms.

regulation of ancillary jurisdiction would be completely autonomous. He predicted that when that happened, it would be important, in order to secure the balance required in regulating ancillary jurisdiction, to ensure that policy considerations of the law of the country where the property is situated did not impair the effectiveness of interim measures of protection.[86] Doubtless, empowering courts to adopt urgent territorial measures of protection regardless of international jurisdictional rules as to the merits of the case is very important as a device in international judicial cooperation, and it does not adversely affect the general principles on international jurisdiction.[87]

8.34 Furthermore, as understood by the European Court of Justice in *Denilauler v Couchet Frères*,[88] '[t]he courts of the place [...] where the assets subject to the measures sought are located, are those best able to assess the circumstances which may lead to the grant or refusal of the measures sought or to the laying down of procedures and conditions which the plaintiff must observe in order to guarantee the provisional and protective character of the measures ordered'.[89]

8.35 It is not possible to underestimate in present times the value that the availability of ancillary jurisdiction in support of foreign proceedings or arbitration represents for international judicial cooperation. The possibility to assist the proceedings on the merits in a foreign court by 'lending remedies',[90] particularly in the case of arrest of ships, by the courts of the country where the ship is located or, more frequently, by the courts of the country where the ship is about to enter, is advantageous to secure cross-border administration of justice and, more importantly, it usually provides a powerful deterrent against elusive debtors.

8.36 Furthermore, international judicial cooperation implies the need to implement worldwide expeditious mechanisms for the recognition and enforcement of foreign judgments.[91] This second aspect of international judicial

[86] D Opertti Badán, *Exhortos y Embargo de Bienes Extranjeros. Medios de Cooperación Judicial Internacional* (Montevideo, Amalio Fernández, 1976).

[87] D Opertti Badán, *Actas y Documentos Segunda Conferencia Especializada Interamericana sobre DIP-CIDIP II*, vol 2 Washington, OAS (1980/81) 52.

[88] Case 125/79, *Denilauler v Couchet Frères* [1980] ECR 1553.

[89] Ibid, para 16.

[90] See in the context of the review of Brussels I Reg the Commission Green Paper COM (2009) 175, 8.

[91] DP Fernández Arroyo, 'Exorbitant and Exclusive Grounds of Jurisdiction in European Private International Law: Will They Ever Survive' in *Festschrift für Erik Jayme* (Munich, Sellier, 2004) 169, 183.

cooperation is examined in relation to the arrest of ships in the following paragraphs.

V. RECOGNITION AND ENFORCEMENT OF FOREIGN JUDGMENTS

In international litigation, the analysis of provisional and protective measures such as the arrest of ships, intended to ensure that the final award[92] or judgment can be enforced by preserving the defendant's property, could not be disassociated from the examination of recognition and enforcement mechanisms in connection with the final award or judgment they are meant to protect. This type of consideration led the international community to introduce a new paragraph on recognition and enforcement of foreign judgments into Article 7 of the 1999 International Arrest Convention, in the case where an arrest has been granted to secure such judgment in a different country from the country exercising jurisdiction on the merits. **8.37**

Article 7 of the 1999 International Arrest Convention is perfectly consistent with the express recognition of ancillary jurisdiction by the Convention in its Article 2(3), and shows the intimate connection between, on the one hand, ancillary jurisdiction and, on the other hand, the recognition and enforcement of foreign judgments. **8.38**

1. The UK Framework

Recognition and enforcement of foreign judgments in this field in the United Kingdom are based on statutes, rules of Admiralty, and common law. The level of assistance needed from the courts of the place of enforcement depends on the country where the judgment originated. Two concentric circles need to be drawn; the first to govern the recognition and enforcement of English, Scottish, and Northern Ireland judgments; the second to govern the recognition and enforcement of judgments within the European Union. Outside these two circles, common law rules and particular statutory schemes apply in England and Scotland. **8.39**

[92] Enforcement of arbitration awards is outside the scope of this book; it is governed principally by the New York Convention on the Recognition and Enforcement of Foreign Arbitral Awards 1958 as applicable in English law (Arbitration Act 1996) and in Scots law (Arbitration (Scotland) Act 2010).

8.40 In the case of judgments within the United Kingdom, the rules are to be found in section 18 of and Schedules 6 and 7 to the Civil Jurisdiction and Judgments Act 1982. As a general rule, a judgment of a court in civil proceedings given in one part of the United Kingdom must be recognized or enforced in another part on registration of a certified copy of the judgment. Registration gives the judgment for the purpose of its enforcement the same force and effect as if the judgment had originally been given by the registering court.[93] This rule excludes recognition and enforcement of provisional measures other than an order for interim payment,[94] and foreign judgments registered for enforcement.[95] One important reform introduced in this sphere by the 1982 Act[96] is the place of an inquiry into the jurisdiction of the original court. Prior to the Act, review of jurisdictional competence was permitted in connection with foreign UK judgments (as any other foreign judgments, since it was the principal criterion for recognition and enforcement under common law), and foreign UK judgments were only recognized if the foreign court had jurisdiction according to the private international law rules of the enforcement court. Yet, the 1982 Act following the Brussels regime, allows review of jurisdictional competence up to a very limited extent. Indeed, in the latter, 'absence of a right to query the jurisdiction of the court of origin is a leitmotif'.[97]

8.41 In the case of judgments of States other than those of the European Union, enforcement is available through two different mechanisms: (a) by an action on the foreign judgment; and (b) through registration, in the case of judgments *in personam* directing the payment of a sum of money, according to various statutory frameworks applicable to judgments of courts of countries parties to various Conventions to which the United Kingdom is a party. The second mechanism is based on reciprocal arrangements with the United Kingdom as a whole, therefore, applicable in English and Scots law generally in the same fashion.[98] The first mechanism is common law based, therefore the differences between English and Scots law in this sphere are equally not very profound.[99]

[93] Schedule 6[6]; sch 7[6].

[94] Section 18(5)(b), (d).

[95] Section 18(7).

[96] Section 19(1).

[97] Elizabeth B Crawford and Janeen M Carruthers, *International Private Law in Scotland* (Edinburgh, Green, 2006) 209.

[98] Administration of Justice Act 1920; Foreign Judgments (Reciprocal Enforcement) Act 1933.

[99] An important difference disappeared when the non-merger rule of English law was abolished by the Civil Jurisdiction and Judgments Act 1982, s 34.

English or Scottish courts may be asked to enforce a foreign judgment against a ship under arrest within their respective jurisdictions. In English law, to recognize and enforce such judgment they will take into account the nature of the foreign proceedings and decide whether in common law terms they were *in rem* or *in personam*.[100] The prerequisites for and the defenses against recognition and enforcement are in principle the same as the general principles in the recognition and enforcement of any other civil judgment, and are equally applicable to judgments in connection with actions *in rem* and *in personam*.[101] The prerequisites are, first, that the foreign court had jurisdiction to hear the claim as recognized by English private international law rules as far as English courts are concerned; and Scots international private law rules as far as Scottish courts are concerned.[102] However, in Scotland the criterion to judge the jurisdiction of the adjudicating court seems to be more internationally-minded since what is required is compliance with a 'broad international standard of justice'.[103] Secondly, the judgment must be final according to the law of the court where it was given. Thirdly, if *in personam*, the judgment must be for a fixed sum; finally, the judgment must not be for tax or a penalty. **8.42**

Following from the foregoing requirements, only in as far as the foreign court jurisdiction is concerned there is a distinction between actions *in rem* and *in personam*. In the case of judgments *in personam*, a court will be recognized as having jurisdiction if the defendant is either present in the jurisdiction of the adjudicating court or submitted to the jurisdiction of the court (English law); 'broad international standard of justice' (Scots law);[104] whereas in the case of judgments *in rem*,[105] both in English and in Scots law, jurisdiction depends on the foreign court having physical control over the *res* at the time of the judgment.[106] Interestingly, since neither the English nor the Scottish courts will enquire into the substance of the **8.43**

[100] Jackson, *Enforcement of Maritime Claims* (2005) 728.

[101] Ibid. Jackson argues that the application of the label 'judgment *in rem*' to Admiralty actions is erroneous since in his opinion 'a judgment declaring a lien to exist is no more a judgment *in rem* than is a judgment recognising a proprietary interest in any asset', para 27.31.

[102] See G Maher, 'Recognition and Enforcement of Non-Scottish Judgments' *The Laws of Scotland, Stair Memorial Encyclopaedia* (SME) (8)153, para 405.

[103] Crawford and Carruthers, *International Private Law in Scotland* (2006) 212.

[104] However, see *Wendel v Moran* 1993 SLT 44 (OH) where Lord Cullen disregarded the place of occurrence of delict as a sufficient jurisdictional basis for the courts of New York (adjudicating court) since the defendant was neither present in the jurisdiction nor submitted to it. He stressed also that insofar as recognition and enforcement were concerned there was no significant difference between Scots and English law, at 48.

[105] *Decrees in rem stands unaided contra mundum* (Crawford and Carruthers, *International Private Law in Scotland* (2006) 205).

[106] Jackson, *Enforcement of Maritime Claims* (2005) 730–2.

foreign judgment, foreign liens will be (indirectly) recognized in England and in Scotland.[107]

8.44 In English law, '... subject to any jurisdiction requirements and where the subject matter falls within the Admiralty jurisdiction, an English court will enforce a judgment *in rem* through an action *in rem*'. '... [A]s it is now recognized that an action *in rem* is against a person, any judgment must be focused on that person. The bringing of an action *in rem* to enforce the judgment must be against the owner of the ship at that time.'[108] Indeed, the only *in rem* aspect of a judgment in an action *in rem* is the title conferred by sale by the court. A judgment conferring title by such sale is 'good against the world' (ie it has *in rem* effects). The enforcement of a sale ordered by a foreign court will be through the recognition of the effect of that sale.

8.45 In English law there is uncertainty about the jurisdiction to accomplish this recognition of the effect of that sale by an action *in rem*. In *The Despina GK* [109] jurisdiction was founded in the Supreme Court Act 1981.[110] Yet, it has been doubted whether the jurisdiction maintained by the Act in respect of pre-Act jurisdiction includes jurisdiction *in rem*;[111] if jurisdiction *in rem* is not available to enforce foreign judgments of an *in rem* nature, the main disadvantage lies in the inaccessibility of arrest. Arguably, though, arrest of the ship in such context would no longer be an interim measure of protection since there is already a judgment.

2. The European Framework

8.46 The European Council in October 1999 established that enhanced mutual recognition of judicial decisions and judgments would facilitate cooperation between authorities and the judicial protection of individual rights, and agreed that the principle of mutual recognition should become 'the cornerstone of judicial cooperation in both civil and criminal matters within the Union'.[112] One of the first EU regulatory measures to result from this effort was the Brussels I Regulation adopted on 22 December 2000,[113]

[107] *Minna Craig Steamship Co and James Laing v Chartered Mercantile Bank of India London and China* [1897] 1 QB 55.

[108] Jackson, *Enforcement of Maritime Claims* (2005) 732–3.

[109] [1982] 1 Lloyd's Rep 553 (Sheen J)

[110] Now renamed the Senior Courts Act 1981 by the Constitutional Reform Act 2005, s 59 and Sch 11 in force 1 October 2009.

[111] Jackson, *Enforcement of Maritime Claims* (2005) 728.

[112] Paragraph 33 of the Presidency Conclusions of the European Council, 16 October 1999 (Press Nr 200/1/99).

[113] Brussels I Reg.

which covers all areas of civil and commercial law except for those that are expressly excluded from its scope.[114]

While an order for the arrest of a ship is in principle within the scope of application of the European framework, since the definition of judgment is wide enough to cover interim measures of protection, recognition and enforcement of an arrest order under the Brussels I Regulation in its present form is an obligation only if a defendant had the opportunity to challenge the measure before it was effected under the law of the Member State that granted the arrest.[115] **8.47**

The underlying principles of the European regime are that, save for specified exceptions, jurisdictional enquiry is for the adjudicating court only. Subject to specific and limited exceptions, once a judgment is given on a civil and commercial matter by a court of a Member State, and is enforceable there, it is to be recognized and enforced in each Member State. Recognition and enforcement within the Brussels I scheme in its present form may be refused only: (i) if such recognition and/or enforcement is manifestly contrary to public policy in the Member State in which recognition is sought; (ii) in the case of default of appearance or lack of 'due process' in the adjudicating court; (iii) in the case of irreconcilability of judgments.[116] The paradigmatic English distinction between actions *in rem* and actions *in personam* is irrelevant in this context, a point made clear in the decision of the European Court of Justice in *The Maciej Rataj*[117] case. **8.48**

VI. THE *LEX SPECIALIS* PROVISION REVISITED

The *lex specialis* provision of the European regime (examined in Chapter 7[118]) should not be limited to direct jurisdictional rules but include indirect jurisdictional rules, ie provisions on recognition and enforcement of foreign judgments. This is where the 1999 International Arrest Convention, and the possibility of its adoption by the European Union, becomes relevant. **8.49**

[114] H Ringbom, 'EU Regulation 44/2001 and its Implications for the International Maritime Liability Conventions' (2004) 35 *Journal of Maritime Law and Commerce* 1.

[115] Note that the EU Commission Proposal would change that state of affairs in the case that the court ordering the arrest was also the court that had jurisdiction to hear the merits of the dispute, allowing for recognition and enforcement of provisional, including protective measures, even if ordered *ex parte* in such cases (new Art 2(a)).

[116] Article 34 Brussels I Reg.

[117] *Maciej Rataj (The Tatry)* (Case C 406/92) [1995] 1 Lloyd's Rep 302 (ECJ).

[118] See Ch 7, paras 7.38–7.52 and 7.107–7.111 above.

1. The 1999 International Arrest Convention

8.50 The 1999 International Arrest Convention has introduced in its Article 7 new paragraphs dealing with recognition and enforcement of foreign judgments in relation to the cases where an arrest has been granted to secure such judgment in a different country from the country exercising jurisdiction on the merits. As mentioned above, this inclusion adds to the coherency amongst the Convention's provisions. Differently from the provision dealing with ancillary jurisdiction (Article 2(3)) which was adopted without considerable discussion,[119] the provision relating to recognition and enforcement of foreign judgments was debated extensively. It may be argued that these different reactions on the part of States representatives evidences that ancillary jurisdiction, on the one hand, and, the recognition and enforcement of foreign judgments following thereof, on the other hand, represent different stages of judicial cooperation between States; the latter continuing to prove more contentious.

8.51 The central issue discussed during the preparatory work pursuant to the 1999 International Arrest Convention was the need for such a provision to fill a gap left by the 1952 International Arrest Convention. It was argued that without a provision of this nature arrest as a provisional and protective measure seemed meaningless.[120] Proposals were made to leave the matter to the law of the *forum arresti*. Fortunately, this 'disruptive' temptation was overcome, and recognition and enforcement were finally provided for in Article 7(5) and (6). These provisions read:

Article 7(5)

> If proceedings are brought within the period of time ordered in accordance with paragraph 3 of this article, or if proceedings before a competent Court or arbitral tribunal in another State are brought in the absence of such order, any final decision resulting therefrom shall be recognised and given effect with respect to the arrested ship or to the security provided in order to obtain its release, on condition that: a. the defendant has been given reasonable notice of such proceedings and a reasonable opportunity to present the case for the defence; and b. such recognition is not against public policy (*ordre public*).

Article 7 (6)

> Nothing contained in the provisions of paragraph 5 of this article shall restrict any further effect given to a foreign judgment or arbitral award under the law of the State where the arrest of the ship was effected or security provided to obtain its release.

[119] *The travaux préparatoires*, see Berlingieri, *Berlingieri on Arrest of Ships* (2006) 536–7.
[120] *The travaux préparatoires*, see Berlingieri, *Berlingieri on Arrest of Ships* (2006) 644–7.

8.52 It is interesting to note that the approach taken by the 1999 International Arrest Convention towards recognition and enforcement, even when it is fully consistent with the purpose of the Convention, is not the only possible approach to the matter. It denotes quite a high standard of international judicial cooperation. A different example is given by the aforementioned 1979 Inter-American Convention on Execution of Preventive Measures. In the latter, the judge adopting the 'urgent measure' exercising ancillary jurisdiction is not obliged to recognize or enforce the final judgment. It is understood that recognition and enforcement of foreign judgments 'is a different stage of international judicial cooperation' (different from the adoption of preventive measures), therefore, ruled by its own provisions and not necessarily connected.[121]

8.53 Notwithstanding the different phases of international judicial cooperation, it is here submitted that the approach taken by the 1999 International Arrest Convention is to be preferred, particularly in Europe, where the predictions of Opertti Badán, who in 1965 submitted that a time would come when the regulation of ancillary jurisdiction would be completely autonomous,[122] have actually become part of the European jurisdictional scheme.

VII. CONCLUSIONS

8.54 Ancillary jurisdiction in the field of interim measures of protection should be regarded as a foundational instrument of international judicial cooperation. The bases of jurisdiction to grant measures intended to ensure that the final award or foreign judgment can be enforced by preserving the defendant's assets or property, could be of a more far-reaching nature than jurisdictional grounds to sustain jurisdiction on the merits of the case in the international arena. This should be perfectly compatible with a well-balanced jurisdictional system.[123] Yet, to be able to perform this supportive role in international judicial cooperation, the intervention of the court exercising ancillary jurisdiction should aim to serve proportionality, expediency, supportiveness, and a good overall management of the case on the merits.

121 See R Herbert and C Fresnedo de Aguirre, *El Arresto de Buques y el Principio de Jurisdicción Mas Próxima* [1993] *Revista de Transporte y Seguros* 165.

122 D Opertti Badán, *Exhortos y Embargo de Bienes Extranjeros. Medios de Cooperación Judicial Internacional* (1976); Opertti explains in the Foreword that the volume largely corresponds to his thesis submitted in 1965.

123 FAP Mann, *The Doctrine of International Jurisdiction Revisited After 20 Years* 186 *Recueil des Cours* 9 (1984) 58.

8.55 Moreover, and with a view to furthering international uniformity in questions relating to the enforceability of security interests in ships, it should be stressed that comparative case-law related to the arrest of ships in this sphere shows that ancillary jurisdiction as examined in this chapter is a fertile field for procedural harmonization.[124] It is suggested that English and Scots law would both benefit if a foreign claimant/pursuer could face similar conditions in order to arrest a ship in England or in Scotland for the sole purpose of interim relief. The current need to start proceedings on the merits in English law, and the fact that ancillary jurisdiction (outside the European and UK frameworks) in Scotland seems to be limited to foreign proceedings or arbitral proceedings that have already been commenced, all jeopardize the protective function of arrest of ships in the international arena.

8.56 Furthermore, the need to secure the effective enforcement of judgments is paramount in an area of freedom, security, and justice as the one envisaged for the European Union and an integral part of the right of access to justice. In the eventuality that the 1999 International Arrest Convention is adopted by the European Union, its recognition and enforcement regime would overlap with the Brussels I Regulation, but they would not collide, since both instruments have a similar approach to the issue of recognition and enforcement of foreign judgments. Thus, in the European context, the 1999 International Arrest Convention would advance international judicial cooperation in the field. In turn, this would enhance maximum efficiency in case management as the recognition and enforcement of the judgment on the merits by the courts adopting the provisional and protective measure is indeed the necessary corollary to the degree of judicial cooperation needed in Europe. However, this is not a decision for the Member States of the European Union[125] to make on their own but for the European Union to make as a matter of competence.

[124] See V Ruiz Abou-Nigm, 'Ancillary Jurisdiction for Interim Measures of Protection in Support of Cross-Border Litigation' (2005) 759.

[125] According to Art 72 of the Brussels I Reg in its present form the preservation of provisions which govern the recognition or enforcement of judgments in Conventions on particular matters is limited to Conventions to which Member States became parties prior to 1 March 2002.

9

Conclusion

I. TOWARDS ADVANCEMENT IN THE ENFORCEMENT OF MARITIME CLAIMS IN EUROPE

This study started from the postulate[1] that the arrest of ships can be said **9.01** to be a truly private international law institution. The international community has taken this view since the 1930s, therefore, harmonization efforts have been put forward in this sphere, and international Conventions have been agreed. The 1952 International Arrest Convention is currently in force in most of the shipping countries. However, the results of this Convention in terms of the harmonization attained in the law of arrest of

[1] 'Any argument in defence or support of a given proposition, however good or bad the argument may be, makes conscious or unconscious use of other propositions, and the status of these in the argument, because they are there consciously or unconsciously taken for granted, is the status of postulates', CJ Keyser quoted in WW Cook, *The Logical and Legal Bases of the Conflict of Laws* (Cambridge MA, Harvard University Press, 1942) 48.

ships as applied in the national courts of the Contracting States is still deficient.

9.02 It has been argued that the approach to procedural issues reflects the fundamental values, sensibilities, and beliefs of a certain society.[2] Such affirmation gets even stronger when it comes to the traditional Admiralty jurisdiction in Great Britain. However, the research supporting this book has been conducted on the premise that different legal systems are becoming increasingly harmonized in the procedural mores. The study shows that the arrest of ships, and its evolution over the centuries, represents an excellent example of the characteristics of a harmonization process in this arena. However, the choice-of-law methodology still has a paramount role to play in this context.

II. THE ARREST OF SHIPS: A DISTINCTIVE INSTITUTION

9.03 The arrest of ships is a very distinctive institution. It is not treated along with interim measures of protection in English law, and it does not adjust perfectly to the law of diligence in Scots law. Its functions, namely, its protective, security, and jurisdictional functions, as examined in this book, go beyond interim relief. However, this book stresses that the characterization of arrest of ships as a provisional and protective measure is a necessary part of the substantive harmonization sought by the international community in this field. In the Conventions, the arrest of ships includes arrest as a protective measure to secure payment of a maritime claim; arrest as a preventive measure to enforce maritime liens; and arrest as a provisional measure to secure the *res*. That is one of the reasons why characterization problems arise, and the need to delineate the scope of arrest of ships as a private international law category becomes clear. After studying these three different types of measure and their different functions, the research shows that it is the provisional character of arrest of ships and not its functions that provides the scope of arrest of ships as a private international law category in the Conventions.

9.04 Notwithstanding the different functions of arrest of ships as examined in this book, the research shows they are very much interconnected; these functions are best understood when considering the relationship amongst them. The protective function is the most noticeable one and without it the

[2] OG Chase, 'American "Exceptionalism" and Comparative Procedure' (2002) 50 *American Journal of Comparative Law* 277.

arrest of ships could not display the other two functions. In turn, the jurisdictional function is, from a private international law perspective, its central one, yet it would not be as effective in the international sphere as a cooperative device if arrest of ships would not give the claimant/pursuer a certain kind of security for his claim; that is the reason why the security function of arrest of ships has been considered as its most relevant one.

III. ENGLISH AND SCOTS LAW: ADVANTAGES AND DISADVANTAGES ON BOTH SIDES OF THE BORDER

While it is often assumed that Scots law will always follow English law in Admiralty matters[3] this book shows that this statement is not necessarily correct; indeed, in the sphere of arrest of ships, it is particularly inaccurate. The differences are not only historical but conceptual. The main difference is that admiralty arrestment in Scots law forms part of the general law of diligence, which has no English counterpart. This has, in turn, advantages and disadvantages on both sides of the borders. Having a conceptual framework helps to understand the different functions and effects of the legal institution; however, these general concepts—with a clear Romanist mark—were not crafted to meet the needs of maritime commerce; whereas that, indeed, can be said about arrest of ships as developed in English law. **9.05**

Most of the differences, however, have been harmonized by the 1952 International Arrest Convention as enacted in the United Kingdom by the Administration of Justice Act 1956, now in England consolidated in the Senior Courts Act 1981. The remaining differences are not so much between English law and Scots law but between arrest of ships to enforce a maritime lien or a mortgage, hypothecation, or other charge of the same nature; arrest of ships to protect the status quo in the case of claims related to possession, title, or forfeiture of the ship herself; and arrest of ships as a true provisional and protective measure, ie a measure to secure a maritime claim. The study shows that such differences are hidden within the international Conventions and within English law; arguably in the former due to the influence of the latter. **9.06**

In English law it is the *in rem* claim that gives arrest of ships to enforce maritime liens distinctive features which, it is submitted, should not be extended to cases where such 'real' linkage between the *res* and the **9.07**

[3] *Boettcher v Carron Co* 1861 23 D 322; *Currie v McKnight* [1897] AC 97 (HL); *SS Blaimore Co Ltd v Macredie* (1898) 25 R (HL) 57, 59; *Clydesdale Bank Ltd v Walker & Bain* 1926 SC 72, 82; *The Goring* [1988] 1 AC 831 (HL) 853.

dispute does not exist. It is also submitted that the indiscriminate approach of English law in this regard is the reason why the main functions of arrest of ships as identified in this book are attributed to the *in rem* claim rather than to arrest in English law.[4]

9.08 In present times substance and interim relief jurisdiction in England depend on the initial service of an *in rem* claim form. Following that, jurisdiction on the merits is previous to the arrest of the ship in English law instead of consequent upon arrest as it is in the international Conventions. Therefore, strictly, there is no *forum arresti* recognized under English jurisdictional rules. The link between arrest and action *in rem* does not make arrest a jurisdictional basis but, instead, the basis is the service of an *in rem* claim form.[5] The paradox cannot be overestimated. The legal system that spread the *forum arresti* and fought for it in the international sphere does not exactly provide for it in present times. Jackson has suggested that, as a consequence of the European jurisdictional regime, jurisdiction on the merits cannot be based on service of the *in rem* claim form but 'may require arrest or submission'.[6] In his words 'this has brought the jurisdictional nature of security [arrest] to the fore'.[7] This study shows that the jurisdictional nature of arrest is inherent to the arrest of ships as a legal institution and this should be recognized in English law in the future in a more straightforward fashion.

9.09 In Scots law, the distinction between the different functions of arrestment of ships is clearer. Furthermore, recent law reform has brought the arrestment of ships in Scotland into line with the latest international trends in the sphere of provisional and protective measures.

9.10 One of the questions considered in this book, *de lege ferenda*, is whether it is more convenient to approach the arrest of ships as pertaining to a broader category (interim relief/diligence/provisional and protective measures) or if it is preferable, for the sake of adjustment to the particular needs of maritime commerce, to treat it as a category of its own—as it is done in English law. The research suggests that the modern Scottish approach that treats Admiralty arrestment within the general law of diligence but as a separate category, ie a special kind of diligence, seems to

[4] To put it another way, in English law arrest as such only displays the protective function; it is for the *in rem* claim as a distinctive Admiralty procedure to display the three, in this order: the security function (issuance of the *in rem* claim form), the protective function (arrest), and the jurisdictional function (service of the *in rem* claim).

[5] Jurisdiction for the arrest as an interim measure of protection, and jurisdiction for the merits of the dispute, have been clearly distinguished in England since *Mike Trading and Transport Ltd v R Pagnan & Fratelli (The Lisboa)* (1980) 2 Lloyd's Rep 546 (CA).

[6] DC Jackson, *Enforcement of Maritime Claims* (4th edn, London, LLP, 2005) 428.

[7] Ibid.

be the best option. The benefits of being part of a more general framework (that of diligence on the dependence) is that there are certain legal effects that belong to the general category, for example the *nexus* (attachment) that arrestment lays over the property arrested, thus, the real right in security that arrestment implies;[8] which in turn gives a preference to the creditor over acts of the debtor and of the competing creditors.[9] Moreover, the judicial authority to grant an arrestment of a ship in Scotland, as a special kind of diligence, is exercised following some of the recognized minimum standards for the granting of provisional measures, such as the need to show that the creditor has a *prima facie* case *(fumus boni iuris)*;[10] that there is a real and substantial risk that enforcement of any decree in favour of the creditor would be defeated or prejudiced by reason of (i) the debtor being insolvent or verging on insolvency, or (ii) the likelihood of the debtor removing, disposing of, burdening, concealing, or otherwise dealing with all or some of the debtor's assets were a warrant not granted (*periculum in mora*);[11] and that it is reasonable to grant the warrant.[12]

IV. THE ARREST OF SHIPS: A PROVISIONAL AND PROTECTIVE MEASURE

This study submits that the arrest of ships as an institution in the international sphere would be advanced by meeting certain minimum standards in relation to the requirements for the granting of provisional and protective measures, such as the need to show a reasonable prospect of success on the merits of the claim, and the urgency of the measure, as well as to provide a cross-undertaking in damages. To bring arrest of ships into line with the referred international standards would advance the ultimate aim of the international Conventions: uniformity in application. **9.11**

On the one hand, this book shows that the apparent conceptualization of arrest of ships as an interim measure of protection in the Conventions has not been as effective as it could have been. Furthermore, the lack of a broader conceptual framework in which arrest of ships could develop as a provisional and protective measure, has represented a setback to uniformity, **9.12**

[8] GL Gretton, 'Diligence' *The Laws of Scotland, Stair Memorial Encyclopaedia (SME)*, vol 8, para 286.

[9] Scottish Law Commission, *Report on Diligence on the Dependence and Admiralty Arrestments* (Scot Law Com No 164) (1998) 186.

[10] Section 15E(1) of the Debtors (Scotland) Act 1987, as amended.

[11] Section 15E(2) of the Debtors (Scotland) Act 1987, as amended.

[12] Section 15E(3) of the Debtors (Scotland) Act 1987, as amended.

and more importantly, has left arrest of ships far behind the most accepted international standards with regard to provisional and protective measures. The research suggests that these drawbacks could be overcome if the autonomous definition of arrest of ships as, first and foremost, a provisional and protective measure, as provided for in the Conventions, was borne in mind whenever the Conventions are to be applied.

9.13 On the other hand, treated as a category of its own, its distinctive features become its defining features, and in this sense the unimportant role of *fumus boni iuris* and *periculum in mora* in English law may find a justification in the pressing needs of maritime commerce. However, this argument is certainly not sufficient to justify the absence of a cross-undertaking in damages in the case of arrest of ships in English and in Scots law; that represents a needless imbalance between the parties to the dispute. The study shows that this feature is a result of the confusion between arrest of ships, maritime liens, and the action *in rem*. If it was possible to look at the three as separable legal concepts, a cross-undertaking in damages by the claimant could be required in the ordering of an arrest of ships as an interim measure of protection; whereas if arrest is sought to enforce a maritime lien through an action *in rem*, it would no longer be treated as an interim measure of protection but as an inherent part (as the preventive phase) of an enforcement procedure. Thus, no cross-undertaking in damages would be required in those cases.

9.14 It is regrettable that Scots law has not taken the opportunity of the recent law reform to enhance this possibility. Having done so would have been consistent with the latest trends in the sphere of provisional and protective measures established by the international community as of late. Surely the decision is grounded in the fear that having done so would have made Scotland a less favourable place to arrest a ship as compared to England. Certainly, policy considerations in this matter outweigh technical ones.

9.15 In Scots law arrestment of ships as part of diligence on the dependence has moved towards a new system of judicial authorization of the diligence, thus following emerging international standards on the field. When the research for this book was in its primary phase, no steps had been taken in Scotland to give legislative effect to the Scottish Law Commission's *Report on Diligence on the Dependence and Admiralty Arrestments*. Fortunately such steps were eventually taken and the Bankruptcy and Diligence etc (Scotland) Act 2007, which improves diligence on the dependence in Scotland and brings it into line with the most accepted international trends in the field, has emerged. Schedule 4 introduced by section 213 of the Act, modifying various enactments relating to admiralty actions and the arrestment of ships, entered into force on 1 July 2010.

V. THE NECESSARY DISTINCTION BETWEEN THE ARREST OF SHIPS, MARITIME LIENS, AND THE *IN REM* CLAIM

English law requires a distinction between the arrest of ships as an interim measure of protection, and ship arrest to enforce a maritime lien. The current relationship between ship arrest and the *in rem* claim has various disadvantages, and it has undermined the correct application of the 1952 International Arrest Convention in English law. This dysfunctional approach to maritime claims severely jeopardizes harmonization. Jackson is of the opinion that the civil law approach is preferable in this regard, ie to abandon the fallacious distinction between *in rem* and *in personam* claims and to confer priority to certain kinds of maritime claims.[13] His analysis has been pivotal to this book. Certainly, the decision of the House of Lords in *The Indian Grace No 2*[14] shows that the system evolves in that direction. However, the research suggests that it would certainly take much more for English Admiralty jurisdiction to depart from its most deeply rooted traditions and to allow for the arrest of ships, in certain cases, to be considered first and foremost as a provisional and protective measure. This book emphasizes the importance of such distinction in the international sphere with a view to enhancing the protective function of arrest of ships in the context of international judicial cooperation. **9.16**

The arrest of ships is a means of obtaining security for a claim. This book examined that assertion from a private international law perspective in English and Scots law as the effects of the security function of arrest of ships in the international Arrest Conventions are left to the law of the *forum arresti*. In turn, the security-related effects in the adjacent field of maritime liens present applicable law problems that do not yet have a definite answer, neither in English and Scots law nor in the international Conventions in the field. The inconsistencies in this sphere cannot be overestimated. One of the arguments advanced in this book is that in modern private international law, where principles rather than legal fictions are necessary, the line between substance and procedure, and right and remedy, should not be drawn arbitrarily as to evade the application of foreign law. Hence, there is no place to consider maritime liens as procedural; moreover, there is no place either to consider the priorities they imply as remedial. Consequently, neither the right nor the priorities intrinsically adjudged to the right should be treated as meriting an automatic reference **9.17**

[13] Jackson, *Enforcement of Maritime Claims* (2005) 240.

[14] *The Indian Grace No 2* [1998] 1 Lloyd's Rep 1 (HL).

to the law of the forum. Both right and priority are inherently substantive and should be subject to the governing law.

VI. THE NEED TO AVOID A FRAGMENTED APPROACH TO THE CHARACTERIZATION OF MARITIME LIENS

9.18 This book suggests that a fragmented approach to the characterization of maritime liens in private international law, either through the distinction between substance and procedure or right and remedy, should be resisted; it enhances the undesirable consequences of 'forum shopping'. In the 21st century a maritime lienee should not be in a position of having his claim substantially satisfied or entirely shut out, depending upon the legal system of the jurisdiction in which the ship is arrested and sold. Against this background, the far-reaching concept of 'procedure' in English law as to cover the existence of maritime liens should be seen as a thing of the past. Furthermore, this book submits that it is inconvenient to refer the connected issues of existence and ranking of maritime liens to different laws; it could lead to incoherencies that would neither advance the policies underlying the governing law nor the law of the forum. The book shows that time is ripe for the re-examination of private international law rules in this sphere, and it is suggested that the fact that in Scots law the functions of arrest of ships are easier to separate should make a difference in its conflict-of-law rule in this regard; ie it should lead to the adoption of a conflicts solution more consistent with the international approach that has distinguished private international law (International Private Law) in Scotland.

9.19 Notwithstanding the foregoing, the research shows that, particularly in the sphere of ranking of maritime claims, 'conflictualism' hardly attains the most appropriate solution to the applicable law issues in this field. The different methodological approaches to choice-of-law in civil and commercial matters indicate that whenever unanimity is not attainable in the international arena so as to achieve a uniform solution in a certain field, 'conflictualism' remains the only option. In the field of ranking of maritime claims, this study suggests that the relationship between the two main methods of private international law works also in the contrary sense. The research shows that in this sphere the 'conflictualism' methodology points at the law of the flag as the only possible option to provide foreseeability and decisional harmony. That is the reason why, following the internationally accepted link between a ship and the country of her flag for registered securities, it has been strongly argued that all issues of property in a ship should be referred to the law of the flag. Nevertheless, one of the arguments advanced in this book is that looking at the reality of ship registration systems, and bearing in mind that sometimes ships nowadays fly flags of convenience, adopting such a connecting factor could be regarded as anachronistic. Moreover, applicable law issues connected to maritime liens could end up being governed by the law of a legal system totally unconnected to the case. Therefore, 'substantivism'[15] imposes itself as the only method to achieve not only foreseeability and decisional harmony but, arguably, also a more equilibrate final outcome obtained via a legal instrument especially created to strike the difficult balance between the interests of all the relevant stakeholders concerned with shipping, namely, financing, construction, ownership, and supplying of ships. Furthering uniformity in this field, however, has proved to be a difficult endeavour; nonetheless, the entry into force in 2004 of the 1993 Maritime Liens and Mortgages Convention is a first step towards that desired goal.

VII. A POSITIVE APPROACH TO CASE MANAGEMENT THROUGH INTERNATIONAL JUDICIAL COOPERATION

Judicial cooperation in the sphere of interim measures of protection in the **9.20**
international mores is paramount. This book examined the doctrinal underpinnings of the distinction between jurisdiction on the merits and jurisdiction for the sole purpose of interim relief. It called the latter 'ancillary jurisdiction' since its main rationale is to be supportive of a good case management on the merits. The 1952 International Arrest Convention has been a pioneer in fostering this distinction in the field of arrest of ships; arguably to confirm maritime law as a fertile field for the development of this fascinating branch of the law, that of private international law. The Europeanization of private international law has brought further advancement of the distinction more generally into English and Scots law. This book suggests that this has the potential to enhance the protective function of arrest of ships. For that actually to happen, arrest of ships should be provided for as a true provisional and protective measure in support of foreign proceedings or arbitration in English and Scots law, without the limits currently imposed by the Civil Jurisdiction and Judgments Act 1982; the need to start proceedings on the merits in English law, and the fact that arrestment in the context of ancillary jurisdiction in Scotland seems to be limited to foreign proceedings or arbitral proceedings that have already

[15] See Ch 1, para 1.32 above.

been commenced, jeopardize the protective function of arrest of ships in the international arena. Hence, there is scope for further development of ancillary jurisdiction in both legal systems in this field with a view to improving the overall case management of international shipping disputes.

VIII. *FORUM ARRESTI*: THE PARADIGMATIC JURISDICTIONAL BASIS IN SHIPPING LITIGATION

9.21 The arrest of ships is a typical jurisdictional basis in international shipping litigation. However, despite being recognized as part of the *lex maritima* of all times it has not been free from criticism. One of the aims of this book was to provide the underpinnings of the exercise of jurisdiction as a consequence of the arrest of ships, and to assess the convenience of its survival in the process of Europeanization of private international law. The main question to be answered was whether arrest constituted a sufficient connection with the forum so as to justify the assumption of jurisdiction by that forum in the absence of any other relevant connections. This book submits that the survival of *forum arresti* as a specific jurisdictional basis for maritime claims, in the context of the Europeanization of private international law, is to be welcomed. By contrast, the assessment is negative when it comes to general jurisdiction in any context (ie the assessment is not limited to the European framework). No arguments can be found to justify the arrest of a ship as a general jurisdictional ground in any case; to put it another way, for the purpose of establishing general jurisdiction there is no room in modern private international law 'to treat a ship as domiciled where it can be found'.[16] Therefore, to maintain *forum arresti* as a general jurisdictional basis denotes a non-balanced system. However, international adjudication of jurisdiction is not an aim of its own, but a way of assuring juridical continuity to international legal relations. Combining a general jurisdictional basis such as the defendant's domicile as an alternative to party autonomy with a thoughtful scheme of specific jurisdictions should avoid a clash between the interests of the claimant and those of the defendant. This is exactly what the European regime has attempted to do. In that context, it is submitted that *forum arresti* in the case of arrest of ships is a specific cooperative forum.

[16] See W Phillimore, *The travaux préparatoires of the International Convention for the Unification of Certain Rules of Law with Respect to Collision between Vessels, 23 September 1910, and of the International Convention for the Unification of Certain Rules Relating to the Arrest of Sea-Going Ships, 10 May 1952* (Antwerpen, CMI, 1997) 400.

A ship is elusive hence the possibility to arrest a ship in a certain port and consequentially ground jurisdiction therein is as important in modern times with ships being owned singly, and flying flags of convenience, as it has always been, due to the speed with which the defendant's main asset could leave the jurisdiction. Many times there will be no connection between the forum and the dispute other than the ship being fixed by arrest in its territory, but in many cases this is the closest connection that the ship and the ship-owner[17] will ever have with any forum. 9.22

As for the counter-argument that *forum arresti* enhances 'forum shopping', this book shows that such a practice is encouraged the most by the law of the forum approach to the conflict of laws rather than by a specific jurisdictional ground such as *forum arresti* in the case of ships. Arguably, in the process of Europeanization of private international law, where the room for considerations as to the appropriateness of the forum in relative terms (as opposed to the abstract rules of jurisdiction prescribed by the regime) is tight, the law of the forum approach to applicable law issues represents a very real incentive to 'forum shopping'. The role of the law of the *forum arresti* has been visited and revisited throughout this book. Outside the natural domain of procedure, and, except for the times when it is truly applied as the governing law, its influence is unhelpful. The research shows that as applied in the context of the 'uniformist' methodology via law of the forum characterization it poses a drawback to the uniformity sought by the international community. Moreover, as a choice-of-law methodology of its own, it benefits only those litigants who are in the position to take the best out of 'forum shopping' opportunities. 9.23

The endurance of *forum arresti* for maritime claims in the crusade against exorbitant jurisdictions in Europe should be seen as the ripeness of a special jurisdictional ground particularly suitable to meet the needs of maritime commerce. Maybe it is time to overcome the myth of general jurisdiction and enhance special jurisdictional grounds.[18] The advantages of the *forum arresti* are blatant: the presence of the defendant's asset (generally its only or main asset) in the forum makes the enforcement of the eventual judgment more expedient. On this basis, the present study 9.24

[17] In modern shipping practice, many fleets operate within large ship-owning groups, owned and controlled by the same parent corporation but with each ship in the fleet or group legally owned by a separate one-ship company. See IM Rizwanul, 'The Arrest of Ship Conventions 1952 and 1999: Disappointment for Maritime Claimants' (2007) 38 *Journal of Maritime Law and Commerce* 75.

[18] On this line see M Twitchell, 'The Myth of General Jurisdiction' (1988) 101 *Harvard Law Review* 610.

submits that the availability of jurisdiction on the merits upon arrest facilitates the sound administration of justice.

9.25 Moreover, the mutual trust principle would also be enhanced if the European Union accedes to the 1999 International Arrest Convention as this would represent the availability of a cooperative jurisdictional ground for shipping litigation to every Member State regardless of their different domestic laws. Hence, one of the difficulties shown in the review of the functioning of the Brussels I Regulation in relation to Article 71 of the Regulation, ie the difficulty in application of this provision due to the fact that different Member States are parties to different specialized conventions, would disappear in this field. This is not to be underestimated considering the importance of the international Arrest Conventions in maritime litigation.[19]

9.26 Finally, it is possible to affirm that *forum arresti* based on the arrest/arrestment of a ship as a jurisdictional basis is not exorbitant but cooperative. It does not jeopardize the balance between the parties; it does not favour one party particularly linked with the forum. The element taken into account to determine competence is essential to the legal relation; is not merely accidental (and in that sense arrest/arrestment of a ship differs from the arrestment of movables as a general jurisdictional basis in Scots traditional law). Its recognition in the international Arrest Conventions shows that the reasonableness test has been passed. This feature is not enough by itself but it is to be considered as one of the tests to determine the legitimacy of a jurisdictional basis. Hence, the adoption of the 1999 International Arrest Convention by the European Union could represent advancement in the enforcement of maritime claims in Europe.[20]

[19] In relation to the importance of the 1952 International Arrest Convention, see the Joint Declaration urging the (then) Community States to accede to the 'most important of all the Conventions on maritime law, namely the Brussels Convention of 10 May 1952' as signed in Luxemburg on 9 October 1978 (H Gaudemet-Tallon, *Les Conventions de Bruxelles et de Lugano Competence Internationale, reconnaissance et execution des jugements en Europe* (Paris, Librairie générale de droit et de jurisprudence, 1993) 155).

[20] Moreover, under Art 267 of the Treaty of Functioning of the European Union the Court of Justice has jurisdiction to interpret international conventions to which the EU itself has become a party. This could represent further harmonization in international maritime law, at least in Europe.

Bibliography

I. BOOKS, JOURNAL ARTICLES, AND BOOK CONTRIBUTIONS

Aguirre Ramírez F, 'Embargo y Arresto de Buques en Uruguay' [2005] *Revista de Transporte y Seguros* 275

Ailes EH, 'Substance and Procedure in the Conflict of Laws' (1940) 39(1) *Michigan Law Review* 392

Alcantara JM, 'Coordination between Maritime Conventions: A Pathological Survey' (1999) 1 *Il Diritto Marittimo* 260

Alfonsin Q, *Teoría del Derecho Privado Internacional* (Montevideo, Martín Bianchi Altuna, 1955)

Álvarez Rubio JJ, 'Los Foros de Competencia Judicial Internacional en Materia Marítima en los Convenios de Bruselas y Lugano' [1997] *Anuario de Derecho Marítimo* 143

—— *Derecho Marítimo y Derecho Internacional Privado, Problemas básicos* (Vitoria-Gasteiz, Servicio Central de Publicaciones del Gobierno Vasco, 2000)

Anderson HE, 'The Nationality of Ships and Flags of Convenience: Economics, Politics, and Alternatives' (1996) 21 *Tulane Maritime Law Journal* 139

Andrews N, 'Civil Proceedings' in PBH Birks (ed), *English Private Law* (Oxford, OUP, 2000)

—— *English Civil Procedure: Three Aspects of the Long Revolution* (Roma, Centro di Studi e Ricerche di Diritto Comparato e Straniero, 2001)

—— 'Provisional and Protective Measures: Towards a Uniform Protective Order in Civil Matters' (2001) 6(4) *Uniform Law Review* 931

—— 'Abuse of Process and Obstructive Tactics under the Brussels Jurisdictional System: Unresolved Problems for the European Authorities, *Erich Gasser GmbH v MISAT* and *Turner v Grovit Cases*' (2005) 1(05) *Zeitschrift für Gemeinschaftsprivatrecht* 8

Antapassis AM, *Les Codes maritimes Grecs* (Paris, Librairie Générale, 1983)

Anton AE, *Private International Law: A Treatise from the Standpoint of Scots Law* (2nd edn, Edinburgh, Sweet & Maxwell, 1990)

—— (and PR Beaumont) *Private International Law* (2nd edn, Edinburgh, Green, 1990)

—— (and PR Beaumont) *Civil Jurisdiction in Scotland* (2nd edn, Edinburgh, Green, 1995)

Apter SA, 'Interim Measures in EC Law: Towards a Complete and Autonomous System of Provisional Judicial Protection before National Courts?' (2003) 7(2) *Electronic Journal of Comparative Law* 37

Asser J, *Maritime Liens and Mortgages in the Conflicts of Laws* (Gothenburg, Gothenburg School of Economics and Business Administration Publications, 1963)

Asser TMC, *Das Internationale Privatrecht* (Berlin, Meidmannfche Buchhanblung, 1880)

Baker JH, 'The Law Merchant and the Common Law Before 1700' (1979) 38 *Cambridge Law Journal* 295

von Bar KL, *The Theory and Practice of Private International Law* (tr GB Gillespie, 2nd edn, Edinburgh, Green, 1892)

Baron G, 'Do the UNIDROIT Principles of International Commercial Contracts Form a *New Lex Mercatoria*?' (1998) 15(2) *Arbitration International* 117

Basedow J, 'EC Regulations in European Private Law' in J Basedow, et al (eds), *Liber Amicorum Kurt Siehr, Private Law in the International Arena, From National Conflicts Rules Towards Harmonization and Unification* (The Hague, TMC Asser Press, 2000) 17

Baughen S, *Shipping Law* (4th edn, London, Routledge Cavendish, 2009)

Beale JH, *A Treatise on the Conflict of Laws*, vol 1 (Cambridge, MA, Harvard University Press, 1916)

Beaumont PR, 'European Court of Justice and Jurisdiction and Enforcement of Judgments in Civil and Commercial Matters' (1997) 46(1) *International and Comparative Law Quarterly* 205

—— (with AE Anton), *Private International Law* (2nd edn, Edinburgh, Green, 1990)

Bekker PH, 'Provisional Measures in the Recent Practice of the International Court of Justice' (2005) 7 *International Law FORUM du droit international* 24

Bell A, *Forum Shopping and Venue in Transnational Litigation* (Oxford, OUP, 2003)

Bell GJ, *Commentaries on the Law of Scotland and on the Principles of Mercantile Jurisprudence* (7th edn, Edinburgh, T&T Clark, 1870; reprint Edinburgh, Butterworths, 1990)

Berger KP, 'The New Law Merchant and the Global Market: A 21st Century View of Transnational Commercial Law' (2000) 3(4) *International Arbitration Law Review* 91

—— et al (eds), *Law of International Business and Dispute Settlement in the 21st Century, Liber Amicorum Karl-Heinz Böckstiegel* (Cologne, Heymanns, 2001)

Berlingieri F, 'Uniformity in Maritime Law and Implementation of International Conventions' (1987) 18(3) *Journal of Maritime Law and Commerce* 317

—— 'The Role of the CMI for the International Unification of Maritime Law' in T Burckhardt and A von Ziegler (eds), *Internationales Recht auf See und Binnengewässern Festschrift für Walter Müller* (Zürich, Schulthess, 1993)

—— 'The 1952 Arrest Convention Revisited' [2005] *Lloyd's Maritime and Commercial Law Quarterly* 327

—— *Berlingieri on Arrest of Ships* (4th edn, London, LLP, 2006)

Bigelow MM, *Story's Commentaries on the Conflict of Laws* (8th edn, Boston, Little, Brown, 1883)

Birks PBH, 'More Logic and Less Experience: The Difference Between Scots and English Law' in D Carey Miller and R Zimmermann (eds), *The Civilian Tradition and Scots Law* (Berlin, Dunker und Humblot, 1997)

—— 'Rights, Wrongs and Remedies' (2000) 20 *Oxford Journal of Legal Studies* 1

Blakemore AW (and CF Chamberlayne and DC Moore), *Handbook on the Law of Evidence* (Albany, NY, M Bender, 1919)

Böckel M, *Einstweiliger Rechtsschutz im MERCOSUR* (Baden Baden, Nomos, 2006)

Boele-Woelki K, 'Unification and Harmonization of Private International Law in Europe' in J Basedow, et al (eds), *Liber Amicorum Kurt Siehr, Private Law in the International Arena, From National Conflicts Rules Towards Harmonization and Unification* (The Hague, TMC Asser Press, 2000) 61

Borchers PJ (and J Zekoll) (eds), *International Conflict of Laws for the Third Millenium, Essays in Honor of Friederich K Juenger* (New York, Transnational Publishers, 2001)

Borrás A, et al (eds), *E Pluribus Unum, Liber Amicorum Georges A L Droz, On the Progressive Unification of Private International Law* (The Hague, Nijhoff, 1996)

Bourguignon HJ, *Sir William Scott, Lord Stowell, Judge of the High Court of Admiralty, 1798–1828* (Cambridge Studies in English Legal History, 1987; reprint Cambridge, CUP, 2004)

Bowtle G (and K McGuinness), *The Law of Ship Mortgages* (London, LLP, 2001)

Boyd R, *Judicial Proceedings before the High Court of Admiralty and Supreme Consistorial or Commissary Court of Scotland* (Edinburgh, C Elliot, 1779)

Braekhus S, 'Choice of Law Problems in International Shipping' (1979) 164(3) *Recueil des Cours* 253

Brice G, 'Maritime Claims: The European Judgments Convention' [1987] *Lloyd's Maritime and Commercial Law Quarterly* 281

Briggs A, 'Conflict of Laws: Postponing the Future?' (1989) 9 *Oxford Journal of Legal Studies* 251

—— 'The Brussels Convention Tames the Arrest Convention' [1995] *Lloyd's Maritime Commercial Law Quarterly* 161

—— 'Conflict of Laws and Commercial Remedies' in A Burrows and E Peel (eds), *Commercial Remedies: Current Issues and Problems* (Oxford, OUP, 2003)

—— 'Forum non conveniens and Ideal Europeans' [2005] *Lloyd's Maritime and Commercial Law Quarterly* 378

—— *The Conflict of Laws* (2nd edn, Oxford, OUP, 2008)

—— (and P Rees) *Civil Jurisdiction and Judgements* (4th edn, London, LLP, 2005)

Brilmayer L, 'Rights, Fairness and Choice of Law' (1989) 98(7) *Yale Law Journal* 1217

Brooke H, (ed) *Civil Procedure* (London, Sweet & Maxwell, 2004)

Brown J, 'The Extinction of Maritime Liens' [2003] *Lloyd's Maritime and Commercial Law Quarterly* 361

Browne A, *A Compendious View of the Civil Law and of the Law of Admiralty*, vol 2 (New York, Halsted and Voorhies, 1840; reprint New Jersey, The Lawbook Exchange Ltd, 2000)

Bucher A, 'La Convention de La Haye sur les accords d'élection de for' (2006) 1 *Revue Suisse de droit international et européen* 33

Burckhardt T (and A von Ziegler) (eds), *Internationales Recht auf See und Binnengewässern Festschrift für Walter Müller* (Zürich, Schulthess, 1993)

Carrascosa González J, 'Medidas provisionales y cautelares en el Reglamento 44/2001' (2005) 3 *Derecho del Comercio Internacional Temas y Actualidades* (DeCITA) 400

Carruthers JM, 'Substance and Procedure in the Conflict of Laws: A Continuing Debate in Relation to Damages' (2004) 53 *International and Comparative Law Quarterly* 691

—— *The Transfer of Property in the Conflict of Laws* (OUP Oxford 2005)

—— (and EB Crawford), *International Private Law in Scotland* (Edinburgh, Green, 2006)

—— (and JJ Fawcett), *Cheshire, North & Fawcett Private International Law* (14th edn, Oxford, OUP, 2008)

Celis Aguilar MM, 'Convención sobre los acuerdos de elección de foro' (2006) 5/6 *Derecho del Comercio Internacional Temas y Actualidades* (DeCITA) 613

Chamberlayne CF, (and AW Blakemore and DC Moore), *Handbook on the Law of Evidence* (Albany, NY, M Bender, 1919)

Chase OG, 'American "Exceptionalism" and Comparative Procedure' (2002) 50 *American Journal of Comparative Law* 277

Chauveau P, *Traité de Droit Maritime* (Paris, Librairies Techniques, 1958)

Cheshire GC, *Private International Law* (Oxford, OUP, 1935)

Chong A (and J Hill), *International Commercial Disputes, Commercial Conflict of Laws in English Courts* (Oxford, Hart, 2010)

Clerke F, *Praxis curi admiralitatis Angli* (Dublin, 1666)

Clermont KM, 'The Role of Private International Law in the United States: Beating the Not-Quite-Dead Horse of Jurisdiction' (2004) Cornell Law School Legal Studies Research Paper No 04-023

Cohen EE, *Ancient Athenian Maritime Courts* (New Jersey, Princeton University Press, 1973)

Collins L, *Provisional and Protective Measures in International Litigation* (1992) 234 Recueil des Cours 19

—— *Essays in International Litigation and the Conflict of Laws* (Oxford, Clarendon, 1994)

—— (ed), *Dicey, Morris and Collins on the Conflict of Laws* (14th edn, London, Sweet & Maxwell, 2006)

Cook WW, '"Substance" and "Procedure" in the Conflict of Laws' (1933) 42 *Yale Law Journal* 333

—— *The Logical and Legal Bases of Conflict of Laws* (Cambridge, MA, Harvard University Press, 1942)

Couture EJ, 'Los embargos y el Tratado de Montevideo de Derecho Procesal de 1889' (1939) 37 *Revista de Derecho, Jurisprudencia y Administración* 247

Crawford EB (and JM Carruthers), *International Private Law in Scotland* (Edinburgh, Green, 2006)

Currie B, *Selected Essays on the Conflict of Laws* (Durham, NC, Duke University Press, 1963)

Cusine DJ (and G Maher), *The Law and Practice of Diligence* (Edinburgh, Butterworths, 1990)

Dahdal A (and P Gillies), 'Characterising the Action *In Rem* in Australia—Recent Perspectives' (2007) *Macquarie Law* (WP 2007-19) 1

Daudpota FK, 'Actions *in rem* Against Ships in Pakistan' (2003) 9(4) *Journal of International Maritime Law* 383

Davenport BJ, 'End of an Old Admiralty Belief' (Case comment) (1998) 114 *Law Quarterly Review* 169

Davies M, 'Choice of Law and U.S. Maritime Liens' (2009) 83 *Tulane Law Review* 1435

De Boer TM, 'The Missing Link: Some Thoughts on the Relationship between Private International Law and Comparative Law' in Boele-Woelki et al (eds), *Comparability and Evaluation, Essays on Comparative Law, Private International Law and International Commercial Arbitration in Honour of Dimitra Kokkini-Iatridou* (The Hague, Nijhoff, 1994) 15

Derrington SC, 'The Continuing Utility of the Action *in rem*' (2007) *Law Quarterly Review* 358

—— (and JM Turner), *The Law and Practice of Admiralty Matters* (Oxford, OUP, 2007)

Devlin P, *The English Rules on Choice of Law with Reference to Maritime Contracts (Charterparties and Bill of Ladings)* (Göteborg, Gumperts Förlag, 1952)

Devonshire P, 'Freezing Orders, Disappearing Assets and the Problem of Enjoining Non-Parties' (2002) 118 *Law Quarterly Review* 124

Dicey AV, *A Digest of the Law of England with Reference to the Conflict of Laws* (London, Stevens, 1896)

Dickinson A, 'English Private International Law Aspects of Provisional and Protective Measures' in M Andenas, H Bukhard, and P Oberhammer (eds), *Enforcement Agency Practice in Europe* (London, BIICL, 2005) 284

—— 'Provisional Measures in the "Brussels I" Review—Disturbing the Status Quo?' (2010) 6 *Journal of Private International Law* 519

Diedrich F, 'Maintaining Uniformity in International Uniform Law via Autonomous Interpretation' (1996) 8 *Pace International Law Review* 303

Dolinger J, *Direito Internacional Privado* (5th edn, Rio de Janeiro, Renovar, 1997)

Donaldson A, 'Some Conflict Rules of Scots Law' (1953) 39 *Problems of Public and Private International Law Transactions of the Grotius Society* 145

Droz GAL, 'Entrée en vigueur de la Convention de Bruxelles révisée sur la compétence judiciaire et l'exécution des jugements' (1987) 2 *Revue critique de droit international privé* 269

Du Pontavice E (and R Rodière), *Droit Maritime* (12th edn, Paris, Dalloz, 1997)

Ehrenzweig AA, *Private International Law: A Comparative Treatise on American International Conflicts of Law, Including the Law of Admiralty* (Leyden, Oceana, 1967)

Einhorn T (and K Siehr) (eds), *International Cooperation through Private International Law: Essays in Memory of Peter E Nygh* (The Hague, TMC Asser Press, 2004)

Espinosa Calabuig R, *El Contrato Internacional de Transporte Maritimo de Mercancias: Cuestiones de Ley Aplicable* (Granada, Comares, 1999)

Evan-Jones R, 'Receptions of Law, Mixed Legal Systems and the Myth of the Genius of Scots Private Law' (1998) 114 *Law Quarterly Review* 228

—— 'Roman Law in Scotland and England and the Development of One Law for Britain' (1999) 115 *Law Quarterly Review* 605

—— 'Mixed Legal Systems, Scotland and the Unification of Private Law in Europe' in JM Smits (ed), *The Contribution of Mixed Legal Systems to European Private Law* (Antwerp, Intersentia, 2001)

Fabano C, 'Maximizing Plaintiff Protection in the World of Asset Freezing and Bypassing the Due Process Requirement of Notice: The Mareva Injunction as an Alternative to the American Legal Remedies' (2002) 9 *ILSA Journal of International and Comparative Law* 131

Farquhar Shand C, *The Practice of the Court of Session: On the Basis of the Late Mr. Darling's Work of 1833* (Edinburgh, T&T Clark, 1848)

Fawcett JJ (ed), *Declining Jurisdiction in Private International Law* (Oxford, Clarendon, 1995)

—— (ed), *Reform and Development of Private International Law: Essays in Honour of Sir Peter North* (Oxford, OUP, 2002)

—— (and JM Carruthers), *Cheshire, North & Fawcett Private International Law* (14th edn, Oxford, OUP, 2008)

Fell ET, *Recent Problems in Admiralty Jurisdiction* (Baltimore, Johns Hopkins, 1922)

Fentiman R, *Foreign Law in English Courts: Pleading, Proof and Choice of Law* (New York, Clarendon, 1998)

—— *International Commercial Litigation* (Oxford, OUP, 2010)

Fernández Arroyo DP (ed), *Derecho Internacional Privado de los Estados de MERCOSUR* (Buenos Aires, Zavalia, 2003)

—— 'Exorbitant and Exclusive Grounds of Jurisdiction in European Private International Law: Will They Ever Survive' in *Festschrift für Erik Jayme* (Munich, Sellier, 2004) 169

—— *Compétence exclusive et compétence exorbitante dans les relations privées internationales,* Recueil des cours, vol 323 (2006) (Leiden, Martinus Nijhoff, 2008)

Fiore P, *Droit international privé ou principes pour résoudre les conflits entre les légitimations diverses en matière du droit civil et commercial* (Paris, Durand et Pedone-Lauriel, 1875)

Forsyth C, *Private International Law* (4th edn, Cape Town, Juta, 2003)

Fresnedo de Aguirre C, 'La Cooperación Cautelar Internacional en el MERCOSUR' in *El Derecho Procesal en el MERCOSUR* (Montevideo, FCU, 1997)

—— 'Embargo de Buques como Medida Cautelar en el Derecho Internacional Privado Uruguayo' (1997) 14 *Anuario de Derecho Marítimo* 385

—— (and R Herbert), 'El Arresto de Buques y el Principio de Jurisdicción mas Próxima' [1993] *Revista de Transporte y Seguros* 6

—— (and V Ruiz) 'El Derecho Marítimo y El Derecho Internacional Privado' (2005) 22 *Anuario de Derecho Marítimo* 189

Garcimartin Alférez FJ, *El régimen de las medidas cautelares en el comercio internacional* (Madrid, McGraw-Hill, 1996)

Gardella A (with L Radicati di Brozolo), 'Civil Law, Common Law and Market Integration: The EC Approach to Conflicts of Jurisdiction' (2003) 51(3) *American Journal of Comparative Law* 611

Gascón Inchausti F, *Medidas cautelares de proceso civil extranjero* (Granada, Comares, 1998)

Gaskell N (and R Shaw), 'Arrest Convention 1999' [1999] *Lloyd's Maritime and Commercial Law Quarterly* 1

—— (and M Tsimplis), 'Admiralty Claims and the New CPR Part 61' [2002] *Lloyd's Maritime and Commercial Law Quarterly* 520

Gassmann R, *Arrest im internationalen Rechtsverkehr: zum Einfluss des Lugano-Übereinkommens auf das schweizerische Arrestrecht* (Zürich, Schulthess, 1998)

Gaudemet-Tallon H, *Les Conventions de Bruxelles et de Lugano Compétence Internationale, reconnaissance et exécution des jugements en Europe* (Paris, Librairie générale de droit et de jurisprudence, 1993)

Gaurier D, *Le Droit maritime romain* (Rennes, PU, 2004)

Gee S, *Mareva Injunctions and Anton Piller Relief* (4th edn, London, Sweet & Maxwell, 1998)

Geeroms S, *Foreign Law in Civil Litigation: A Comparative and Functional Analysis* (Oxford, OUP, 2004)

Gierke O, *Deutsches Privatrecht*, vol 1 (Leipzig, Duncker u. Humblot, 1895)

Gillies P (and A Dahdal), 'Characterising the Action *In Rem* in Australi—Recent Perspectives' (2007) *Macquarie Law* (WP 2007-19) 1

Glenn HP, 'Legal Cultures and Legal Traditions' in M van Hoecke (ed), *Epistemology and Methodology of Comparative Law* (Oxford, Hart, 2004)

Gloag WM (and JM Irvine), *Law of Rights in Security, Heritable and Moveable: Including Cautionary Obligations* (Edinburgh, Green, 1897)

Goldrein I (ed), *Commercial Litigation: Pre-Emptive Remedies* (London, Sweet & Maxwell, 2005)

Goldschmidt W, *Derecho Internacional Privado* (Buenos Aires, Depalma, 1992)

Goode R, *Official Commentary to the Cape Town Convention on International Interest in Mobile Equipment and Protocol thereto on Matters Specific to Aircraft Equipment* (Rome, Unidroit, 2002)

—— (and H Kronke, E McKendrick, J Wool), *Transnational Commercial Law* (Oxford, OUP, 2004)

Gordon WM, 'A Comparison of the Influence of Roman Law in England and Scotland' in D Carey Miller and R Zimmermann (eds), *The Civilian Tradition and Scots Law* (Berlin, Dunker und Humblot, 1997) 135

Gras NSB, 'A List of Local Customs Due in the Port of Ipswich' in *The Early English Customs System: A Documentary Study of the Institutional and Economic History of the Customs from the Thirteenth to the Sixteenth Century*, vol 18 (Cambridge, CUP, 1918)

Gretton GL, 'Diligence' *The Laws of Scotland, Stair Memorial Encyclopaedia* (SME) (8) 17 (101–399)

Griggs PJS, 'Uniformity of Maritime Law: An International Perspective' (1999) 73 *Tulane Law Review* 1551

—— 'Obstacles to Uniformity of Maritime Law, The Nicholas J. Healy Lecture' (2003) 34 *Journal of Maritime Law and Commerce* 191

Gutteridge H, *Comparative Law: An Introduction to the Comparative Method of Legal Study and Research* (Cambridge, CUP, 1949)

Hall JE, *The Practice and Jurisdiction of the Court of Admiralty* (New Jersey, The Lawbook Exchange Clark, 2005)

Hare J, 'Of Black Books, White Horses and Sacred Cows: The Quest for International Uniformity in Maritime Law' (1999) British Maritime Law Association available online at <http://www.bmla.org.uk/documents/of_black_books.htm>

Harris J, 'Understanding the English Response to the Europeanisation of Private International Law' (2008) 4 *Journal of Private International Law* 347

Hartley TC, 'The European Union and the Systematic Dismantling of the Common Law of Conflict of Laws' (2005) 54 *International and Comparative Law Quarterly* 813

—— 'The Hague Choice-of-Court Convention' (2006) 31 *Edinburgh Law Review* 414

Hayden RP (and KC Leland), 'The Uniqueness of Admiralty and Maritime Law: The Unique Nature of Maritime Liens' in (2005) 79(5)–(6) *Tulane Law Review* 1227

Herbert R, 'Objeto y Método del Derecho Internacional Privado' in D Opertti Badán et al, *Objeto y Método en el Derecho Internacional Privado* (2nd edn, Montevideo, FCU, 1990)

—— (and C Fresnedo de Aguirre), 'El Arresto de Buques y el Principio de Jurisdicción mas Próxima' [1993] *Revista de Transporte y Seguros* 158

Hess B (and T Pfeiffer and P Schlosser) (eds), *The Brussels I Regulation 44/2001, Application and Enforcement in the EU* (Beck Hart, 2008)

Hill CJS (ed), *The Arrest of Ships Series* (London, LLP, 1985–88)

Hill J, 'The Exercise of Jurisdiction in Private International Law' in P Capps, M Evans, and S Konstadinidis (eds), *Asserting Jurisdiction: International and European Legal Perspectives* (Oxford, Hart, 2003) 39

—— *International Commercial Disputes in English Courts* (3rd edn, Oxford, Hart, 2005)

—— (and A Chong), *International Commercial Disputes, Commercial Conflict of Laws in English Courts* (Oxford, Hart, 2010)

Hoffmann J (and S Kumar), 'Globalization: The Maritime Nexus' in *Handbook of Maritime Economics* (London, LLP, 2002)

Hood K, *Conflict of Laws within the UK* (Oxford, OUP, 2007)

Hutton N, 'The Origin, Development, and Future of Maritime Liens and the Action *in rem*' (2003) 28(1) *Tulane Maritime Law Journal* 81

Inglis IG, 'Jurisdiction, the Doctrine of Forum Conveniens, and Choice of Law in Conflict of Laws' (1965) 81 *Law Quarterly Review* 380

—— 'Arrest of Ships in Scotland' in C Hill (ed), *The Arrest of Ships Series*, vol 4 (London, LLP, 1987)

Irvine JM (and WM Gloag), *Law of Rights in Security, Heritable and Moveable: Including Cautionary Obligations* (Edinburgh, Green, 1897)

Jackson DC, 'Fitting Maritime Jurisdiction into Europe or vice versa?' [2001] *Lloyd's Maritime and Commercial Law Quarterly* 219

—— *Enforcement of Maritime Claims* (4th edn, London, LLP, 2005)

Jados SS (tr), *The Consulate of the Sea and Related Documents* (Alabama, University of Alabama Press, 1975)

Jenard P, 'Report on the Brussels Convention' (1979) OJC/59/60

Jitta DJ, *La méthode du droit international privé* (The Hague, Belinfante, 1890)

Joerges C, 'Europeanization as a Process: Tensions between the Logic of Integration and the Logic of Codification' Conference Paper, Conference on Europeanization of Private Law held at the European University Institute, Florence, 24–25 October 2003

Johnson A, 'Interim Measures under the Draft Principles and Rules of Transnational Civil Procedure: Some Reflections from the English Perspective' in *The Future of Transnational Litigation, English Responses to the ALI/Unidroit Draft Principles and Rules of Transnational Civil Procedure* (London, BIICL, 2004) 112

Jolowicz JA, 'On the Comparison of Procedures' in JAR Nafziger and SC Symeonides (eds), *Law and Justice in a Multistate World, Essays in Honor of Arthur T. von Mehren* (New York, Transnational Publishers, 2002) 721

Juenger FK, *Choice of Law and Multistate Justice* (Dordrecht, Martinus Nijhoff, 1993)

—— *The Problem with Private International Law* (Roma, Centro di Studi e Ricerche di Diritto Comparato e Straniero, 1999)

—— *Selected Essays on the Conflict of Laws* (New York, Transnational Publishers, 2001)

—— 'The lex mercatoria and Private International Law' (2001) 5 *Uniform Law Review* 171

Kahn-Freund O, 'General Problems of Private International Law' (1974) 143 *Recueil des Cours* 139

Karatzas TB (and NP Ready), *The Greek Code of Private Maritime Law* (The Hague, Martinus Nijhoff, 1982)

Kennett W, *The Enforcement of Judgments in Europe* (Oxford, OUP, 2000)

Kerameus K, 'Provisional Remedies in Transnational Litigation' in I Andolina (ed), *Trans-national Aspects of Procedural Law: World Congress on Procedural Law, Taormina 17–23 settembre 1995*, vol 3 (Milan, Giuffrè, 1998) 1169

—— 'International Procedural Harmonization and Autonomous Interpretation' in K Siehr and T Einhorn (eds), *International Cooperation through Private International Law: Essays in Memory of Peter E Nygh* (The Hague, TMC Asser Press, 2004)

—— 'Scope of Application of the ALI/Unidroit Principles of Transnational Civil Procedure' (2004) 9(4) *Uniform Law Review* 859

—— 'Actual Problems of Enforcement Law in the European Union' in B Bachmann et al (eds), *Grenzüberschreitungen: Beiträge zum internationales Verfahrensrecht und zur Schiedsgerichtsbarkeit: Festschrift für Peter Schlosser zum 70 Geburtstag* (Tübingen, Mohr Siebeck, 2005)

—— 'Procedural Approximation and Legal Pluralism in the European Union' in T Andersson (ed), *Parallel and Conflicting Enforcement of Law* (Leiden, Nijhoff, 2005)

Kessedjian C, 'International jurisdiction and foreign judgements in civil and commercial matters' *HccH Prel Doc 7* (1997)

—— 'Note on Provisional and Protective Measures in Private International Law and Comparative Law' *HccH Prel Doc 10* (1998)

Klett S, 'Las medidas cautelares en el ámbito del derecho internacional privado. El régimen del Código General del Proceso' in A Landoni Sosa (ed), *Curso sobre Medidas Cautelares* (Montevideo, FCU, 1999)

Kriz JM, 'Ship Mortgages, Maritime Liens, and Their Enforcement: The Brussels Conventions of 1926 and 1952'. Part One [1963] *Duke Law Journal* 671; Part Two [1964] *Duke Law Journal* 70

Kronke H, 'Most Significant Relationship, Governmental Interests, Cultural Identity, Integration: "Rules" at Will and the Case for Principles of Conflict of Laws' (2004) 3 *Uniform Law Review* 467

—— 'The Scope of Party Autonomy in Recent UNIDROIT Instruments and the Conflict of Laws in the MERCOSUR and the European Union' in *Liber Amicorum Opertti Badán* (Montevideo, FCU, 2005)

—— (and R Goode, E McKendrick, and J Wool), *Transnational Commercial Law* (Oxford, OUP, 2004)

Kumar S (and J Hoffmann), 'Globalization: The Maritime Nexus' in *Handbook of Maritime Economics* (London, LLP, 2002)

Lagarde P, *Le principe de proximité dans le droit international privé contemporain* (1986) 1 *Recueil des Cours* (vol 196) 9

Lainé A, *Introduction au Droit International Privé* (Paris, F Pichon, 1888/1892) vol 1

Lasok D (and PA Stone), *Conflict of Laws in the European Community* (Oxford, Professional Books, 1987)

Leland KC (and RP Hayden), 'The Uniqueness of Admiralty and Maritime Law: The Unique Nature of Maritime Liens' in (2005) 79(5)–(6) *Tulane Law Review* 1227

Levack BP, *The Civil Lawyers in England, 1603–1641: A Political Study* (Oxford, Clarendon, 1973)

Lipstein K, 'Characterization' (1999) 3 *International Encyclopaedia of Comparative Law* (ch 5)

López Rodríguez AM, *Lex Mercatoria and Harmonization of Contract Law in the EU* (Copenhagen, DJOF Publishing, 2003)

Lorenzen EG (ed), *Cases on Conflict of Laws* (St Paul, West Publishing, 1937)

Lowe JAG, 'Maritime Securities' *The Laws of Scotland, Stair Memorial Encyclopaedia* (SME) (20) 118 (273–315)

Lowenfeld AF, *International Litigation and the Quest for Reasonableness: Essays in Private International Law* (Oxford, Clarendon, 1996)

McArdle AD (ed), *International Ship Arrest: A Practical Guide* (London, LLP, 1988)

MacCormick N, 'Law as Institutional Fact' in N MacCormick and O Weinberger, *An Institutional Theory of Law: New Approaches to Legal Positivism* (Dordrecht, Kluwer, 1986) 63

McGovern N, 'The Role of Inter-Governmental Organizations in the Development of Private International Maritime Law' in T Burckhardt (with A von Ziegler) (eds), *Internationales Recht auf See und Binnengewässern Festschrift für Walter Müller* (Zürich, Schulthess, 1993)

McGuffie KC (and PA Fugeman, PV Gray), *Admiralty Practice* (London, Stevens, 1964)

McGuinness K (and G Bowtle), *The Law of Ship Mortgages* (London, LLP, 2001)

McKendrick E (and H Kronke, R Goode, J Wool), *Transnational Commercial Law* (Oxford, OUP, 2004)

McLachlan CA, 'Second Interim Report on Provisional and Protective Measures in International Litigation', Report of the Sixty-Seventh Conference, Helsinski (London, ILA, 1996)

—— 'The Continuing Controversy over Provisional Measures in International Disputes' (2005) 7 *International law FORUM du droit international* 5

McMillan ARG, 'The Theory of Arrestment *ad fundandam jurisdictionem*' (1922) *Scots Law Times* (News) 89

—— *Scottish Maritime Practice* (Edinburgh, Hodge, 1926)

Macphail ID (T Welsh (ed)), *Sheriff Court Practice* (3rd edn, Edinburgh, Green, 2006)

MacQueen HL, *Common Law and Feudal Society in Medieval Scotland* (Edinburgh, EUP, 1993)

Maekelt T de B, *Teoría General del Derecho Internacional Privado* (Caracas, Academia de Ciencias Políticas y Sociales, 2005)

Maher G (and DJ Cusine), *The Law and Practice of Diligence* (Edinburgh, Butterworths, 1990)

—— 'Recognition and Enforcement of Non-Scottish Judgments' *The Laws of Scotland, Stair Memorial Encyclopaedia* (SME) (8) 151 (400–10)

—— 'Diligence on the Dependence: Principles for Reform' [1998] *Juridical Review* 188

—— 'Diligence on the Dependence: Reform Needed' (2004) 27 *Scots Law Times* (News) 167

—— (and BJ Rodger), 'Provisional and Protective Remedies: The British Experience of the Brussels Convention' (1999) 48 *International and Comparative Law Quarterly* 306

—— (and BJ Rodger), *Civil Jurisdiction in the Scottish Courts* (Edinburgh, Green, 2010)

Mance J, 'The Future of Private International Law' (2005) 2 *Journal of Private International Law* 185

—— 'Is Europe Aiming to Civilise the Common Law?' The Chancery Bar Lecture 27 March 2006

Mancini PS, 'Prelezione al corso di diritto pubbllico marittimo insegnato nella R. Università di Torino nell'anno 1852–1853' (speech given on 29 November 1852) in PS Mancini, *Diritto internazionale—Prelezioni, con un saggio sul Machiavelli* (Naples, Marghieri, 1873) 93, 105–6 (tr) PJS Griggs, 'Obstacles to Uniformity of Maritime Law, The Nicholas J. Healy Lecture' in (2003) 34 *Journal of Maritime Law and Commerce* 191

Mandaraka-Sheppard A, *Modern Maritime Law and Risk Management* (2nd edn, London, Informa, 2009)

Mankowski P, *Seerechtliche Vertragsverhaltnisse im Internationalen Privatrecht* (Tübingen, Mohr, 1995)

—— (and Ulrich Magnus (eds)), *Brussels I Regulation* (Munich, Sellier, 2007)

Mann FAP, *The Doctrine of Jurisdiction in International Law* (1964) 1 vol 111 *Recueil des Cours* 1

—— 'Uniform Laws and the Conflict of Laws' (1979) 95 *Law Quarterly Review* 346

——*The Doctrine of International Jurisdiction Revisited After 20 Years* (1984) 2 vol 186 Recueil des Cours 9

Marciano A (and J-M Josselin) (eds), *The Economics of Harmonising European Law* (Cheltenham, Elgar, 2002)

Marsden RG (ed), *Select Pleas of the Court of Admiralty*, vol 1, The Court of the Admiralty of the West (AD 1390–1404) and The High Court of Admiralty (AD 1527–45) (London, B Quaritch, 1894–97)

Mason A, 'Harmonisation of Maritime Laws and the Impact of International Law on Australasian Maritime Law' (1999) 2 *Il Diritto Marittimo* 637

Mathiasen J, 'Some Problems of Admiralty Jurisdiction in the 17th Century' (1958) 2(3) *The American Journal of Legal History* 215

Maxwell D, *The Practice of the Court of Session* (Edinburgh, Scottish Courts Administration, 1980)

Mears TL, *Analysis of M. Ortolan's Institutes of Justinian: Including the History and Generalization of Roman Law* (London, Stevens, 1876)

Meeson N, *Admiralty Jurisdiction and Practice* (3rd edn, London, LLP, 2003)

von Mehren AT (and DT Trautman), *The Law of Multistate Problems: Cases and Materials on Conflict of Laws* (Boston, Little, Brown & Co, 1965)

Meili F (and AK Kuhn), *International Civil and Commercial Law as Founded upon Theory, Legislation and Practice* (tr AK Kuhn, New York, Macmillan, 1905) (English-speaking edition of Das internationale Civil-und Handelsrecht auf Grund der Theorie, Gesetzgebung und Praxis)

Mendelssohn BA, 'Delimitation of Right and Remedy in the Cases of Conflict of Laws' (1935) 16 *The British Yearbook of International Law* 20

Meston MC, 'Some Aspects of Scottish Admiralty Practice' (1964) *Juridical Review* 1

—— 'Admiralty' *The Laws of Scotland, Stair Memorial Encyclopaedia* (SME) (1) 197 (401–18)

—— (and WDH Sellar), *The Scottish Legal Tradition* (Edinburgh, Saltire and Stair Society, 1991)

Michaels R, 'The Functional Method of Comparative Law' in M Reimann and R Zimmermann (eds), *The Oxford Handbook of Comparative Law* (Oxford, OUP, 2006) 339

—— 'Two Paradigms of Jurisdiction' (2006) 27 *Michigan Journal of International Law* 1003

Miranda P, *História e Prática do Arresto ou Embargo* (Sao Paulo, Saraiva, 1929; reprint Campinas, Bookseller, 1999)

Moore DC (and AW Blakemore and CF Chamberlayne), *Handbook on the Law of Evidence* (Albany, NY, M Bender, 1919)

Muir Watt H, 'Law and Economics: quel apport pour le droit international privé?' in *Etudes offertes a Jacques Ghestin: Le contrat au début du XXIe sičcle* (Paris, Librairie Générale de Droit et de Jurisprudence, 2001)

Mukherjee PK, 'The Law of Maritime Liens and Conflict of Laws' (2003) 9(6) *Journal of International Maritime Law* 545

Muther T, *Sequestration und Arrest im Römischen Recht* (Leipzig, Hirzel, 1856)

Myburgh P, 'Uniformity or Unilateralism in the Law of Carriage of Goods by Sea?' (2000) 31 *Victoria University of Wellington Law Review* 355

Nadelmann KH, 'Jurisdictionally Improper Fora in Treaties on Recognition of Judgements: The Common Market Draft' (1967) *Columbia Law Review* 995

Nafziger JAR (and S Symeonides) (eds), *Law and Justice in a Multistate World: Essays in Honor of Arthur T von Mehren* (New York, Transnational Publishers, 2002)

von Neuhaus PH, *Die Grundbegriffe des Internationalen Privatrechts* (Tübingen, Mohr, 1976)

Ng J, 'How Closely does the Chinese Law of Ship Arrest Resemble International Maritime Practice and the Ship Arrest Conventions?' (2006) 12(5) *Journal of International Maritime Law* 337

Niboyet JP, *Manuel de Droit International Prive* (2nd edn of the same title of A Pillet and JP Niboyet, Paris, Recueil Sirey, 1928)

Nicholas B, *An Introduction to Roman Law* (Oxford, Clarendon, 1975)

Niemeyer T, *Zur Methode des Internationales Privatrechts* (Leipzig, Duncker und Humblot, 1894)

Nieschulz S, *Der Arrest in Seeschiffe: Eine rechtsvergleichende Untersuchung des deutschen, niederländischen und englischen Rechts* (Hamburg, Lit, 1997)

North PM, *Essays in Private International Law* (Oxford, Clarendon, 1993)

Nygh P (and F Pocar), 'Preliminary Draft Convention on Jurisdiction and Foreign Judgments in Civil and Commercial Matters' (2000) Prel Doc 11 HccH

Offerhaus J, 'Netherlands Maritime Law and The Conflict of Laws' Conference delivered before the Norwegian Maritime Law Association in Oslo on 25 April 1955 *Arkiv for sjorett* 2 (1954/57) 618

Opertti Badán D, *Exhortos y Embargo de Bienes Extranjeros. Medios de Cooperacion Judicial Internacional* (Montevideo, Amalio Fernández, 1976)

—— 'Reconocimiento y Ejecución de Sentencias Judiciales Extranjeras' (1976) OAS Ser.K./XX.2 CIDIP II/3

Panagopoulos G, 'Substance and Procedure in Private International Law' (2005) 1 *Journal of Private International Law* 69

Peel E, 'Forum non conveniens and European ideals' [2005] *Lloyd's Maritime and Commercial Law Quarterly* 363

Petrochilos GC, *Procedural Law in International Arbitration* (Oxford, OUP, 2004)

Pfeiffer T (and B Hess and P Schlosser) (eds), *The Brussels I Regulation 44/2001, Application and Enforcement in the EU* (Beck Hart, 2008)

Philip A, 'Maritime Jurisdiction in the EEC' (1977) *Nordisk Tidss-Krift for internationale ret* 121

von Planck JW, *Das deutsche Gerichtsverfahren im Mittelalter: nach dem Sachsenspiegel und den verwandten Rechtsquellen* (Braunschweig, 1879; reprint Hildesheim, Olms, 1973) vol 2

Planitz H, *Studien zur Geschichte des deutschen Arrestprozesses, Der Arrest gegen den fugitivus in Zeitschrift der Savigny-Stiftung für Rechtsgeschichte* (Abteilung, germanische, 1913 vol 34 49)

Price G, *The Law of Maritime Liens* (London, Sweet & Maxwell, 1940)

Prichard MJ (and DEC Yale) (eds), *Hale and Fleetwood on Admiralty Jurisdiction* (London, Selden Society, 1993) vol 108

Ready NP (and TB Karatzas), *The Greek Code of Private Maritime Law* (The Hague, Martinus Nijhoff, 1982)

Rees P (and A Briggs), *Civil Jurisdiction and Judgements* (4th edn, London, LLP, 2005)

Reid KGC (and R Zimmermann) (eds), *A History of Private Law in Scotland*, vol 2 (Oxford, OUP, 2000)

—— 'While One Hundred Remain: TB Smith and the Progress of Scots Law' in E Reid and DL Carey Miller (eds), *A Mixed Legal System in Transition: T.B. Smith and the Progress of Scots Law* (Edinburgh, EUP, 2005)

Ringbom H, 'EU Regulation 44/2001 and its Implications for the International Maritime Liability Conventions' (2004) 35 *Journal of Maritime Law and Commerce* 1

Robinson GH, *Handbook of Admiralty Law in the United States* (St Paul, Minn, West Publishing Co, 1939)

Rodger BJ (and G Maher), 'Provisional and Protective Remedies: The British Experience of the Brussels Convention' (1999) *48 International and Comparative Law Quarterly* 306

—— (and G Maher), *Civil Jurisdiction in the Scottish Courts* (Edinburgh, Green, 2010)

Rodière R, *Le Navire* (Paris, Dalloz, 1980)

—— (and E Du Pontavice) *Droit Maritime* (12th edn, Paris, Dalloz, 1997)

Rose N, *Pre-Emptive Remedies in Europe* (London, Longmans, 1992)

Rosenne S, *Provisional Measures in International Law: The International Court of Justice and the International Tribunal for the Law of the Sea* (Oxford, OUP, 2004)

von Rudorff H, *Zur Rechtsstellung der Gäste im mittelalterlichen städtischen Prozess: vorzugsweise nach norddeutschen Quellen* (Breslau, Marcus, 1907) vol 88

Ruiz Abou-Nigm V, '*The Lex* Mercatoria and its Current Relevance in International Commercial Arbitration' 2 *Derecho del Comercio Internacional Temas y Actualidades* (DeCITA) (2004) 101

—— 'Ancillary Jurisdiction for Interim Measures of Protection in Support of Cross-Border Litigation' (2005) 4 *Uniform Law Review* 759

—— (and C Fresnedo de Aguirre), 'El Derecho Marítimo y El Derecho Internacional Privado' (2005) 22 *Anuario de Derecho Marítimo* 189

Russell KA 'Exorbitant Jurisdiction and Enforcement of Judgements: The Brussels System as an Impetus for the United States Action' (1993) *Syracuse Journal of International Law and Commerce* 2

Sack AN, 'Conflicts of Laws in the History of the English Law' in *Law: A Century of Progress 1835–1935* (New York, New York University Press, 1937) vol 3 342

Sadikov ON, 'Conflict of Laws in International Transport Law' (1985) 1 *Recueil des Cours* (vol 190) 191

Santomauro P, 'Sense and Sensibility: Reviewing *West Tankers* and Dealing with its Implications in the Wake of the Reform of EC Regulation 44/2001' (2010) 6 *Journal of Private International Law* 281

von Savigny FC, *Private International Law and the Retrospective Operation of Statutes. A Treatise on the Conflict of Laws and the Limits of their Operation in Respect of Place and Time* (tr W Guthrie, 2nd edn, Edinburgh, Clark, 1880)

Scott A, 'Substance and Procedure and Choice of Law in Torts' [2007] *Lloyd's Maritime and Commercial Law Quarterly* 44

Schlosser P, 'Report on the Convention on the Association of the Kingdom of Denmark, Ireland and the United Kingdom of Great Britain and Northern Ireland to the Convention on Jurisdiction and the Enforcement of Judgments in Civil and Commercial Matters and to the Protocol on its Interpretation by the Court of Justice, signed at Luxembourg, 9 October 1978' *Official Journal of the European Communities* (1979) C 59 (OJC/59/1979)

—— 'Jurisdiction in International Litigation—The Issue of Human Rights in Relation to National Law and to the Brussels Convention' (1991) *Rivista di Diritto Internazionale* 5

—— 'International Judicial and Administrative Cooperation' (2001) *Recueil des Cours* 284

—— (and B Hess and T Pfeiffer) (eds), *The Brussels I Regulation 44/2001, Application and Enforcement in the EU* (Beck Hart, 2008)

Shany Y, *The Competing Jurisdiction of International Courts and Tribunals* (Oxford, OUP, 2004)

Shaw R (and N Gaskell), 'Arrest Convention 1999' [1999] *Lloyd's Maritime and Commercial Law Quarterly* 1

Siehr K (and T Einhorn) (eds), *International Cooperation through Private International Law: Essays in Memory of Peter E Nygh* (The Hague, TMC Asser Press, 2004)

Siig KM, 'Maritime Jurisdiction Agreements in the EU' [1997] *Lloyd's Maritime and Commercial Law Quarterly* 362

—— *Arbitration Agreements in a Transport Law Perspective* (Copenhagen, DJOF, 2003)

Slater AG, 'Forum Non Conveniens: A View from the Shop Floor' (1988) 104 *Law Quarterly Review* 554

Smith TB, *British Justice: The Scottish Contribution* (London, Stevens, 1961)

Smith W, *Maritime Practice, Adapted to the Sheriff Courts of Scotland* (Edinburgh, T&T Clark, 1832)

Snyder F, *The Europeanisation of Law: The Legal Effects of European Integration* (Oxford, OUP, 2000)

Stewart JG, *A Treatise on the Law of Diligence* (Edinburgh, Green, 1898)

Story J, *Commentaries on the Conflict of Laws* (Boston, Hilliard, Gray & Co, 1834)

Stürner R, 'Anglo-American and Continental Civil Procedure: The English Reform as a Model for Further Harmonization?' in M Andenas, N Andrews, and R Nazzini (eds), *The Future of Transnational Civil Litigation, English Responses to the ALI/Unidroit Draft Principles and Rules of Transnational Civil Procedure* (London, BIICL, 2004) 11

Talice JR, 'Objeto y Metodo en el Derecho Internacional Privado' in D Opertti Badán et al, *Objeto y Metodo en el Derecho Internacional Privado* (2nd edn, Montevideo, FCU, 1990)

Teare N, 'The Admiralty Action *in rem* and the House of Lords' [1997] *Lloyd's Maritime and Commercial Law Quarterly* 33

Tellechea Bergman E, *La dimensión judicial del caso privado internacional en el ámbito regional* (Montevideo, FCU, 2002)

Terry P, 'Convention of Accession of Denmark, Ireland and the United Kingdom to the Convention of Jurisdiction and Enforcement of Judgments in Civil and Commercial Matters' (1980) 4 *Journal of the Irish Society for European Law* 31

Tetley W, 'The Lack of Uniformity and the Very Unfortunate State of Maritime Law in Canada, the United States, the United Kingdom and France' [1987] *Lloyd's Maritime and Commercial Law Quarterly* 340

—— 'Charterparties and Choice of Law' (1992) *Il Diritto Marittimo* 1146

—— *International Conflict of Laws: Common, Civil and Maritime* (Montreal, Blais, 1994)

—— *Maritime Liens and Claims* (2nd edn, Montreal, Blais, 1998)

—— 'Arrest, Attachment and Related Maritime Law Procedures' (1999) 73 *Tulane Law Review* 1895

—— 'Mixed Jurisdiction: Common Law vs Civil Law (Codified and Uncodified) Part I' [1999] *Uniform Law Review* (3) 591 and 'Part II' [1999] (4) 877

—— 'Uniformity of International Private Maritime Law—The Pros, Cons and Alternatives to International Conventions—How to Adopt an International Convention' (2000) 24 *Tulane Maritime Law Journal* 775

—— 'Maritime Liens in the Conflict of Laws' in JAR Nafziger and SC Symeonides (eds), *Law and Justice in a Multistate World: Essays in Honor of Arthur T. von Mehren* (Ardsley, NY, Transnational Publishers, 2002) 439

—— *International Maritime and Admiralty Law* (Quebec, Blais, 2003)
—— *Marine Cargo Claims* (forthcoming, 4th edn, 2008 available at <http://www.mcgill.ca/maritimelaw/books/> (last accessed 19 August 2007))
Thomas DR, *Maritime liens* (London, Stevens, 1980)
Trautman DT (and AT von Mehren), *The Law of Multistate Problems: Cases and Materials on Conflict of Laws* (Boston, Little, Brown & Co, 1965)
Tsimplis M (and N Gaskell), 'Admiralty Claims and the New CPR Part 61' [2002] *Lloyd's Maritime and Commercial Law Quarterly* 520
Tu G, 'Finding a Proper Nexus for Constructing Specific (Special) Jurisdiction Regarding Commercial Contract and Tort Cases: A Comparative Study of the US and European Approaches' (2009) 5 *Journal of Private International Law* 243
Turner JM (and SC Derrington), *The Law and Practice of Admiralty Matters* (Oxford, OUP, 2007)
Twiss T (ed), *The Black Book of the Admiralty* (London, Longman, 1871–76; 2nd reprint New Jersey, The Lawbook Exchange Ltd, 1998)
Twitchell M, 'The Myth of General Jurisdiction' (1988) 101(3) *Harvard Law Review* 610
Van der Plas C, 'The Limits of the Judicial Function and the Conflict of Laws' (2006) 53(3) *Netherlands International Law Review* 439
Verheul JP, 'The Convention Relating to the Arrest of Seagoing Ships of 1952: Some Questions' (1983) *Netherlands International Law Review* 383
Wächter CG, *über die Collision der Privatrechtgesetze verschiedener Staaten* (Pt 1), 24 Archiv für die Civilistische Praxis 230 (1841); (Pts 2, 3 and 4) 25 Archiv für die Civilistische Praxis 1, 161, 361 (1842)
Welwood W, *Sea Laws of Scotland* (Edinburgh, Robert Waldegrave, 1590; reprint Scottish Text Society *Miscellany Volume* (1933))
West M, 'Arbitrations, Admiralty Actions *in rem* and the Arrest of Ships in the Hong Kong SAR: in the Twilight of The Indian Grace (No. 2)?' [2002] *Lloyd's Maritime and Commercial Law Quarterly* 259
Westlake J, *A Treatise on Private International Law, or the Conflict of Laws* (London, Sweet & Maxwell, 1858)
Wiswall FL, *The Development of Admiralty Jurisdiction and Practice since 1800 an English Study with American Comparisons* (Cambridge, CUP, 1970)
Wool J (and E McKendrick, H Kronke, R Goode), *Transnational Commercial Law* (Oxford, OUP, 2004)
WWC, 'The Function of Writs of Prohibition' (1919) 28 *The Yale Law Journal* 482
von Ziegler A (and T Burckhardt) (eds), *Internationales Recht auf See und Binnengewässern Festschrift für Walter Müller* (Zürich, Schulthess, 1993)
—— 'Particularities of the Harmonization and Unification of International Law of Trade and Commerce' in J Basedow et al (eds), *Liber Amicorum Kurt Siehr, Private Law in the International Arena, From National Conflicts Rules Towards Harmonization and Unification* (The Hague, TMC Asser Press, 2000) 875
Zimmermann R, 'Roman Law and European Legal Unity' in AS Hartkamp et al (eds), *Towards a European Civil Code* (2nd edn, Nijmegen, Kluwer Law International, 1998) 21

Zuckerman AAS, 'Mareva Injunctions and Security for Judgment in a Framework of Interlocutory Remedies' (1993) 109 *Law Quarterly Review* 432

II. OTHER DOCUMENTS

Report of the Scottish Committee on Jurisdiction and Enforcement (The Maxwell Committee Report)

Acts and Documents, Second Specialised Inter-American Conference on Private International Law—CIDIP II (Washington, OAS, 1980/1981)

Documents of the Second Inter-American Specialised Convention on Private International Law CIDIP II—The Inter-American System (Treaties, Conventions and Other Documents) vol 1, Part I (1976) vol 2 (1981) (OAS Washington)

'Discussion Paper on Diligence on the Dependence and Admiralty Arrestments' (Scot Law Com Discussion Paper No. 84, December1989)

'Arrestment of Ships Securing Claims against Demise Charterers' (Scot Law Com Consultation Paper, March 1990)

'Discussion Paper on Extra-Territorial Effect of Arrestments and Related Matters' (Scot Law Com Discussion Paper No. 90, 1990)

Resolution No. 1 adopted by the 20th Conference of European Ministers of Justice, Budapest, 11–12 June 1996

The travaux préparatoires of the International Convention for the Unification of Certain Rules of Law with Respect to Collision between Vessels, 23 September 1910, and of the International Convention for the Unification of Certain Rules Relating to the Arrest of Sea-Going Ships, 10 May 1952 (Antwerpen, CMI, 1997)

'Report on Diligence on the Dependence and Admiralty Arrestments' (Scot Law Com Report No. 164 (1998))

'Enforcement of Civil Obligations in Scotland' (Consultation Paper Scottish Executive)

Principles of Transnational Civil Procedure ALI/Unidroit as adopted in 2004 (2004) 4 *Uniform Law Review* 758

Index